"Rikki Klieman is a bold voice for women's self-assertion and self-reliance. . . . An articulate, take-charge professional role model, Rikki helped sweep woe-is-me victim feminism into the dustbin of history."
—Camille Paglia, author and professor of humanities and media studies at the University of the Arts

"Rikki Klieman, a great trial lawyer famous for her captivating final arguments, has delivered a frank, revealing, and spellbinding memoir about her life in and out of court, as well as on and off Court TV."
—Barry Scheck, attorney and cofounder of the Innocence Project

"Rikki worked, struggled, and succeeded. She's a dynamic advocate, a caring person, and now a true partner with her powerful husband."
—Gloria Allred, attorney at law; partner, Allred Maroko & Goldberg

"*Fairy Tales Can Come True* is rich with resonance. It is at once a cautionary tale and a compelling story for anyone who has grappled with, or is interested in, the steep price of success, and what the word finally means."
—John Lescroart, author of *The First Law*

"Rikki has written that rarest of celebrity memoirs, one that feels utterly real. She has produced a book that is as vivid as her life."
—Jeffrey Toobin, legal analyst, CNN and *The New Yorker*

"Rikki Klieman has a unique view of life and the justice system. You get it all in *Fairy Tales Can Come True*."
—Michael Connelly, author of *Chasing the Dime*

"When they finally catch up with me, soaked in blood and holding a viscera-covered knife—a dead waiter at my feet—Rikki Klieman is my first phone call. A terrific book."
—Anthony Bourdain, author of *Kitchen Confidential*

FAIRY TALES CAN COME TRUE

HOW A DRIVEN WOMAN CHANGED HER DESTINY

RIKKI KLIEMAN

WITH PETER KNOBLER

ReganBooks
An Imprint of HarperCollins*Publishers*

HarperCollins books may be purchased for educational, business, or sales promotional use. For information please write: Special Markets Department, HarperCollins Publishers Inc., 10 East 53rd Street, New York, NY 10022.

FIRST EDITION

Designed by Kelly Hitt

Printed on acid-free paper

Library of Congress Cataloging-in-Publication Data

Klieman, Rikki J., 1948–
    Fairy tales can come true : how a driven woman changed her destiny / Rikki Klieman with Peter Knobler.—1st ed.
        p. cm.
    ISBN 0-06-052401-4
    1. Klieman, Rikki J., 1948– 2. Women lawyers—New York—Biography. I. Knobler, Peter. II. Title.

KF373.K553A3 2003
340'.092—dc21
[B]

2003041443

03 04 05 06 07 WBC/RRD 10 9 8 7 6 5 4 3 2 1

To Bill, for twenty-five years and a day

—R.K.

❦

To Daniel and Jane

—P.K.

If you asked me what I came into this world to do,
I will tell you: I came to live out loud.

—Émile Zola

⬦

And life gets more exciting with each passing day.
And love is either in your heart or on its way.

—"Young at Heart," Carolyn Leigh and Johnny Richards

CONTENTS

PREFACE

It happened over and over again.

I'd be on trial, working from 5:00 in the morning until 11:00 at night, totally focused on my job. There wasn't a day the whole year when I wasn't trying a case, preparing a case, or blessedly pleading one out. Pretty much the only thing I did that was good for myself from Monday through Friday was take a break and go out at 6:30 each morning for a forty-minute run. I slept with the case's six-inch-thick brown accordion folder on the floor next to my bed, so if I woke up tossing and turning in the middle of the night, as I was regrettably prone to do, I wouldn't have to pad around my home to work on it.

I would finish my court week at 4:30 P.M. on Friday, get back to the office in a frenzy, unable to decompress from the demands of the trial itself, and start throwing my papers around, trying to get the stuff to fit in my bag. I was living in Boston but had to deliver a speech the next day to a group of lawyers somewhere in America, and I couldn't be without my papers filled with quotes, humor, and drama.

We had a ritual. Every Friday evening after work, my criminal defense lawyer friends and I would gather at an upscale French restaurant, Maison Robert, and begin to unwind. A criminal defense attorney always has someone's life in her hands, which has its appeal but can lead to stress in large drafts. We would drink for hours, after which I would stagger home and at some point find myself in the kitchen saying, "Oh my God, I forgot to eat." I'd pop a Lean Cuisine in the microwave sometime near midnight to make sure I had some carbohydrates in me to absorb the alcohol. I'd take an Alka-Seltzer, two B vitamins, four glasses of water, and a sleeping pill, and pray for a few hours of uninterrupted sleep.

I would wake up at dawn. I wasn't worried about the speech I was going to give; I had given that speech so many times before. In fact, I thrive on public speaking; it gives me an audience and an absolute certainty that I am making a difference in other people's lives. When I am onstage I am transported to some other place. The larger the group, the more the energy—from me to them, from them to me.

It was the process of getting there that was awful. I had my garment bag and makeup kit already packed and my travel outfit laid out. I would grab a cab, stagger onto the plane in my navy blue slacks and a blazer, and fall dead asleep before the plane left the tarmac. I don't even remember saying hello to the flight attendants; I was out cold.

A few hours later I would wake up startled, drink a bottle of water, and see how much time I had before landing. It was usually not much. Sometimes I'd have a moment in my schedule to clean up before the function at which I was speaking, but usually I was being met at the gate, which meant I had to get off the plane looking sharp, together, and competent.

I could do that.

I squeezed into the minuscule airline bathroom, stripped down amid the stainless steel, and put on my good clothes. Sweating in that confined space, standing with one foot on the toilet seat, my elbows bumping the doors while I put on my stockings, this was not the moment to sneak a quick peek in the mirror. It was just insane.

My travel kit was stocked with Visine, Evian spray, toothbrush and toothpaste, a thick moisturizer for the flight, and my makeup. I'd done enough of these quick-change routines to be able to do my face in three and a half minutes. Back then my hair was long and straight—the Joan Baez/Buffy Sainte-Marie look—so I saved a couple of minutes by only having to brush it through. Finally a fast check—a dazzling smile. "Showtime!" Very Roy-Scheider-as-Bob-Fosse in *All That Jazz*. I was ready.

I would emerge from the bathroom and return to my seat.

If this happened once, it happened a hundred times—the man sitting next to me, and it was inevitably a man traveling on business, would say, "Wow, Cinderella, what a difference!" or "How did you do that?" I would chat him up—"What do you do? Here's what I do"—to see if I could land some business for my law firm. Airplanes are a rainmaker's heaven.

Briefcase in hand, slinging my garment bag over my arm like a princess gathering her train, I would strut off that airplane as if I didn't have a care in the world. My assigned Bar Association escort would be right at the gate. We'd rush off to the car and head to the conference.

I know how to make people like me the way some people know how to be a good date; I pepper them with questions. "Hi. What do you do?" I did not have to give out information about myself as long as I could do a thorough direct examination in the car. People like to talk about themselves and I encouraged them.

By the time I arrived at the conference center I would have gathered myself. Truly glad to be there, I would meet the hosts and guests, a group that started out as a majority of men but grew over time to be a preponderance of young women lawyers looking for a role model. I would shake a lot of hands, smile, talk, sit for a meal, then stand up and deliver my speech. I carried a tattered yellow legal pad with notes for my various presentations to make me feel secure, but I really didn't need it.

While I was onstage I was in heaven. I was flying. Life couldn't have been better. I was in the moment, unafraid to be at risk, daring to be my best. I was teaching. I was performing. Often I would talk about "theater in the courtroom," the concept of creating an involving drama while winning over the jury. I would involve the audience in a show of my own, and at the end I enjoyed the applause.

What an adrenaline rush. "Well, of course," I'd tell myself, "this is why I travel every weekend. This is the bee's knees. This is what I live for!"

In the Q&A afterward, young lawyers would bombard me with questions. It was always about success, success, success. I was thrilled to be a role model. I loved their energy, and I was more than happy to share what I knew with a new generation of attorneys, particularly eager women.

But after the rush comes the crash. When the discussion ended, if I was on the eastern seaboard, I would fly straight home. Same deal: Hit the airplane and hit the pillow. In the years when I was married, I felt I should at least try to be a wife, so when I got back, my husband and I would go out to dinner and I would talk about the speech or listen to tales of his weekend. When I was single, I would go home and collapse.

If the conference was in Los Angeles or Las Vegas or Denver, however, I had no choice; I had to stay overnight. I dreaded the overnight, it meant I had to be scintillating at length. There are many fine things to do and people to meet in Phoenix or San Francisco or Seattle, but I spent entire evenings during which I smiled and laughed and could not remember a single word one person said to me. I looked good; I was living glamorously; I was making a difference in people's lives—but I was dead. I hit top and bottom at the same time. All I wanted to do was either get back to the office and work or go home and climb into bed. Sometimes there would be a man there, sometimes not.

one

"MISS REMARKABLE"

MY PARENTS CALLED ME "MISS REMARKABLE" EVEN BEFORE I WAS BORN.

Jeannette Wiener and Ben Klieman met in 1926 when they were both sixteen years old. My father's parents had brought him to the United States from the Ukraine when he was two; my mother was born in America to a father who had migrated from the same general area and a mother who insisted, since she was born in the United States, that she was a "Yankee." They married young and lived the immigrant life. My father was in the garment business; he bought

Hanes hosiery, Wrangler jeans—American goods—from manufacturers and sold them to retailers. He was a middleman in the *schmatte*
trade, trying to make a living. My mother was a housewife. In her
younger days she worked for Fannie Mae Candies. She had a wonderful sense of color and texture, and found her decorating flair, I'm
told, when she created the company's displays and windows.

My parents adored each other. "Jeanne K," as my mother was
known, was charismatic and full of style. And in the Chicago neighborhood where they lived, it was widely known that Ben and Jeanne
were passionately in love.

But they couldn't have children. They tried and tried but could
not conceive. In a culture where parents slaved and sacrificed so that
their children could have a better life, Ben and Jeanne were denied
that reason to live.

At the age of thirty-two my father was drafted into the infantry in
World War II. A Jewish boy in the infantry. He saw serious action in
the Philippines and New Guinea, where he was under fire on the
beaches and in the jungle; each day he survived was a miracle. And
with his life constantly in danger, he wrote love letters to his wife,
which she kept forever.

When Ben returned home from the war, he and Jeanne again
tried to build a family. No success. After trying for seventeen years,
they gave up hope. But if they couldn't conceive a child of their own,
they also couldn't conceive of *not* having a child. World War II had
just ended, and there were thousands of children in desperate need of
loving parents, so Ben and Jeanne considered adoption. And as often
happens when couples think about welcoming a child into their lives,
they must have relaxed. My mother got pregnant. She was thirty-
seven years old. Family lore has it that they had an argument one
morning, and when my father came home to apologize he took my
mother to a hotel for a passionate reunion, where, as a joke, they reg-
istered as Mr. and Mrs. John Smith. I was conceived that night. The
story is probably apocryphal, but it's sweet nevertheless.

The extended family was ecstatic. Family was vital, particularly
after millions of Jews had been wiped off the earth during the war.
Every Jewish child was a cause for celebration. A distant cousin

wrote to Ben and Jeanne, "After all these years, this is a miracle child who will do something remarkable." They took that to heart, and even before I was born I became known as Miss Remarkable. I was truly the answer to my parents' prayers.

From the time I was born my mother told me I could be anything I wanted to be. I could grow up to be president of the United States, she said. All I had to do was work for it. I believed her, and as Miss Remarkable, I had a strong desire to be a perfect child. So if my mother asked me to do something, I was going to make sure I did it perfectly.

Until I was four my family lived in an apartment above a Mexican variety store on the North Side of Chicago. My closest friends were the two sons of the owner and my two male cousins. My cousin Gerry was four months younger, and we were raised like twins; his brother, Bobby, who was a few years older, ran us ragged.

One day, when I was about three years old, my father was at work and my mother was determined to find a toy western army fort to give to Bobby for Christmas. (Our family was quite ecumenical. My mother's only sister, Doris, married an Italian, and my mother's brother converted to become a Baha'i. Because I was exposed to so many different religions, I was taught to treat people equally no matter what they believed.) My mother could not find a babysitter, but she didn't plan to be gone for long. She plunked me on the couch, clicked on the little Philco TV, left some milk and cookies on the coffee table in front of me, and gave me a couple of toys to play with. "I'm going to the store. I have to find a present for Bobby," she said. "I'll be back in a little while. I want you to sit here until I come home."

The couch was a burnt orange color, and its nubby fabric felt itchy on my legs. I played with the toys, watched the television, ate the milk and cookies. I didn't move from that couch. An hour passed. I had to go to the bathroom, but I stayed where I was. My mommy had told me to stay there, and I was the perfect child.

My mother swept in several hours later. I heard the key turn in the lock of the door, but I didn't get up to greet her. I wanted her to see that I was still on the couch. She took off her coat and gave me a big hug.

"You stayed here all day?"

"Yes, I did." I beamed through my discomfort.

"I'm so sorry I was late," she apologized.

"Can I go to the bathroom now?"

"Oh, my God."

My mother was horrified, but I was proud. She had expected me to act like an adult. This had been a difficult task, and I had performed it well. I really had shown my mom that I could do what I was told. I was perfect.

I was nuts.

When I was four, we moved into a co-op building on Chicago's Northwest Side—four apartments to a building, two per floor, with a hallway down the middle and a big backyard—in a newly built neighborhood called Budlong Woods. My mother had a wonderful eye—in another life she would have been an interior designer—and our apartment was a showpiece, though done on little money. With the help of my uncle Joe Ventrella, a housepainter and an artist who had married Mom's sister, she fashioned a long mural that turned our hallway into an Italian garden wall, complete with blue sky and wispy clouds. They stenciled Pennsylvania Dutch figures on the kitchen cabinets that made us feel as if we were outdoors. My mom bathed the screened-in porch with candlelight for spring and summer dinners alfresco.

Mom was an excellent cook with a flair for presentation. With unmatched dishes and glassware from the Salvation Army (boy, was she ahead of her time!), linen tablecloths, and colored cloth napkins with napkin rings, our evening meals were special for all of us. My pet beagle and I, with his paws and my hands perched on the windowsill, would watch for Dad to come home from work. At 6:30 precisely my father would come through the door, swing me around, give me a big hug and a kiss, scratch the dog, walk to the kitchen to kiss my mom, and then go wash vigorously for dinner. (It was a ritual, as if he was washing the dirt and the blood of his wartime experiences off his hands.) He never failed to tell my mother how nice the table looked.

Dinner conversation was lively, as the three of us talked about one another's day. Perhaps this early experience is why dinners throughout my life have been geared to relaxation, laughter, communication, and connection. Afterward, we often watched television together, roaring to Sid Caesar and marveling at the variety of Ed Sullivan's entertainers. Clint Walker caught my eye as Cheyenne Bodie, an attraction that has stayed with me these many years.

And every night before I went to bed, my mother would stroke my forehead, pat the dog who was cuddled in the crook of my knees, and ask, "Rikki, what are you thankful for today?" And each night I would have to give that question some thought and find an answer.

My father worked all day, so I spent most of my time with my mother, and from a very early age she began to work my brain. We didn't have a car, so we got around town on the Chicago Transit Authority (CTA) buses. Before I started going to school, well before *Dick and Jane*, I learned how to read from these trips. Chicago is organized on a grid, and I would memorize the names of the streets and the numbers of the blocks. We would go north from Madison— M-A-D-I-S-O-N—from 0 to 400 to 800, all the way to 6000. In Chicago there are a hundred numbers to a block and eight blocks to a mile, so if we go from 0 to 2400 how far have we gone? I also learned the street names and was proud to recite them. This was my first lesson in memorization. My mother used every opportunity to train my mind. She encouraged me to read, and I always had my head in a book. I liked it.

I also liked to dance. I began taking ballet lessons when I was four. I was in toe shoes by the time I was twelve. Ruined my feet forever. My father said, "If you have to have something ugly about you, it may as well be your feet." I added acting classes when I was ten. How my father paid for those lessons, I do not know. We had little or no money, but I always seemed to have wonderful clothes, and if I wanted to take another class or buy another book, my parents found a way to support me. I didn't know until years later that my mother shopped at the Goodwill thrift store, Montgomery Ward's warehouse, and the bargain basement at Goldblatt's, where she could buy dresses three for a dollar.

I went shopping for Christmas with both my parents. We walked into a toy store and I looked at everything on the shelves. "Now, tell me, what are some of the things you like?" my father asked. "You tell me and I'll tell Santa, but Santa can really only bring you one." One was fine with me.

A born actress, I loved to perform—I sang, I danced—and was happy to be the center of attention. Every day after school I would sit and watch *The Mickey Mouse Club* on television. I had my ears and my T-shirt (it read "Rikki Jo," and I still have it), and I was devoted. I wanted to be a Mouseketeer more than I wanted to breathe.

I was in Florida when I found out that I was "pretty."

My father had to go to Miami to work with a group of manufacturers who were meeting there. This was the perfect opportunity for our first family vacation. A new ice cream parlor had opened in the Saxony Hotel, and we went there to meet Al Weinstein, one of my father's customers. Al Weinstein was a rough, tough New Yorker with a deep Miami tan, a head full of shocking white hair, and a cigar that constantly dangled from his mouth. I'd heard stories about Al. He would tell his wife, "I'll be back in a little while," then hop on a plane to a racetrack in another state for a couple of days. He was a character. When I met Mr. Weinstein, he took my face in his hands, opened my mouth, pinched my cheeks, and said to my father, "Ben, you saved a lot of money." My father looked at him quizzically. "No nose job, no braces. She's a beauty!"

So I was a beauty. It was widely agreed. My parents did a wonderful job of making me believe it. I was remarkably fortunate to acquire such self-esteem at a very early age. Of all the gifts my parents gave me, this may have been the most valuable.

I was eight years old and I knew that boys were attracted to me. I began to realize the enormous power that pretty girls possess. I liked it.

In elementary school I was a good student. No matter the subject—English, social studies, arithmetic—I was Miss Remarkable, and I had to be the best. Our Florida trip did not fall during my school vacation, so I had to miss about a week of classes. My parents valued education over play, so they went to my teacher and got my week's worth of homework assignments. I may have been on vacation, but every day I put a sign on my door: PLEASE DO NOT DISTURB BEFORE 10. HOMEWORK BEING DONE. I didn't come out until I was finished. I could have been angry about missing mornings in the sun, but I felt very grown-up. And yet, I suspect I missed a certain unbridled part of my childhood: how controlled I was in my need to be seen as a responsible adult.

My teacher in the fourth grade at Jamieson Elementary School was Mrs. Friedman. She liked me because I worked hard. Mrs. Friedman tested us on arithmetic every week. As we finished, we raised our hands to signal we were done and were assigned a number, from one for first to twenty-five, or however many kids were in the class. Then we exchanged notebooks, Mrs. Friedman read the correct answers, and we were given another number equal to the number we got wrong. The best score you could receive was one: first to finish, zero wrong.

Everybody knew that I did well on these tests, and I had no fear on the first day we were quizzed on multiplying four-digit numbers. I opened up the problem notebook—I remember it was green—and began.

I had a problem, all right: This test wasn't easy. I had been able to multiply double- and triple-digit numbers without difficulty, but when it came to multiplying four numbers on top by four on bottom and then adding to arrive at the answer, I found I could do the work accurately, but it was taking me what felt like an eternity to complete. I tried to focus on the work, but midway through the exam I knew I was going to finish in the bottom half of the class. This had never happened before; it wasn't going to happen now.

I forced myself to throw up. Through dint of will I made myself vomit so I would be sent home sick and would not have to finish the test; I would not finish out of the money; I would not fail.

It worked. Nobody knew my secret, and I wasn't telling. I was still at the top of my class. (This wasn't the last time I would use this trick. I found that if I couldn't achieve maximum success in school and later at work with my mind in certain situations, my body could save me by failing. How sad.)

When I was ten years old, we moved to Hollywood Park, another northwest Chicago community. I changed elementary schools and was trying to figure out where I fit in. The popular girls—as only the pretty ten-year-old girls can be—wanted me to join their little group. I was very flattered; everyone wants to be popular. But then there were the geeky, smart girls, and I liked being with them just as much. I could have faced a fifth-grade crisis, but instead of forcing myself to make a choice, I floated between the groups and considered all of them to be my friends. I was more comfortable with the eggheads, but I straddled both worlds. Fortunately, another girl, Leatrice Hauptman, floated between them, too, so I had some company.

I was taking acting lessons in downtown Chicago at the Jack and Jill Players. Dance lessons were given in the same building at Adams and Wabash, and voice lessons were only a block away. I was still traveling with my mom, commandeering her every afternoon, but my mother had things to do. As much as she enjoyed spending time with me, sometime after I turned twelve she asked, "Can you go by yourself?" Was I ready for this level of independence?

Sure I was. I took the CTA bus after school, transferred to the elevated train to the Loop, did my lessons with my schoolbooks in my lap en route, took my classes, and retraced my steps back home. I felt very accomplished. The vast majority of my friends had never even been to downtown Chicago, and I was going four times a week by myself. Today, letting a twelve-year-old girl ride the subway alone at night might be considered child abuse, but life then was so much more innocent and safe.

At Jack and Jill we put on plays, and I also studied ballet, though I wasn't a good ballerina; the discipline was entirely too structured for me. In the same building was a dance school where a man named Tommy Sutton taught jazz and modern dance. I asked my parents whether I could take his class. Tommy was black, and in some circles the idea of a twelve-year-old white girl studying dance with a black man in Chicago's inner city was unusual in 1960. My parents encouraged me, and I flourished. Tommy was a great teacher, and when I discovered jazz dancing my body took off. I would become truly transported, almost possessed. Who knew that was in me?

All of the students in Tommy Sutton's class were older than I was. I was dancing with adults, and I loved the feeling that I could handle the responsibility and respond on their level. Movement in an adult world was comfortable; it gave me room to grow, and the grown-ups helped me flourish.

My father's side of the family was the more religious, so we celebrated the Jewish holidays and rituals at his parents' apartment. My mother imparted a less traditional upbringing, reading religious parables and the Old Testament with me, but she believed that much of organized religion caused intolerance and discrimination, so I was not sent to either Hebrew school or Sunday school. My mother was not a joiner, so she wouldn't even allow me to become a Brownie or a Girl Scout. But she thrived on my girlfriends, listening to them, talking with them, guiding their dreams. My friends were as special to her as they were to me.

Many of my friends went to summer camp, but because my parents took such an active part in my life, they preferred that I spend my summers with them. Aunt Doris and Uncle Joe and my cousins Gerry and Bobby joined us for summer weekend trips all over Wisconsin and Michigan: swimming in Lake Geneva, sightseeing in Oshkosh, lying on the beach in Kenosha. My family's two favorite Chicago haunts were Arlington Park, where we watched the thoroughbreds run, and Riverview Park, where we rode the roller coasters and took spins on the carousel. To this day, give me a ride on a wooden coaster or a merry-go-round full of carved horses, and I am in heaven.

Two and a half blocks from my house was Hollywood Park, where all the kids hung out at night on spring and summer weekends when it was warm. Dozens of teenagers, sometimes hundreds, would gather and just hang. When I turned thirteen, my girlfriends and I hung out there, too. Most of the kids were high schoolers older than we were, maybe fifteen or sixteen, but we became regulars and learned the routine. About a half mile away, across the Chicago-Lincolnwood line, was a fun park with a miniature golf course, several batting cages, and an ice cream stand. At some point each evening there would be a mass migration from Hollywood Park to the cages. You'd walk over, have a milk shake, stand around, talk, flirt. One night I watched a boy in the cages, hitting.

He was strong, in great shape, average height, with smooth, tan skin and dark brown hair. He looked good and he was connecting. He must have seen me watching, because when he was done swinging, he came out and watched me. When he walked over, I could see he was much older than I was; he was one of the big boys.

"Hi, I'm Eugene Green."

He was sixteen years old, he drove a mint-condition Pepsodent–green-and-white '53 Chevy, and I fell for him at that moment. I was dazzled. I saw him the next night at Hollywood Park and he told me he wanted to take me out.

"You know I'm thirteen, right?"

"I want to date you." I was new to such things. I had had boyfriends by then, but we always traveled in a pack—lots of boys and girls together, some in couples, some not. The idea of going out *in a car* with a boy who was light-years ahead of me in social development both scared and intrigued me. I could handle it, I thought, just like everything else. As if reading my mind he said, "Because of our age difference I have to get your parents' permission." He drove me home and I introduced him to Mom and Dad.

Gene and my parents had a discussion outside my presence. This was unusual; I took part in most of the conversations in our house, especially those that centered on me. I was excited and flattered and filled with emotion for this boy. After fifteen minutes of nervous waiting, I was brought into the room. Everyone was serious but smiling. Gene said to my father, "I know that I'm much older than Rikki, and I'll respect Rikki's age. I will not act improperly in any way. I want to be able to take Rikki out in my car and do social things together without having to sneak around. If that's okay with you, that's okay with me."

My parents were amazed by this youngster. As protective as they were of their remarkable daughter, they were impressed with this unusual boy. They gave him their blessing. We could date.

When Gene left, my father and mother sat and talked with me

about acting responsibly. And they didn't mean just sexually; I'm sure my father did, but sex was never discussed in our house. It just wasn't. "We expect you to be a responsible individual," my mother told me. "You're very grown-up and we expect you to act the way we've taught you, with good sense. We expect to be informed where you are going and with whom you are going, and we expect you to be home at a reasonable hour."

Gene fell madly for me, and I for him, as only adolescents can do. What was a sixteen-year-old boy doing with a thirteen-year-old girl? My parents had raised me to be mature beyond my years, and I had been striving to be an adult almost from the time I was born. Gene's interest was no surprise to me or to my friends. I was not the usual thirteen-year-old, and I didn't want to be.

Gene Green was a revelation. That summer we spent almost all our free time together. The only couple I knew well was my mother and father, and they were very romantic—they were old people and they held hands! But Gene wanted me to discover the world. He took me to museums and art galleries; we went to the theater. He opened up my mind. We read books together and talked about them. My head was expanding, and I adored the fact that Gene was so smart and handsome and charismatic. He was a gorgeous, athletic boy in a '53 Chevy who was also an aesthete! He was my mentor, my guide. (He was, in fact, the template for all the men to come; I would be dating Gene Green, in one form or another, for the rest of my life.) I felt passionate toward him, but at such a young age I didn't know what real passion was. Gene did, but he kept his promise to my parents; his behavior was entirely appropriate.

We dated all summer, and then, when it was time for us to go back to school, he dropped me completely. He told me he was going to. The seventh and eighth grades were in the same building as the high school, and he was going to be a junior. "I don't want to go to school," he said, "and be taunted by my friends for dating a child. I'll see you in the spring."

I was stunned. I didn't know what to say. "My birthday is May thirteenth," I sputtered.

"I'll see you then."

I was devastated. The front door of our house had a window in the shape of a triangle, and I stood and looked out that window for days, waiting for him to tool up in his car, longing for him, sobbing. My pet beagle bayed to match my misery.

Gene never came. But on my next birthday there he was, and we started all over again.

We followed this pattern all the way through high school. Gene would leave whatever girl he was dating on May 13 and come to me, and I would get rid of the boyfriend I had at the time and go back to Gene for the summer. On the day after Labor Day, Gene would leave me. I was devastated every September; I kept thinking it wouldn't happen again. And then it did. It was just like the theater: audition, rejection, move on to the next opportunity. But sometimes I got the part, and I understood that three months with Gene were worth the rejection and heartache. Such intense pleasure was worth all the pain.

The summers were wonderful. We cared for each other deeply, and Gene shaped my idea of who I was and what place men had in my life. There were always boys around. After the first time Gene dropped me, I knew I would find someone for whom I genuinely cared until he came back. I treated guys the same way guys treated girls: I had my lessons and my school activities—when I wanted to be with my boyfriend, I was with my boyfriend *and only then*. Except for Gene. I lost free will around Eugene. I didn't like his abrupt endings, and I didn't like the forced winter silence between us, but if that's how a boy dealt with a girl, I could deal with boys that way, too.

We dated even after Gene graduated from high school and went away to the University of Illinois. I visited him. I guess it didn't embarrass him to be seen with a high school girl in college. Ultimately we drifted apart. I fell madly in love with a new guy my freshman year in college. Then I fell for someone else my sophomore year, and eventually Gene lost his hold on me. There was no great breakup; we just ran our course. He made me happy and he made me smarter, then he hurt me, then he made me happy and he made me smarter, then we did it all over again. I was attracted to his power and to the way he expanded my mind. It was what I learned to look for in a man.

Not long after my family moved to Hollywood Park I began making friends and visiting their homes. One afternoon I came home with a question. "Mommy," I asked, "why don't you have a number on your arm? All the rest of the mothers do." I was ten years old. My mother sat me down at the kitchen table, put out a glass of milk and a plate of cookies, and told me about the Holocaust. This was the first I had heard of it. She told me about Hitler and the concentration camps and the killing of six million Jews. The Holocaust became a subject of burning interest throughout my life. I was a true believer in the power of the mind, and I could not understand how people of high intellect and great culture could join together in an attempt to exterminate an entire race. That youthful idealism has stayed with me, and I remain conscious that, simply because of my birth right, I am a part of a group that others may hate and even want to destroy. I maintain a fierce pride in my origin that even my parents did not instill.

My mother told me there was prejudice in the world, and that some people could only feel better about themselves if they looked down on someone else. "It is terrible," she said. "Remember on our trip to Florida, we talked about the rivalry between that Negro waiter and the Cuban busboy?" It was our first conversation about bigotry. There would be many others. Over the years, my studies brought me closer to an understanding of racial and social injustice.

Hollywood Park was filled with Holocaust survivors. They found one another and they founded their own community, one held together by a shared searing experience. Having willed themselves to live through hell, and having arrived at what must have seemed to be the promised land, the survivors were determined to embrace the future. The drive of these parents to have their children succeed was extraordinary.

Von Steuben High School was 95 percent Jewish. The boys were going to be lawyers, doctors, and CPAs; the girls were going to college to get a big ring from a Jewish lawyer, doctor, or CPA. The school had no athletic fields, no football team. There was no premium for being a sports star or a cheerleader; you got status at Von Steuben for being chosen for an advanced placement or honors class. Intellectual success begets professional success; this was believed with biblical fervor.

Bonnie Typlin, my good friend from the egghead group, wanted to be a doctor. Imagine, a girl wanting to be a doctor. Even in our school such ambition was unheard of, but my mother encouraged Bonnie, telling her, "You can do this; you can overcome the obstacles. A bright girl like you can become a doctor. Certainly. You're smart; you're devoted. Have faith in yourself; you can become anything you want to be. You want to be a doctor—be a doctor." It was the same thing she had been telling me all my life. When Bonnie graduated from medical school, my mother could not have been more proud. Bonnie and I remain the closest of friends. She is a sister, a confidante, an extraordinary woman.

My mom was captivating. She walked into a room so full of life that she almost shone, as if she herself were full of light. My friends dropped by our house all the time and everyone wanted to talk to her. My boyfriends loved her. Boys would go on dates with other girls and then come to our kitchen at midnight for a bowl of cereal. My mom would sit with them. "How was your date? Did you have a good time?" Kids treated her like a friend, not a parent.

But my mother, who was almost thirty-eight years old when I was born, was over fifty by the time I got to high school, and I didn't recognize her beauty. As I became prettier she let herself go, putting on weight and choosing to buy clothes for me rather than fix her teeth. I got the shoes, she didn't; I got my hair done, she didn't. She seemed to decide there was only so much beauty available to the family and she wanted me to have it all. She lived through my attractiveness.

I was getting good roles at Jack and Jill—Peter Pan in *Peter Pan*, the Cowardly Lion in *The Wizard of Oz*, Emily in *Our Town*. At the age of sixteen, I was fortunate enough to get my Actors' Equity card in summer stock by playing Tiffany Richards in *Mary, Mary*. I had a crush on Bob Balaban, a young actor whom I had met at summer theater. (I even stole a kiss backstage during the finale of *The Sound of Music*.) I could dance, but I was a mediocre singer at best, so musicals were a frightening challenge.

When I thought about colleges, I wanted to go to a good theater school. I considered Yale, Stanford, Carnegie-Mellon—all top schools with excellent theater reputations. But my parents were concerned that I would neglect my studies in pursuit of my career. Their drama school of choice was Northwestern University in Evanston, Illinois, which had a noted theater arts program. Northwestern produced many good actresses and provided a full academic education as well. It was also only forty-five minutes by train from downtown Chicago.

But I was ready to get out into the world; I did not want to feel tied to the homestead. My parents were not insensitive to my feelings. My parents had never owned a car, but they bought me a white Corvair. Unsafe at any speed, but who knew? Even though freshmen weren't allowed to have cars on campus, it would add to my freedom. They told me, "You don't have to come home on weekends. We'll treat you as if you are in another city. But we would both be happier if you went to Northwestern." They had raised me to be intellectually independent and had granted me extraordinary liberty, but when the time came for me to leave, they couldn't bear it and wanted me within arm's reach. And I loved to be near them. I was not a rebellious child; I was trying to be perfect.

Every dollar my father had saved in a life of hard work was going into my college education. Everything. He had struggled and slaved and put together the money as an act of love and sacrifice. As much as I wanted to get away, I couldn't ignore their feelings. Northwestern was an excellent school; I would receive good theater training and a solid education. If it was so very important to my parents to have me close at hand, I could make that sacrifice. Not that my sacrifice was in any way comparable to theirs; I was going to a great school and I was going to act. With my mother and me in the backseat and my father up front, my aunt Doris drove her red Volkswagen Beetle to the Northwestern campus. After inspecting my dorm room, my parents kissed me and drove away.

two SORORITY RUSH

DON'T KNOW THAT MY ROOMMATE HAD EVER MET A JEW, BUT HERE I WAS, AND ACROSS the hall was another dark-haired Jewish girl from Kansas City. Our dormitory *shtetl*. I didn't think anything of it; my high school had been almost entirely Jewish. I was busy getting oriented to college life, and in autumn 1966, when I arrived on campus, freshman orientation at Northwestern University was dominated by sorority rush week.

"Sororities are discriminatory organizations," my mother told me. "They're cliquish and they're not nice to people." She was dead set against my rushing. But the Greek system was so ingrained at the school that campus social life depended on it, and my life had always been extremely social. If everyone else was going to rush, so was I. On the morning rush week commenced, I received the schedule of houses I was to visit and I set out to join the sisterhood.

I didn't want to join the Jewish sororities. I had the sense that they hovered together for protection and I didn't feel the need. If I was going to join a house, I wanted some variety. In this completely new environment I wanted a broader spectrum of friends.

The wall-to-wall carpeting at Delta Gamma was deep green, like a fairway. I was dressed in a green-and-blue plaid kilt, matching twin sweater set, and black ballet flats, but from the moment I walked in, it was clear that I was not welcome. The women were all wearing Villager clothing similar to mine, but for me this outfit was a costume; for them it was a uniform. They were all tall and blond and Christian, and not one made a move to greet me. Other young women were escorted to small clusters of gamine young ladies who talked with them to see if they were sister material, but I was left to stand by myself. I looked around the room. I was the shortest girl there, and the darkest, and the only one standing alone in the vestibule. One look had decided that I wasn't a Delta Gamma.

When someone finally did guide me to a group standing in the middle of the lounge, the girls scattered like straw in the wind. All these blondes wanted no part of me. I wasn't worth their time. Soon I was alone again. I wished the floor would open up so I could vanish into the rough.

I was shaken. No one had ever snubbed me before—far from it. Still, I told myself, maybe I had simply walked into an unfortunate but aberrant selection of women. There were other sororities.

I made the rounds of the rush parties and was given the same cold treatment at Kappa Alpha Theta, Kappa Kappa Gamma, everywhere. I rushed at the three top tall-blonde-popular houses, and by the end of the day I understood quite clearly that I was not going to be invited back for a second round. I was so shaken that even when I found someone to talk to, I could hardly speak.

By the time I returned to my dorm room I was in tears. I didn't fit in. I must not be attractive. I must not be what they want. I didn't know what clothes to wear; I was fat, dark, stupid, ugly. I had nothing to offer. The possibility of antisemitism did not dawn on me.

I was afraid to talk to other freshmen about my terror. What if they had been accepted? Would they stop speaking to me, too? Was I beneath them? I was all alone, with no direction home. In one afternoon my sense of who I was had been completely stripped from me, along with my self-worth. I hadn't even started classes, and my college life was already over.

But I continued to rush. I so desperately wanted to be accepted. I didn't have a vision of college without this kind of belonging. Finally, I walked into the Alpha Chi Omega house, where I found a dearth of statuesque blondes. ACO was home to both devastatingly attractive women and ordinary college girls. Women came up to me and asked questions; they let me tell them about my acting background and what I had done in my life. And they liked me. I was so grateful that this Gentile house had accepted me that I joined them. I was so scared of being an outsider that I would have kissed their feet in gratitude.

My mother was horrified. Not that I told her about the rejections. I simply said, "I like these people, and they like me. There are theater majors in this house; they care about academics; they are very nice and I would like to do this."

"Rikki," my mother said, "I'm sure no colored person is there." (She was using the terminology of the day. My mother was as close to color-blind as a person could be in 1966.)

"You're right, Mom. But I'm rushing anyway."

I bought a couple of Villager skirts and a pair of penny loafers and began to acclimate to campus life. I worked hard academically, of course. I joined the theater and read for several parts.

In high school I had never felt it necessary to grab the spotlight; it had found me naturally. At Northwestern, so very unappreciated, I found there was a need in me to be recognized. I liked the applause I received onstage, and I wanted that same warmth from the people around me. So I applied to become a member of the Wildcat Council, a group selected on academic merit and personality to give campus tours to alumni and prospective students. If you were on the Wildcat Council, you had made it. Driven to succeed, I was excited when they chose me.

Northwestern's trademark on-campus event each spring was Freshman Carnival, a weekend-long extravaganza that raised money and gave everyone an excuse to party. For anyone who wanted to be noticed, the power job was Carnival cochairman. Every year one girl and one boy were elected to the position. It was not an honorary title; the Carnival cochair needed the vision to organize the event, the ability to handle the details to make this huge production run smoothly, and the personality to galvanize the student body into having a wailing good time. The cochairman became a recognized campus leader, a celebrity, a distinguished freshman with a big future. And you had to campaign for it. People ran for Carnival cochair as if they were running for student council president. One of my sorority sisters, Allison Platt, said, "I think you should run."

I didn't need a lot of convincing. I needed to regain my self-esteem, and Allison's confidence in me was a great start. I wanted to show that even though I wasn't a tall blonde from Edina, Minnesota — a Kappa Kappa Gamma — I was still a force to be reckoned with.

Allison, it turned out, was the James Carville of campus elections. She and a cabal from our dormitory helped me organize an elaborate campaign, which was not simply a matter of putting up construction-paper posters in the dorms. I had to be everywhere, do everything, introduce myself to the entire campus, and get them to like me. I had to attract the spotlight and then shine in it. I was an actress; I could do that. And with Allison's help, I did. I announced specific ideas to make our Freshman Carnival an event our class would remember for a lifetime. I used the campus newspaper. I shook hands with all the tall blondes and their boyfriends, and talked to people I'd never met and asked for their vote. And everywhere, I made sure people knew my name.

And I won.

Having gotten the job, I worked diligently and Freshman Carnival went off without a hitch. By the end of freshman year I was back on my feet. Thank heaven. I had been so scared.

When I returned home to Chicago I found myself in the middle
of the Summer of Love. It was 1967; the Vietnam War was expanding and so was the opposition to it. I read the paper, watched the war
on the news, and talked to my parents and friends. It became clear to
me over time that the United States had no business being in Vietnam: No international dominoes were going to fall on American
shores, and boys my age were dying over there for no good reason.
When I returned to campus in the fall of 1967, I was much more
politicized than when I'd left. I wasn't going to trash an ROTC building, but I was going to march in protest. I did not drive to Washington, D.C., that fall to march on the Pentagon; political activism was
still brand-new to me. Boys began arriving on campus with long hair
and blue jeans instead of the standard uniform of khaki trousers,
white polo shirts, and blue blazers, and the girls' Villager skirts and
circle pins were being replaced by jeans and turtlenecks. I paid a lot
of attention to the changing world around me.

Even my sorority was changing. For the first time, several black
girls had actually rushed ACO. When we held our annual meeting to
discuss potential new inductees, some sisters analyzed the pledges on
their merit, but a large portion of the sisterhood objected strongly to
every black nominee. The meeting never became heated (we never
had heated discussions about anything), but these girls dug in
strongly, their objections running deeper than the reasons that were
aired. Finally, the chapter voted to accept one person of color, almost
because we thought we had to. Not everyone was happy with the
decision. "I wouldn't want to brush my teeth next to her," said one of
my sisters. An entire wing mumbled in assent.

That night I called my mother. "You were right," I told her. I
didn't take a public stand, and, if asked, I suspect my fellow ACOs
would have felt they were being remarkably progressive by pledging
even one black girl. I didn't want to live in such an exclusionary
world, however, so I resigned from the sorority. No one else seemed
to take it as seriously. I kept some of my sorority friendships, though
for the most part, I was out on my own.

I auditioned for *A Man for All Seasons* and thought I read fairly
well. Then this blond freshwoman came in and took my breath away.

As she read, every inflection, every gesture was perfect. She wasn't flashy, she didn't demand a thing from the audience, but I couldn't look away. Whatever it takes to completely command attention on a stage, she had it. I watched her wrap herself in that role and I had an epiphany. I understood, perhaps for the first time, that there were some things I could do and some things other people were better at than I was. I had never seen a more talented actress. (Apparently she could do comedy as well. When Shelley Long landed the part of Diane on *Cheers*, I was not at all surprised.)

I landed my first important lead in a college play later that year: Catherine in Tennessee Williams's *Suddenly, Last Summer*, the Elizabeth Taylor role. (By that time I was letting my hair grow, and it was working its way down my back in the manner of Joan Baez, Bob Dylan's consort, the queen of folk music.) I was thrilled, and I worked intensely to bring that character to life. She was sexy and in turmoil. I understood that.

I became more politically active as I learned more about the war. Senator Eugene McCarthy was running for president, and I handed out flyers and stuffed envelopes at his local campaign headquarters. But I became a turncoat when Senator Robert Kennedy's candidacy began its ascendancy. I was among the many students around the country who rallied to him. I marched; I signed petitions; I did whatever a college student could do to move the country in a better direction.

Martin Luther King Jr. was assassinated and we marched in his honor. Bobby Kennedy was assassinated and we were devastated. Everyone was in tears. Changing the world was going to be considerably more difficult than we had thought.

During this time of upheaval, Northwestern was calm but simmering. The administration did what it could to prevent the explosions that were disrupting Columbia, Berkeley, and other campuses across the country. In one of my social science courses, for the final exam the professor asked us to write about our reactions to Kennedy's death and their relationship to what we had learned that year. I thought that the assignment was a master stroke.

I was at home in the summer of 1968, when the Democratic

National Convention was held in Chicago. The only reason I didn't get teargassed in Grant Park during the police riot was that I had a girlfriend come in from out of town that night and my mother took us to dinner. My father, who was away on business, assumed I was demonstrating. He called home very concerned that I had gotten my head cracked open.

Junior year was more of the same: campus activism, classes, theater. I was getting good grades and good parts. It was a vital time to be young and on campus, and my friends and I enjoyed it to the maximum.

A group of theater majors had been working on an experimental play for months. Very avant-garde, lots of ensemble improvisation, under the direction of a progressive professor named Joe Brockett. Incense burning, elaborate imaginative dance—a performance I would probably cringe at today but at the time I thought it was completely fabulous. My parents took the train up to see me on opening night and came backstage afterward and praised me to the skies. In their eyes I could do no wrong.

After the play we went out for dinner, then I drove my parents home and headed back to Evanston, where the cast party was being held at the apartment of my boyfriend, a scene designer who shared the two-bedroom place with another student in the theater department. When I arrived I was pleased to find the small apartment filled with a couple dozen people standing around drinking wine, talking animatedly about the craft of acting, emoting as only theater people can, and listening to Blood, Sweat & Tears blaring on the stereo.

BLAM! The Evanston police broke down the door with a sledgehammer.

"All right, everybody up against the wall!"

My boyfriend wanted to know what the hell was going on. The cops showed him a search warrant, then spun him around and lined him up with everyone else. They were looking for hundreds of pounds of marijuana. They knew it was in here. Just shut up and do as you're told.

The cops separated the men from the women. The guys were plastered against the living room wall; the women were herded into one of the bedrooms, where a female officer screamed at us to be quiet and stand still. I could hear police in the other room bellowing at the men. One by one the girls were brusquely body searched. I was wearing navy blue slacks and a long blue jacket with a mandarin collar and little silver buttons down the front. Why do I remember that?

The whole world seemed to stop in that moment: The cops were screaming, tearing through the apartment, opening drawers and pulling up seat cushions in their search for contraband. And Blood, Sweat & Tears kept spinning 'round. No one had turned off the music; it just played and played. I was terrified.

It was March 1969. According to most of my friends, any college kid who wasn't smoking pot at that time just wasn't paying attention. But there was no pot—that is, none to speak of—in the house. Not in anyone's pockets, not in the ashtrays, nowhere. Hundreds of pounds? After a thorough search, the police came up with a minute quantity in a medicine vial, residue scraped from two dried pipes, and a bag of seeds in the kitchen pantry.

"All right, you're going in."

They carted us down to the police station. None of us had ever been anywhere near the inside of a jail. They fingerprinted us, rolling our tips in ink just like on *Dragnet*. They took mug shots, not eight-by-ten glossies but the real thing. We were booked. I was stunned. I was the perfect child. I was not supposed to be there. This was going on my permanent record.

"I have to go to the bathroom," I told the officer standing next to me. "I'm really going to be sick."

"Stay where you are."

He would not let me go. Maybe he didn't believe me; maybe he didn't like pot-smoking college girls with hair down to their waist; maybe it was against regulations. I don't know. I threw up right on his feet. He didn't like me even more after that.

Then they threw us into the cells.

When I finally got to make my phone call it was the middle of the night. I certainly didn't wake up my parents. I called Roger Friedman, a charismatic student leader, and by the morning he and his contacts had raised enough money to bail us all out.

I called my parents as soon as we were released. "Mom, I got arrested."

"Rikki, I couldn't sleep last night," my mother said. "I had the feeling something bad was happening to you." She and I had such a strong connection that I fully believed her.

We made headlines in all the papers that morning. PROFESSOR, STUDENTS ARRESTED IN DRUG RAID. I was embarrassed for myself; I was embarrassed for my parents; I had brought shame upon my family. I was miserable.

The boyfriend of a woman I had worked with that summer was a criminal defense lawyer. "You're going to need two lawyers," he advised when I called. "One for the people who were visiting and one for the guys who live in the apartment. The best drug lawyer in Chicago is George Pontikes. He is legendary for getting people off. Call him."

I had never heard of George Pontikes, but he had heard of our case by the time I called and he agreed to represent my boyfriend and his roommate. Mr. Pontikes agreed that the larger group could be represented by Al Armonda, the attorney I had originally called. He accepted the case.

The first thing they did was move for a change of venue. Evanston was a very small community, and the publicity surrounding our bust had been thunderous. Considering the media carpet bombing and the potential for pretrial publicity to influence the jury, the judge transferred our case to the City of Chicago Narcotics Court, where the city's expanding docket of drug cases was decided. Within months we were ready for trial.

A few days before our initial hearing in Chicago, we convened to discuss our case in Al Armonda's downtown office. Drug cases were his business. He was calm, perhaps even eager. I was scared. I could be convicted. I could go to prison. I would never be an actress; I would never get a job; I would be a disgrace. And I wasn't the only one who was scared: One of the other girls who had been arrested was from Ohio; she had come in to see the play and been invited to the party by a friend. She had to fly in for the hearing and hardly knew any of us. She was petrified. I didn't know what was happening to me, so I asked a million questions. Armonda tried to lay out the facts, present us with all of the possible results, and give us a perspective that, because of our limited experience in this area, perhaps we did not have.

Our case would be heard by Judge George Wendt. This was fortunate, Armonda said, because Judge Wendt had little tolerance for small potatoes, he was interested in more far-reaching cases. Judge Wendt was also unlikely to put such generally upstanding citizens as ourselves in jail for so minor an offense. Nothing was certain in court, Armonda told us, but he had a strong feeling that we were not in jeopardy. Feeling a little relieved, we trooped to the courthouse.

The City of Chicago Narcotics Court was on the South Side, on the corner of Twenty-sixth and California, in the same area as the Cook County Jail. The hallways were filthy and reeked of urine. I went to the bathroom before court convened and found there were no doors on the stalls. Our privacy was public. I sat there facing a mirror and was shocked at the severity of my surroundings. Under harsh fluorescents I saw myself and everyone else in that row, and they were all in my predicament. We were free . . . for now. What would I face if I was convicted?

We were charged with possession of narcotics, which really meant "being present where marijuana is found," a felony in Chicago in 1969. People were being sent away for drug possession all the time. I could be a felon! I tried to control my fear.

The courtroom was a processing center through which hundreds of drug cases were marched every day. Among the defendants, our little group of college kids had virtually the only white faces. Almost everyone charged looked poor; their clothes were ripped or filthy. I watched the court officers strut their fiefdom like squires before whom we were specks of dirt.

Al Armonda turned out to be a showman. His expensive suit contrasted quite consciously with his surroundings, as if anything connected to him must by association be clean. He addressed the court, and if I can't recall all of his words verbatim, some phrases have stayed with me for years. "Your Honor," he said, "look at these students from the noted center of higher education, Northwestern University. Look at these people and how they appear. These aren't drug smugglers; these aren't drug abusers; they're good, clean kids."

Judge Wendt almost flew off his bench. "Are you saying, Counselor, that a rich, well-dressed young man or woman should receive more lenient treatment under the law than a poor black defendant? Is that what you are saying? Because if it is, your clients are in a lot of difficulty."

I was going to jail forever. I had put my life in the hands of a cocky lawyer and he had sent me up the river. All my father's savings—gone. My family's good name—gone. My mother and father had invested everything they had in me, and I had let them down. Not only had I been far from perfect, I had brought them shame. Shame! My life was over. We were dead.

Al Armonda was desperately trying to backpedal when George Pontikes rose slowly from the defendants' table. If Armonda was Perry Mason, the rumpled, older Pontikes was Columbo. (I was twenty-one, and he appeared old to me, but he may have been forty, not seventy.) He stood not so much to save a colleague from a judicial harangue as to amiably clear up a minor misunderstanding. Comfortably, like a man in slippers in his den, he addressed the legal nuances. No, he told the judge, we were not innocent because we were well dressed; we were not guilty because the government had no case. Two pipes and a bag of seeds did not warrant incarcerating a dozen people who knew nothing about them, nor could the government prove ownership by anyone charged.

Pontikes had appeared before Judge Wendt many times. When he entered the courtroom, I had noted that he knew the court clerk personally and all the bailiffs by name; the institutional brusqueness that was so intimidating to me had softened for him. I had the strong feeling that his reputation as a winner had been earned. People treated him well out of respect, not fear. It was also clear that his words and position carried weight and that he was familiar with the manner in which Judge Wendt thought. The judge accepted his explanation, and the crisis was averted.

George Pontikes was my image of what a criminal defense lawyer ought to be. He was a freedom fighter and a true counselor; he cared about his clients and advised us wisely. He knew how to work through the law, and he thought this case was a true injustice. He was living proof that there was some honor to the legal profession.

We didn't go to trial that day, nor the next time we appeared before Judge Wendt, nor the third. At some point, from the bench, the judge said, "None of these people could have gotten high from what was in that apartment." Eventually the case was dismissed. Two pipes and a bag of seeds was far less than what was necessary to jail a dozen people, but it was Chicago, and one never knows how these things come about. I do know that my knees buckled when I heard the decision, and that all of us rushed outside and stood around screaming for joy.

Under Illinois law, once a case is dismissed a defendant can file to have his or her record expunged and mug shots and fingerprints returned and to regain the legal right to say truthfully on any application that he or she has never been arrested. I applied. My prints and photographs came back and I was granted that right.

But it was not so much the legal right as the moral propriety that concerned me. I truly believed that being present where marijuana was kept was a sin, whether or not it was illegal. I had sinned and I deserved a black mark in my life.

My day in court stirred me. The trial of the Chicago Eight—or the Chicago Seven, depending on one's perspective on the severing of Bobby Seale's case—began in 1969, and I drove from Evanston to downtown Chicago several times at some ungodly hour in the morning to stand on line for tickets to this strange circus. I had been a peaceful protester, but I was nonetheless passionate about stopping the war. I marched in Chicago when the United States invaded Cambodia, I protested when National Guardsmen shot students dead at Kent State University, and I was involved in the student strike that shut down classes at Northwestern. My politics were liberal, not violent or radical.

I also thought this trial would be good theater, and I was not disappointed. Abbie Hoffman and Jerry Rubin were fun pranksters, and it didn't take a genius to see that Judge Julius Hoffman had no control of his courtroom. Abbie and Jerry goofed on him, goofed on the process, and goofed on the system. Judge Hoffman never figured them out.

I thought Tom Hayden had a significant political mind, but because I was not a violent person I could not follow his beliefs to their ultimate conclusion. I was no revolutionary. My hero in that group was Rennie Davis, the head of the National Mobilization Committee to End the War in Vietnam. When he told the prosecutor, "I hope after this trial . . . that you and I can sit down and talk about what happened in Chicago and why it happened. . . . I would like to do that very much," I understood him completely. Despite the fact that he and the prosecutor were on opposing sides of the courtroom, Davis felt they might understand each other because they both were pursuing the same goals: law and justice. I was awed by that sentiment.

In much the same vein, I took a course at Northwestern in First Amendment freedoms, taught by Professor Franklyn Haiman. What a revelation! I became engrossed by the case law we read and couldn't wait for class each week. I loved understanding how the law worked, and reading about and discussing the intricacies of the Constitution. Because I had seen them in action—and inaction—with my own eyes, I felt a deep need to know what freedom of speech, freedom of the press, and freedom of assembly really meant. Professor Haiman brought the law to life for me.

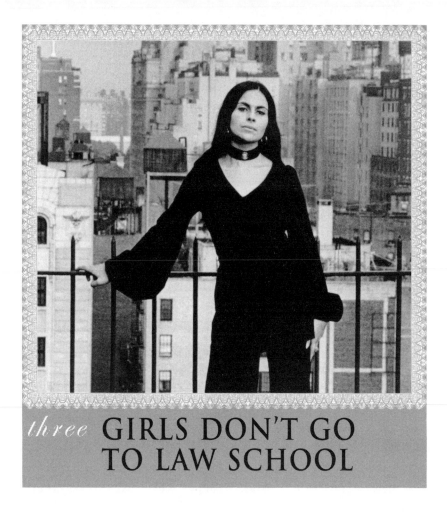

three GIRLS DON'T GO TO LAW SCHOOL

WHEN I GRADUATED IN 1970, I WAS DETER-
MINED TO GO TO NEW YORK, THE CENTER
of the theater world, and become an actress. The family of my great
friend Andy Frances, a student actor/director/producer whom I had
dated at Northwestern, lived in Stuyvesant Town in New York City.
Andy's mother, Evan Frances, allowed me to move in with the family
in Manhattan for the summer in exchange for my helping with the
chores. I worshiped Evan Frances. She was a very prominent, highly
opinionated, highly successful, highly driven journalist. At the time,

she was special projects editor of the *Ladies Home Journal,* and she even gave me a job helping her to edit stories. I was pleased no end. When I ultimately moved out of the Franceses' home and got an apartment with another aspiring actress, I remained in close touch with Evan. She became my role model, almost like a second mother to me, and remains so today. Well into her eighties, she is as vibrant and feisty as ever.

I took acting classes and put together a portfolio, then looked for an agent. I read *Backstage* and *Variety* as I made the rounds of auditions. I was a Kelly girl and took every temporary typing job I could get. I waited tables and worked at whatever I could find while I was trying to get my big break.

I got a call to model for a commercial and arrived at the studio to find one guy standing there with his camera. No lighting assistant, no production assistant, just him. I walked in and thought, What am I doing in this room? Very quickly he became physical. I pushed him away with a force I did not know I had, yanked the door open, ran down the stairs and out of the building, and didn't stop running for blocks.

This type of encounter happened several times. I learned to search for signs, to be particular about which calls to go on and which to turn down. For an actress to refuse work, the scene had to be very threatening. But even legitimate producers gave me a song and dance, trying to get me into bed. One literally chased me around his desk, and when he couldn't catch me, said, "You're much too moral to be in the theater. This is how it's done." Not with me, it wasn't.

I liked going to bed with men. I am a very sexual creature and for me sex is an act of intimacy. I certainly had my share of partners, but I chose to have sex on my terms when I wanted to be with a particular man. In that way I was very much like a guy; I chose my sexual partners according to my own desires. The choice was mine. I was responsible for my own body, and I never used sex as a bartering tool. I feel as strongly about this today as I did when I was young. As women, *we* decide what we do with our bodies, and we take responsibility for our decisions. I was not at all averse to having sex with men, but bartering my body for an acting job would have meant my self-esteem had sunk to an all-time low. I had a healthy self-esteem. I didn't need to do that.

I finally got a job in a bus-and-truck-company production of *Stop the World—I Want to Get Off*, touring little towns from the East Coast to the Midwest for several months. This was grueling work for very little money. I did get to go onstage and sing and dance, but since I couldn't sing much in the way of harmonies, I became tremendously frustrated. My back hurt constantly, and when it went out, as it did a number of times, people massaged me in the wings just so I could make it through the performance. I was afraid to admit to myself that this really wasn't the way I thought a life in the theater would be.

My father and I had agreed when I came to New York in June 1970 that I would give acting one year, after which we would have a discussion as to whether I wanted to continue to pursue it. "If it hasn't gone your way," he told me, "I think you would be better off in life looking at another profession." He didn't want to see me waiting tables when I was sixty-five, still hoping for my one big break. A year went by and I had not made a mark. When spring 1971 came around, he was willing to give me another year. It wasn't actually "give me," since I had promised myself that one way or another I would pay back the money he had paid for college.

Then I landed the golden audition. Francis Ford Coppola was casting *The Godfather*. I believed I was the perfect actress to play Apollonia, the Sicilian peasant woman whose beauty hits Michael Corleone like a thunderbolt. This could be a career-making part, I thought. Marlon Brando was starring; Diane Keaton and James Caan had roles. I dressed appropriately, put my portfolio with my résumé and head shots under my arm, and took a subway to midtown. I walked to the office building where the audition was being held and stepped onto the elevator.

When the door rolled open, my heart dropped. Sitting and standing in a line that snaked around a corner and wound down the linoleum hall were a hundred of me—two hundred of me!—all attractive, dark-haired, five-foot-two-to-five-foot-eight Mediterranean types aged fifteen to forty years old, all with ready portfolios and thunderbolt smiles. I stood at the end of the line. Soon more women were standing behind me.

We waited. Some of the women kept to themselves and tried to keep up appearances. Others told stories. Most of these stories were about their successes: "I played Maria in *West Side Story* in Atlanta"; "I was in the road company of *Hair*"; "I played Ophelia at Yale." They were all great actresses; they had all gotten uniformly great reviews; they had all impressed this producer and that director. And they were all out of work. Some of the women telling these stories had been searching for roles — *had been on this line!* — for fifteen years.

These were truly attractive women. I thought they were pathetic. And I thought, This could be me if I don't get this part, telling my credits to a pack of beautiful losers. I just didn't want to be them. I didn't want anyone to feel sorry for me the way I was feeling sorry for them. I looked up and down the hall. The line was moving.

Two hours passed. When my turn arrived, I put on my most confident face, walked in smartly, handed my photo and résumé to the woman at the door, and read my lines for the producers. I thought I read quite well, at least for thirty seconds. They said, "Thanks, we'll call you if we need you."

I had no idea what I was going to do with my life, but I knew I was not going to do this ever again. I was the child of Depression parents, and my fear of poverty was overwhelming. I was working odd jobs and saving every penny, and I could not bear the thought that I might be living this way for the next twenty or forty years. I was willing to not succeed. (I did not mention the word *failure*.) I was not afraid of rejection; I was willing to go forward. But at some point in your life there comes a time when you say, "I don't want to do this anymore. I don't need to succeed at this anymore. This is crazy." By the time I got back to my apartment I had reached that point.

I didn't want to fail, and I didn't want to quit. I had to find a way to leave without defining my departure as failure. As I had done in the fourth grade, I used my health.

For nine months my doctor had been telling me I had an ovarian cyst that ought to be removed. It wasn't cancerous, but it was a dermoid cyst that could eventually grow to the size of a grapefruit. I called my parents. I neglected to mention the audition. "You know, I really think I should have this cyst out. It's time. I'm going to call Dr. Alpern and arrange it. I'll do it after my birthday."

"Are you sure?" my mother asked. "You want to leave New York? What about your career?"

"Well, you know, the cyst is really bothering me."

That afternoon I bought a steamer trunk and began piling my stuff inside. I told my roommate I was going back to Chicago for surgery and paid several months' rent while she found another girl to share the apartment. I shipped the trunk and went home. I let that cyst cue my exit.

I was once again living in my parents' house. I had a month to wait before my surgery was scheduled. Meanwhile, I had all day, every day, to figure out what to do with my life.

I called Professor Franklyn Haiman at Northwestern. While I had thrived in the drama department, I had never felt more alive than when I was taking his class on First Amendment rights. I asked whether I could visit him on campus.

Classes were still in session, and the campus was bustling. He must have known why I was there. I didn't waste his time.

"All my life, Professor, I've wanted to be an actress. Everything I've ever done, from the time I can remember, was to be an actress; it's the only thing I ever wanted to do. I thought I was pretty good. I thought I could make it work, and when I went to New York it was terrible."

"You haven't even been there a year," he said. "Don't you think you should give it some more time?"

"No. It's a dissipated way to make a living. I can't sing to save my life. I'm a good dancer, but it's already taking its toll on my body. My back is a mess. I think I'm a really good classical actress, and I want to do serious drama, but it could take years to get a part. I'm afraid of being broke." I about broke down. "I think I have a good mind. . . ."

"You have a really good mind," he consoled me. After a year of rejections I was glad to hear something nice.

"I think I should use it for other things."

"Well, what do you want to do?"

"I don't have the faintest idea." It was true. Without my vision of myself as an actress I was bereft of a vision of the future. We discussed teaching, which was a logical career choice for women in the seventies. I mentioned how interesting I had found the communications courses I had taken with him. Studying communications in graduate school was another option.

"You'd be a very good teacher," he agreed. "And graduate school also sounds worthwhile." He paused as he ran his mind over what he knew. "How about that First Amendment course? You did very well."

"I loved that course. That was my favorite course in college!"

"Why don't you think about going to law school?"

I had never given it a moment's thought. "Girls don't go to law school," I told him.

"No, but women do."

My mother loved the idea. "Why not? You'll be great." Professor Haiman had explained that I would need to take the LSAT exam. "You'll take the test; you can live here; you'll recuperate. . . ." My mother had always told me I could do anything. She did it again.

My father wanted to know how I was going to afford three years of law school. "I don't know how you're going to do this financially," he said. "I don't have any money to send you." He was worried that what I was suggesting was simply impossible, and he was scared for me because he had nothing left to give.

"I'm sure I can get a scholarship or a loan, but I'll worry about that later."

I had asked Professor Haiman to recommend books for me to read while I was recuperating from surgery. He suggested *Crime in America* by Ramsey Clark. I began it in the hospital and continued it at home. The recovery process took eight weeks, and I was babied through it. First I could walk only one block each day, which meant I had a lot of time to read. Clark's book mentioned an organization in New York City called the Vera Institute of Justice, which produced criminal justice research projects that I found intriguing. The institute had begun an extraordinary reform effort called the Manhattan

Court Employment Project, the goal of which was to reduce recidi-vism and increase productivity and public safety by finding employ-ment for inmates released from jail. Vera was also a champion of the Bail Reform Project, which promoted releasing defendants on their own recognizance if they could show substantial roots in the commu-nity.

With so much time on my hands I pulled out my trusty Smith-Corona portable typewriter and began flooding the institute with let-ters asking for a job. It was June; the LSAT exam was given at the end of July, and I wouldn't know my scores until September, at which time the law schools would be full. I would have to work an entire year before starting law school, and I was determined to work at Vera.

What little I knew about the legal system pointed me in the direc-tion of criminal or Constitutional law; it was theatrical. George Pon-tikes had shown me how to work a local courthouse, and the Chicago conspiracy trial had been federal theater of the absurd. My world involved people and politics, so it was natural for me to want to work at Vera.

I took the LSAT at the end of July and then threw on my back-pack and hitchhiked to Colorado with my new boyfriend, Jeffrey Lane. We stayed with one of my college roommates and had a high old time for a month, and when my mother called to say that the Vera Institute wanted to interview me, we hitchhiked back. The Vera Institute had a position at the Appearance Control Project that involved working with the district attorney's office on a statistical study of police witnesses. I was young and fresh off the picket lines. I said, "You know, I really wanted to work on the defense side." I didn't want to work with the government; as a child of the sixties I was sus-picious of that type of authority. They told me, "This is the only job available. We don't know when another will open up." I agreed to come to New York for an interview.

Evan Frances put me up. I looked presentable as I walked through the employee entrance on Leonard Street into 100 Centre Street, a municipal building cliché, with institutional wood doors topped by opaque glass that seemed like half a slam would knock down. I searched the stone corridor for the institute's door. Inside, I was greeted by a woman in her mid-twenties who was talking to a devastatingly handsome black man. He looked at me and said, "Hire this woman." She laughed.

"I guess you passed the Dick Lowe test."

Dick Lowe, an assistant district attorney, smiled at me as he left the office.

I was interviewed by Samuel Herrupp, the project director, who asked whether I could stay in New York for a few days while the institute made its decision. I had mixed reactions. I was excited as could be to have an opportunity to work in the law community, but I didn't know whether I wanted to associate with these people. Still, if they were all like Dick Lowe it might not be so bad.

The Appearance Control Project hired me, and I spent 1971–72 working intensely on a study with a group of fewer than a dozen other, predominantly single women. We were the Vera girls, and pretty much the only women in the courthouse. I had the time of my life.

The project involved researching and reviewing the existing system of calling police and civilian witnesses to court to testify for the prosecution. Police officers were routinely sitting around the courthouse killing time for hours and sometimes days, waiting to be called to the stand. Some didn't mind, they were getting paid for doing nothing, but not only was it costing the city tremendous amounts of money—overtime pay for cops coming to court on their days off or vacation days—these were hours and days these officers were not on the streets protecting and serving the public. And, in fact, most cops *did* mind; they preferred being out there doing their jobs to sitting on benches drinking coffee in the courthouse. Plus, the civilian complainants would often get worn out by the process and eventually refuse to prosecute their cases. If your purse was stolen or your pocket was picked, why waste four to ten days of your life returning to a courthouse? If the Vera Project worked, they might have to come only once before justice could be done.

We gathered the statistics, analyzed the problems, and created a system under which cops would be called only for the hours they

needed to testify and only on their shift. The civilians were assigned a
real hearing date, not a pretend one laden with continuances, so they
could go to work or take care of their families.

This was my first experience with the police from their side of the
barricade. I thought I knew everything about police officers from my
demonstration days, and a few of my notions were correct. As I
worked intensively alongside these men, I found that a few were out
of control: They drank too much and liked to talk about their cases in
ways that were contemptuous of both the criminals and the public.
But at heart, I was utterly wrong. I learned that most cops took their
jobs very seriously and put themselves in harm's way for a living.
They wowed me. They were smart; they were committed; they lived
for their jobs: They believed they were destined to protect and serve,
to keep our world safe and secure. They were the real heroes of our
society. It didn't hurt that they were handsome and fun, living in a
wiseacre culture in which each story is better than the one before.
They loved women. And they thought I was a peach.

I met Joe Coffey, one of the greatest detectives in the history of
the New York Police Department. He broke the Hell's Kitchen gang,
the infamous Westies, and later went after mob bosses Paul Castel-
lano and John Gotti. Detectives are talkers, and Coffey was a talker
extraordinaire. He would swirl into a criminal courtroom and,
through vivid storytelling and true New York character, turn it into
his private theater. As a reward for helping him with some academic
paperwork, as I did for many others who were working on advanced
degrees in criminal justice, he put me in his unmarked car and took
me on a ride-along to Fort Apache, the legendary precinct in the
Bronx. I understood that there was a lot not to love about some cops,
and then there were the Joe Coffeys on the force, the professionals
who were going to make a positive difference in policing. So—
surprise, surprise!—I loved cops. I became their biggest cheerleader.

My impression of prosecutors was born of my drug bust experience and the Chicago Seven conspiracy trial. I thought the criminal
justice system was full of men—and prosecutors were almost always
men—who worked for the DA's office because they could not get

jobs elsewhere. Wrong again. The Manhattan district attorney was Frank Hogan, and his office was filled with the best and the brightest. His lawyers were graduates of Harvard and Yale and had left the biggest law firms to work for him. Hogan had a reputation: He was going to do justice. He was proactive, and his first line of talented attorneys attracted more talented attorneys, and so on, until his office was the gem of the system. People who wanted to use prosecutorial discretion wisely to make a difference in the safety of New York worked for Hogan.

In Hogan's office I found my first female role model in the legal arena—a young, beautiful, tough-as-nails assistant district attorney named Leslie Crocker Snyder. She was the first female ADA to be permitted to try homicide cases, and I would watch her work with awe and admiration. The vision of her confidence, competence, and poise guided me through several formative years. She ultimately became a famous New York judge, and my friend. Years later she presided over my wedding.

When I finished work each day, I would ask my boss Sam Herrupp whether I could go into the courtrooms and watch other trials in progress. I was transfixed. I forgot for a moment the filth in the corridors and smell of urine in the hallways; in my mind I had entered the halls of marble. I felt privileged to watch these people at work, and I wanted to be just like them.

I once again stayed with Evan Frances and her family. I put away every penny I possibly could. I never took a cab, only subways and buses; sometimes I even walked. My mother was still shopping the bargain basements for me, so I had work clothes. I had friends; the Vera girls were a close-knit group doing fun work together.

I was going out with two very different men. I was crazy about Jeffrey Lane. Jeffrey was brilliant and beautiful beyond words, with lots of blond hair that fell down around his ears, green eyes, a fabulous body. Very athletic, carried himself like an aristocrat. Jewish. A very sexy guy. He was going to Boston University School of Law, and we saw each other on weekends. We were twenty-two years old and . . . intense. But I was working in New York and I was meeting a lot of people, which was tempting.

It was natural for me to become attracted to someone who was smart as well as good-looking. I found an ADA named Dick Miller, who had a prematurely white shock of hair and sparkling blue eyes, and was as Irish as Irish could be. He was a bit rough around the edges and had a working-class background not unlike my own. Without even raising his voice, he owned the courtroom. I fell for him, too.

What a year: paradise in the courts, a life in New York, and two exciting men, both of whom I cared for deeply.

I could not make up my mind between them. What ultimately decided it for me was the fact that Dick Miller wanted to get married.

I didn't want to get married! I was twenty-three years old, and I was going to be a criminal defense lawyer; marriage would change everything, especially to a man like Dick, who was going to want children right away. Jeffrey didn't want to get married, so I chose Jeffrey.

I was accepted at Boston University School of Law. Harvard turned me down, which I, in my hubris, thought was a terrible mistake on its part. I went to Boston thinking, I should be across the Charles River. My class was full of baby boomers, many of whom had worked for several years or come back from Vietnam. It was 1972, the year of Watergate and the oral argument in *Roe v. Wade*, of journalists and lawyers. Everybody wanted to be either Woodward and Bernstein, or radical attorneys William Kunstler and Leonard Boudin. We were extremely competitive, and I'm sure all my BU Law classmates thought we should have been at Harvard, but we weren't. Despite our good education, many of us were bitter because we weren't at the school of "the chosen." Some of us used that resentment as career fuel.

Jeffrey had been at the top of his class and was tremendously helpful in teaching me how to approach my studies. Law school does not put a premium on answers, he informed me; the value is in the method you use to find them. One does not obtain a right or wrong solution; one's solution may or may not be workable. I had never been exposed to this way of thinking; I was a "right-answer" girl and I had a hard time adjusting. Through hours of talk, Jeffrey helped me adapt to these concepts.

After the first few months I realized that although law school was going to be difficult, and some students were going to perform better than I was, I would survive and thrive. My daily on-campus routine began when my first class convened at 9:00 in the morning and ended when the library closed at 11:00 at night. I kept my books in a locker because I didn't want to take them with me. That was my rule: When I'm home, I'm home. But I wasn't home for long. I studied all day, every day. Jeffrey was also a devoted student, so we would study together all week and go to the movies on weekends. We were deeply in love and very passionate, but we didn't have much time to devote to each other.

At Jeffrey's suggestion I joined a study group with students from my class. We gathered together simply because we sat next to each other in the classroom—whichever seats we took the first day, that was it. The professors entered, taught, and exited, while the students remained fixed and fearful.

My study group functioned not unlike the cast and crew of a play. We divided the work, took full responsibility for our own assignments, and shared the results. We were devoted and scared. Law school was extremely competitive, and our demand for excellence, combined with a compelling blend of insecurity and downright fear, brought our group to a high degree of competence. One of us rose to fourth in our class of 340. I was number forty-five.

I was so scared and so focused on doing well in law school that I didn't realize how unfocused I had become on Jeffrey. By my second semester our close-knit relationship had unraveled. Because all my time was spent studying, I became friendly with a student in my section named Alexander Wesman. I met him in the library, where else? Everybody called him Sandy. Sandy and I often wound up having lunch together and discussing the only thing anyone ever talked about: the law.

Like most of the men I had dated, Sandy was attractive, but in a different way. He was lanky, with long black hair and a mustache, and was given to wearing very tight jeans, a denim shirt, and cowboy boots. Where most of my study-group friends were over-the-top serious, Sandy talked about driving race cars and playing football in col-

lege. He was down-to-earth and funny. What started as a study partnership became something more. Without quite meaning to, I began
weaning myself from Jeffrey and moving toward Sandy. This was a
surprise to many of my friends. Jeffrey was the person I was supposed to be with: academically serious, brilliant, tenacious. Sandy
was a regular guy.

Jeffrey and I ended stormily at the end of the spring semester. It
must have been quite a scene, because I have completely blocked it
out. I had followed him to Boston, but things had changed. I do know
that he was furious and took the breakup hard. Jeffrey did not return
to school the following year. I was shocked—he was clearly on the
path to becoming a terrific lawyer—and I felt terribly guilty.

Not being able to remember the details of my breakup with Jeffrey was the first instance of what would become a continuing pattern. I have an elephantine memory for detail, yet it is clearly true
that I block out unpleasant endings of relationships. I idealize the
men I'm with and what they mean to me, and I revel in our good
times; yet when I leave them it pains me to think of myself as a person
who could be so hurtful, so I choose not to remember. I was always
moving forward, and I could not think of myself as a woman who put
either my career or another man ahead of the man I was with. I
became willfully blind.

I took a job that summer at the New York City Board of Correction, a watchdog agency over the Department of Correction. Sandy's
family lived in the New York suburb of White Plains, and I went up
there on weekends. They seemed nice and were pleased to meet the
new girl their son was dating.

One weekend Sandy and I took off. I didn't tell anybody where
we were going, but we drove to Connecticut and took a room at a
motel for a real lovers' tryst. We felt furtive and edgy and romantic in
ways that we really hadn't up to that point. Alone and away, we could
be private and let loose. After a year in law school, this kind of release
was a long time coming.

That weekend, Sandy's father had a heart attack and died.

Sandy's mother couldn't find her son. She called my apartment,
but I wasn't there; she called Sandy's friends, but they didn't know

where he was, either. That was the point: We had gotten away. For untold hours after his father died, Sandy was out of touch. Mrs. Wesman was frantic. Finally she found his best friend, who was the only person who knew our whereabouts. We were shacked up in a motel when Sandy heard the news.

Suddenly, there I was, part of the grieving family. I was at Sandy's side, helping to console his mother, helping Sandy deal with the funeral arrangements, meeting the relatives, sharing grief. What had been a budding two-month romance was catapulted into a relationship far more serious than we had ever intended, and we were helpless to stop it. I wanted to be there for Sandy, I wanted to be a good person, but I could see that we were moving at a speed we had not at all anticipated. I was thrown into the role of daughter-in-law. It wasn't anybody's fault—death will do that—but I went from the girl-friend to fiancée in what seemed like a matter of minutes.

In the fall we returned to school, and, as silly as this sounds, the next thing we knew we were getting married. We were in our second year of law school, and we were planning a June wedding, and I didn't know how any of it had happened. Neither did Sandy. Circumstance had made me a member of the Wesman family, so it seemed natural to formalize the arrangement. We were swept up in a series of events we couldn't seem to control.

My mother had met Sandy and thought he was a great guy. I called home and told her he was going to be my husband. She said, "What are you doing? Why are you doing this now? You left New York because you did not want to get married and compromise your career. So why?"

"I don't know."

"You don't know?!" She was beside herself. "Don't you think you ought to think about this?"

I couldn't think about it. If I thought about it for even a moment, I would see that we were not the right people for each other at this point in our lives. We were wonderful friends and good study partners, and we were caught up in a firestorm of emotion and loss and guilt. I simply could not find a way *not* to marry him. We had gone too far.

"We're just going to do this, Mom," I said.

Sandy and I planned our June wedding; it would be held in his parents' garden in White Plains, a year after his father's death. We organized it ourselves—chose the caterer, selected the decorations, hired the band.

The only point of contention was religion. Sandy's mother was Catholic, and his father, Alexander Wesman Sr., had been Jewish; Sandy had been raised in both traditions. My family's Thanksgiving table was like the United Nations, and we celebrated both Christmas and Hanukkah.

As the groom-to-be's surviving parent, Mrs. Wesman wanted us to be married by a priest. I was horrified. I refused. She insisted. Sandy and I had several discussions about it. "How about a priest and a rabbi?" he suggested. "How about two?"

"No."

"Well, this is a good compromise."

"I can't explain this to you," I told him. "It's not rational. I am not getting married by a priest. That's just the way it is." With my nonreligious upbringing, I wasn't even particularly comfortable being married by a rabbi. "Why can't we just go to a justice of the peace?"

Finally, a compromise presented itself that satisfied Sandy, me, and his mother, up to a point. One of Mrs. Wesman's next-door neighbors was a cantor at the local temple. He would perform the ceremony. And that is how we planned to be married, in a lovely garden setting before friends and family on a warm day in June 1974.

My parents and my aunt Eve, my father's younger sister, were staying at a hotel in White Plains, and the night before the wedding, after the rehearsal dinner, I visited with them.

My aunt Eve played a large role in my life. When my parents were first married, they moved into his parents' home, and my mom became almost a second mother to her new sister-in-law. She taught Eve how to dress and carry herself with style. Eve was a very attractive girl, but in her twenties she developed ulcerative colitis, had an ileostomy. My father used his small savings to pay for Eve's nursing to give her hope. She responded with tremendous love for him and, when I came along, for me. Aunt Eve was the one who took me to my first play, toured museums with me, and spent afternoons with me at the movies. Aunt Eve always had boyfriends, but she remained single throughout her life, determined to take care of herself. A strong, independent, charismatic woman, she was a great source of inspiration. She was my true role model. Like my mother, Aunt Eve told me I could be anything I wanted to be. She encouraged thought, discussion, and action. I relied on her advice for years. I still do. She and my mother both counseled me on men, sometimes giving me more information than I needed to know.

At some point my mother and I were alone.

"Mom," I told her, "I don't want to do this. I can't go through with it."

She was something less than sympathetic. "You should have thought about this sooner," she said. "I talked to you about this before."

"I can't do it. I just can't do it. My career will be over before it begins."

"Maybe it's prewedding jitters," she allowed. "A lot of brides feel this way the night before. Maybe you'll feel differently in the morning."

I woke up the next morning and I didn't feel differently. I didn't want to get married. But I thought, Maybe it's a bride thing. Maybe brides just do this. Maybe it's fear of lifestyle changes. I'm an anxious person anyway; my whole family is full of anxiety. I set all this in motion; I created this wedding; I really need to finish this. I am going to get married, and I'm going to be a good wife.

I got through the ceremony and the wedding reception. Everyone told me I looked lovely. Sandy's mother was happy. I think it's significant that I don't remember my wedding night. I was so angry with myself for losing control of my life. Here I was, married, weighed down by all of marriage's demands and expectations, when what I really wanted was a successful career. It was insane. How did I get here? At the end of the day, Sandy and I were exhausted and drained, and we just fell into bed.

It is very important for law students to land a major internship in the summer after their second year of study; that job is an avenue to a permanent position and a foothold on a successful career. We looked in Boston; I got many substantial offers, but Sandy didn't. We looked in New York, with the same result. Finally, we both landed jobs in Chicago. I was accepted at the large and prestigious corporate law firm Isham, Lincoln and Beale. I wanted to make a career in criminal defense law, but why not see what this experience would bring? Essentially, I got the job he wanted. This wasn't good.

I was a married woman when I went back to BU that fall, but our life did not run smoothly. I was tenacious and I outdid my husband. I didn't want to, but I did. Sandy was smarter, but I was a better student. My grades were excellent, and that caused friction in our marriage. We were both competitive people, and I never liked to be bested by anyone, but I wanted my new husband to succeed more than I wanted to succeed myself—a remnant, I suppose, of an old-fashioned culture—which became patronizing.

Things came to a head when we took a transactional analysis business-planning course together. I have no head for business. I had trouble with tax law because, for the life of me, I couldn't understand why people wanted losses in their portfolio—wasn't the whole point of investing to make money? I found it nearly impossible to construct a business plan. Sandy understood the course work perfectly. He had a mind for business and knew how to move numbers around to create real transactions. He was a great businessman, and when we studied together he explained enough of the course for me to parrot back on the examination. Going into the final exam I was terrified that I would fail the course.

I got a better grade than he did.

Our balance was all off. One part of me wanted my husband to outshine me. And he wanted to outshine me. But he knew and I knew that I was going to find some way to get ahead; after all, I was "Miss Remarkable." Everything I said sounded wrong. We knew our relationship was doomed.

I loved Sandy as a human being, but on an emotional level I was so angry at myself for getting married that I took it out on him. We had been friends before we were lovers; now I turned increasingly cold and over the course of two semesters we came apart. Withdrawn and uncommunicative, I showed little emotion; in fact, the only thing I showed any interest in was getting good grades and a good job. I was impossible.

By the end of law school we acknowledged we had made a mistake. One day Sandy simply said, "Why don't we just face facts, Rikki. This is not working. I really love you; I really want everything in your life to be good for you. But this is not working for either of us. Let's save ourselves from any more pain."

Thank God. I had felt guilty for being in a motel room with Sandy when his father died; I saw our marriage as a debt I owed to Sandy and his family. In retrospect, I know he felt the same way. But to marry a truly decent human being out of obligation was a huge mistake. My guilt was compounded by the realization that I had not faced up to the situation and corrected it myself.

I thanked Sandy for taking charge. And I agreed.

How was I going to tell my parents? I had gotten arrested in college, I had failed as an actress, and now I had screwed up my marriage. I would be a divorcée. In my parents' world, this would be as bad as getting busted for drugs. Worse. I didn't want to be a divorcée, but I didn't want to be married, and more than anything I didn't want to disappoint my parents. I was the perfect child. How was I going to tell them I was getting a divorce?

I didn't. I moved out of our apartment and into a place with four guys, all law students. They cleared out an attic and Sandy moved me in. The guys made my room pleasant by plopping a huge stuffed Snoopy on the bed as a welcome mat. I held on to it for dear life each night as I slept. There were no histrionics, no arguments. In essence, Sandy and I both sighed with relief. We didn't have many possessions to squabble over, and almost from the time I moved out we became friends again. We just never should have been married so young.

I didn't tell my parents. I was such a coward. I never lied to them; I just didn't tell them the truth. Every week they asked, "How's everything?"

"Fine."

"How's Sandy?"

"Fine."

Sandy began seeing another woman. I was so grateful. I wanted Sandy to be happy, and I wanted to stop feeling guilty about marrying him. I finally told my parents the truth.

It wasn't the kind of news I wanted to deliver by telephone, so I did it in person. I flew to Chicago and gathered my parents in their living room. "Mom, Dad, I've got something important to tell you." I suspect that is a phrase of some menace coming from the mouth of one's child. I soldiered on. "Sandy and I have separated."

My father asked, "Are you okay?"

"I'm fine."

My mother asked, "Is Sandy okay?"

"It wasn't really right for us. It just wasn't right. Mom, you knew that from the beginning."

My father's eyebrows went up. Apparently my mother had secrets of her own that she didn't share with her husband.

"He's seeing another woman now, and he seems to be doing well," I said. "He's happy. Really, it's better for both of us." I didn't lie. I didn't tell them that Sandy had left me for another woman, which would have made him a cad and thus taken the onus off me for having been a failure as a wife. But whatever they wanted to infer from my statement was acceptable. Interesting phrasing. I was becoming a master of communication.

The divorce was easy; there was nothing to divide except the photographs. And it was done. My marriage — gone.

four MENTORS AND MEN

THE LAW REVIEW IS THE MOST PRESTIGIOUS
ORGANIZATION AT A LAW SCHOOL. IT IS THE
domain of the academically elite. Law Review members get the best
clerkships when they graduate, followed by jobs at the best law
firms. Two factors determine a student's selection to Law Review:
cumulative grade point average and a written essay. I was not among
the top ten in my class, but I was ranked highly enough to be permitted to write my way on—which I did. I was invited to join the Law
Review.

I turned it down.

During my first year of law school I had participated in moot court. My classmates and I were assigned to teams and given a case file; we wrote an appellate brief and then argued the case before a panel of judges. I loved moot court; it was acting, performing. I knew if I could not distinguish myself in any other way, I could excel there. I had found my niche.

I turned down Law Review to participate in advanced moot court. This was unheard of, but I had my reasons. How do you go to the head of the class? You persevere in the area where you are best suited, and my area was moot court. On Law Review, without top-ten grades, I would have been one of many. My most vital goal was to become notable. If I performed well in moot court and was chosen to be on the national team, I would draw significant attention. And I could claim two successes instead of one on my résumé: "Although invited to join the Law Review, I chose to devote my efforts to the advanced moot court program."

Things worked out as planned. In the autumn of our third year, while we were still married, Sandy and I and Harry Conklin were chosen to represent Boston University in the national moot court competition. We were competing before panels of the best lawyers and judges in a bracket against the other New England law schools, including that school across the Charles River. We advanced to the semifinals, which were being held in a courthouse in Cambridge.

Ours was the last round of the day, and among those on the bench hearing us were the novelist and attorney George V. Higgins and U.S. District Court Judge Walter J. Skinner. Afterward there was a reception in the courthouse for all the participants.

I had read Mr. Higgins's book *The Friends of Eddie Coyle*, and was excited about the prospect of speaking with him. He was a real writer. A celebrity! I was moving through the crowd on my way to find Mr. Higgins when I met Judge Skinner. "I thought your argument was excellent," he told me. "You are a talented advocate." I thanked him. "Have you considered applying for a federal clerkship?" he asked.

I had not; I didn't think there was any point. The most prestigious job one could get coming out of law school was clerking for a federal judge. The position was a stepping-stone to a significant career. But only the top 5 percent of students in the class were encouraged to apply, and the competition was fierce. I was in the top 14 percent, but if the judges were crunching numbers only, I stood no chance. Judge Skinner had heard me present my case, he had not seen my transcripts. "I assume you would qualify," he told me. I smiled at him.

"Well, perhaps it was fortuitous that I was sitting on your panel of judges," he continued. "One of the two law clerks whom I hired for next year contacted me today and said he is not coming because he is taking a federal appellate court clerkship. I was going to go back through my files of the others whom I considered, and I would like you to interview with me. Would you do that?"

So sometimes even judges have to hold a last-minute rush week. "Of course," I said. "When would you like to see me?"

"Tomorrow. Five o'clock."

"I'll be there."

I was vibrating. What an honor! I had to step aside for a moment to regain my senses. Then I continued my hunt for George V. Higgins.

I gushed when I found him. "I've read your book! Aren't you wonderful. I'm so excited. I was so happy you were on my panel. I can't get over this!" I just know I sounded girlish and stupid and ridiculous. Apparently Higgins found my rambling very charming.

"It's a pleasure to meet you, too."

"If I get my book, will you autograph it?"

"You can come by my office anytime." He gave me his business card. "I'd be happy to do that."

The following day I had a second interview at Goodwin, Proctor & Hoar, a major Boston law firm. I was taken from office to office, partner to partner, in the annual dance of potential associates. By the time I got out I was running quite late.

I was wearing my interview dress—a fitted, fuchsia turtleneck number I had bought on sale at Loehmann's to impress prospective employers—off-white stockings and bone-colored high heels. Feminine but not sexual. The fact that I was wearing a fuchsia dress to interviews now astounds me; then it seemed attractive and classy. My long, black hair billowing behind me, I was running down the street toward the federal courthouse.

The wind was blowing, it was cold, and I was late when I dashed into the lobby and searched frantically for the judge's chambers. My watch said 5:45 when I found it. My hair was all over the place and my nose was running as I knocked on the judge's door. I was wiping my nose with my left hand and rapping with my right when he opened the door in my face.

"Boy, what a way to make an impression."

Judge Skinner laughed. "Come on in."

I presented my résumé, my letters of recommendation, my writing sample. Judge Skinner was a very distant man. In Boston they would describe him as an Irishman who always wanted to be a Yankee. He asked me very appropriate questions, then gave me hypothetical situations and asked how I would solve them. I thought I did well. He said he would get back to me within a week.

My mother had taught me the value of a handwritten note promptly delivered, so I rode the T to Boston the next morning and dropped one off with the judge's secretary. I really wanted that job. How could I clinch it? Robert Kent, a professor at BU Law, was an intellectual force to be reckoned with and knew many judges. I had taken his course in Constitutional law and I made an appointment to see him in his office. When I arrived, I politely asked him to write a recommendation that I could forward to Judge Skinner.

"No."

I was stunned. This job was within my grasp. Why would he refuse to help me get it?

"Because you are not in the top five percent of your class."

"But I'm really smart."

"Yes, you are. You're just not that smart."

"I'm going to get this job," I said firmly. "I'm going to be very good at it."

"You don't have that kind of intellectual capacity."

Why was he doing this? "You know, I got a very good grade from you," I persisted.

That did not seem to sway him. "Only people at the very, very top of their class should be federal law clerks," he intoned.

I walked out furious. I did not know Professor Kent well; he was simply an influential faculty member. But his influence was not going to be used in my favor.

I didn't know how else to get where I wanted to go. Finally, I just cast my fate to the wind.

A week later I got hired.

How was I going to tell Sandy this one? Why would I even have that thought? Of course, Sandy was gracious and supportive . . . as he always had been.

At graduation, I was chosen by the dean and faculty to receive the Sylvia Beinecke Robinson Award for significant contribution to the life of the law school. Miss Congeniality. I was surprised and thrilled. This award recognized not only intellectual excellence but, far more significantly, the importance of one's place in the community. School consisted of more than the classroom, just as there was more to life than the courtroom and more to the legal system than the letter of the law. I shared the award with another student, Mary Lee Wolff, and we were both tremendously excited to be recognized.

Judge Skinner's courtroom was on the fifteenth floor of the federal courthouse. It was a large room, the ceremonial courtroom where events for dignitaries were held. Down the hall, the judge's chambers were austere but warmed somewhat by drawings and paintings of sailboats; sailing was the judge's first love. The clerks' office was to the right. Big windows, a lot of light, a long rectangular table dominating the room. My fellow clerk was another recent law school graduate named Rick Pichette, and we spread out our papers and were always at work. Rick and Rikki. We should have had straw hats and canes.

To avoid duplication of effort, Judge Skinner assigned each of us to individual cases. We would read through the papers—motions for summary judgment, motions to dismiss—and write memoranda outlining the legal issues on both sides. Some judges allow their clerks to draft all their opinions, but this was only Judge Skinner's second year on the bench, and we were his second set of clerks (judgeships were for life; clerkships lasted one year), so he preferred to be quite hands-on. The judge would reason the case through and write the opinion. On occasion we had some influence by adding a theory from the case law to buttress his point of view. But as time passed and we earned increased responsibility, he began to tell us the result he felt was ultimately appropriate and ask us to write a draft opinion. This was rare and very heady. I think he may have been humoring us; in the end it was always his draft, not ours, that went out.

I was very impressed by Judge Skinner. He was fair; he thought about evidentiary and sentencing issues. The judge enjoyed being a teacher and loved intellectual repartee. In the midst of a trial he would come into chambers and talk about motions before him with Rick and me. The fact that he actually encouraged these debates in which his clerks' opinions seemed to matter was uplifting to me. He was a tremendously smart man, and I enjoyed the challenge of working for him.

Every day, either Rick or I would attend the trial in progress while the other did research; we would switch after several hours. If the trial was particularly interesting, both of us would attend and then just work late.

Federal court is inspiring. This is the way law is supposed to be practiced, with all of its majesty, pomp, and circumstance. I think I get taller when I enter a federal court.

Every judge had a pair of law clerks; we worked in close proximity, so many of us became friendly. I met the court clerks and marshals and probation officers who gave the place character. They were the kind of people I had grown up with; I wasn't raised around judges. I grew up among the clerks and bailiffs of the world. The courthouse was a wonderful fraternity of people, and I use that word advisedly; I was the rare female in that world. They were all guys, and it felt like my year as a Vera Girl all over again. Even the defendants were members of that frat. I was leaving the courthouse at 11:00 one night and there hanging out on the steps was the lead defendant in an organized crime loan-sharking case, "Skinny" Kazonis. Skinny had a bad reputation; you really didn't want any part of Skinny. I was walking out of the building and he called to me. "Miss!" I turned around quickly as he approached. I must have blanched. What did Skinny want with me?

"You know," he said, "you shouldn't be out here alone at night. It's late; you shouldn't be a woman alone."

He was a defendant, I was a representative of the judge, I didn't know whether I should talk to him or not. I didn't know what to do.

Skinny took action. "I'm gonna get you a cab," he said. "You stay right here." I stood on the steps for several minutes while he flagged one down, then opened the door, helped me inside, and closed it behind me.

I came to work the next day in fear and trembling that I had done something wrong, made inappropriate contact, ruined the trial. I told the judge. He started laughing at me.

Through the clerks I came to know several other judges, and I made a point of visiting them as often as possible, or speaking with them at various court functions, and discussing points of law. I wanted to understand the big picture. School busing was an all-consuming issue in Boston at the time, as was jail reform. Legal rulings were changing the way life was being lived, and it was interesting to me that judges were finding new ways to use their power.

I was also intent on becoming an effective attorney. "Which lawyers do you respect in the criminal defense and civil bars, and why?" I asked every judge I talked to. Which qualities were particularly important? I wanted to create myself as a lawyer but there were virtually no women attorneys in the courthouse, and I was almost entirely without a female role model. (While influential, my contact with Leslie Crocker Snyder in New York had been fleeting.) The lawyer who appealed to me most was Joe Balliro.

He was in his fifties, a little more than stocky, a man whose defendants were often accused of having significant positions in the hierarchy of organized crime. He looked like his clients. But when he spoke, you heard Shakespeare. Balliro had an extraordinary voice—mellifluous, flowing, his diction perfect. The clerks, federal marshals, and court stenographers all clearly thought this man was worthy of respect. You could see it when he walked into the courtroom; he was friendly and in command. In Judge Skinner's court many lawyers would spring up and say, "Objection! May I approach the bench?" The judge would say no. When Joe Balliro asked to approach, he approached.

Joe Balliro was the dean of the criminal defense bar in Boston.

What gave him this power? "Balliro is perfectly ethical. His word is his bond," Judge Skinner told me. "He doesn't make frivolous objections; he doesn't make frivolous motions. He tries his cases to win. He knows the difference between a big issue and a small issue. He's a brilliant cross-examiner. He is one of the great defense lawyers."

I wanted to be just like him.

Judge Joseph Tauro added another perspective. "The lawyers who really know how to work the federal court know the probation officers, know the marshals, know the people who can make their life easier—*and they treat them with respect.* I can tell a lot about a lawyer from how my court clerk feels about him. If my clerk thinks he is a good guy, then I know he's a good guy." There's an old adage: "Judges can hurt you but clerks can kill you." It's true.

The courthouse camaraderie was terrific. In social situations the guys took care of me. At the Christmas party, if someone had too much to drink and was coming on to me, any one of the clerks would be there to make sure I was out of harm's way. I was also looked after at work. Some lawyers think they can get to a judge through his law clerk. Being Judge Skinner's only female clerk, I was approached regularly. If during recess a lawyer tried to ingratiate himself with me and somehow get me to influence the judge about an opinion, I would tell him, "I really cannot discuss this with you." If he persisted, I would go to the lobby and summon Rick: "You've got to come out here." The lawyer would disappear.

I made lasting friendships. I was curious and humble in the presence of the judges and magistrates, who knew so much more than I did. I was not flirtatious or inappropriate, but friendly and inquisitive. My year as a clerk was progressing productively.

I did stop by George Higgins's office to have my book signed. Higgins was not only a bestselling writer, but also a former assistant United States attorney and a successful practicing criminal defense lawyer whose clients included G. Gordon Liddy and Eldridge Cleaver. He was about eight years older than I was and had world experiences far beyond mine. I immediately found him enormously entertaining, charming, witty, fun. I waited for him to make his move, and on Valentine's Day 1976 he had a dozen roses delivered to me in the courthouse chambers. I opened the card, read his sweet note, and put the flowers on my desk.

When Judge Skinner saw the bouquet, he went ballistic.

"George Higgins sent you flowers here?" he demanded. The judge was a proper man with a short fuse. His neck was turning red as his voice rose. "Are you dating him?"

"No, I'm not." I could see the judge was upset but I didn't understand why.

He didn't believe me. "Why would he send you flowers if you're not dating him?"

Actually, I had had no idea that I appeared on George Higgins's radar sufficiently to warrant his sending me flowers. I was surprised by the gesture, and I liked getting flowers, so I was quite pleased. "We became friends," I explained. "I met him when I met you. I've been to his office a number of times. Yes, I've had a drink with him on occasion."

The judge remained furious. "You can't do that with a lawyer who practices in front of me!"

"I don't have a relationship with him!" I insisted.

"That doesn't matter. There is impropriety. There is the *appearance* of impropriety. You are compromising me. This is entirely improper!"

I was getting smaller and smaller in front of him. Clearly I had not understood the impact of what I'd done. Not only did the judge think I was a liar, he made it clear he thought I was thoroughly lacking in judgment. Such a public gesture. Roses at the courthouse, indeed. For a clerk, few infractions were worse.

Judge Skinner was so angry he sputtered. "You have to take care of this right now. . . . You have to call him. . . . This is unthinkable! Now I know why judges don't hire women clerks!" His robes flying, he stormed out of the room.

I was stunned by the heat of his response. He could have simply told me, "Rikki, in light of my job as a judge and yours as my clerk, you should not be seeing him"; or, "Look what you've done; in order to avoid the appearance of impropriety I now must recuse myself from his cases"; or, "You have made my life extremely difficult." Instead, he blew a fuse.

What I did not understand was that Judge Skinner had taken a chance by hiring a female law clerk. His colleagues, who had neither taken that initiative nor followed his lead, had doubtless told him it was an unwise or unfortunate or foolish thing to do. And now they had been proved correct. I was one of only a few women in the courthouse and I had screwed up royally.

I called Higgins. "I am really very sorry," he said. "I didn't mean to get you into any trouble. It never would have dawned on me. . . . I'll talk to the judge."

"That might not be the best idea right about now."

"I'll write him a letter. I did not mean to compromise you; I did not mean to compromise the Court." He paused. "Frankly, I didn't mean to compromise me, either." He laughed. "Well," he said, "as long as he thinks we're going out, do you want to have some dinner?"

Why not? I could tell the judge that we weren't dating from now until doomsday and he wouldn't believe me.

We did go to dinner, and whether by choice or happenstance, Higgins did not appear before Judge Skinner for the rest of that year. And we did start a relationship.

Higgins was thirty-six; I was twenty-eight. He was extremely accomplished. He had a wicked wit and a great belly laugh. He was also a handsome man with curly brown hair, light eyes, and an upturned Irish nose. We spent a couple of weekends on Nantucket in the summer of 1976 aboard his sailboat, *The Litigator,* fishing for blues

and entertaining his friends. It was quite a party boat, what people
called a "Bloody Mary boat." His friends were entertaining and
impressive as well. Among them were the extraordinary *Boston Globe*
political columnist Marty Nolan, the author David Halberstam, and
the playwright John Guare. I listened to their conversations, and was
learning every moment. The fact that I was permitted to talk with
them at all, let alone as an equal, was extremely heady.

Into this group came a reporter for the *Cape Cod Times* named
Mike McPhee, also a friend of George. Not a bad beat he had landed.
Like me, Mike was the kind of person who attached himself to people
he admired in order to listen to and learn from them. And then there
was the way he looked. He came aboard the boat one morning, and
the second I saw him the wind picked up. Wow. He looked like
Robert Redford. Shock of dirty blond hair, craggy face, a bit more
puckish, handsome with character. He was only a few years older
than I was, and I was very attracted to him.

Timing is everything. George had just lost a good friend and was
taking care of his widow, Loretta Cubberley. Rather than abandon
her to her grief, George invited Loretta to the clambakes and lobster
dinners our group was enjoying. As we sat in the sand and drank
wine and watched the sunset the first time she and I met, it became
clear to me that George was becoming quite devoted to this woman.

I came back to Boston from one of these weekends and called
McPhee. "It was great spending time with you," I said. Then I took a
leap of faith. "I know I'm attracted to you. I think you're attracted to
me. So, what are we going to do about it?"

I was right. He told me, "I don't know, what do you think?" We
were silent for a moment. "But have you noticed that George seems
attracted to Loretta?"

Great minds think alike. We decided I would talk to George. "If I
can arrange this"—What would I call it? I had only been with
George a few times—"separation that makes things easy, can I come
to see you next weekend?"

He said, "I'm here."

I called and invited myself over to George's office. How was I
going to approach what could be an awkward breakup? Why not go

with what's in front of me. "We would both have to be deaf, dumb, and blind not to realize that you are attracted to Loretta and I'm attracted to McPhee," I said. George and I were still in the early stages of dating, this did not have to be wrenching. "Can we make this work without having any bad feelings toward each other?"

George looked at me.

"Done!" His grin was fabulous.

What an easy negotiation. Know your parties, trade value for value, make both sides happy. I spent the next weekend with McPhee and George eventually married Loretta. He loved her madly until the day he died.

McPhee was renting an attic apartment overlooking the beach. We could hear the bell buoy at night. What a great place for a summer romance and what a great time to have this wonderful job.

I had won the Robinson Award in law school; I had succeeded in moot court; I had been a federal clerk. I was on the path to success. At the end of our term, all my fellow law clerks were interviewing for jobs in prestigious corporate law firms. Although my goal was to be a criminal defense attorney, I fell into line with them. I developed a four-to-eight-year plan. I would work at a corporate firm for two to four years, honing my writing and negotiating skills while learning how to be a civil lawyer; then I would go to a U.S. attorney's office for several years, prosecuting crimes and obtaining trial experience; after that I would become a defense lawyer. Conventional wisdom had it that this was the yellow brick road. I began interviewing.

Judge Skinner had watched me study Joe Balliro. "What are you doing?" he said. "You really want to be a criminal defense lawyer. Well, go be a criminal lawyer." I told him about my plan. "That's all very rational," he told me, "but the best piece of advice I can give you is to do what you want to do. You don't want to go to one of these law firms. You never wanted to do that."

It was good advice. I chose to ignore it. I was offered a position at Hale & Dorr, the most prestigious litigation law firm in Boston. They seemed a slight bit looser than most of the city's Yankee firms. I was on my way.

While I was having a fabulous summer in Nantucket with Higgins and McPhee, I was also seeing a man I had met at the end of law school in 1975. I had seen him go in and out of classrooms from time to time. He looked like my kind of guy, so one day I went up to him and asked his name. It was David Levin.

While I was clerking, David was getting his post–law school master's degree in tax law. David was a trust-fund baby. At the age of twenty-one he and his siblings came into more money than I will make in a lifetime. The interest from his trust was well into six figures annually.

Money was not my goal. I wanted to be financially secure, but I was going to do it on my terms. Rich or poor, the people I was attracted to were the ones who had charisma. David had charisma in abundance. With jet-black hair in a Jewish Afro, ice-blue eyes, olive skin, and a long, lean body, he was the physical embodiment of seventies male cool. We were dating on and off even before I was seeing McPhee, and the more time I spent with him the more I liked him.

David's hobby was hot-air ballooning, and sometime in July he said, "Look, I'm going to move out to Colorado. I'm starting a new venture. I've purchased this tract of land and another guy and I are going to open a ranch for guests. We're going to call it the Balloon Ranch."

"Great!"

"I'm driving out there. You're off in August. Why don't you come with me?"

"Okay."

McPhee and I were just a summer romance. Neither he nor I was looking for something permanent. That's how it was in the seventies. We had fun, then moved on. We parted as friends.

David and I drove across the country. We picked up David's business partner, a balloonist named Linc "Z" Baum, and arrived at the ranch in the San Luis Valley, a couple of hundred miles south of Denver. There were acres and acres of land and a beat-up old barn. David was going to start his business from the ground up; he began by knocking down the barn.

David's father, Martin Levin, and his grandfather before him were builders in northern New Jersey. In the 1950s it would have been very hard to move outside of Newark and into the Oranges without finding a Martin Levin or Levin family home. David had been raised in that business, so knocking down and putting up buildings was part of his heritage. We began to construct a compound on the Balloon Ranch.

There was a gang of us, all David's and Linc's friends. We put up Sheetrock and nailed nails and built a two-story lodge with bedrooms upstairs to sleep twenty and a hotel kitchen and a lovely vaulted living room quite befitting the balloonists who would be staying there, people who liked heights. A hundred yards from the main house would be a stable with horses. This was a revelation for me. I had never worked with my hands before, and I had fun. I played with Linc's Newfoundland dogs and didn't think a thing about the world of the law. After all, I could still become the finest woman trial lawyer in the country . . . thirty days from now.

One morning the industrialist Malcolm Forbes, a hot-air balloon enthusiast who owned a home nearby, zoomed in on his motorcycle with a bunch of his pals to see what we were up to. He looked around and told David, "You can put this up for two hundred thousand dollars. If I was going to build it, it would have cost two million."

I was so absorbed in that world that I called Hale & Dorr and said, "I look forward to starting with you, but if I may, I would like to join you one month later than I had originally planned." The firm didn't object. Many people extend their summer before becoming an associate; it's the last chance for a vacation before going to work twenty-four hours a day. So thirty days became sixty days.

David's father and stepmother had scheduled a photographic safari to Africa. "Would you like to come with your girlfriend?" they asked him. He accepted and we left the building for several weeks of international travel. We went to Israel, Africa, Greece, London. We toured the game parks of Kenya and Tanzania, the four of us with a guide and driver, taking photographs and standing in awe and wonder at the continent's beauty. And everywhere we went we traveled in a style and with an opulence to which I will never have the opportunity to become accustomed again. The Levins' wealth was unimaginable to me. Their willingness to spend and share that wealth was extraordinary.

I had grown up with and developed a fair amount of sophistication, but my trip with David and his family was an eye-opener. I liked the idea of extensive traveling with interesting people on an unlimited budget, though I had more modest goals. I told David, "One day I'm going to go into a store and I'm going to buy a dress without looking at the price tag."

This was a profound moment for me. To this point, my quest had been for fame, for the acknowledgment that would come from my being the best female criminal defense lawyer in the United States. Now another element had been introduced: money. I wanted to earn enough of my own money to be able to buy treasures like these for myself.

When we returned to the States I realized it was time for me to go to work. I said good-bye to David and flew back to Boston and Hale & Dorr.

But my perspective had changed. I was no longer certain I wanted to pursue a conventional career path. I visited Judge Skinner to discuss my future.

"I'm supposed to start at Hale & Dorr next week. I'm really concerned that I've made a mistake and you were right."

"Well, what's the solution?" he asked.

"I guess I shouldn't start. I came back from this wonderful trip, and I've looked at my life. I want to be a criminal defense lawyer, but at Hale & Dorr I'm going to get locked up working till midnight, writing memos, never doing the work that I love." The wrong path was stretching out in front of me.

"Well, then, you should tell them. You are not doing them any favors if you go work there for a year or two years and just leave and never come back. Why should they spend all that money training you if you have no intention of working for them? If this is how you feel, you ought to go tell them."

I was not at ease when I walked into the Hale & Dorr hiring partner's office my first day on the job. A short fellow with a pleasant smile, this man was no doubt expecting me to thank him for the opportunity to work at the firm and to promise to put in the long hours and great effort necessary to succeed there. I told him, "This may sound immature, it may sound to you like a woman who changes her mind—and I do not want to create a bad reputation for women whom you may hire in the future—but I have thought this through over the time I have delayed in coming here, and I truly think that I should not start." He looked at me as if I were crazy. "You are going to invest a lot of time and money and effort in me, and it is clear to me that I won't stay here long because what I want to do—what I have always wanted to do—is become a successful criminal defense lawyer."

He was not the hiring partner for nothing. "Rikki," he said soothingly, "we want you to be here. Hale & Dorr may not be what you think it is. Why don't you try us for a while and see how you like it? We do some criminal work in the white-collar area; why don't you keep an open mind?"

I didn't want to be a bad girl. A lot of effort goes into the hiring of associates, and I didn't want to feel responsible for his work having been in vain. I had made a commitment, and my word ought to be my bond. It took only three minutes for him to convince me to stay. I felt too guilty to back out. The same guilt had led to a marriage that had lasted less than a year. I should have known better.

I was miserable. I had betrayed myself; I had betrayed my vision of the future; I had been weak and malleable in ways no good attorney should ever accept. After a weekend of remorse, I walked into the hiring partner's office and resigned again. "I know what I agreed to only a week ago. But I wanted to please you, and I was really afraid I was hurting the cause of women. This is all silly. Let me just finish the projects I have started, then I'll go. It'll take a couple of weeks. You don't have to pay me."

The partner was searching for a reason to explain my irrational behavior. "Is it about Hale & Dorr?" he asked. "Is it about being a criminal defense lawyer? Or is it something in your personal life?"

Ah-ha, I thought; I know how to get out of this very easily.

"Now that you bring it up," I said, "I have been seeing a man in Colorado, and I would like to go out and spend time with him and

perhaps take the bar and practice law out there." I had never, not for
one second, had that thought until the words came out of my mouth.

The partner brightened; confusion left his face as if he had wiped
it away with a moist towelette. "Oh!" he exclaimed. "Now I understand! Of course. Why didn't you say that in the first place?"

Such prejudice. Men in law firms could not understand that a
woman might reject their business, or the place of business in which
they had so much invested, because she wanted to explore other professional opportunities. What they *could* understand was that a girl
would leave because of a man! I had fulfilled every stereotype of the
spouse-hungry female, and by playing to type I effectively freed
myself and prevented them from being mad at me. They could say to
themselves, "We clearly made a mistake by hiring a woman who
obviously only wanted to go off somewhere and get married. Good
thing we found out so early." I hadn't gone in there with that intention, but I certainly had seized the opportunity when it was offered. I
probably set back the cause of women at that firm for years, and I
was sorry about that, but I was out of there.

I worked for two weeks, for free. I finished, to the letter, all my
assignments. A pariah, I endured people giggling behind my back.
(They even wrote a jingle about me: "What has three I's and three K's
and stays for three days?") My last day I said good-bye to the people
with whom I had worked. They were very sweet, treated me like a
child, thought I was smart but inane, frivolous, not to be taken too
seriously. I was packing my briefcase when one of the Hale & Dorr
partners, a man named Blair Perry, came storming through the door.
Perry was a little guy, no more than my height, gray hair, tortoiseshell glasses sitting halfway down his nose. He was very exercised
and he put a finger in my face. "Let me tell you something, Missy!" he
sputtered. "You will never work in this town again! Don't even think
about coming back to Boston!"

I looked at him, aghast. "Mr. Perry, I am truly sorry you feel that
way." He was not interested in listening. He turned on his heel and
stomped out of my office.

What was I going to do now? I walked right over to Judge Skinner's chambers. He was amused that the way I found to exit Hale &

Dorr was to ruin the cause of women at the firm forever. I didn't find that quite as amusing as he did. "What are you going to do now?" he asked.

"I don't know. I've got to find a job that gets me where I want to go."

"Maybe you should have thought of that before leaving Hale & Dorr."

"Maybe I *will* go to Colorado." I was not worried. I had been a federal clerk; I had been hired by Hale & Dorr; I had many options.

Sure.

I got home and called David. "Let me tell you what I just did."

He was completely sympathetic. "If you want to come out here, come on out; you can stay as long as you like. If you want to take the bar out here, that's fine. You can figure it out." I was in Colorado within the week.

What a beautiful setting. The Balloon Ranch sat in the San Luis Valley. To the east, the Sangre de Cristo Mountains were purple and majestic; the high-desert plains, while not actually fruited, were quite lovely as well. Our bedroom was on the second floor of a separate house David had built for us, and in the morning, if I wasn't helping guests into the balloons or flying in a balloon myself, I would take a cup of coffee and sit on the balcony and watch the sun rise.

What did I do all day? We worked on the ranch, we worked with the guests. I was a jogger, and among my greatest pleasures was making the run to the mailbox, which was about two miles down the road. And I spent time with David, which was wonderful.

David's father, Martin, was relatively newly married to his second wife, Vivian. I do not know whether this story is entirely true, but I understand that after many years of marriage, Martin finally left his wife, David's mother, and moved into the Pierre Hotel in New York City. He called Vivian, whom he and his entire family had known for decades. She left her family and joined him. It was a bizarre yet romantic tale, and they were a remarkably happy couple. David loved all his parents. The four of us truly enjoyed one another's company.

Following Martin and Vivian's lifestyle blueprints, David and I stayed in sumptuous suites in Reno and Lake Tahoe that had televisions in the bathroom, a luxury I had never seen before. We visited David's brother in Marina del Rey and spent time in San Francisco. The family's exquisite home on the Palisades in New Jersey featured a fabulous vista of New York City and a superb collection of modern art on the walls. (Vivian's bathroom opened into a protected area filled with greenery. I still love the idea of sitting in the bath and facing the outdoors.) We spent a week on their yacht in Palm Beach, Florida, docking only to eat at fine restaurants.

Vivian delighted in opening up my life. In Florida she took me to the Palm Aire health spa, gave me a tour of the grounds, and showed me how to treat myself royally. In London she took me to my first steam bath and treated me to my first massage. I remember how thrilling it was to her that I had never had a massage.

Martin and Vivian were remarkably generous. They gave me a Cartier watch for my birthday. They presented me with an original Elsa Perretti heart from Tiffany on a chain of "diamonds by the yard." And not only were they generous, they were nice. They became my friends, my family. They lived well but without airs. Mind you, they were regular people—a family of builders—who happened to have made a lot of money.

The Levin family funded two trusts. One endowed David and his two siblings with a yearly income from the time they turned twenty-one. The other distributed funds to charities. David and I talked at great length about the idea of my running the charitable trust as a job one day. And what a job that would have been: doing good with all that money.

Martin and Vivian wanted David to marry me. We loved each other. He was smart. We talked all the time. We read books, talked politics, played backgammon, loved the movies. We had an exhilarating sexual relationship. David was a terrific, terrific guy, and I liked being a member of this lovely family. There cannot be a woman in America who would not have wanted this life. And for my part, I would have been the perfect daughter-in-law; they were a Jewish family and I was a Jewish girl. Not to mention a lawyer. What could be bad?

I did believe David and I would eventually marry. I would be an attorney and we would live in Colorado and I would practice law and be married and wealthy. How ideal was this! I took a bar review course in Denver in preparation for the Colorado bar exam. The community of lawyers there stimulated me, and just as important, I could hang out with them. (One of the prep course teachers, a former disk jockey named John Moye, used rock and roll to illuminate corporate law. "Tell Laura I Love Her," I will always remember, is an express grant of authority, and the story of "Dead Man's Curve" is really about a contract offer and acceptance. All from the law firm of Ray Peterson Jan & Dean.)

David let me use his Mercedes for the commute, and on weekends I used to drive the several hundred miles back and forth playing Joni Mitchell tapes at full blast. The life we lived was truly a life of plenty.

I took the bar exam and faced a decision. What was I going to do with my life? I had this life of fun and frolic all on David Levin's money; I would never have to work, not for a moment, if I didn't want to. I cannot overstate the comfort that thought gave me, a child of Depression-era parents. One day I could administer the Levin trust and do good deeds. After interviewing with the Denver public defenders' office and the district attorney's office, I felt quite certain I could find work there. And if I didn't want to work, I could just play on the Balloon Ranch and travel with David. I would have a built-in family and wonderful in-laws. How rare. A handsome, loving, productive, sexy husband. Everything about that life was seductive. I was fully prepared to live it.

I was invited to a law clerks' dinner for Judge Skinner that was being held in Boston on marathon weekend in the spring of 1977. This would be fun. We would celebrate the judge, and I would see old friends, walk around Boston in the springtime, watch the marathon, and head back to Colorado. It would be a nice break, a pleasant couple of weeks. I accepted.

Boston in the spring is heart-wrenchingly beautiful. Particularly on marathon weekend, when crowds are bustling and people are running through the streets. I walked everywhere. Down on the Charles

River people were rowing and the dogwoods were in bloom. On Boston Common and in the public garden, the smell of the lilacs filled me with an intense longing to live there again. As I walked I felt as if I were in the throes of love. I was breathless about the whole city of Boston.

At the dinner I saw all of the Skinner crew. I had been away for months, but the courthouse scene had been rolling along without me. Rick Pichette and his wife, Thea, who was also an attorney, held the event at their home. I had a lovely moment of collegiality with the judge and his wife. "Well, Rikki," he asked, "what are you going to do?"

I really was not prepared to hear what came out of my mouth. "I have to come back here." And once I said it I knew it was true: "I *have* to come back here. I can't explain it, but my heart belongs to Boston."

Was I insane? There was nothing unsettled between David and me, no trouble spot that might spread and destroy us. I loved him. He loved me. But two weeks in Boston had unearthed my real need to make my own success. I had been trying to hide from the fact that the only person who could support me and take care of me was me. As seductive as the Levin family lifestyle was, I didn't want to be someone who depended on a man for my financial security or my professional life or my personal life. My mother had told me long ago, "The only person who never leaves you is you." I needed to do what I spent all those years going to school for. I had struggled to go to law school, and I was not going to get married, have kids, and throw away my career, which is what would have happened. I was passionate about my work, my vision, my success. Compromise was not an option. I could not possibly scale the cliff before me, take a few years off to have babies, and then resume my place on the wall. My career would have plunged to its death, and taken me with it. I owed that career a chance. I had school loans to pay, and they were my responsibility. After putting myself through law school, I understood what a sacrifice it had been for my father to put me through college, and now I owed it to both of us to make good. Somehow, in my head, a law career in Denver contingent on David's largess was not the same as being a criminal defense lawyer on my own in Boston.

I had been calling David every night just to chat, and I called him after the dinner, not really knowing what I would say.

"Hi, how are you?" I began.

"Fine."

"How's everything?"

"Great. The ranch is fine. Business is all right. When are you coming home?"

"I'm not sure." How could I say this? I plunged forward. "David, I love you. I love your family. I love our life." He must have known some blow was to follow because he was silent. "But somehow I need to know I can do something on my own." Again, no response. He was a lawyer, too. He listened. "I need to know I can have a career that is really mine, one not dependent on your money, on your family. I need to see, for me, if this is even possible. If I come back to Colorado and continue to live on the ranch and even go up to Denver and practice, I will never know. I will always be living as your wife in your world on your funds. Since I've decided to become a lawyer, since I decided to go to law school, I think I need to see how this works for me."

David was incredibly silent. I was swimming in uncharted waters: the cold depths of honesty.

"Why can't you do that in Denver?" he asked.

"If I'm in Denver I'd feel beholden to your money. I know you've never made me feel that way. I know that. But I can't be a successful, self-sufficient woman unless I see if I can do it apart from you. I can't. And I know it's something I have to do."

"But I don't want you to." He sounded so lost.

"I don't want to do it, either. I love you. But I don't want to say to you in five years, or ten, or twenty, 'I never had a career, and I never did it because of you.' I don't want to do that to us." Again, silence. I dropped the other shoe.

"I have to stay here. If I go back to Colorado, even to get my things, I'll be right back where I started; I'll never get back to Boston. If I set foot in that house I know I won't leave. The only solution is for me to find a place to live here. I'm going to ask you to send me my clothes and let's see what happens."

"You don't even know if you can get a job."

"I'll get a job."

His head must have been whirling. Mine was. I was crying. He was crying, too. "I'll send your stuff," he said, "but if you are going to stay there, you're not coming back here. You have to make this choice."

I didn't believe David's words were actually an ultimatum. Part of me believed that I could go back if I wanted to. I loved him, he loved me; we could always resurrect what we had had. He wasn't getting married anytime soon. I certainly wasn't. I thought I was invincible. I thought I couldn't screw up my life. I truly believed that I could have it all. I just had to do it in stages. Sure, I could have this fabulous life one day if I wanted it, but I wanted it on my own terms, which meant that first I had to know who I was.

The other part of me was terrified.

My heart ached. "I've made the choice. I have to stay here now."

I was emotionally spent. I loved David and I loved our life. I knew absolutely no matter how successful a lawyer I became I would never approach that lifestyle. You can become rich, but what the Levins had was wealth. What a risk. I was losing the relationship; I was losing the security; I was losing the money. How foolhardy. And for what?

I knew that too. As I looked at myself, in the far reaches of my mind, in places that I really never wanted to explore, I thought of myself as a dilettante. Living on the ranch, traveling the world, abandoning the law — I was being frivolous. And if there was any image of myself I would not tolerate it was that I was frivolous. I had been a serious youngster, a serious child. I had dedicated myself to becoming an actress and then a lawyer. I had earned my degrees and won a federal clerkship. Somehow I felt that if I lived the life David was offering, I would be throwing all of my accomplishments away. Hopping on jets and boats at a whim and flying hot-air balloons all day — how do you not look at that as play? This was not my image of who I was supposed to be. It was very seductive, but it was not who I was supposed to be.

I was fearless. I would become a great lawyer. It absolutely did not occur to me that I might not succeed.

I was staying with Rick and Thea, and when I got off the phone I went to them and cried like a baby. "What have I done?" I sobbed. "This is crazy. Have I done the right thing?"

I understood my rational thought process, but I was in complete denial about my feelings. It was one thing to choose to leave the man I loved and wanted to marry, a wonderful human being who could keep me in a style for which any other woman would sell her soul, in the name of career. It was quite another to dare to look inside my heart and to feel the turmoil that my choice had created.

Unlike Sandy, David wouldn't still be my friend; that would be too difficult. This was total separation. If I stayed on the ranch, I would be David's possession forever; I would have no identity. I would be a part of his life; he would not be a part of mine. I would have no life of my own.

I needed to leave David to seek my destiny, but in that choice I felt I might be doing myself real damage. By striking out on my own I feared I was dooming myself to an emotionally barren life. I felt an enormous sense of loss for what might have been. I thought about my parents, and David's father and stepmother, and the power of the love those couples shared. Yet I did not seem able to reach within myself and find that love. Much of me feared I never would. Perhaps I was incapable of their type of total commitment, that willingness to submerge oneself in the life of another. This realization made me very sad. Even if I achieved a rewarding professional life, I might still be emotionally bankrupt. I hoped in my heart of hearts that this was not to be my fate.

Rick and Thea both gave me a hug and at some point I fell asleep. The next morning I got on the phone. I knew what I wanted. I wanted to try cases. And the only way to do that was to work in a district attorney's office.

five **"I CAN DO THIS"**

THE HOTTEST DA IN MASSACHUSETTS WAS BILL DELAHUNT. HE WAS PROGRESSIVE AND liberal, and he had created significant new programs such as a juvenile diversion project that took defendants under the age of seventeen out of the criminal justice system and placed them in supervised activities that helped both them and their communities, as well as a domestic violence unit that provided a safe haven for battered women. Delahunt did not believe that a prosecutor's office should be simply reactive; his office was proactive, changing behavior at the earliest stages. Few law enforcement professionals had heard these words in 1977.

Prior to Delahunt's ascension, district attorneys' offices anywhere in Massachusetts outside Boston were largely part-time operations. They as much as had party-line phones. ADA jobs were often political patronage given to insiders' friends. Lawyers could be ADAs and maintain their civil practices. And whether you were a cop or an ADA, it didn't hurt to be Irish. Delahunt was changing all that. He had recruited the best and the brightest and was revitalizing the Norfolk County district attorney's office.

I called to apply for a position, and after being funneled from extension to extension I was finally told there were no jobs available. In fact, there was a waiting list of some considerable length, and no openings were expected in the foreseeable future.

I called George Higgins. "I've decided to stay in Boston. You told me all about Delahunt, and I want to work for this guy. I can't get a job interview." He said, "I'll call you back in ten minutes." Ten minutes passed. He called.

"I've got you an interview tomorrow at noon. You're going to see the DA himself. Bring your résumé. Good luck."

I called Joe Oteri. Like Joe Balliro, he was a great father of Boston criminal defense attorneys and one of the city's leading lights. I had met him many times during my clerkship. "I want to go work for Delahunt," I said. "I couldn't get an interview. I just called Higgins, who got me one. Can you help me out?"

"Yeah, I'll call him for you."

I walked into Bill Delahunt's office on a Friday. He was leaning back in his chair, wearing khakis, a polo shirt, and Top-Siders, which were propped on his desk. We hit it off immediately.

"You couldn't come any more highly recommended than from Higgins and Oteri," he said. "The truth is, though, I just don't have a job for you. Because of budget constraints, we only have a certain number of slots allocated to begin with and they have all been filled." I must have looked crestfallen, which I certainly was. But we talked about my acting career and Northwestern. I asked many questions about the new programs he was instituting in his office. It didn't take a minute for me to be sure that this was a man I wanted to work for. Apparently, he was equally certain about wanting me on his staff.

After about a half hour he said, "I'm going to make a deal with you." A deal from a prosecutor. He was very adept at making these. "I want you to work for me. There are very few women in the criminal justice system, and you're going to be a star. I know it, and I want you to be a star in my office. I will give you the next job that comes up, the next vacancy I have, before anybody else. Do you need a job today?"

"I don't have much money," I admitted.

"Can you go back and call Higgins, call Oteri? Can they give you work? It may take three months, five, six months, I don't know, but I'm giving you the next job."

I was elated. "I'll make it work," I assured him.

Now all I had to do was find a way to eat for the next half-year. Higgins was writing; he had no job available. I called Oteri, who said, "I'd like to help, but I just don't have a place to put you." I decided to call Joe Balliro. I didn't know him. I had only admired his work from a distance.

"Mr. Balliro, I don't know if you'll remember me. I used to be Judge Skinner's clerk."

"Oh, the girl with the long black hair. What can I do for you?"

"I was just offered a job by Bill Delahunt . . ."

"That's great," he said. "He's terrific. You'll get good experience there."

". . . but he doesn't have a position for me yet and I really need to work."

"Why don't you come see me on Monday and we'll talk."

Although Balliro maintained a small office in a suite with other lawyers near the courthouse, he began his day in the dining area of his apartment at Harbor Towers, a white luxury high-rise building on Boston Harbor, near the aquarium. I put on one of the two dresses I owned and met him there. The coffee was brewing, papers were spread on a round table, and the talking pace was vigorous. That day, I met his associate Joan Schmidt, who did Balliro's matrimonial work. Joan and I were immediately drawn to each other—two eager young women who wanted to learn, to work, to succeed.

I told Balliro I would work for him for nothing. "Please don't ever say that," he said. Then he gave me a job that didn't pay much more.

But it was a great job. Balliro was an institution. His firm was a mom-and-pop operation but they were everywhere. People knew, if you have a problem in the Boston area, call Balliro. Joe was getting older, however; he was tired of going to the jails to meet clients, and he was tired of driving around to the district courts that dotted Route 128 to handle all the little cases that added up to make him money. Why did he need to run up to Lowell or Newburyport or Concord to do some misdemeanor case? Did he really need to be present at a probable cause hearing in Salem when he knew there would be probable cause found to bind the defendant over for trial? Balliro saw me as a source of cheap labor, someone who wanted to learn and was willing to work like a dog. He was a very perceptive man.

I borrowed a car, not having enough money to buy one. And I did the Route 128 loop. All the bad-check cases, the drunk-driving citations—I was there. The Charles Street jail in Boston was a hellhole, reeking of urine and the funk of the street; I couldn't wait to get inside to interview a client. To me, this was incredibly glamorous and rewarding work. I was constantly busy, on my toes every moment of every day, and I was thrilled to be there. I had a small part of people's lives in my hands, and I was completely in my element.

And on top of that I got to watch Joe Balliro work.

He walked into the courthouse as if he owned it. He knew every bailiff by name; he had a word for every judge, every clerk. He knew the rules of evidence and the rules of procedure as if he had written them himself. Decades of trial experience had honed his skills, and he knew exactly when to object and when silence was more effective. He knew how to address a jury to make them take him at his word. He knew which witnesses to cross-examine with kindness, which with a stiletto, which with a hammer. Every day was a lesson. I thought I had reached the pinnacle of my life, to sit at the knee of Joe Balliro. What a lawyer. What a scholar. What a magnificent presence in the courtroom. I would have paid to work with him.

In recognition of my work, and because he wanted to show some confidence in me, Balliro brought me in as a second chair in a counterfeiting case being tried before Judge Frank Freedman in federal court. Big-money case, organized crime–type defendants. I prepared all the paperwork—trial briefs, witness summaries, questions for the witnesses. Joe stretched me to the max as his second. I didn't complain.

At some point Balliro mentioned that he had a sentencing hearing in Louisiana that the judge would not continue; therefore, he would have to miss a day in court. We knew where the trial was going; we were pretty sure that the witness on the stand that day wasn't going to make or break the case. So Joe asked the client if he would consent to my representing him in court and cross-examining a witness in Joe's absence. By that time I had spent considerably more time with the defendant than Joe had, because that kind of hand-holding is exactly what an associate does. The client agreed. I was going to be Joe Balliro for a day.

My witness was an FBI fingerprint analyst. Talk about being suckered; Joe knew full well that a lawyer really can't cross-examine a fingerprint expert, because of the nature of fingerprints—you can't cross-examine them; they're either present at the scene or they're not; their points and whorls correspond or they don't. I, on the other hand, was not possessed of this knowledge. What did I know?

I went to the law library and read all night. I needed to be immaculately prepared. In those days before DNA testing, fingerprint analysis was the courtroom's most exact science. I had never cross-examined a witness before a big-time jury. Years of a man's life were at stake if I had a bad day. I didn't want to look like an idiot in court.

I invented the wheel, or so I thought. Halfway to sunrise it dawned on me that no one can tell when a fingerprint arrived on a surface, only that it exists in the present. "A fingerprint on a can or a glass could last for years, isn't that correct, Special Agent Jones? You don't know when the fingerprint was put there, do you? You could never know when the fingerprint was put there, could you, sir?"

I arrived in court the next morning in absolute fear, but I approached the podium and presented myself with a swagger. I crossed that witness looking as confident as I could be and conducted what I now know is the only fingerprint cross-examination a lawyer can ever do without looking like a fool. I asked my questions, got my answers, and sat down. My heart was racing.

The lawyer to my right, representing a co-defendant, smiled at me. "That was great," he whispered.

At the morning recess, another co-defendant's lawyer said, "When you need to object, I'll poke you. You get up and say, 'Objection,' and by the time you've said it, I'll write down the grounds so you can tell the judge."

"Thank you." And that's how the day went. By the end of the session I was in heaven. I thought, I'm in the money. This is my life. I can do this.

Another great benefit of my job was the fact that Joe Balliro shared office space with one of the great trial lawyers of all time, F. Lee Bailey. Traveling as he did from case to case, Bailey was rarely there, but I made a point of asking his assistant for permission to introduce myself. His personal office was configured like an amphitheater, like a law school classroom. I walked down several tiers to his desk and shook his hand. I thought I was in the presence of God.

I worked for Joe Balliro for four months and was at the top of my game. I forgot all about Colorado. I became totally focused on being a lawyer.

In August, Bill Delahunt called with a job. "It may open up next month. You can start as a district court assistant," he said. I was bubbling when I told Joe. He saw things differently. "You don't need to go to the district courts, you've been in the district courts virtually every day for months. You should go straight to superior court. You tell him that."

Like an idiot, I called Delahunt back. When Joe Balliro said, "Jump," I jumped. "Mr. Balliro said for me to tell you that I have tried a number of district court cases before . . ." I named several judges. "Mr. Balliro thinks that if you have a position you should put me into superior court."

Delahunt started laughing. A big, booming laugh. "I'm sure everything you are telling me is the truth." He couldn't contain another guffaw, perhaps at my utter lack of guile. "But I don't have a position in superior court. I have a position in district court."

"How long will I have to be in district court?"

"A year or two."

I told Balliro. He said it was a waste of my time.

"But I want to try cases and I want to work for Delahunt."

Life works in mysterious ways. I was walking down the street no more than a few days later when I ran into Peter Agnes, a fellow who had been a law clerk at the supreme court of New Hampshire at the same time I had clerked for Judge Skinner. We stopped and traded job stories for a few minutes, and I told him how I was first on Delahunt's waiting list at the DA's office. "I have a thought for you," Peter said. "Do you know who John Kerry is?"

"Of course. Vietnam Veterans Against the War. Threw his medals over the White House wall. He's been a hero of mine for years."

"Well, John Kerry is about to become John Droney's first assistant district attorney for Middlesex County. You might want to go work with him." John Droney was an old-line political guy in Cambridge, and I couldn't imagine why anyone would want to work there rather than cast one's lot with a comer like Delahunt. "Kerry is going to totally revamp that office. He's recruiting. He's taking people out of big law firms, and people like you in the federal court and me at the state supreme court, and he's going to make Middlesex the best DA's office in the country. I'm going there. Maybe you don't have to go into the district court; maybe you can go into the superior court."

When I told Balliro, he said, "What do you have to lose? You've got a job with Delahunt in a month or so. Why don't you call up Middlesex and see if you can get an interview?"

"Why don't *you* call up Middlesex and see if I can get an interview?"

"I feel a little odd about it. I'm close to Delahunt."

"Not that close."

Balliro called John Droney, praised me to the skies, and got me an appointment.

When I arrived at the Middlesex offices in East Cambridge, you could see things were happening. Cubicles were being built, phones were being installed; there was movement and heat. I was shown into Kerry's office. With a wall of windows framing him, John Kerry, at six foot four, was a tall, cool drink of water.

He came around his desk and, smiling, shook my hand. I judge people by their handshakes. Women, for instance, often have poor ones—weak, limp, unforthcoming introductions that say, "I have no right to be here." This is the sort of thing that can be taught, however. A woman can make a strong first impression by reaching forward confidently. Kerry had a great handshake: firm, solid, inviting.

It was a good move, coming around his desk to greet me. A desk is a false barrier that inhibits rapport, and when Kerry sat down with me at a round table, we were already communicating.

Why wouldn't he want to hire me? My academic credentials were good, and I had clerked in federal court and gained intensive case experience working for Balliro. Plus, I was a woman. There was a glaring shortage of women lawyers throughout the country, more glaring in DA's offices. If Kerry was actually attempting to reinvent the office, he needed women with him.

I was very honest with Kerry. I told him I admired his activist history, and I detailed what I had learned from Skinner and what I had done with Balliro. He got a big laugh out of my three-week stint at Hale & Dorr. There was a district court job waiting for me from Delahunt, I said, "But I'll come work for you. I will tell you today that I will take this job if you give me a superior court position."

I had no idea what I'd walked into. Kerry and Delahunt were competing for attention, respect, success. Delahunt's Norfolk was a small county, while Kerry's Middlesex ran, as some say, from Cambridge to Canada. Kerry said he was going to make every single advance Delahunt was proposing, and more. He was successfully recruiting lawyers who made large salaries at prestigious law firms to come to work for him for a pittance.

But he didn't have a superior court position available, either. "I'm going to try to create one for you," he said.

I ran back to the office and reported to Balliro. "You did the right thing," he said.

When Kerry called several days later, he was as good as his word. "I have a superior court position for you. It starts right after Labor Day." I was overjoyed.

"This is wonderful," I bubbled. "I am so honored. I would very much like to work for you, but in all fairness, I feel I have to call Bill Delahunt to see if he can match the offer. I have a history with him, and I think that would be the honorable thing to do."

Kerry was not quite so understanding. "You either take this now or you don't," he informed me.

I wanted to work in superior court. Kerry was offering me exactly what I wanted, but wasn't I supposed to go to Delahunt, because he had accepted me first? I did not want to disappoint one man to satisfy another, but I wanted this job and, faced with an ultimatum, I didn't feel I had any other choice.

"I accept," I told Kerry.

I was a bit stunned when I put down the phone. Had I compromised my principles for the sake of a position? Balliro made me feel better. "Delahunt can't match the offer," he said convincingly. "He doesn't have the spot right now."

I called Delahunt, guilt-ridden; again I felt like a bad girl who'd done a bad thing. "I have no superior court position," he confirmed, "and I don't know if I'll have one for a year or two. You have no choice; you have to take it. But mark my words: I am going to let you be his star, I'm going to watch everything you do, and I'm going to come steal you back in a couple of years."

I was pleased at the compliment and thankful for his understanding.

When I joined the Middlesex DA's office, I found that Kerry had two other women ADAs joining his staff at the same time, Christine McEvoy and Carol Ball. I liked them both, but I really hit it off with Christine immediately.

Christine was a very pretty woman, very Irish, with sparkling blue eyes and a pointy little nose. She had been attractive all her life. There is a camaraderie among attractive, professionally accomplished women. Women who are confident of their competence, who know inside that they are worthy of their reputations, carry themselves with strength and dignity. This is particularly so in the legal profession, which is very much a man's world. How is a woman going to be a trial lawyer unless she possesses the confidence that she can talk to and persuade people? To be a litigator, a performer, instead of a bookish attorney working over trusts and estates, one needs that backbone of confidence. When this is coupled with a certainty of one's attractiveness it becomes "presence." I have always taken to women with presence. They are not insecure about their looks or abilities; they have traveled parallel paths and worked hard to arrive at their successes; they know the effort they have expended; and they appreciate the difficulties they have had to overcome—difficulties that other people, and, unfortunately, most other women, do not know exist. Buoyed by this mutual understanding, we find no need to put one another down.

Like blondes and women with large breasts, attractive women lawyers are constantly faced with the assumption that their success was achieved because of their looks. It's okay to be competent and powerful if you're ugly or even moderately good-looking. But if your looks attract real attention, people say you must have gotten your job because you slept around.

I realize this sounds terrible: "Don't hate me because I'm beautiful." But the fact is, certainly as I was entering the Middlesex DA's office in September 1977, the pettiness was widespread and unmistakable.

Which is why I was so pleased to learn that, in Christine, I had found a colleague. We had gone through law school at a time when there were few women in the classes, and we had endured and thrived and created ourselves as lawyers with no female role models, always chopping our own way through the legal jungle. We were instinctively happy to see each other.

I was driven; I was going to get to the top fast. John Kerry demonstrated how it was done. I worked from 8:30 in the morning until 10:00 at night, but I can't remember a time when he didn't arrive before me or stay after I left. He was a shining example of dedication.

I began trying cases virtually as soon as I came on board. In those days, by Massachusetts law, if a misdemeanor defendant lost a case before a judge in district court, he had the right to appeal the trial de novo, "as new," and start all over again before a jury in superior court. Around the courthouse it was called getting "two bites of the apple." The most effective way to train ADAs was to start them out on these misdemeanors. Working for Balliro I had had a taste of working on the other side of the courtroom; now I was prosecuting misdemeanor jury cases such as assault-and-battery and petty theft.

My first case involved a defendant in an automobile collision charged with reckless driving. I tried it like a murder case. I walked in and introduced myself to the clerk, the uniformed court officers, everyone who worked in the courthouse. These were the guys who could make or break my life. I chatted with them; I bought them coffee. Joe Balliro's lessons had not been for nothing.

The trial was as simple as could be. I produced a diagram of the accident scene; I stated the facts of what had happened, who had been in the car. I had the guy dead to rights. I was a tiger, relentless in the pursuit of justice.

At recess I asked the court officers, "Was that okay? Is there something else I should do?" They were nice people; they told me I was terrific. I certainly felt terrific. I felt I was where I ought to be, in a courtroom, in front of a jury, at home.

Somewhere around my third trial I finished my examination of a witness and said, "Your Honor, the Commonwealth rests." The next step would be a motion from the defense for a directed verdict, a standard defense motion at the end of every prosecution case, saying that even when you look at all the evidence solely from the light most favorable to the prosecution, the prosecution had not proved the elements of its case and the judge should direct a verdict in favor of the defendant. That motion is routinely denied, after which the defense puts on a case, if it chooses to do so. The judge called a recess.

"Psst."

Johnny Vita was trying to get my attention.

Johnny Vita was a court officer who seemed to have been there since the courthouse was built. I had met him when I'd been a defense lawyer, and he knew how ambitious I was. I had asked him thousands of questions about rules of evidence, and how to approach certain lines of inquiry with specific judges, and where to stand when I was dealing with a jury. He and the other court officers knew the answers; this is what they did, and since they had seen the law practiced both well and poorly for decades, they were experts.

"What?" I asked.

"You never identified the defendant."

"What do you mean? I had all kinds of witnesses saying he did this, he did that."

"You have to have somebody point him out directly by name and say, 'Your Honor, may the record reflect that the witness, Mr. Jones, has identified the defendant.'"

I was aghast. He was right.

"You're going to get directed out."

What a disgrace. My third trial and my negligence was going to let a guy walk.

"Unless the defense lawyer missed it, or the judge missed it," he added helpfully.

"What do I do?"

"You could ask to reopen your case in chief," he said, "but I don't think the judge is going to let you do that if you just forgot."

Johnny had found a fatal flaw. "Maybe you'll get lucky."

I went back into the courtroom petrified. How would I explain this utter incompetence to John Droney and John Kerry?

I did get lucky. The defense missed it, the judge missed it, and as soon as the first defense witness hit the stand for cross-examination I had him identify the defendant. I won the case and have Johnny Vita to thank for my law career.

My drug arrest in college had propelled me to become a criminal defense lawyer. George Pontikes was my image of the lawyer-warrior, fighting for justice not with a saber but with an intellectual understanding of the law and the passion of a true believer. In light of my own past, when I was a prosecutor at the Middlesex DA's office, I refused to work on simple drug possession cases. This was the seventies and they were plentiful. I did handle one, however, against a young man who was arrested with a group of friends for possession of pharmaceutical cocaine with intent to distribute. They were taking it from a local druggist and, as I recall, using most of it themselves. The case went forward in 1978, and while he was under indictment and out on bail, this man and his wife and infant son were walking on the beach in the rain. A moment after his wife handed him their son she was struck by lightning and killed. Ultimately, he came before the court. These cases usually demand jail time but I agreed that, because of his circumstances—he would either stay out of jail and be a single parent or be incarcerated and lose his son to the child welfare system— he should be given a probationary sentence. After much discussion, the district attorney and the judge agreed.

The defendant raised that boy to be a fine young man. He sent me a picture of his son every year from 1979 to 1995 and never forgot what I had done for his family. Neither did I. If I had not been arrested myself I could not have understood how such an event could ruin a person's future. I did for him what George Pontikes had done for me. I'd had the opportunity to save a life, to help form a life, and it was one of the finest moments of my career that I put aside prose-cutorial zeal and became a gladiator for the defendant.

After several months of these trials and errors I graduated to rape and armed robbery cases. I wanted to get to homicide, the high-water mark for a prosecutor. When you were assigned to try a murder case you had made it. Usually this took several years, but I was working hard and fast. I had places to be.

The receptionist was nervous when I got to work one mid-December morning. This was unlike her. A receptionist at a district attorney's office has heard it all; she couldn't care less. Now she was fluttery. "You need to call your mother," she told me. I walked into my office. Christine McEvoy followed me in and closed the door. "Call your mother," she said. I picked up the phone and dialed.

My mother was screaming. "Your father is dead! He's dead!" She was keening, frantic, hysterical. "You've got to come here right away."

"I'll be there today." I tried to calm her but she would not be calmed. She was alone in the house with my father's corpse and she could not stop screaming. I stayed on the phone with her. "Do you have anyone who can come be with you?"

"Your uncle Joey is coming."

"Good." She continued to wail and I tried to keep her occupied. I'd be there right away, I promised. I attempted, without much suc-cess, to soothe her. I had cases to try, but they were out the window. "I'll call you as soon as I know what I'm doing." When my mother had regained a little of her composure I told her I loved her and that I would see her that night. Then I hung up.

My father hadn't been sick. Of course, he didn't exercise, he ate terrible food, but so did most Jewish men his age. At my law school graduation he'd had to sit after he had walked any little distance, but I'd seen no sign that he was in peril. He had had a heart attack in his sleep and died. He was sixty-seven years old. My mother was in shock.

My parents had been married for forty-six years. My mother adored my father; he was her reason to live. What would become of her?

I must have looked at risk myself. Chrissy had been told by the receptionist and decided to mother me and take control. She said, "You're in no condition to put this together. Just sit here for a minute." She called the airline and made a reservation within minutes. As she picked up the phone I began to cry. This time I couldn't stop. I had last seen my father that summer at my aunt Doris's funeral. My mother had now lost a sister and a husband within months. I would have seen him in two weeks for Christmas; now I'd never see him. I hadn't said good-bye; I hadn't been prepared; I hadn't thought of the world without him.

I had lived through deaths; I had even lost relatives. But there had only been my father, my mother, and me. Now there was only my mother and me. I was enveloped in a sense of loss and could think of nothing else. I was allowed that luxury because Chrissy was doing my business.

She took me home and helped me pack; she got the ticket; she put me on the plane. When I collapsed into my seat my loss truly drained me, but I needed to remain strong. I knew that, as demanding and demonstrative and efficient as my mother was, she could not possibly live without my father. He had been planning to retire at sixty-two, then sixty-five, then seventy. My parents' generation lived for retirement, for the time when they would buy a Winnebago and go out west, or live on a houseboat. My father had postponed it time and again; now he and my mother would never have time alone. I could not conceive of the shape my mother must be in, and I knew I would have to postpone my own grieving to take care of her.

The house was full of friends and relatives when I walked in. When she saw me, she allowed herself to let go once again. The depth of her grief scared me: I had never before seen someone who truly did not want to live.

My mother wanted me to deliver the eulogy.

"Mom, I don't know if I can."

"Well, you have to."

It was only after his death that I began to understand my father's worth and the depth of affection people had for him. I knew he was gentle and soft-spoken and took care of things quietly. I was witness to his honesty; for example, when he was in New York on business and took me to dinner, he would fill out an expense report for half the bill, excluding my meal. Apparently, the business appreciated his brand of integrity. I was greeted with an outpouring of support for this blue-collar guy from his well-to-do business friends—manufacturers and owners of clothing companies—who flew in from New York so as not to miss his funeral.

I spoke. "My father must be remembered as he really was," I said. "His faults: perhaps he was too good, too honest, having too little false pride. A man who heard others say bad things about a person, who could always find a response of something good about them. In my thirty years I can honestly say that I never heard a bad comment.

"A man who called himself a conservative, who could still be curious about my ideals during my radical days and go to see a student strike at Northwestern University and listen and understand.

"A man who knew death, sorrow, and pain, and never spoke of it. A man who knew love, goodness, and unselfishness, and always showed it. A quiet man who embodied honesty, gentleness, and, most of all, personal integrity.

"If there is a heaven up there, and at these times we must have some belief to sustain us, my childlike vision sees him sail through those pearly gates, since there is not one black mark against him. He sits on the highest, lightest, fluffiest pink cotton-candy cloud— deserved because of his goodness, because he really was 'Gentle Ben.'"

My mother sent a written copy of the eulogy to "the boys," now middle-aged men, who had served with my father in the Philippines and with whom my parents had corresponded at Christmas for years. She received many letters in return, telling stories of his heroism, the lives he had saved, how they had called him "Pop" because at thirty-two he had been so old, and recounting what a source of inspiration he had been. I had not heard any of these stories; my father, quiet man that he was, had never talked about the war.

I was gone for a week. When I returned, I went back to court and never stopped. I charged through every case John Kerry handed my way. If I had worked hard before, after my father died I was relentless. I talked to my mother every few days; she was inconsolable and I feared she was suicidal. "I want to die," she told me. "I don't know how I'm going to live." She cried all the time. I could not grieve for my father, I didn't have time: I had to be strong for my mother and I had to work. I visited home as often as time would permit, which wasn't often enough. Finally I invited her to Boston. I had just moved into a truly theatrical duplex in the Little Italy section of the North End, and my mother, bless her heart, used a large part of the small pension my father had left her to furnish it.

What a wonderful gesture, and what joy we both had putting my place together. The apartment was spectacular, with hardwood floors, built-ins, twenty-eight-foot ceilings, and a spiral staircase, and she used her exquisite interior design talents to help me set it up. We called it my "Paradise apartment" and she stayed with me for a couple of months. The time we spent in each other's company was restorative, and by the time she returned to Chicago she was at least willing to stay alive.

My father had been dead a very short time when I prosecuted my first attempted murder case. (In Massachusetts, the charge is "armed assault with attempt to murder.") The path to a homicide case can take years for a young assistant district attorney, but I had gotten this close in months. I prosecuted *Commonwealth v. Edward Martin*.

In the Boston suburb of Chelmsford, a summer block party had attracted hundreds of high school and college kids and then started to get out of hand. A call went out to the police for assistance. Before the cops came on the scene, a stranger arrived, got into a scuffle, pulled out a handgun, and fired. A high school football player was shot. The victim, bleeding on the ground, was severely disabled and almost died. The shooter took off. The police canvassed the crowd and interviewed the victim at the hospital. They obtained positive eyewitness identification and then arrested a suspect, Edward Martin. Martin's alibi: He was at home with his wife.

Edward Martin was the last person one would think of as a shooter. He was a well-respected member of the community who had worked for the town itself. He had never been in trouble with the law and had a decent reputation. In fact, he was a police buff. The cops found a scanner in his home that monitored police frequencies, allowing Martin to listen as law enforcement officers were summoned to fires, accidents, robberies, shootings. People saw him do it; he said he wasn't there. He was a solid citizen with an alibi and no motive.

The police taught me ballistics. They set the scene ably and gave me sound and timely IDs from reputable witnesses. In my mind, clearly Martin had done it. Now I had to convince the jury.

This was the most important case I had ever tried. I needed to present it at its finest. I needed to connect with the jurors and make them believe me. How best to do that?

During my opening statement I didn't stand right up by the rail. I had seen lawyers make that folksy gesture, like a neighbor leaning over the back fence to make contact. That was too close. I wanted to establish physical and emotional communication, but the jurors didn't want me in their box, and I didn't want to invade their space. I approached but stayed six or seven feet away. They were comfortable, and I was still within their sphere.

I believed firmly that as on stage no movement in the courtroom should be superfluous. Every movement should have a purpose, and that purpose is to attract the jury's attention. I understood intuitively and from my theater training that one has the ability to walk to serve this end. I planted myself center stage before the jury box. I did not use a podium; everyone used a podium and I wanted to be unique. I also didn't want that piece of furniture between me and the jurors. I stood before them and got centered, literally centered—mentally, emotionally, physically—with my feet about six inches apart, facing them directly. I took a breath and found they were waiting for me to speak. I used the silence by extending it.

When I finally did speak they were all watching, all with me.

Primacy and recency, what a lawyer says first and what she says last, are what a jury remembers. I opened with the story. I took them into the block party in great detail; they could see it, hear it. The party got rowdy; Edward Martin arrived, pulled out a gun, and shot the victim. What we didn't know is why.

I looked at them. They looked back at me. I walked from the center of the room to a point at the end of the jury box, again about six feet away. I said nothing while I was walking. You don't speak while you walk in a courtroom, you make the jurors follow you with their eyes and their minds until you stop, turn, and speak to them directly once again. I stopped, turned, faced them, and told another part of the story. When I had finished, I walked silently to the other end of the box so that both sides of the jury could feel close to me. Then I spoke again.

I certainly wasn't above acting out a case. I played all the parts, and as I performed I convinced the jury that what I was saying was true. It was theater: the willing suspension of disbelief.

We all have a host of voices in our bodies. You don't speak to a child the same way you speak to someone across a tennis court. You don't speak to your husband or wife or significant other the same way you speak to a colleague at work, and you don't speak to that colleague as you would to an employer. You don't speak to the bus driver the same way you speak to your best friend. You have all these voices, and I found the ability to create tension in a courtroom by controlling my tone. I spoke quickly when I needed, and slowly when it served my purpose. If my object was to make the point that an eyewitness had plenty of time to see an action, I spoke very deliberately, making the time . . . slow . . . down. If I wanted the jury to feel something go by in a nanosecond I spokeinahurry.

This was a revelation: I could do theater in the courtroom! I maintained the drama and the tension for both jurors and onlookers.

I had the facts, I had the witnesses, but without a motive my case was difficult. Look at him. Who would believe Edward Martin would shoot someone? His lawyer was as convinced of his innocence as I was of his guilt. The case went on for several days.

I discussed *Commonwealth v. Martin* with John Markey, a fellow ADA and at the time my boyfriend. He said, "Put yourself in his shoes." It was brilliant advice. I took on the role of Edward Martin. What did I find?

Eddie Martin loves cops. He spends hours in his room with the squawking police scanner, listening to police officers talk about exciting events all over his neighborhood. His life is ordinary, the cops' lives are exciting and he is excited by them. He wants to be a cop. He's a smart guy, he figures he could do their job better than they could. He hears the call—there's a wild party that needs taming. What a rush it would be to respond to this emergency. These kids, they're tearing up the town. How will the cops handle it? I know what I'd do.

I know what I'd do.

That's what motivated Eddie Martin. He knew what he'd do! He put his gun in his belt and headed over to be a cop.

But he wasn't a cop. He had no training; he had no policing expertise; all he had was his desire and a weapon. And when he got there he wasn't treated like a cop but like the civilian he was, interfering among a bunch of kids.

I know what I'd do.

He shot someone.

That was my theme. That was my closing argument. The jury found Edward Martin guilty.

I won my first big trial—an attempted murder case. It made the papers, the media picked it up. I became a high-visibility, up-and-coming ADA. I worked case after case, honing my skills.

The best way to learn to be a trial lawyer is to watch the great ones at work. I spent as much time as possible in the courtrooms observing my betters. If I heard that an excellent lawyer was arguing a case in our courthouse I would put my work aside and go sit in the gallery and soak up his or her style and substance, even if it meant I had to go back to my office and work until midnight.

I was committed. Instead of reading novels at night I read transcripts of legal cases. I combed our library for Joe Balliro's cases and Joe Oteri's, and I took notes and jotted down particularly effective question-and-answer combinations. I found the greatest lawyers and their best moments, and I devoured their work.

I paid particular attention to two women trial lawyers who had immediately preceded me in the criminal justice system in the greater Boston area, Andrea Gargiulo and Alice Richmond. Richmond was an assistant district attorney in Suffolk County (Boston), a special assistant attorney general, and later became president of the Massachusetts Bar Association. Gargiulo was a pioneer in the Middlesex DA's office, a very smart and attractive brunette so tough that she was known around the courthouse as the Dragon Lady. That is not usually a compliment, but her fearsome crosses were legendary, and I suspect she preferred winning like a dragon to losing like a pussycat. I found her cross-examination undermining the testimony of a psychiatrist in an insanity defense case particularly compelling and remarkably succinct.

Massachusetts law says that a defendant may be found not guilty by reason of insanity if as a result of a mental disease or defect at the time of the occurrence, he could not distinguish right from wrong or could not conform his conduct to the requirements of law. Gargiulo broke the law down into four parts: mental disease or defect; at the *time* of the occurrence; could not tell right from wrong; or could not conform or stop himself. The defense will consistently find a psychiatrist who is willing to testify that the defendant has such a disease or defect. If she says the defendant is psychotic or schizophrenic or bipolar, that testimony is not going away. No psychiatrist on the witness stand is going to change his or her opinion; that's not going to happen. What a good prosecutor must do is undermine that opinion.

"The occurrence took place on January second, didn't it, Dr. Johnson?"

"Yes, it did."

"You weren't called into this case until August second, right, Dr. Johnson?"

"Correct."

"So between January second and August second you never met the defendant?"

"Right."

"Between January second and August second you had no idea what he looked like?"

"Right."

"You had no idea how he appeared to others?"

"Right."

"You had no idea what he sounded like?"

"Right."

"The only idea you have is what you have read in the records of the institution?"

"Right."

By separating the defendant in the present from the defendant in the past Gargiulo took apart the issue of time and rendered the expert witness's testimony completely irrelevant. The mental state of the defendant as he stood before the court and the jury was of no consequence under the law, only his state of mind at the moment of the crime. After this cross, this witness had been stripped and simply could not state with any degree of credibility what the defendant's mental state was at the only time pertinent. Gargiulo followed that by analyzing the events. What was the defendant's mental state immediately before this occurrence? Immediately afterward? Could he distinguish right from wrong or conform his conduct to requirements of law at those times? The psychiatrist had no way of knowing, and again was taken out of the equation. If a young lawyer followed Gargiulo's legal footprints, he or she would look very much in control. I certainly did; I stole the examination outright and used it to great effect in cases that I won.

I spent fifteen months prosecuting increasingly high-visibility cases, and sure enough, in November 1978 Bill Delahunt was on the phone.

"I told you I was going to call you in a couple of years. I've got a superior court opening after the first of the year, and I want you to take it. I'm going to pay you more money than Kerry is paying you, and I want you to come here."

Whatever I was making per year with Kerry in Middlesex, Delahunt was going to double it in Norfolk. People don't stay in DAs' offices forever. Kerry understood and gave me his blessing. I jumped.

ILL DELAHUNT WAS A MASTER OF THE
MEDIA. WHILE I HAD MY MIND ON TRYING
the cases in the courtroom, he had a wider focus. He understood that
his success as a district attorney, an elected position, depended not
only on his winning cases at trial but also on earning and keeping the
public's trust and admiration. And who controlled access to the public? The media.

We discussed this often. I wanted very much to succeed, and I was
extremely interested in gaining every advantage. Bill Delahunt became

my mentor. "Whether you are in the public sector, in a district attorney's office, or in private practice," he explained, "you must always give fair time to the press. If you don't, they'll kill you." A thorough grasp of the mechanics of handling the media was vital, he told me.

"You have to remember that you must always deal with the *Boston Globe* and the *Boston Herald* equally. You may have a personal preference, one over the other, or a relationship with an individual reporter. You may find a reporter whom you trust and you may be inclined to bring him or her into your confidence to break a story, but you must make that decision judiciously. These papers are competitors, needless to say; you cannot slight one for the other, otherwise one or the other will hold a grudge forever. Sometimes you are better off holding a press conference, which they can both attend, so neither will be offended."

He schooled me. "With television people, you should always invite them to your office as a pool, for the same reasons. And you never wing it. You must prepare a set speech before every press conference, even if it is only a few sentences. It never matters what questions the press asks—the question never matters, *only the answer matters*: On the six and eleven o'clock news they never air the question; they only air the answer." When I sometimes forgot this lesson, Delahunt would take me aside and critique my performance.

"You need to decide before you appear in front of the cameras exactly what are the three, and no more than three, points that you want to get across. And no matter what they ask you, you can deflect them to give them your three points.

"You always have a story with a beginning, a middle, and an end, even if it is one sentence. You never leave it incomplete," he emphasized.

"Keep going forward. You are always prosecuting your case with the press. Always out there. You are on the offensive."

He was good.

Delahunt's first assistant, the chief, was Bob Banks. Bob was gracious enough to let me share his office, and we got along famously. He seemed much older than I was, though what did I know; I was thirty years old and I probably thought he was fifty, though he may well have had only ten years on me. He had worlds more experience. Bob had been a public defender for many years and been recruited by Delahunt himself. He was a burly, red-faced man with light blue eyes and a great big smile. He will no doubt hate this description, but he reminded me of the uncle we all want to have, the one we look forward to seeing on holidays who gives us that great grin and a big bear hug. He was also a brilliant trial lawyer and an excellent administrator. We had two desks in the office, two phones, and I enjoyed the opportunity to listen to him negotiating pleas or discussing motions with his adversaries.

He was on a first-name basis with almost everyone to whom he spoke. Unlike so many attorneys, who feel compelled to push their version of the facts on whomever they encounter, Bob was a listener; there would be long pauses during which I would see him listening in earnest to the person on the other end of the line. Finally he would say, "What do you mean by that?" Clearly this would take the speaker off guard. "Yes, when you say that the rape victim is not to be believed, what can you show me?" Pause for an answer. "I'm willing to listen to you, I'm willing to discuss dismissing the case, but you've got to show me something; you can't just tell me about it."

He, too, took time with me. Bob taught me the value of individual cases: this is worth ten years, this is worth six months. A burglary during the day when no one is home is considered minor; a burglary at night when the occupants are asleep is a home invasion, to be punished to the full extent of the law. He was also a talented cross-examiner, and I would often go to court to watch him work. He asked short, simple questions that sounded like statements. All the witness should ever be doing, he demonstrated, is answering yes. Don't drag it out for days, just get in and get out. He was very focused, with both a great strategic and a great tactical sense, and we had a fine friendship. There was much to learn in the Norfolk County DA's office.

Delahunt gave me a lot of leeway in prosecuting my cases, and I was all over the map, trying homicides and arson and rape cases, even investigating horse-race fixing. And I got lucky. In 1980 Massachusetts decided to allow cameras in the courtroom.

Now I could really perform.

There has been great controversy over the effects of live television coverage of trials. Initially, many feared that lawyers would play to the cameras; judges would be moved to one extreme or another by their presence; defendants would become pariahs for being charged with a crime in full view of their communities. I disagreed then and I disagree now. I took it as a chance to shine, to do my best work in front of a large and interested audience. Most lawyers did the same, and as a result I believe the presence of cameras in the courtroom has caused lawyers to become better prepared—for many reasons, among them ego, vanity, commerce, and honor.

Among the most ardent opponents of cameras in the courtroom were members of the criminal defense bar, who would say, "Oh my God, if the camera comes in the rights of my client are going to go down the tubes." They were wrong. Judges act better when the camera is trained on them. Judges who are arbitrary and capricious, judges who will do the most horrible things to a criminal defendant, will not dare do so in real time and on tape viewed by the general public and the legal community. In fact, the camera is the best assurance a defendant has against a judge who will act truly unconscionably.

What the camera does show is good lawyering and bad lawyering. What it doesn't show is what goes on in the court's back rooms, where, for instance, some defendants in death penalty cases are given representation you would not want for a traffic ticket. There is no spotlight trained on that.

So not only was I trying high-visibility cases, I was highly visible while trying them. If there was a significant criminal case in Norfolk County, I was usually involved in one way or another. I was becoming, in Boston, a Very Famous Lawyer.

One of my most famous cases was one we knew we were going to lose.

Carmen Lazzaro was a nineteen-year-old construction worker who lived in Westwood, Massachusetts. On Labor Day weekend in 1980 he had an argument with his father at the job site, drove home, brooded in his house, grabbed a meat cleaver, got back into his car, stuck the knife under the driver's seat, and drove north on Route 128 in rush-hour traffic.

He hit one car. He hit two cars. He hit a third car and knocked its passenger, a businessman from Lexington, off the road, then pulled onto the shoulder to see what he'd done. When the driver got out, Lazzaro backed up and ran over the man on the ground, breaking both his legs, then sped away.

He continued to drive on, swerving into people, smashing cars wildly. Labor Day weekend, rush hour, a crazy person was playing real-life bumper cars on Route 128. Drivers could see the carnage in their rearview mirrors and began careening out of his way. Lazzaro hightailed it for five miles, creating a wake of collision and chaos, then literally drove off the highway near Route 135 in Needham and slammed into a tree.

His car smoldering, Lazzaro sat in the driver's seat, not moving.

Gregory Kiff, a passerby, saw the accident, got out of his car, hopped the median, and navigated four lanes of traffic on foot to see if he could help. He didn't know anything about the carnage that stretched for miles in the other direction. All he knew was that a guy hit a tree and needed help. Good Samaritan that he was, he rushed to the car window.

"Are you all right?"

Carmen Lazzaro looked him dead in the eye, got out, and cleaved Kiff from head to toe. He hacked at him, wailing, while Kiff crumpled to the ground, screaming in agony.

Other motorists had gotten out of their cars and were coming to help, and now they were screaming, too. What could they do? The man had a meat cleaver; they weren't getting anywhere near him, so they yelled for him to stop.

Lazzaro quit slashing while Kiff was still miraculously alive. He ran and jumped into one of the cars left open by another Good Samaritan who had stopped to help him, then zoomed away again. He drove a few more exits and eventually a police car pulled up behind him. The blue light flashed; the siren called. Lazzaro slowed his stolen car and came to a stop at the bottom of an off-ramp. The police surrounded him, guns drawn. When they got to him, Lazzaro's first words were, "You should kill me for what I just did out there."

The case came to Delahunt's office and he handed it to me. At first I thought it was a slam dunk. After all, Lazzaro had admitted to police just minutes after the act that he knew what he had done and that it was wrong. In Massachusetts we had a phrase "police at the elbow," which meant this: If a police officer was at your elbow, right next to you, would you still perform the act? If you would not, that was proof you could conform your conduct to the requirements of the law. Lazzaro literally had police at his elbow when he spoke.

Delahunt knew otherwise. Being no fool, the district attorney said to himself, "This is a huge case; these are horrendous injuries; this is going to be all over the news . . . and I'll bet the guy is really crazy."

Kiff lived. And because there had been no death, there could be no prosecution for murder in the first degree. In the Commonwealth of Massachusetts, jury trials are mandatory only in murder-one cases; otherwise the defense has the right to ask that the case be decided by a judge. Any jury was going to convict. The *Boston Globe* was calling Lazzaro "The Meat-Cleaver Motorist." All we had to do was bring Gregory Kiff to the stand to testify about his injuries, show the jurors pictures of Kiff almost hacked to death, and follow that with the man Lazzaro ran over. "The crime was so heinous, who cares about the insanity defense? No matter what those shrinks say—they say they're all crazy—we're gonna convict." That's exactly what a jury would have thought and done.

But the defense was smart. Lazzaro's lawyer was Martin Cosgrove, about whom Judge Skinner once said, "Marty Cosgrove has the most disarming shuffle I have ever seen." He wore thick glasses; he was totally rumpled; his shirt was hanging out; his shoes had a hole in the bottom; he looked like he needed a shave. It wasn't an act—that was who he was. And he was brilliant. Cosgrove waived the jury, and the case was assigned to Judge Robert V. Mulkern. Judge Mulkern had been a superb criminal defense lawyer and was an independent thinker who would definitely not be swayed by public opinion. If Lazzaro was not guilty by reason of insanity, Judge Mulkern had the strength and character to obey the law and rule in his favor.

Our doctors examined Lazzaro in preparation for the trial. Dr.

Martin Kelly, a fine forensic psychiatrist who almost always testified for the government, came back and told me, "Rikki, he is bonkers."

"What am I going to do?" I asked.

"I don't think you'll find one psychiatrist who will say that he is sane under the law." That would be a first, but Dr. Kelly was serious. "You're going to try it the way you should try it," he said. "You're going to try it by the numbers; you're going to do everything you can to convict him. The victims deserve your best. But you are going to lose."

Apparently, without his family quite understanding what was happening to him, in his late adolescence Carmen Lazzaro had become schizophrenic. Some time earlier he had lost control and begun slashing tires madly on the street, but when the police responded they had not considered the act to be anything other than teenage vandalism. This time Lazzaro had had a totally psychotic episode. Still, I had to try the case. His victims lived from one end of Route 128 to the other, and they deserved my support.

The district attorney's job is to prosecute crimes and protect the rights of victims, to make people feel safe in society. I tried to undermine the insanity defense, but the medical evaluations were so proximate to the moment of the crime that I could not call into question their timing. And without a doctor who would testify that Lazzaro was not insane, this was a very difficult case to make. I presented the horrific facts in detail and with passion, but when Judge Mulkern indeed found Lazzaro not guilty by reason of insanity and sentenced him to be held for treatment at Bridgewater State Hospital and not released until he was determined to be no longer a danger to society, we were obliged to tell the public and the victims that justice had been served. What else could we do?

My back went out.

I'd had back problems since I was a girl. When I was sixteen, I took a leap into my partner's arms during a dance rehearsal in summer stock. He dropped me and I fell on my coccyx. It acted up at the theater in London during the summer of 1969, and I was flat on my back for a week. In the mid-seventies I was trying on a pair of slacks in a department store dressing room in Atlanta, bent down, and could not get up. I had to lie on the floor for an hour before I could rise and be wheeled onto a plane back to Boston.

This time was worse. I was having dinner with several people at my friend Joan Schmidt's apartment, and as I reached for the salt I couldn't move. I couldn't stand; I could barely sit; I couldn't walk. They managed to get me home, but in the morning I could not rise out of bed. I had never felt such pain. It shot from my spine all the way down my right leg in spasmodic lightning bolts of sciatica. I crawled to the phone and called my doctor, who said he would meet me at the hospital. Somehow I was brought there, since I was physically incapable of getting there on my own.

A myelogram showed that I had a herniated disk in my spine and was in heightened spasm, so the doctors filled me full of painkillers and Valium and waited until it stopped. It was clear to my orthopedist that I needed surgery, but I refused. I didn't have time for back surgery; I needed to be in court. I stayed in the hospital for ten days, at which point things had cleared up sufficiently for me to go home, provided I popped every pill they prescribed.

I wasn't exercising, I wasn't eating properly, my body could barely support me. I was in pain every moment of every day, but I went to work; there were cases to be won. I took my morning megadose of medication and lay in the backseat of a friend's car as he drove me to work each day. I did my paperwork and managed to stand up in court long enough to try my cases, then I lay in the backseat all the way home. My forty-four-step walk-up was too much for me, so I moved in with Joan for a while, because her apartment in Harbor Towers had an elevator. That summer my boyfriend, Jay Flynn, took a share in a house on Cape Cod, and on weekends he picked me up in his arms like a bundle of kindling and carried me down to the beach, where I lay until he carried me home. I didn't know how I was going to survive. But I kept on working.

My mother began sending a sheaf of newspaper clippings about a treatment in lieu of surgery called chymopapain injection, which was performed in Canada but had been outlawed in the United States. Even in Canada one needed a referral from an established orthopedist or neurosurgeon to begin the process. I spoke with my physician, who sent me to an orthopedist, who refused to authorize the procedure. My uncle, who lived in Alexandria, Virginia, sent me to an orthopedist who believed in the treatment; he saw me on a weekend and approved it. Finally, when the pain was excruciating and I was starting to lose control of my bladder, I gave in. I called that doctor and told him, "You've got to get me up there right away." One phone call later he told me, "If you can get to Hamilton, Ontario, in forty-eight hours, you can have it done this week." I called my mother, who said she would meet me there.

The situation was complicated by the fact that the procedure cost five thousand dollars; being illegal in the United States, it was not covered by medical insurance. I was making a salary somewhere above twenty thousand dollars a year and simply did not have that kind of money in the bank. I didn't have that kind of money, period. On top of that, the Canadian hospital would not take a check. I needed cash.

I called my mother. "If I can borrow the money from Daddy's pension," I said, "I'll work to pay you back."

"Rikki." I don't think she was angry, perhaps a little disappointed in my lack of faith in her. "You never have to pay me back. This is for your health and I'm glad that I have it to give to you."

But she was in Chicago, and I needed the money immediately. Even a check would take time to clear. I had to go where the money was. I called a man I had met through Attorney General Frank Bellotti and Bill Delahunt, a man who had been generous while raising funds for various charities, and asked for a huge favor. If he could loan me several thousand dollars for one week, I told him, I would pay him back with the funds my mother would give me. Out of no obligation to me, but out of respect for my two mentors Bellotti and Delahunt and his belief in my potential as a lawyer, this wonderful benefactor messengered five thousand dollars to my apartment that afternoon. In cash. It was one of the great acts of kindness visited upon me in my entire life. With that money I could have the chymopapain injection and perhaps walk again without pain.

My boyfriend, Jay, flew with me to Hamilton. He exchanged my

U.S. dollars for Canadian at the bank and deposited me at the hospital. My mother arrived, and she and Jay met the doctor with me.

Dr. Murray looked at my myelogram, asked me to stand, which I could not, and explained the procedure. As I understood it, after administering a significant dose of intravenous Valium, he and his team, using the myelogram as a guide, under surgical conditions, would inject me with the chymopapain, a substance made from papaya, which would, like a Pac Man on a rampage, devour the herniated portion of my disk while leaving the rest of my body inviolate. Dr. Murray was very encouraging. He quoted extensive research on the subject and assured me that the treatment was quite effective and legitimate, its illegality in the United States notwithstanding. "The pain down your leg will be entirely gone when you emerge from this procedure," he assured me. In its place, he explained, would be the most excruciating pain in my back I had ever felt in my life. This would be my body's reaction to the introduction of the new substance. He and his team would minimize its effect with drugs, but I should be prepared for the pain to last between twenty-four and thirty-six hours, after which it would leave forever and I would walk out of the hospital a cured and pain-free woman. I thought, Yeah, right. But I really did not feel I had a choice; I could not live this way for much longer.

While I was in the hospital, Jay and my mother were out becoming famous friends. Whatever there was to do in Hamilton, Ontario, they did it. They found the good restaurants, they walked the streets, and saw the sights. I was lashed to a gurney and they were hitting the town.

By the time I woke up, Jay was calling her "Mom." He was a vodka drinker, and as he sat in my hospital room with his orange juice and vodka in a thermos, my mother brought me dark-chocolate-covered peppermint sticks, and they had a fine time while I was sweating out the back pain. Dr. Murray had not overstated it in either length or degree; I was in agony for a full day and a half. And then he said, "Get out of bed." I said, "I can't." He said, "Oh, but you can!" I swiveled, put my feet on the ground, walked up and down the corridor, put my clothes on, and off we went. If I were Catholic I'd say I had been to Lourdes.

Dr. Murray told me to stay away from work for a month. He prescribed a rehabilitation regime for me to perform each day, including walking for miles and swimming laps. To regenerate the nerve tissue I took enormous quantities of B and C vitamins. My mother stayed with me, and Jay slept over occasionally, although sex was out of the question. The pair of them would go grocery shopping. My mother made me meals, and all I had to concentrate on was getting back my health.

That was too much to ask. Instead of luxuriating in my forced freedom from work by reading or stretching out and relaxing, I thought, I'm going to lose my career. Out of sight, out of mind; I'm in trouble. Immediately before my collapse I had been working on a huge case, and I was terrified that it would be taken from me. I could not lose this case. I could not lose *control* of this case. It was going to be the biggest case of my career to date; I could not be sick! And, of course, the more anxious and concerned I became, the more my body spasmed, the more I needed my Valium; the more Valium I had in me, the less I was able to work. It was a vicious cycle, and I was incapable of breaking out of it.

There was a street festival in our North End neighborhood one Sunday—people marching, arcade games on wheels, the Madonna on a float with dollars pinned to her, little stands set up selling all kinds of delicious Italian food. Jay went down and came back with a sausage, pepper, and onion sandwich for me. I usually enjoyed this street delicacy, but this time I wasn't very interested. It sat there, wrapped in white paper, smelling up the apartment. My mother looked at me. She picked it up.

"Will you just enjoy the sandwich!" she said. "Stop thinking about missing work. All you want to do is get back to work because you are afraid that something will happen with your job. You don't live in the present for one moment."

I took a bite but didn't say a word. That was my way. And I did not listen. I went about my business, preparing to return to court. Time passed awfully slowly.

In the hospital in Hamilton my mother had met a very handsome older man who looked just like John Wayne and had taken a liking to her. The day I got out of bed they had been talking, and it was clear even in my addled state that this gentleman was mesmerized by my mom. They were quite animated, and I could tell from a distance, just by his body language, that he found her fascinating. He asked for her phone number before we departed. Some weeks later I asked, "Why don't you see this fellow?" On top of being good company, apparently he was extremely wealthy.

"I have no intention of ever going out with a man other than your father," she told me. "I never went out with a man before your father, and I'm not going to go out with a man after your father."

But my father, no matter how much we loved him, was gone, and this man seemed both exquisitely eligible and extremely interested. "Mom," I said, "I think you're wasting your life."

"It's my life," she snapped. "In my life, I have only loved your father and that is the way it shall always be, and I don't expect you to understand that."

I didn't understand her sudden intensity. "Why not?"

"Well, look at your life. Have you ever been without a man for more than three days?"

I was surprised. I had always had boyfriends; she was well aware of that—we certainly talked about them often enough—and I thought my mother had approved. "No," I said. "I don't think so."

"Well then, you will never be able to have a relationship like your father and I had. And frankly, I feel sorry for you."

My parents had adored each other. One would walk into a room and the other would light up. I hadn't found that kind of devotion with anyone, and I think my mother did feel badly that such a soulful connection was missing from my life. But she was saying more, and it was this that I took exception to.

She was saying I should have stayed married to Sandy, that it was wrong for me to have divorced, that my drive toward a career was taking me down a path of which she simply did not approve. I was always looking for something extra; for me, there was always someone more exciting personally or something more compelling professionally than the vision of settling down with one man and starting a family. My mother had once told me, after I had left one boy for another, "For a wonderfully smart young woman, sometimes I think you have no common sense." She was a woman whose relationship to her husband had been the primary focus of her life. My primary focus was not my relationship with men but my relationship with my work. What my mother valued was love, and now in essence she was telling me that my life would never amount to anything.

She may have been concerned for me; she may have felt that the longer I went forward with my career the less chance I would have of finding the nurturing relationship she wanted for me; she may have been expressing a feeling that had bothered her for a long time. But what I felt was anger and resentment. Wasn't she the woman who had told me I could be anything I wanted to be? Hadn't she nicknamed me Miss Remarkable, and wasn't it exciting that I was going to impress the world? Hadn't she made it clear that I was the person who should make my own decisions? Well, what I wanted, after being an assistant district attorney, was to be a famous criminal defense attorney. Marriage could wait. Children? Who knew? My mother, who understood me so well, did not understand my drive for a career. As much as she loved and adored me, it was clear in that moment that she didn't understand me. I was angry. I was hurt. I was alone.

What did I do? I threw myself back into my work.

On May 18, 1979, four Brookline teenagers, Ralph Langdon, sixteen; Peter Mattimoe Jr., sixteen; Mark Eliasson, fifteen; and Brookline High School football star James Corbett, seventeen, had been drinking at a couple of end-of-school parties and wound up outside a pizza parlor in an area called Cleveland Circle, on the border between Norfolk and Suffolk Counties, Brookline and Boston. The Cleveland Circle movie theater had let out a few blocks away, and people were walking home in the spring air. The four teenagers formed a gauntlet through which people had to pass. As a pair of college-age young men walked between them, one of the four yelled, "Spic!" and shot his foot toward them in a karate move.

The high school boys had been drinking. Maybe they could tell the difference, maybe they couldn't, but the young men they yelled at were not of Hispanic descent; they were Iranian students studying at

Boston University. One of the boys kicked back and then ran, pursued by Corbett. The other, a twenty-year-old engineering student named Ali Majidi, was surrounded and overwhelmed. What began as a fistfight became much more serious when Ralph Langdon took a knife from his pocket and started stabbing Majidi. He stuck in the knife many times. Depending on which eyewitness one believes, Mattimoe either did or didn't continue to punch Majidi and hit him with a U-shaped metal bar while Langdon was stabbing him. Majidi was punched in the head, and when he fell to the ground, kicked in the legs and back and chest. Mattimoe swore that he was pushed backward and wound up against an iron fence, knocked out cold with a concussion; that was Mattimoe's story, and he was sticking to it.

Eliasson was kicking and punching Majidi for all he was worth, and Langdon kept on stabbing. They beat him and beat him and beat him. Eyewitnesses looking down on the fracas from their apartment windows called the police, and when the boys heard the sirens they scattered. They were gone.

Ali Majidi was dead on arrival at Beth Israel Hospital with three stab wounds to the chest and three in the back.

Mattimoe was not unknown in those parts and was identified, tracked down, and brought to the police station with his mother. He told his story and was even taken to the hospital to evaluate and treat his concussion. As kids often do, he took the police to the scene of the crime and reenacted it for them. He showed where he, Langdon, Eliasson, and Corbett met up afterward. From Mattimoe they identified Ralphie Langdon, who was Ralph Langdon Jr., the son of a Brookline police officer. The detectives who caught the case went to the Langdons' home, notified the father, and took the son into custody. The other boys were brought in shortly thereafter.

Delahunt assigned the case to me.

This was a vicious killing for no reason. I felt responsible to the dead young man and to the Massachusetts community to see that the boys who killed him were punished to the full extent of the law. Although all the boys were underage, with the exception of Corbett, who was not directly involved in the assault on Majidi, I felt it would be a travesty and an injustice if they were tried as juveniles—their maximum sentence would be incarceration at a secure Department of Youth Services (DYS) facility until their twenty-first birthday, after which Majidi would still be dead and they would be out on the street. These kids had committed a very adult crime, and I was determined to see them tried as adults. I took Corbett to the district court in Brookline for a probable cause hearing. His murder charge was dismissed, which was no surprise.

The Brookline police were furious: Ralphie was one of theirs, a cop's son. Boys will be boys; he was only sixteen; why ruin his life; give the kid a break. One would think that police, of all people, would want to see a killer punished, but whether it was clannish loyalty or an unwillingness to enforce the law evenhandedly or simply a display of support for a brother officer, they showed tremendous anger when I made it clear I wanted Langdon, Mattimoe, and Eliasson transferred to adult status. One detective on the case, Robert Allen, stood by me in the prosecution. He had been at the scene and knew the facts; he had taken charge from the beginning and would not be swayed from his duty by personal considerations or the notorious blue wall of silence. For that I will be eternally grateful.

It was almost impossible at that time for a prosecutor to get juvenile cases transferred to the adult court. At a closed hearing, a prosecutor's mandate was to convince a judge that the teenager in question could not be rehabilitated within the confines of the juvenile system and deserved to be treated as an adult for his crime. That law had been established to handle underage recidivist offenders who had been in and out of the Department of Youth Services and kept committing crimes. It was not meant for kids with no prior record who had never been in the juvenile system. Still, I was both outraged and determined, and I didn't want to lose.

A tenacious and thorough detective named Brian Howe was assigned to this case by the State Police Unit that investigated homicides for the Norfolk County district attorney's office. He was an ace, and he was willing to do whatever I wanted within the bounds of the law to get these kids transferred. "I want to know everything everybody knows about these kids," I told him. "I want to know every neighbor, everybody they ever went to school with. I want to talk to every teacher. There's nobody I *don't* want to talk to, and I want someone to tell me that these kids were marked for violence."

Detective Howe was old-school; he felt as I did, that these kids ought to be treated as adults, and he went into overdrive. For months he collected information, and when I entered the hearing room I knew more about these kids than if I had raised them. There was nothing we didn't know, from the moment they were born until that morning. Every person they ran into, every girl they talked to, any time they threw a snowball, what they wrote in their English composition papers, what their teachers observed about them, what kids in the school yard said about them, what the police thought was going on in their homes . . . we knew about it.

The Supreme Judicial Court of Massachusetts eventually looked at our findings and reported in an opinion, *Two Juveniles V. Commonwealth (and a companion case)*, 381 Mass. 736 (1980):

"Juvenile A, concededly the person who repeatedly stabbed the victim, exhibited no remorse after the homicide. Two weeks before the second part of the transfer hearing, he was again arrested and charged with an assault by means of a dangerous weapon. . . . He had been suspended from school in 1978 for painting racial epithets on the school walls. . . . [He] also had a problem with alcohol abuse.

"There had been incidents of aggressive behavior in which Juvenile B was involved . . . and he was also a drug and alcohol abuser. Prior to the time of the homicide, he had been arrested for assault and battery, breaking and entering with intent to commit a felony, larceny. . . . He was found not to have responded to any rehabilitation he had been offered. Juvenile B was found to be the assailant who had used the metal bar in the homicide.

"Juvenile C was found not to have exhibited any appreciable remorse by word, act or expression. [He] was found to have been the instigator of altercations with other people prior to the homicide. He had previously rejected all counseling and therapy despite recommendations that he accept assistance. Not only was he found to have a proclivity to violence, but also to have a strong antipathy to minorities. He was heavily involved in self-defense training and interested in military weaponry."

I didn't want these kids on the streets.

We prepared extensive legal briefs for the judge, arguing force-fully that even though these boys had not previously been appre-hended, their actions before the night of the killing combined with the randomness and viciousness of the attack to create a probability that no stay in a state-run juvenile facility was going to rehabilitate them. The fact that they had not been incarcerated previously did not earn them a free ride on a particularly heinous crime.

The transfer hearing ran several days. I was passionate in pursu-ing my case. Ultimately, Judge William Scannell was convinced. They would be charged as adults.

"This is a miracle!" Bill Delahunt exclaimed when the decision came down. "I thought this was impossible. No one could have done this. This could change the way juveniles are dealt with in Massachu-setts. I'm very proud of you!"

I was thrilled with his praise and very pleased with the decision. "Thank you," I told him. "We need to do justice for this student, and we certainly don't need to look like we are abandoning him and his family by virtue of the fact that he is Iranian."

But as proud as I was of my work, there was no joy in my victory. I was going to treat these children as adults, knowing that I might be sending them to prison for the rest of their lives for something they did one night when they were teenagers. And as much time as I had spent getting to know these boys in order to prosecute them, I also began to like them. They were kids who had problems, boys who had been extremely violent on one particular night, but they were also children with difficult paths through life and no one to lead them to safety. They became people to me; I knew who they were. As a prosecutor, I never wanted to know that much about a defendant again.

So my achievement was tinged with sorrow. I knew from both a legal and a political perspective that what I had done was correct, but once I had done it I wished I hadn't.

Richard Gargiulo, the husband of Andrea Gargiulo, my predeces-sor in the Middlesex DA's office, represented Ralph Langdon and came to me to work out a plea agreement. If Ralphie were found guilty of first-degree murder as an adult he was facing life in prison without the possibility of parole. And he could be found guilty. Eye-witnesses in the apartment building saw him from above. He was blond and noticeable. They called him "light and bright": "The kid with the light hair"; "The kid with the bright hair." Richard knew he had to plead it; he could not risk seeing this boy incarcerated for sixty, seventy, or eighty years. We negotiated at some length concerning what the appropriate punishment should be and finally agreed. Langdon pleaded guilty to manslaughter.

How smart I thought I was. How foolish. It never dawned on me that by pleading Ralph I had totally ruined my case against the other two. Ralph was the kid with the knife; he had actually stabbed Majidi. The worst Eliasson and Mattimoe could be found guilty of now was manslaughter, and it wasn't going to be easy. I was too green to realize the hole I had dug for myself. Nevertheless, I tried my ever-loving heart out.

Peter Mattimoe was represented by one of the great Massachusetts criminal defense attorneys, Daniel Featherston. Featherston was tall and lanky, a strange physical specimen. When he gestured, his wingspan reminded me in many ways of a vulture's. Or Ichabod Crane. Yet he was a brilliant orator who understood drama. His mellifluous voice soothed the jury as he delivered his message, and his message in this case was that Peter Mattimoe was out cold when Ali Majidi was killed. Mattimoe had been well coached before he got on the witness stand to testify in his own behalf. Witnesses testified that he had participated in the battering, but he denied it, and although I wasn't buying it, Featherston made that denial believable.

Mark Eliasson was represented by Frank Levy, a lawyer more at home in civil cases, who quietly and appropriately followed Featherston's lead. Levy had an aura of integrity that would certainly help his client.

The trial brought extensive media coverage, as would be expected. When I told the jury slowly and dramatically that as Majidi staggered at the scene Mattimoe and Eliasson "beat him and beat him and beat him," the emotion behind the phrase caught the public's attention and brought home a degree of violence one could not see in the faces of these boys who had been cleaned up for the proceedings.

We made headlines as Brookline and much of Boston chose sides. Even before we began, Daniel Featherston wanted to break legal ground in questioning the jury. In Massachusetts, as in the federal system, lawyers do not question prospective jurors, judges do. Lawyers may suggest questions for the judge's approval, but it is the judge's responsibility to question the jurors. Featherston came into court with ten to twenty pages of multiple-choice questions through which he was hoping to glean the jurors' attitudes. He wanted to ask prospective jurors whether they agreed "most" or "least" with questions like "I believe that all suspects should receive Miranda warnings at the earliest possible moment" and "I think the police should be permitted to encourage a suspect to volunteer information before issuing the Miranda warning."

This had never been done in Massachusetts legal history, but Judge William Young, a superb jurist with great integrity, thought Featherston's questionnaire was innovative and helpful in determining the actual thinking of jurors instead of each side's usual reliance on such stereotypes as "truck drivers are in favor of the prosecution and teachers favor the defense." Judge Young found the questionnaire a valuable exercise and allowed it.

I thought the questionnaire was brilliant in its tilting of the scale toward the defense, who would be getting vastly more quantities of information than they had ever had. And I was apoplectic over one particular element. The most outrageous of Featherston's questions asked for the juror's opinion on whether "most prosecuting attorneys have a sadistic streak." He was putting an egregious image into the mind of the jury before I even opened my mouth. I thought that crossed way over the line of propriety, and I let him know about it. He and I went after each other and it got very personal in chambers and in the hallways between sessions. He was angry with me and I was angry with him. Yet in the courtroom we fought with the dignity and decorum the court demanded. He did characterize me as "an avenging angel" in his closing argument, but I probably deserved it.

Detective Allen, facing withering pressure from his brother Brookline officers, stood tall in his testimony. Detective Howe's investigation had revealed a pattern of violence that indeed demanded

adult treatment. I argued forcefully for a guilty verdict of manslaughter in a joint venture, as these boys did combine in their effort to do
Majidi terrible harm. Majidi was dead, and no matter the defendants'
intentions, they had killed him and ought to be punished. Featherston said Mattimoe was not even conscious and Levy said Eliasson
just made a mistake. The trial lasted for two weeks.

The all-white jury deliberated for six and a half hours and came
back with a verdict of guilty of assault-and-battery with a dangerous
weapon.

I was devastated. Featherston and Levy were elated. A verdict of
anything less than the indictment is a loss for the prosecution and a
win for the defense. That's Trial Law 101. I was livid. But at least
they had been tried as adults and would serve their sentences in the
harsh reality of an adult prison.

After the verdicts, Judge Young set a date for sentencing. At that
hearing Featherston pulled a full-court press. As well prepared as I
had been for the juvenile hearing, he trumped me at the sentencing.
He came to court with compelling reasons why, when it came to sentencing, these kids should be treated as juveniles. He had a litany of
excuses for his young client, backed up by facts. It was like listening
to the lyrics of "Officer Krupke" from *West Side Story.* I was mesmerized by his bravura performance but I was not amused.

I thought this had already been decided. They had been tried as
adults; they had been found guilty as adults; they should be punished
as adults. The judge did have the option to sentence them as juveniles,
but I did not think there was a remote possibility in Christendom of
his using it. I didn't dignify that concept by even considering it.

Judge Young sentenced Mattimoe and Eliasson as juveniles.
They would go to a Youth Services facility until their twenty-first
birthday. He then awarded the same sentence to Langdon.

I was furious. When the sentence was read and the gavel came
down, I stormed out of the courtroom. I blew open the double doors
with my left hand and flew into the corridor screaming! Eighteen
months of my life! I could have tried this case in juvenile court a year
and a half earlier and gotten the same result. How dare Judge
Young! I had slaved over this case for *a year and a half* and he took

away my work! This was *my* work! And Brian Howe's work! How dare he!

But how odd life can be. Several years later I was meeting some friends for drinks at the bar at the Bostonian Hotel. I walked in and pulled up a chair. We were having a grand time when someone came up behind me and tapped my shoulder. I looked up and there was Mark Eliasson, dressed in a bellman's uniform. I stood up.

"Ms. Klieman," he said. "How are you?"

"Mark." I was caught off guard, perhaps a bit apprehensive. "What are you doing here?"

"I'm working here now," he answered. There was something about his voice that was unusual.

"How are you doing?"

He said, "I'm doing great. You know, I really needed to go to jail." I looked at him. "The best thing that happened to me was winding up within the system. I don't know how violent I might have been. I heard everything you said at that hearing. I heard *everything* you said. You know what scares me now is you were probably right about me, even though I hated you at the time."

I knew what was unusual about his voice; it seemed calm.

"I'm really going to be a productive member of society," he told me. "I'm going to show you that the judge gave me a chance and I'm really, really going to produce."

I hugged him. "I wish you well. I am very sorry I couldn't see the possibility in you and Peter. I'm so glad someone else did."

"It's okay," he said. "You were just doing your job."

"Boy, that's pretty forgiving of you." I hugged him again.

Some years passed and I found myself in 1987 at a wedding at another elegant Boston hotel. I was sitting at dinner when a very handsome, well-dressed young man approached my table. "Ms. Klieman, how are you?" It was Mark Eliasson again. He had become this prestigious hotel's food-and-beverage manager. I gave him a great big hug. "I'll never forget you," he said.

"I'll never forget you," I promised. "But you shouldn't remember me for anything good."

"No. I'm just a better person now."

He brought tears to my eyes. He *was* a better person, a better person than I. He taught me so much about the human condition. His gesture of goodwill toward me was an unselfish, magnanimous act. His kindness was my gift. I thank him here and always.

I have been told that Mark's career prospered and he entered the hotel system's management hierarchy. How truly wonderful. I hope to see him again one day.

How wise was Judge Young. How biased was I. The hubris of a young prosecutor, to think that I knew so much, that I had such power and zeal to put a young man in prison forever without any effort at rehabilitation. If we cannot rehabilitate our young people, who can we ever rehabilitate? Placing prosecutorial power in the hands of people perhaps too young or too lacking in life experience is sometimes not wise. Judge Young, being far older and more seasoned—and more learned—than I, understood that we could not give up on these children; we needed to give them another chance.

Unfortunately, right now society seems to be going in the opposite direction, jailing increasing numbers of teenagers rather than making any real attempt to bring them into our national family. As a society we ought not stand for putting twelve-, thirteen-, and fourteen-year-olds in prison without the possibility of parole. It's inhuman; it's unthinkable; it's uncivilized. I did not know that then, but I know it now. I had fought against putting Mattimoe and Eliasson into the juvenile system, because I was certain they could not be rehabilitated; yet Judge Young wanted them there, correctly, because he was certain they could. As a prosecutor, I could see only the crime. Although I knew all about the defendants' lives, I could not see their humanity.

Over the years Daniel Featherston and I became friends. He died in 1996. I was living and working in New York, but I flew to Boston to attend his memorial service. I would not have missed it. What a good lawyer, what a passionate advocate for his clients, what a pillar of the bar that man was. Whenever I hear the strains of "Danny Boy," which was sung at his funeral, I shall always remember that giant of a man.

seven **A WOMAN AT THE BAR**

ARLY IN MY CAREER, AS I TRAVELED FROM COURTROOM TO COURTROOM, FROM JUDGE to judge, observing the law being practiced and learning my craft, I asked the people I respected how I could make my mark. One federal judge advised me, "You could truly establish yourself as a lawyer of importance if you became active in the world of continuing legal education. That is, as you hone your skills and become more proficient as a lawyer, you then go on to teach others. This will also create a niche for you as an expert in your field." He also suggested I become involved with the Boston and Massachusetts Bar Associations because both were looked upon as organizations of quality. People developed reputations in the legal community, he explained, by virtue of their activities there. One could work on committees, then become a member of the board of governors, and move up the chain. I took that advice quite literally.

I began while working at the Middlesex County district attorney's office by attending the two-week National Institute for Trial Advocacy summer program as a student. There I learned the rudiments of trial practice: how to give an opening statement, how to conduct a direct examination, how to do a cross, how to examine an expert. The head of my section at the program was Judge John Paul Sullivan, with whom I studied trial practice at Boston University School of Law. After two years he asked me to assist him as a member of the faculty, again following in the footsteps of Alice Richmond, who had been his first female assistant, and in addition, perform a demonstration of trial techniques for the class. Usually, the most senior faculty were chosen to give demonstrations to show how the exercise was supposed to be done. I was extremely flattered to have been asked.

In 1979 I was asked to join the faculty of the Intensive Trial Practice Institute (ITP) at Harvard Law School. I was honored and thrilled. Harvard brought in esteemed professional people from around the United States—famous trial lawyers and a few academics—for intensive three-week courses that took place in September and January. The attorneys who gave the demonstrations were decades older than I was and arrived at the apex of their reputations: Charles Ogletree, Marshall "Pete" Simonds, Jake Stein. At the time, there were few women on the faculty or in the classes.

I was ambitious but I recognized the fact that I was a kid, a baby lawyer. I did whatever they wanted me to do. If the day consisted of something as mundane as demonstrating how to establish a chain of custody—When you seized the drugs, Officer, what did you do with them? And after you put them in an envelope, what did you do next? And after you placed your initials on the envelope, where did you take it?—I did it. When teaching, I soaked up the knowledge of other faculty. I attended their lectures and took notes as furiously as the students did. There is rarely a right and wrong way to do things in trial practice; however, some strategies and tactics are more effective than others. I wound up with a notebook full of tips and devices to improve my performance.

Chicago federal defender Terry MacCarthy's instructions concerning opening statements were a revelation. I had routinely begun my openings by saying, "May it please the court. Your Honor, Madame Forelady, ladies and gentlemen of the jury. My name is Rikki Klieman. I am an assistant district attorney of the Commonwealth of Massachusetts. Now, as an assistant district attorney, I am the prosecutor in this case. That is a person who, for the government, the Commonwealth, will introduce the Commonwealth's case. What I say is not evidence; it is simply a summary, an overview of what the Commonwealth intends to introduce in its case." I would go on like that, familiarizing myself and the legal fundamentals to the jurors, at some length.

I learned from the ITP masters that I had it all wrong. A lawyer's first and last words to a jury are critically important. *Most* important. Why would I ever waste those precious initial moments on that nonsense? The one thing an effective attorney needs to do is to tell her story from the beginning. Who cares what my title is? It doesn't matter that I am going to present a summary. Present the summary! And the *last* thing a lawyer ever wants to tell a jury is that what she is saying is not evidence!

The ITP course was a life-changing experience.

A year or so later, I was asked to work as co-counsel in a demonstration with John Keenan, who had been the head of the Homicide Bureau in Manhattan DA Frank Hogan's office and later became a federal judge for the Southern District of New York. I was quite intimidated to serve as his colleague, but we functioned well and the demonstration was a success. Afterward a very formidable fellow approached and had a few words with me.

Albert Krieger was one of the top criminal defense lawyers in the United States. Working out of New York, he tried huge cases and rarely lost. He had represented the Native Americans involved in the 1973 uprising at Wounded Knee as well as members of the Bonanno crime family; he would later defend John Gotti. Krieger believed in teaching and refining criminal law. He was one of the early members of the National Association of Criminal Defense Lawyers, and his brilliant reputation swirled around him like a hurricane.

A strong, muscular man, Krieger carried himself with grandeur, and I was convinced that he was even larger than he appeared. His head was shaved, and with his piercing eyes he looked like a cross between Yul Brynner and Kojak. His voice was an operatic instrument, a booming baritone with a resonant bottom, and he used it with power. When we discussed Albert Krieger, students and even some faculty would imitate his distinctive style: "And the right of the defendant to effective assistance of counsel is an inalienable right." It's a voice that would be at home in a cathedral. I'm sure he talks like that when he's having breakfast.

Mr. Krieger approached me and said, "Ms. Klieman, when are you going to be a criminal defense attorney?"

"I hope sometime soon," I said. How pleasant that he knew my name.

"How soon?" he rumbled.

"I don't know, about a year or so."

He reached into his breast pocket. "I want you to make a promise to me. I am going to give you my business card. I don't want you to lose it. I want you to promise me that as soon as you become a criminal defense attorney you will write to me and remind me of this conversation, because I want to bring you to the National College for Criminal Defense. I want you to teach. I have never seen a woman lawyer do what you do. You have a lot of people to serve. There are women out there who have no role model, and you can be their role model. As soon as you become a defense lawyer, you call me."

I was flattered, elated, just completely tickled. I put his card in a safe place. The day would come.

I continued trying cases and I became extremely comfortable in court. The courthouse became my home, my community, almost my family. I knew the court officers, the judges, the attorneys, and I lived among them with great enthusiasm. I was working, winning, having a wonderful time.

For the most part I wore dresses to court rather than suits because I was comfortable in my feminine-yet-competent persona. One morning I had been presenting a case to the grand jury and arrived at the first criminal session at the Norfolk County courthouse a few minutes late. That didn't matter; there were routinely fifty cases cramming the court calendar, and if a prosecutor wasn't immediately available when his came up it simply went to the bottom of the list. The cases were being heard by Judge Frank Keating that morning in what is known as the Sacco and Vanzetti courtroom, the one in which that historic case was tried. It is an imposing room under a high dome, and the place was abuzz with lawyers and clients and family of clients, the ceaseless, echoing din of preparation and anxiety. I breezed through the swinging double doors and began the long walk down the center aisle to the well of the court, as it is called, beyond the rail before the bench.

"Oh, Miss Klieman." Judge Keating was peering over his eyeglasses as I approached. "How nice of you to join us today."

All of a sudden I was walking in silence. The whole room went still, as if a noise track had been wiped clean. This didn't happen often. The defense attorneys and ADAs, who all depended on the judge's goodwill for a significant element of their success, froze. There is something oddly compelling about the anticipation of seeing a prosecutor get crucified.

"You grace us with your presence today."

I didn't say a word. I surely did not want to pull the whiskers of this legal lion. The judge was furious. What I had taken to be a routine practice he was apparently deeming a deep insult. He looked at me gravely.

"What a lovely dress," he said. "Perhaps you will do a pirouette for me."

Clearly he was baiting me. This was 1980, the heyday of heightened feminism, and from the bench he was asking for a dance. He was doing nothing if not provoking me to bridle. How could I get out of this one?

"With pleasure, Your Honor." I smiled, held my briefcase in one hand, stretched out my ballerina arms and did a little twirl.

"Would you like me to do it in reverse?" I swear I was giggling.

Judge Keating grinned. "By all means." I twirled backward. He started laughing. "Well done."

"I can dance, too!"

He chuckled. "All right, let's call your case."

From that day forward Judge Keating would do anything for me. There was never a time in all the years I subsequently appeared before him that he would not have done whatever I needed, whenever I needed it. If I was going to be late because I was at another courthouse, and I showed him respect by calling his clerk to ask for several hours' continuance, my case was put aside. If I was going to plead a client guilty and presented a good reason to support my sentencing recommendation as opposed to my opponent's, he ruled for me. It's amazing what a little pirouette will do.

Today, more than twenty years later, most women attorneys would report him to the Judicial Conduct Commission. Even in 1980 some women would have stood on feminist pride, taken offense at his demand, and said, "I will not!" I thought of myself as a serious person and a competent lawyer, not someone who deserved to be trifled with. And what Judge Keating was doing was, yes, sexist. But in that moment I had the choice to make him either my friend or my enemy. I chose to make him my friend. How difficult a decision was this for me? Not difficult at all.

Women in my age group who have risen to the top of their professions have one thing in common: We know how to play. We like men as people and are not cut to the quick by every occasional insensitive, sexist, stupid remark. We will never act in a way that is demeaning, but we will find meaningful ways to act. How ultimately foolish it would have been to attack a judge who himself felt attacked or disrespected. Instead, we both played and we both won.

Powerful women may be even a bit flirtatious with colleagues or adversaries, but never with judges, jurors, or clients. Never. We can afford to be feminine, but we cannot afford to be sexual. Years earlier, Judge Skinner had told me, "You can be thought of by every male juror as his mistress or his daughter. I suggest you choose the latter."

A friend of mine who practiced in Boston was possessed of a *Playboy* centerfold–type body and made a practice of dressing like a high-class call girl when she came to court. I talked to her until I was blue in the face about how neither judges nor her colleagues and adversaries nor juries were taking her seriously because of her dress code, but she chose to lead with her sexuality as opposed to her competence, and didn't want to hear about it from me. In the courthouse I had male friends and acquaintances who were respectful and protective of me as both a lawyer and a person. I thought my friend's style did severe damage to her career. If I had come to court in a slinky, low-cut dress showing a lot of leg, if instead of my chaste pirouette I had shaken my hips or performed a runway shimmy, that would have been entirely inappropriate. I remained well within the bounds of good taste. But if someone says "What a nice dress!" are you going to report him for sexual harassment? How preposterous!

Still, sensitivity persists. The Commonwealth of Massachusetts conducted a gender bias study in the courthouse, which put everyone on edge. The best response came from a court officer, who handed me a printed note: "You look very beautiful today. Please destroy this card." I laughed out loud.

When I was in the prosecutor's office in Middlesex, the criminal defense lawyers, prosecutors, and cops hung out at the Esquire, a Cambridge bar owned by a guy named Manny. Burgers, steak tips, chicken wings, and a lot of drinking. We worked long hours in total immersion and at the end of the day when everyone was tired, we went out to play. We had a life; we were public prosecutors. When we were on trial we worked all the time; when we weren't it was always, "Come on, let's go to Manny's."

I palled around with a group of four or five guys, including my officemate, Kieran Meagher. We were a tight bunch, "that group at the end of the hall," and if we weren't on trial on Friday afternoons we would get in our cars and go off the reservation for long lunches at the Hilltop Restaurant on Route 1 that served steaks and salads for about eight bucks. We found some little Italian restaurants in the North End and went for pizza at Regina. These guys were my friends, my brothers. They talked in front of me the way guys talk. War stories back and forth. If some woman walked by with big breasts, they didn't let the fact that I was a woman stand in the way of their verbal appreciation. As far as they were concerned, I was a guy. Chrissy McEvoy, Carol Ball, myself, and maybe a few women public defenders were the distaff contingent, but basically we were guys to these guys, and that was nice. I loved being with them, being one of them; I loved being part of their lives and feeling like I was a member of the trial bar. When I left Middlesex for Norfolk, the place was Rossi's in Dedham, but the scene was the same. It's a lawyer's ritual: work hard, play hard, drink hard.

In the summer of 1981, as I approached my fourth anniversary as a prosecutor, I went to my mentors, District Attorney Bill Delahunt and Attorney General Frank Bellotti, and said, "I think it's time for me to go." Conventional wisdom had it that, unless you were fashioning a career in public service, you were a prosecutor for four years and then moved on. Five years was too long; six or more and you couldn't make it in the "real world." I had learned to be a prosecutor, but my vision of myself had always been as a criminal defense attorney. I had developed my courtroom skills; now I wanted to use them for the defense. "I'm not quite sure exactly who I should go with," I said. "Do you have any ideas?"

Bellotti said, "You've had white-shoe law firms offer you jobs before and after your federal clerkship. I think you ought to write a business plan for them about starting a criminal trial division."

"That's never been done," I told him.

"Precisely."

We brainstormed the idea. What could I bring them?

Delahunt said, "You could service the clients' kids when they get arrested for drunk driving. You could service the clients in white-collar crime situations, which are occurring with increasing regularity. White-shoe firms don't know how to do criminal work; they have to send it out. Now they wouldn't. There's a large amount of business there.

"You could also give young associates significant opportunities by instituting a program to accept pro bono homicide cases." In fact, a classic question from the most highly sought-after young law school graduates in those days was "Do you do pro bono work?" Now a firm could answer in the affirmative. "This would be a strong incentive to attract the best new talent," Delahunt continued. "All those kids who want to be trial lawyers but in actuality will be writing interrogatories and complaints and never seeing a courtroom, they would be given unprecedented opportunities."

Bellotti also felt that in order to become a strong trial attorney I ought to learn good civil practice; I should know how to draft a complaint, an answer, and interrogatories; I ought to know how to take depositions. I had never done any of this as a prosecutor. At the same time I was leading a criminal trial division, the firm could bill me out and make money on my time on civil matters, and I could learn my civil craft.

I wrote the business plan and made phone calls and plumbed my contacts, and, after spending months interviewing with every litigator and department head in the firm, was offered a job at the Brahmin law firm Choate, Hall & Stewart.

I began in September 1981. One of the first phone calls I made was to Blair Perry at Hale & Dorr.

"Mr. Perry, it's Rikki Klieman."

"Oh, how are you!" He was full of good cheer.

"I assume you know that I've been working in Boston."

"Yes, I read about you all the time." My work as a prosecutor had made me something of a celebrity.

"Well, I just wanted to tell you I started a criminal trial division at Choate, Hall & Stewart, and I think it's going to be very successful."

Perry tried to drum up some business for his firm. He said, "You should have come and talked to us at Hale & Dorr!"

"Mr. Perry, you may recall that at one of my last moments at Hale & Dorr, you put your finger in my face, called me 'Missy,' and said I would never work in Boston again. I knew one day I would make you eat those words."

He just laughed. Then I laughed and said, "Okay, I forgive you. You forgive me?"

"Yes."

I ran into Blair Perry in the courthouse from time to time during the next few years and we always exchanged greetings. Ironically, Hale & Dorr and Perry later had a parting of the ways.

I learned how to take depositions by getting creamed during the first session I conducted on my own. The other side could see that I didn't know what I was doing, and they ran roughshod over me. I did not know how to control the proceedings. I had no idea how to stop the questioning from going places that were not in my client's best interest, and at the end of the day I knew I had not done a good service to the people who were paying me. I went straight to a partner and asked for transcripts of what he considered great depositions. I placed them next to my bed and used them to develop my craft. Quickly the trade secrets were revealed.

Depositions are all posturing. There is no judge in the room. A witness is brought in who may or may not be a party to the lawsuit, and the other side is permitted to ask him or her questions concerning anything that might possibly at some point be relevant to the case. You must probe deeply with follow-up questions. You must always be listening to the answers and pursue all unanticipated avenues of information. You don't ask your client anything—why add to the other side's information bank?

Even the physical layout of the room is significant. It became clear to me that taking a deposition was all theater. Staging, timing, and presence were key. The question I began to ask myself was, Where is the power? Onstage, I'd been taught to "find my light" in order to have all eyes upon me. In a courtroom the same rules applied. This was merely another stage. Sometimes an attorney wants all the attention; sometimes she wants others to forget she's there.

I developed a set of physical and mental requirements for a successful deposition. My client must be seated next to the court reporter so his words are understood clearly and there is no need for the reporter to interrupt his concentration with "What? What? Can you repeat that?" I must be seated next to my client so I can hit, kick, or nudge him when I need him to stop. At the same time I need to be sufficiently distanced from him so I can judge his state of mind, see if the questioning or the questioner is getting to him.

I want the questioner seated as far away as possible, not only on the other side of the table but, if I can arrange it, way down at the other end. Conversely, if I am questioning a witness I want to be right on top of him. Physical intimidation and intimacy are the two most effective means of extracting information from a person who does not want to give it to you. If I am being sweet, if I can establish a comfortable body language with a witness, I can come away with sizable amounts of the information I need. Some male lawyers pound their fists on the table during depositions, point fingers in the witness's face, and scream. They can be quite terrifying, and quite effective. I could never do that. I'm too small; it would be ridiculous. If I want to intimidate, I might slam a book closed or throw it down on the table in disgust. I might act as if I am reading something the witness once said, then close the pages, look at him, and ask, "Didn't you say . . . ?" He, of course, may believe I have his words right in front of me, even if I do not.

If my client is to be deposed I establish at the very beginning of the session that there will be a bathroom break every hour. The opposition invariably complains, usually along the lines of "You've got to be kidding." I tell them, "I need to use the bathroom once an hour." I don't need to use the bathroom once an hour; I need to go whack my client once an hour when he is doing something stupid.

A basic rule of depositions is that an attorney may object for the record, but her client must answer the question. A judge will decide later whether the information is admissible. If the questioning attorney is getting into an area that I truly believe is inappropriate, improper, irrelevant, embarrassing, or scandalous, I have no problem saying, "We're stopping. You're not going there. You are not going to get to ask these questions. They will never be permitted. You are just doing this to harass the witness." Obviously, one does not make these accusations frivolously. The other side—ninety-nine times out of one hundred in my Choate, Hall & Stewart days he was a man—will be irate and say, "I have a right to ask the question."

"No, you don't."

"Yes, I do." Now that's effective lawyering.

"Fine, let's go to the courthouse. Let's go to the judge." That often stops them; few lawyers really want to disrupt the flow of their deposition by getting up from the table and heading for court. They will trade individual questions to maintain their momentum. I am the guardian of my client; if I feel the other side is truly harassing him, I will say, "We're out of here. We're gone," pick up my stuff, and leave. The trick is to actually do it; the opposition has to know they can't call your bluff and win. The chances of my ever going to the judge are no more than two percent, but I am going to show that I will not be intimidated by some big, strong guy no matter how hard he argues or how loudly he shouts. I will persist.

I learned effective deposition techniques quickly. My tradecraft developed as each month passed.

One aspect of the corporate law firm I did not immediately understand was the concept of billable hours. Because I was my father's daughter, I could not understand the ethics involved in billing for more hours than there are in the day. Choate, Hall & Stewart, like most other law firms, broke the hour into minimum billing components. For instance, if the minimum component was a quarter hour, a lawyer could conceivably conduct five separate three-minute conversations in that time and bill the clients for a combined seventy-five minutes. I understood and accepted this; a minimum component was reasonable. But I saw lawyers billing for hours when they went to the bathroom, ate lunch at their desks, got some air, went to the bank. One associate said, "Well, you're doing some work for a bank, right?" "Yes." "Whenever you need extra hours for your billable day, just bill them to the bank."

"I can't do that."

"Everybody does that."

"That is unethical. That is astounding!"

He explained the concept: "You've got to bill the hours, right? And if you are working on a project, maybe you think about it on your way to work, you think about it in the shower. It is okay."

"No, it is not okay." Nevertheless, this is the way the system often works. White-shoe law firms pressure their associates, or partners for that matter, to bill an impossible amount of hours, resulting in their charging the living daylights out of their clients.

I made several good friends at Choate, Hall & Stewart. Don Farrell, a specialist in bankruptcy law, helped explain that field to me because I simply did not understand it. He and another lawyer, Richard Trembowicz, were my buddies. We worked impossible hours, arriving at the office every morning, six and a half days a week, at 7:30 and often leaving at 10:00 at night, then convened at a restaurant called Gallagher's and shared stories over a couple of drinks before heading home. Dewar's and water was my poison. Just a couple of drinks, or was it "just one more"?

My goal when I joined Choate, Hall & Stewart was eventually to make partner, to earn financial security as well as success. To that end, I was initially most interested in establishing my place in the firm's hierarchy by creating a criminal trial division. The partners had agreed to the concept and I pursued it. Among my first moves was to apply to the federal court to be placed on the federal appointed counsel list, from which lawyers were selected to defend indigent defendants when the public defender had a conflict. For instance, in a case involving multiple defendants, the public defender would be assigned one and the rest would be parceled out to lawyers from large firms or small firms experienced in criminal defense, who would take these cases at a minimal rate—thirty dollars per hour, clearly pro bono work. These lawyers were often former prosecutors with trial experience. Money was not the object; you actually worked at a deficit. These were exciting, complex trials before outstanding judges. The lawyers on the appointed list had to qualify and be approved. The prestige level was extremely high, and those who were accepted were considered masters of their craft.

In a parallel move, I applied to be placed on the murder list at the superior court. The standards for this list were just as stringent. One needed recommendations from adversaries and judges, from your boss, from your former boss. The application process was elaborate, but anyone who wanted to be a trial lawyer, particularly on the criminal side, wanted to be on both of these lists. I certainly did. I applied for both and was accepted, and shortly after I arrived at Choate, Hall & Stewart I got the call. I was asked to take an appointed case.

Excited is too meager a word to describe my feelings. This was federal court. This was where the great criminal defense lawyers practiced *real* law! *I was going to try a case in federal court!*

Joseph Salvatore DiCarlo, my defendant, was sitting in the holding cell and when he saw me he was not pleased.

"You're a real lawyer?" Sal, as he was known, was a "dees, dem, dose" conversationalist. He was a little guy, not much taller than I was, but very round. He looked like a stereotype of a member of the mob. He was being charged by the Organized Crime Strike Force with federal offenses, including conspiring in a truck-hijacking ring.

"I'm a real lawyer, Mr. DiCarlo."

"I don't want a broad to represent me."

I wasn't going to let a little thing like old-school intransigence get in the way of my first appointed case. "Mr. DiCarlo, let me tell you something." He looked at me directly. "You will be happier having me represent you than any other lawyer. Just trust me. We'll go down to the bail hearing and we'll see how you feel."

"What makes you think you're a good lawyer?" he grumbled.

"Because I am a woman and I've had to work twice as hard as any of these men." He didn't care. "I think that, in the course of this case, I'll work twice as hard as any other lawyer. I've tried a lot of cases, more than any of these men, whoever they're going to be. I've prosecuted murder cases. If I know how to prosecute cases from beginning to end, I know how to defend cases, too."

Sal was unconvinced. "You're too pretty to be a lawyer."

I told him, "I think that might work to your advantage."

The prosecutor, who I thought was a friend, sandbagged me at the bail hearing by simply doing his job. If I hadn't before, I now understood that this was very much for real. And I was surprised when I read the indictment and found that the case was to be tried before Judge Skinner. I told Sal I had been the judge's law clerk. "What does that mean?" he asked. I explained and said Judge Skinner had a great deal of respect for me. Sal grunted, "I'm liking you better already."

(Judge Skinner disclosed this relationship and made clear to all present that I would get no preferential treatment. Neither Sal nor the prosecutor objected.)

DiCarlo was charged along with four other defendants, and all the lawyers gathered together weekly to compare strategies. We were very collegial. After getting the hang of the case we agreed to hang together. The entire trial hinged on the words of one man, John Zucchari Jr., who had allegedly been involved in the purported hijacking and had decided to turn state's evidence. Our defense was that this man was lying. He had reason to lie: He was getting a deal from the government—he would get out of prison sooner, whatever the usual trade-off that cooperating witnesses come up with. Our job was to convince the jury that our clients were, in essence, being framed by this confessed felon in return for favorable treatment.

I called Joe Oteri with the news of my appointed case and he was excited for me. His partner Martin Weinberg, known as "the motion guy," was an ace with the paperwork and volunteered to help me. This was the precomputer era for criminal lawyers, and Marty and I spent hours riffling through his filing cabinets. He asked questions and then pulled on-point motions out of the drawers for me. Oteri, Weinberg, and Jimmy Lawson, their third partner, functioned as two brothers and a dad to get me ready for this case. These guys were real trial lawyers!

Criminal defense lawyers in Massachusetts in 1981 rarely gave opening statements. The reason was traditionally sound but ultimately flawed. In the old days, there was no such thing as reciprocal discovery. Although the defense would file motions to receive, and would obtain, discovery material from the government—witness statements, grand jury testimony, police or agency reports, expert opinions, and "Brady material," which is exculpatory evidence—with certain exceptions such as an assertion of an alibi or an insanity defense, the government could not extract such information from the defense.

But by 1981 the rules had long since changed, and there was more opportunity for the government to probe the defense case prior to trial. Still, traditional defense attorneys in Massachusetts were reluctant to let the government know the thrust of their defense. Or, they would say, their defense might change depending on how the prosecution's case went. I thought such a position was absurd. Over time I came to believe that for a defense attorney not to open directly after the prosecutor might even approach malpractice.

I had read about the Kalven and Zeisel study of Chicago juries, which found that 80 percent of jurors have made up their minds as to the guilt or lack of guilt of a defendant at the end of the opening statements. It did not seem to be good strategy to allow the prosecution's assertions to go unchallenged at a time when they were having the greatest effect. On the eve of the trial, I brought this concept to the group of defense lawyers, who all had far more experience than I did, and told them I would like to make an opening statement.

"What?!"

The general consensus was that I was being ridiculous, that no one ever did this. We discussed the concept quite heatedly, and finally I'd had enough. "If you guys aren't going to open," I told them, "I am. You can just sit there and listen, that'll be fine, but I have an obligation to my client to make this opening."

This made the fellows extremely nervous. Finally I said, "How about this: We all have the same defense; we all feel the same way. Why don't I open for all of us? I'm the only female; it's kind of logical that you'd choose me to open."

(To which Joe Oteri said, when I told him, "Yes, conclusively proving the conspiracy!")

They agreed, in part because I suspect not one of them had ever actually delivered an opening.

I opened. Oteri and Marty Weinberg came to watch me. I was spirited in my defense.

Five citizens are accused of a crime based on the word of a proven liar, I told the jury, a man who would buy his freedom from the government simply by placing the blame on others. If he gave one story, someone might think it was true. But here you will hear some five different versions of his own imagination. He provides versions one and two to the FBI; he provides versions three and four to the grand jury; and he will provide a fifth version to you, ladies and gentlemen . . . just watch. He sat at his own three-week trial and got little bits and pieces of information from which to concoct a story to get him out of a federal prison. He contacted the FBI—he wanted to show he had something to sell. He wanted his "Get Out of Jail Free" card. He used suspicion and turned it into accusation. Don't you turn suspicion into conviction.

When I finished, I could see Judge Skinner smiling despite himself. I felt like a daughter performing at her first dance recital in front of her father.

My first criminal defense case began. I had charts; I had diagrams; I had documentation for every inconsistent statement the informant had made. Massive charts: He said this on this date; he contradicted himself on that date. I was in the zone. I didn't care if I slept or ate. Time flew by and all I cared about was my case.

Sal, it was clear to me, was one of the most guilty-looking men you could find at a defense table. Call it profiling, call it ethnic prejudice, call it what you will, but if all the jury did was look at him, they were sure to convict. I had no intention of putting him on the witness stand, so his voice and speech patterns weren't a problem, but he carried himself like a thug, which was lethal. Sal needed to look like a gentleman. He wasn't going to lose the weight; he wasn't going to lose the look. How could we change his image in the mind of the jury?

The jurors, defendants, and lawyers traveled inside the courthouse in one another's orbits. We walked the same corridors; we shared the same elevators; we ate in the same cafeteria. The jurors saw me. They saw Sal. It occurred to me that I had a wonderful opportunity to stage a play in which Sal DiCarlo was a likable character.

I met with him in my office and said, "Sal, don't ask me the reasons for this, beyond the fact that I'm going to tell you that the jurors see everything you do. You don't need any other explanation. This is what I want you to do." Sal didn't flinch. "Every day that we go to trial, you meet me at my office first. We walk to the courthouse together."

"Okay."

"When you meet me, you take my briefcase, especially if it's a big briefcase. I want you to take the briefcase," I repeated. "When we get to the courthouse you open the door for me."

"You don't have to tell me to open the door for a lady. I know when to open a door." Sal the soldier was a gentleman.

"You carry the briefcase through the halls and we go upstairs to the cafeteria. Then you put down the briefcase. I want you to help me off with my coat, put it on a chair. I want us to walk through the line together talking about the weather or anything else."

"Like what?"

"The Red Sox are fine, but nothing about the case."

"Right."

"When we get to the end of the line I want you to pay for my breakfast. If you don't have the money"—he was an indigent defendant— "I'll give you the money. But it looks like you pay for breakfast."

"Okay. Whatever you say. But I don't want you giving me money. I'm not taking money from a broad. A lady, I mean."

"I understand," I said. "Now, when you're in the back of the elevator, you make sure that the ladies get out first."

Sal was insulted. "I know how to treat a woman," he told me. "I *know* how to treat a woman."

"In the courtroom, Sal, I want you to pull out my chair for me. And when you sit next to me, we talk. I want you to treat me like you would treat your mother, your daughter, your sister. Do you understand that?"

"I understand."

The trial lasted seven days. We walked to the courthouse together every morning and Sal performed brilliantly. Absent any other means, I needed him to transcend his physical appearance by virtue of how he treated me. The fact that he did know how to treat a lady, and that I responded to him appropriately, worked wonders. I knew we were being observed and I felt we were being well received.

I was anxious before I delivered my closing. This was the first time I had ever made a closing argument for a defendant, let alone a summation in a federal court. Joe Oteri and Marty Weinberg were both in the gallery, silently cheering me on. I wrote much of my presentation from material I found in their files. I had taken notes on what was called the Edward Bennett Williams closing, particularly concerning the presumption of innocence, and I was quite impassioned when I spoke it in court.

"[T]oday, Joseph Salvatore DiCarlo is a fortunate man . . . because [he] has been on trial in an American court. In an American court, he does have his presumption of innocence that you have heard so much about today. It's not a slogan, nothing you print on the wall and forget about it. It's the essence of our system. Because he has the ability to be in this court and let the government say all. He has the ability to stand there and say, 'Accuse me, government, and I will stand proud, and I do not have to answer you' because, I say to you, members of the jury, that the testimony against Joseph Salvatore DiCarlo, which rests primarily on that of John Zucchari Jr., is not worthy of belief, but it should not even be dignified with a response."

I moved to another position before the jury and could feel their eyes on me. I stopped, turned, and addressed them again. "I can only leave you with a couple of last thoughts. There are two cornerstones to our criminal justice system. Again, these aren't idle words. One is 'proof beyond a reasonable doubt,' and that means that each and every one of you has to have an abiding conviction of Mr. DiCarlo's guilt, and you can't, I suggest to you, you *cannot*, on the quality of this evidence, have an abiding conviction of his guilt because you must pause or hesitate when you consider Mr. Zucchari's testimony." Having been in his courtroom for a year, I knew Judge Skinner would use the phrase "pause or hesitate" in his instructions to the jury and I made certain to include it when I crafted my argument.

"And I say to you, please, I urge you, when you go in there, don't compromise. If you have a reasonable doubt, hold onto that doubt. Don't trade a defendant for a defendant. Don't trade a count for a count. If you have that doubt, hold onto it and listen and talk with your fellow jurors. Because this man and these other men, this man's liberty here is at stake. Liberty is too indivisible and too precious to be bargained away in a jury room.

"[T]here are lawyers who are far older and better than I, and for those of you who have heard these words before, please forgive me. I

will say it again, because in this case it's really true. They tell you you
can't buy justice because it isn't justice, and they tell you you can't
buy love because it isn't love you get. And they tell you you can't buy
truth because then what you wind up with is truth with a cloud over
it. But you can buy testimony. And that's what the government did in
this case."

The jury retired to deliberate. The defendants remained at the
courthouse. Assuming the panel would be out a long while, perhaps
days, we defense attorneys repaired to the Le Meridien Hotel bar to
wait for the verdict. Oteri and Weinberg joined us. We didn't know
what to expect. The case had been stacked against us from the beginning, with a turncoat witness and elaborate government conspiracy
theories that wove the five defendants into a seamless tapestry of
organized crime. The guys were congratulating me on my closing
argument; I was congratulating them on theirs. We were congratulating each other as we ordered up one round after another.

We had been bellying up to the bar for no more than a couple of
hours when a call came. The jury was coming back; they had a verdict. That was quick. What did it mean?

"Oh, my God, I have liquor on my breath!" I dove into my purse
for the toothbrush I always carry, then ran to the bathroom and
brushed my teeth frantically. I chewed gum with a vengeance as I
threw on my coat and ran across Congress Street in my high heels to
the courthouse.

The jury came back "not guilty." For everybody, across the board.
Not one of the defendants was convicted of even the slightest crime.
Oteri said, "Tell the court reporter you want a bound copy of your
closing argument, because you may never see another acquittal in
federal court in your lifetime. Get it now." I did, and it served as a
wonderful memento of the moment I made the transition from prosecutor to defense attorney.

eight THEATER OF THE COURTROOM . . . FOR THE DEFENSE

SPENT MUCH OF MY TIME AT CHOATE, HALL & STEWART WORKING ON CIVIL CASES. I didn't understand bankruptcy law but I was doing that, too. I wrote memos and briefs; drafted motions, complaints, and interrogatories; attended depositions and motion hearings. I met with clients, worked with clients, slaved for clients. The clichés about law firm associates working like Bob Cratchit are true. I worked fifteen-hour days six and a half days a week because there were only so many billable hours and we had to bill them all. I lost sight of my goal of becoming a respected trial lawyer. When I was an assistant district attorney, I knew I wanted to learn tradecraft and become a famous criminal defense lawyer. But at Choate, Hall & Stewart I didn't know what I was after. In concept I wanted to be a partner, make a lot of money, and run a criminal trial division, but in practice I was being ground to dust under the crushing paperwork.

I really wasn't happy unless I was trying a case, so my heartbeat fluttered when a clerk of the Suffolk Superior Court called to tell me I was being appointed to represent a man who was accused of murder.

There is nothing sexier than trying murder cases. What is the worst possible crime? Murder. What is the crime most central to the mainstream culture of television, books, movies? Murder. What crime is irreversible, irrevocable, irresistible? Murder. There is a killer fascination for homicide.

If you are a real trial lawyer, you want to try the biggest cases; you want to wrap yourself in the fabric of a difficult character; you want the klieg lights of publicity. You want a murder case. And because most criminal defendants accused of murder are poor, the most effective means of handling a murder case is to get on the murder list. Massachusetts was not a death penalty state, so a person's life was not literally in your hands, but the fact that you were responsible for a defendant's liberty for the rest of his or her life did hold the same drama. I had been appointed and anointed.

I rose and paced, as I do when I am excited, and informed the clerk that I would be honored to accept. The defendant's name was Michael Chandler, I was told, and he had been a fugitive but was now in custody. "So I guess bail is out of the question?"

When I called to ask for information before I met my client, the ADA prosecuting the case, Paul Connolly, said, "Your guy plunked a bullet into this kid and killed him. He got out on bail and then ran away. They captured him in New Hampshire with all kinds of guns. It's not an easy case."

The Charles Street Jail, which I had visited when I was working for Joe Balliro, had not gotten any friendlier. If you were stupid enough to wear jewelry when you visited, you hid it in your purse and secreted it with your coat in the scarred brown lockers that clanged against one wall. I filled out the visitor's form, then walked through the metal detector, past a glass door that opened after you stood motionless before it and thudded closed behind. The floors had a smell of sweat and fear that the thick bleach swabbed on by inmates only made more funky. The closed room where lawyers met with their clients housed a wooden table and a couple of chrome-legged chairs with torn Naugahyde seat covers.

Michael Chandler was very polite. In his arrest photo he looked extremely menacing, unkempt, with a wild beard, biker hair, and a motorcycle jacket. In person he stood about six feet tall and his hair was now short and thoroughly dark — a solidly built white guy.

He asked about my experience. I walked him through my résumé. I asked him about himself and his family. I did not ask him what happened.

I don't ever want to be put in a position in which I cannot put a defendant on the stand if I choose to do so, and I cannot put a defendant on the stand if I have any thought that he is perjuring himself. If he tells me a story on day one, and when I receive and show him all the discovery materials he comes up with a new story on day twelve, I won't put him on. There may be lawyers who will. I won't. So I didn't want to hear it from him on the first day.

Chandler was compliant, but firm about his innocence. What he said from day one through his testimony at trial was "I never meant to kill this guy. This really was self-defense."

When I reviewed the discovery material I agreed.

In most cases a defense attorney does not have a defendant who is going to take the stand. When a defendant testifies in a criminal case, the burden of proof psychologically shifts from the government to the defendant. It shouldn't, but it does. The only thing those jurors are interested in from that point forward is, Do I believe the defendant? They lose track of the concept of reasonable doubt, which is the government's actual burden of proof. If they don't believe the defendant, they do not even think about reasonable doubt; they convict.

The only case in which a defendant must always testify is self-defense. The only person who can tell you the fear that was going through his mind at the time of the killing is the defendant. So my rule is, you "never" put a defendant on, except when it is necessary, which is in a self-defense case or some other extraordinary circumstance when the particular facts call out to mandate it.

Are there times when clients will shade the truth? I believe perhaps they sometimes tell me what I need to know and withhold what I don't, and that is just fine with me, unless it backfires. For instance, when facing a sexual assault allegation, a client may "forget" to tell me about those other women who are waiting in the wings, who then tell the jury about other times, other places, other forcible encounters. That is a loud backfire.

It is not necessary to put on a defense. A defense attorney tries the government's case, putting the prosecution's proof to the test. If I can bring the jury to understand that the government does not have the quality of evidence to convict my client beyond a reasonable doubt, the government loses. When the defense puts on a case, the jury starts balancing stories and forgets about the burden of proof and the presumption of innocence.

I read the discovery material, shared it with Chandler, and only then asked him to write out a statement of what he said happened.

Michael Chandler, it turns out, does not know how to tell a lie. It became clear to me what happened on the day of the killing.

Chandler, twenty-six, lived with his wife Linda and their son Michael Jr. in Dorchester. On March 14, 1982, along with several friends and relatives, Linda took Michael Jr. to the St. Patrick's Day parade in South Boston. Later, Michael and Linda met up at a dinner their families held traditionally. Around 8:00 they decided to go home. It was a lovely night so they decided to walk.

As they were strolling on a South Boston street they met up with a group of South Boston boys, Southies, who had just come pouring out of a bar. With his beard, long hair, and motorcycle jacket, Chandler looked different—he was not one of them. One of the guys bumped into Linda, who was tiny, and started swearing. Chandler told him to take it easy and keep on going. The next thing he knew someone had thrown a bottle at him. Then another. Then a steel milk crate. The crowd around him grew increasingly menacing, the noise deafening in the developing frenzy, and legitimately scared for her safety, Chandler told his wife to run. He saw someone, broken bottle in hand, charging at him. He told the guy to drop it, but the kid kept on coming, swearing, not caring.

Chandler had a license to carry a gun, and he was carrying one, a .357 Magnum. He pulled it out of his holster, shouted, "Don't come any closer!" and fired a warning shot in the air. Another bottle flew toward him. The kid with the bottle did not stop; he lunged forward. Chandler, a marksman, tried to shoot him in the shoulder, but the bullet went scrambling around in the boy's body and hit the heart. Chandler ran. The kid died.

Chandler and his wife kept running, hearing bottles crashing behind them and people yelling. They got to a vacant lot and heard, "Halt! Police!" Relieved, still alive, Michael crouched over Linda to protect her. They put their hands in the air.

When the police picked him up, Chandler did not know the boy was dead. He was belligerent. Why should he be arrested, he shouted from the paddy wagon, they're the ones who should be arrested! At the police station Chandler consented to and gave an audiotaped confession, still pissed off, still not knowing the kid had died. He sounded like a thug. "A .357 Magnum is the third most powerful handgun in the world!" he bragged.

The following morning Chandler was taken to the South Boston District Court and was finally told that the boy he had shot was dead. He couldn't believe it. His entire confession had been given without any knowledge that he had killed someone.

What I had here, it seemed to me, was the purest of manslaughter cases. He had killed a person using excessive force when he felt that his life and the life of his wife were in danger. It could not be clearer.

But there were problems. Why was he carrying a gun? One of his jobs, it turned out, was distributing "adult" magazines, and sometimes he had to go pick up the money. Oh, great. Character references? He was a member of a motorcycle "gang," or "club," depending on the spin. Oh good, really good. After his arrest he had escaped and was recaptured in New Hampshire. Yikes!

I knew that on St. Patrick's Day in South Boston Chandler

thought he himself was going to die; he thought his wife was going to die. He had fired a warning shot. He didn't think the kid would keep coming at him. There were more of them than there was of him.

In my opinion, Chandler would not be acquitted, even though his was a pure case of self-defense and defense of his wife. But a broken bottle versus a .357 Magnum? To a jury it would look like excessive force. I asked whether, if I could work out a plea to manslaughter, he would take it. He had me explain it to him.

I did not think a Boston jury would walk him out, and while I firmly believed that the logical verdict was manslaughter, there was the possibility that he could be convicted of murder, for which he would have to do life in prison without possibility of parole. After much agonizing—he had been walking down the street with his wife one minute, a gang of punks had attacked him the next, and now he could be going to prison for twenty years—he told me to see what I could do.

Connolly said, "No. Did you ever see a picture of him when he was arrested? The guy is a thug."

"What did that have to do with his walking with his wife in South Boston?"

"I am not going to give you a manslaughter plea, at least not with the kind of time you want. Forget it."

"All right then," I told him. "We are going to try this case and I am going to win. This is a manslaughter case, period. We can put it to rest right now."

"No way."

The case was assigned to a judge who was new to the criminal court and did not live in the city of Boston. That didn't mean much to me except that he might not be sufficiently familiar with the Boston culture to grasp what it meant to be someone who looked like Michael Chandler on the provincial streets of South Boston on St. Patrick's Day 1982. It could be tough over there. *I* wouldn't have gone to South Boston late in the afternoon on that St. Patrick's Day. Too many drunks, too little tolerance; you've got to be nuts. To add a wrinkle, the judge had been a civil trial lawyer, then a civil court judge. He had never before sat on a criminal case. I was very concerned that he was not going to get it.

"Before we pick a jury," I said in court, "I want to put something on the record." The judge agreed. "I want to put on the record the fact that I have tried to work out a manslaughter plea in this case. I am telling you, Your Honor, that the result in this case is going to be a manslaughter verdict. We could stop wasting everyone's time right now. It's a clear case of excessive-force self-defense. My client is willing to plead to manslaughter and we really should plead this case."

The judge turned to the prosecution. "Mr. Connolly?"

"It is a murder case."

"Fine. Let's get the jury."

They charged Michael Chandler with murder one—premeditated. The lesser included offenses that the jury would consider were murder two (intentional but without premeditation) and manslaughter (excessive force used in self-defense). The penalty for murder one was life in prison without the possibility of parole; for murder two, life with the possibility of parole after fifteen years; for manslaughter, zero to twenty years. In Massachusetts, a nonlife sentence has a maximum and a minimum, with eligibility for parole beginning at two-thirds of the minimum sentence. If the facts warranted, the jury would have the choice to deliver one of four verdicts: guilty of any count or not guilty.

Having been a prosecutor, I thought Connolly was not only wasting his time and mine but needlessly causing pain to the family of the victim. Why put them through the anguish of a trial if the result was clear? I understood that prosecutors are sometimes under pressure from victims' families, who feel their loved one was murdered and must be avenged. But when I was a prosecutor I did not feel the need to bow to that pressure if it was inappropriate. Rather than simply get a conviction or exact revenge, a prosecutor is supposed to do justice. The district attorneys for whom I had worked, John Kerry and Bill Delahunt, believed that explicitly. We thought we were doing justice. How naive of me. In other counties, in other states, justice seemed quite irrelevant; winning was paramount. That is why so many prosecutors' offices overcharged crimes, hoping for a conviction. I was not schooled that way, and I was and continue to be appalled when it happens.

Despite the fact that the logical verdict in this case was guilty of manslaughter, I still felt I had a chance for a not-guilty verdict. If the jury believed Chandler when he said, "I did it to protect my wife. I did it to protect myself," they could conceivably acquit him.

Chandler had to testify. The jury needed to get a visceral sense of the danger he felt in Southie that night. I knew, however, that he was an explosive guy. His audiotaped confession demonstrated his temper; when challenged, Chandler was the type of man who would yell back. He was tough, hard, belligerent—not a particularly appealing witness on his own behalf. There was no doubt in my mind that in Connolly's cross-examination the prosecutor would do everything in his power to push my defendant over the edge. If Chandler went ballistic on the witness stand, our defense would be shot to pieces.

And yet he was very polite with me. I needed to get him on the witness stand, have him tell his story, and prevent him from exploding. We needed to work.

I told the guard at the Charles Street Jail that I wanted to play "flinch" with Chandler.

"You want to play what with who?"

"You remember that game when you were a kid, where you put your hands out, palms up, and someone put their hands on top of yours, and the object was for the person with his palms up to lift a hand and move as if to slap the other guy and see if he flinched? You remember that game?"

"Yeah."

"I want to play the flinch game with Michael Chandler."

"Lady, are you out of your mind?"

"Trust me."

"He is four times your size. You're going to slap him in the face? He is going to knock you out, and I am not going to be responsible."

"This is important for me to do."

He hitched his pants. "You want me to watch?"

"If you feel better watching."

"Frankly," he said, "I'd rather not. I'd really rather not even know you told me this."

I walked into the client room. Soon they brought in Chandler. He was not happy in prison, but he was surviving.

"Michael, you remember the flinch game?" I explained the rules.

"I want to play it with you," I said. The guard had stepped away from the door. "I'm going to be the person who goes first. Sometimes I might even slap you. I want to see that I can do that and you're not going to react."

"Okay." He didn't seem like he wanted to deck me.

"Now, I have to make sure that if I slap you, you're not going to say I assaulted you."

He shook his head. "I don't know why we're doing this, but okay."

"Just to protect myself"—he looked up as I spoke—"would you sign something for me?" He put his signature on a release form without question.

I played the flinch game with Michael Chandler several times a week for three weeks. Sometimes I would move my hand toward him as if to slap him but would not make contact. Other times, I smacked him. Not often, but more than a few times. We would play it for a few minutes and then I would put him through a mock cross-examination as if I were the prosecutor. I was not trying to be subtle.

"I need you never to flinch . . . and never to hit me back. Whatever the prosecutor throws at you, the worse it gets, the calmer you get. We are playing for your life." I would move as if to smack him again, then get in his face with my cross. I had been a prosecutor; I knew how to rile a witness. I didn't hold back. He did. As hard as I hit him, with both my hand and my words, he never struck back.

In my opening statement to the jury I again emphasized the presumption of innocence. "He, Chandler, comes before you and says the government must prove him guilty. He need not offer one shred of evidence in his own defense, but he will. He is here to tell you what really happened on that tragic evening, an evening he will never forget as long as he lives. A senseless death occurred, and Michael Chandler too mourns that death and must live with it every day of his life. But if the incident happened as simply as the Commonwealth tells the tale, we need not be here today."

The prosecution mounted its case. Chandler's angry confession, played in court, sounded remorseless. But he clearly stated that he shot his attacker in the shoulder to stop him. I showed that Chandler did not know he had killed the young man until the next day, and that he then reacted with remorse, which took away the taint of the frightening audiotape. It no longer showed a cold killer; it was a record of an irate man who had just been set upon by a pack of drunken guys.

Connolly was very good with his evidence. The .357 Magnum is a cold- and dangerous-looking weapon. Chandler himself had called it the third most powerful handgun in the world. It looked big, and was made even more threatening because Connolly wouldn't go near it. He never touched the firearm; with a long, thin, telescoping silver pointer he indicated the trigger, the barrel, and the stock from a distance, implicitly saying, "This is a killing machine. This is *Michael Chandler's* killing machine."

A defense attorney must defuse the worst piece of evidence against her. How could I undermine this imagery?

I held the gun with both hands and put it to my breast. I cradled it, toyed with it, walked around the courtroom with it, casually handled this .357 as if it were a Dale Evans/Roy Rogers cap pistol. The old saw is "Physical evidence doesn't lie, only people do." But in reality, a good lawyer can change the effect of a piece of physical evidence by putting it into a new physical context and using it to her own advantage. If a lawyer is conscious of the theater in the courtroom, she can take the worst evidence against her, turn it into a prop, and make it appear vastly different in the jury's eyes than it did only a few minutes earlier.

I cleaned Chandler up for the trial, and when he took the witness stand—clean-shaven, hair short and trim, wearing a suit that fit and seeming as if he had worn one before—he looked like a choirboy. We had prepared for the fact that Connolly was going to make some comment about his appearance; Chandler was simply going to acknowledge that it had changed—not fudge the answer, not tell the court that his lawyer had suggested the alteration, simply state, "I changed my appearance." Sure enough, Connolly attacked on the point.

Putting his mug shot in front of him, Connolly said with some heat, "This is what you looked like, Mr. Chandler. This is what you looked like!" To the Boston jury hearing the case and looking at the picture, the message could not have been more clear: This is a dangerous man; this man is not like us.

"Yes," Chandler agreed.

"And now you have changed your appearance!"

"Of course I have changed my appearance. I felt I should look as presentable as possible." The simple answer was "Yes." Why had he strayed from our script? Was he going to break now? Had his composure been shattered? He turned and looked at the jury, then said to the prosecutor, "They are making a decision with my life."

He had gotten it. Everything we had done, all our talk, all our preparation had been absorbed. I hadn't suggested that he turn to the jury, he had done that on his own. The moment was riveting. I watched the jury look at him with fresh eyes.

They came back with manslaughter. As they should have.

At the sentencing hearing the judge was angry. I was on record as saying that manslaughter was the proper verdict, and my client was on record as being willing to accept his responsibility in the matter; only the prosecution's overreaching had prevented us from saving the court, the state, the lawyers, and the families of both men several weeks of trial and tribulation. In an act of considerable outrage, not to mention courage, the judge sentenced Chandler to less than we had asked for in our plea negotiation.

I didn't hear from Chandler once he went to prison, nor again years later when he got out. I don't expect to. Criminal defendants do not like dealing with their lawyers after their trials, even the ones you walk out of the courthouse. It was a bad time in their lives; they do their time and don't look back. I hope he and his wife are well and prospering. I came to care for them a great deal; they were part of my life. At that time they were my whole life.

The courthouse was like a small town, and word was getting around. The mantra: Anything less than the crime charged in the indictment is a victory for the defense. I had used a series of unusual tactics and

I had won again. One of the happy results was that I began to try more cases. I received another murder assignment, and I started to be approached by organized crime clients and others accused of smuggling major amounts of marijuana. Big smuggling cases. Boat-loads of marijuana.

I loved my marijuana-smuggling clients. They were just like me and my friends. They were middle-class kids; some went to college, some didn't. But instead of becoming lawyers or writers or CPAs, they went into marijuana smuggling. It was a business. They were not violent; they did not carry weapons. They were nice guys who had simply chosen a different line of business than most Americans. And they had a great spirit about them. They were charming; they were intelligent; they were fun! The marijuana business, from the sixties through the seventies and into the eighties, was filled with kids who looked like your stockbroker. They were good clients; they arrived because my reputation preceded me, they were obedient, they listened to me, they respected me.

And I could win with them. That was very enticing. At the time there was still a functioning Fourth Amendment protecting citizens from unreasonable searches and seizures, and because law enforce-ment was often slipshod or arrogant, a good lawyer could actually file a motion to suppress evidence—a statement, a confession, or the drugs themselves—and have it accepted and the case thrown out. Today, the case law has become far more narrow, and these motions are rarely granted, but in the eighties the marijuana trade was not only big business, it was big business for lawyers up and down the eastern seaboard.

The cocaine trade was entirely different. In the 1980s the cocaine business was booming, and while there was significant money to be made, it was very clear to me that a lawyer dealing with clients accused of cocaine smuggling was forced to handle cases the way those people wanted or not at all. Rather than listen to their lawyers, the clients dictated how they wanted the case tried; they said who was going to plead guilty and who wasn't. They ran the case and they made me very uncomfortable. This is, of course, a vast generalization, but some of those people truly scared me. There was a Colombian codefendant in one of my cases who I thought would slice my throat as easily as talk to me. I was not ready to go over that edge and I did not want to become involved. Keeping one's distance was no easy task, particularly for a woman.

As he had asked, I did call Albert Krieger when I became a criminal defense attorney. He was as good as his word, which did not surprise me, and wrote a letter recommending me and Howard Weitzman for positions on the faculty of the National College for Criminal Defense (NCCD), which would be holding a weeklong summer session in July 1982. (Weitzman became famous for his magnificent and successful defense of John DeLorean. He was O.J. Simpson's first lawyer, who withdrew when his client decided to talk to the police. He later became executive vice president of Universal Studios. We are friends to this day.)

The NCCD had a superb reputation as an institution that truly created trial lawyers. Its faculty was an array of the most successful and influential people in American criminal law, including Bobby Lee Cook, "Racehorse" Haynes, James Montgomery, Eugene Pincham, Judge Robert Rose (now deceased), Michael Pancer, Dale Cobb, Terry MacCarthy, Larry Pozner, and Roger Dodd. As a direct result of Krieger's introduction I was invited to teach, and I was honored and thrilled to participate.

In May of that year I had met the legendary Bobby Lee Cook at what was billed as the Superstar Seminar in Atlanta. Joe Oteri introduced us over cocktails. Bobby Lee was the lawyer upon whom the television character Matlock was based. A smart, sharp, transcendently canny attorney in his mid-fifties with a white goatee, he looked like a cross between Uncle Sam and Abe Lincoln. Long and lanky, he stood maybe six foot two, maybe taller. He made a habit, I don't know why, of wearing extremely expensive seersucker suits that were just a little too short in the leg—high-water pants—as if the tide would be rising any minute and he didn't want to get his trousers wet. Floods. He smoked a pipe constantly, and the front of his jacket was a cotton field of ashes. He was beyond fabulous.

Bobby Lee was a southern gentleman. "My dear," he drawled

when we were introduced, "I am so charmed to meet you." Likewise, I'm sure. Bobby Lee just charmed me to pieces. As he and I and a tableful of lawyers were having dinner, dozens of people gathered to sit at his knee and hear him spin stories of his legal conquests. I found he was also scheduled to teach at the NCCD. "Won't that be nice," he said sweetly. "We can teach together."

The National College for Criminal Defense was convened in Houston that summer. In addition to teaching trial techniques each day, I was to conduct a demonstration in the art of delivering a closing argument, and because one's physical appearance in the courtroom can contribute just as much to attaining a goal as one's legal reasoning, I planned to dress for the occasion. I would not enter a court, nor would I lead a class, wearing blue jeans. I packed carefully for my week as a faculty member. In fact, I packed two bags, one containing my best courtroom clothes, the other my sweatpants, sneakers, and workout togs.

Neither was coming down the airport carousel. I was standing in the Houston baggage claim area waiting and waiting and my luggage was simply not there. All the other passengers on my flight had collected their bags and gone on their way, and I was standing alone, getting more anxious by the moment. Who strolled in but Bobby Lee Cook.

"Ms. Klieman, how are you, my dear?"

"I'm just fine, Mr. Cook," I lied. "How are you?"

"Please," he said. "Bobby Lee." He surveyed the circling conveyor belt. "What are you waiting for?"

"My luggage hasn't come out." The waiting area, once crawling with travelers anxious to grab their belongings and get out of there, was still. You could hear the hum of the carousel as it made its empty circuit. I thought I would start to cry.

"What am I going to do? I have no clothes. Our classes start tomorrow. How am I going to teach?"

The baggage chute rumbled. One of my bags tumbled down. My gym clothes. That was it.

Bobby Lee was unperturbed. "First," he said, "let's just go in and file the little claim." He took my arm and walked me into the airline office, where I filled out the lost-baggage forms. I was very upset. I could not afford to lose my entire work wardrobe, and I certainly could not afford to lose this opportunity to participate in the life of the legal community.

"Look, darling," Bobby Lee said with great warmth, "I'll take you over to Neiman Marcus and I'll go buy something for you to wear tomorrow . . . and the next day. And by then, maybe your luggage will have arrived."

"No, no, no." I hardly knew this man. "I can't have you do that. I can buy my own clothes."

He waved his hand. My objections were summarily overruled. "I know what little you are going to buy. I'm taking you shopping."

I had no choice in the matter. At least not according to Bobby Lee.

I didn't shop at Neiman Marcus. I had spent four years earning a civil servant's salary at the district attorney's office, and I had school loans still to pay. I had only worked at Choate, Hall & Stewart for less than a year, and while I was now making decent money I was still looking at price tags, and the price tags I was looking at weren't on Neiman Marcus clothing. Not even close.

Bobby Lee walked me to the women's wear floor and stopped before a mannequin draped in a Diane Freis dress. He said, "This would look just fine on you." It was an elegant, silky dress, beige and white, with a ruffle at the bottom and puffy, three-quarter sleeves. It had two big pockets, and I liked pockets. He told the saleswoman, "I want this dress in her size." I stopped him.

"I can't really afford a dress like this." In those days a Diane Freis dress cost seven hundred dollars. I was buying dresses for fifty bucks at best, if I wasn't with my mother in the bargain basement. This was way out of my league.

"I can," he said.

I told him, "I'm going to pay you back."

"Yes, you are. You're going to be a fine lawyer. You're going to have plenty of money. You've got that white-shoe, silk-stocking Boston law firm for now; eventually you'll have plenty of money."

I tried on the dress. It fit beautifully.

Bobby Lee was a clotheshorse. He shopped the store looking at the patterns, feeling the material. He bought me a suit, then said, "Well, we've got to get you some shoes."

In the shoe department he headed straight for the Ferragamos. "These are the shoes to go with that dress."

"Mr. Cook, I can't."

"Bobby Lee. Just call me Bobby Lee. No 'Mr. Cook.'"

"All right, Bobby Lee. But how am I going to pay you back?"

"You'll pay me back." He bought the Ferragamos. "I guess you've got to go get yourself some stockings and some underwear. I'll let you pick that out yourself."

When I had made my selections he gathered the purchases and paid the bill. Then he took me to a drugstore. Talk about a man who understands women! "You need those toiletries, you know. You need a hair dryer; you need a hairbrush; you need makeup. You just take this little basket and you get everything you need." I stepped toward the aisle. "Don't you skimp on anything!"

I walked into the hotel laden with Neiman Marcus bags. I felt like Cinderella in a fairyland.

The week at the National College for Criminal Defense was among the best of my life. I was thrilled to be among these legends, and I concentrated extremely hard to impress them. I worked on the closing argument of my mock trial, *Bosveld*, as if it were the most important trial of my career. It had been used in previous years, so I reviewed audiotapes of the lawyers' closings and then wrote, rewrote, and rewrote my argument again. I taught every day from 8:30 in the morning until around 6:00 in the evening and then went and drank with my colleagues and soaked up their stories and their collegiality.

I learned an excellent cross-examination technique from Eugene Pincham, a lawyer and judge out of Chicago. His voice was an instrument. "The car was red, wasn't it?" he intoned at his witness. The person on the stand, not wanting to provide any assistance to the defending attorney, said, "Well, when I was walking to the grocery store I saw a car."

"The car was red, wasn't it?"

"Well, I'm walking to the grocery store and . . ." He didn't answer the question. He didn't want to.

Gene Pincham looked over his half-glasses at the witness. "Do you have trouble with your hearing?" The witness either remained silent or said no. "This is a simple question," Pincham said, maintaining eye contact. "Repeat after me: 'The car was red, wasn't it?'" No witness could evade that cross-examination. Gene Pincham and so many of the NCCD faculty were masters of their craft.

Every night the student lawyers would prepare their performances of each assignment. The following morning they would hear a lecture on a topic—opening statements, direct examination, cross-examination, examination of an expert, closing arguments—and then break into smaller groups of approximately ten to do exercises and have their work critiqued by faculty advisers. Around 4:00 in the afternoon, two faculty members would perform a demonstration of the material that had been discussed that day. A lecture and the next day's assignment would follow. The faculty then convened to discuss the day's events: who was doing well, who was not, who needed help. This was a very verbal process.

At the end of the week Bobby Lee approached me. "Can you write as well as you speak?"

I said I thought I could.

"Well . . ." He was smiling at me. "I'd like to give you a little test. Do you think in Massachusetts you can get some Georgia law books?"

"I'm sure I can."

"I just lost a murder case and I'm taking it up on appeal. Let's see what you can do. I'll send you the materials; you can write the brief."

Shortly after I returned to Boston I received boxes of trial transcripts and discovery materials for a case called *Georgia v. James Williams*. James Williams, otherwise known as "Big Jim," had been accused of killing a young man named Danny Hansford in his mansion in Savannah, Georgia. Williams had claimed it was self-defense, but the government charged that he had phonied up the crime scene to make it look like self-defense when in actual fact he had plotted to kill Hansford. What was not said, what was apparent but had been danced around by everyone involved, was that Williams and Hansford had been lovers.

I read the materials and investigated this case in the same manner I had pursued the closing argument in my mock trial: with everything I had. And as I read, I found a piece of evidence that didn't make sense to me.

Big Jim Williams had testified that he shot Hansford in self-defense and that on April 3, 1981, a month *before* the killing, Hansford had flown into a rage and fired a shot through the floor of Williams's house. A Savannah police officer had testified that when he was called to Williams's mansion on April 3 he had seen the bullet hole in the floor, but that he "could not determine if that was a new type of gunshot or was an old one." The same officer was called to the scene on the day of the murder. Bobby Lee had asked the district attorney if that officer's written report of the killing included information that would in any way contradict his trial testimony. The prosecutor responded that it did not.

Not long after the guilty verdict, Bobby Lee had received an envelope in the mail from an anonymous source within the district attorney's office. It contained a complete version of the police officer's report on the day of the killing, including a line stating that on April 3 he had found "a fresh gunshot on the floor" of Williams's house. That line had somehow never found its way into the report furnished to Bobby Lee.

Pursuant to a case called *Brady v. Maryland*, it is a violation of the Constitutional right to due process of law for a prosecuting attorney to conceal exculpatory evidence. Clearly grounds for a mistrial.

I wrote the brief with the help of a young lawyer. We worked methodically, incessantly, and sent it off to Bobby Lee. He signed his name to the document and filed it with the court. Saying it would "not approve corruption of the truth-seeking function of the trial process," the court reversed the conviction and James Williams got a new trial. This story was told at some length and to good effect by John Berendt in his bestselling book, *Midnight in the Garden of Good and Evil*. In the movie, Kevin Spacey was a perfect Big Jim.

After the case was reversed, Bobby Lee called. "I think it is time for you to see Big Jim." I flew down to Savannah, one of the most beautiful cities in America, and Bobby Lee escorted me to a Georgia mansion that really was beyond beautiful. Art and antiques dominated the decor, a stunning stairway swept from the entranceway to the floor above. And behind that remarkable home lay a carriage house in which Big Jim housed much of his tasteful collection of antiques and jewelry. Bobby Lee and Big Jim ushered me back there. Choate, Hall had already been paid a handsome fee for my work, but Cook and Williams did not feel I had been thanked properly. "Jim and I would like to give you a gift for the holidays," Bobby Lee said graciously. He asked Williams to bring out his estate jewelry. "You and I are going to pick something out, together with Jim's approval." Jim nodded his assent. "Don't you go be a piker on me, now. Don't you go pick out some insignificant little thing here. We have to do this right."

So now in my safe-deposit box sit four extraordinary baubles, my gift from Big Jim and Bobby Lee.

Bobby Lee also kept giving me work. He called one day to tell me that he was going to meet a fugitive from justice, recently on the run from a federal marijuana-smuggling indictment in Florida. He believed the man's wife was also indicted, and he wanted me to meet him in Atlanta, where we would reconnoiter at a hotel near the airport. I would represent the wife; he would represent the husband. How could I resist?

We knocked on the door of the airport hotel room and were met by a fellow named James Erp and his wife, Linda Parker. They told us the tale. Erp was under a huge federal indictment as the kingpin of a marijuana-smuggling operation in and around Florida. Perhaps a dozen other defendants were involved, including his wife. Erp was scared and wanted to turn himself in, but he wanted the right lawyer for the job. He had come to Atlanta because he had heard of the great Bobby Lee, and he wanted Bobby Lee to take the case. I was then treated to one of the great lawyering spectacles: Bobby Lee Cook negotiating a fee.

"Jim," he began, "you know, this looks like it is going to be a lengthy trial. I am going to have to file a lot of motions; I'm going to have to deal with the fact that you might be in jail. We don't know; we'll try to get you bail. You have lots of roots in the community; you have family there; you have a business there. But this is going to be a lot of my time, so I need a fee of . . ." He named a figure substantially into six figures.

Erp didn't flinch. "I can come up with that in a little while."

A little while was not satisfactory. "No, no, no," said Bobby Lee. "I bring you back; I file an appearance; I want the money." He was saying, in essence: I am not going down there and having you stick me with a big trial without getting all the money first. If I don't get it now, I'm never going to see it.

"I've got a plane," Erp said. "I've got a boat. I can give you that."

"I ain't in the aviation business and I ain't in the water business." Bobby Lee was quite certain. "I'm in the lawyer business and I run my business on money. I don't run my business on stuff. You got a boat, you got a plane, you get someone to convert that to good cold cash. If I have that in my hand I will represent you, and for that amount of money I'll have Ms. Klieman here represent your wife. You get two of us for the price of one." Erp said he would see what he could do. "Well, you've got about seventy-two hours. You see what you can do."

Bobby Lee got the money.

Even a minimal amount of research produced the inescapable conclusion that Linda Parker was not guilty. Whatever business may have been going on around her, she'd had no part in it. She was truly an innocent bystander. Because I had been swept up in my own circumstances while I was in college—arrested for being in an apartment "where marijuana was kept"!—I took this case personally. Even though, as a defense lawyer, I had no burden of proof, I embraced the awesome responsibility of proving this woman not guilty. This was why I had become a criminal defense lawyer, and I would be devastated if I failed.

Though I defended drug cases, I believe drugs are one of the great problems of the modern age and am passionate about the need for drug-abuse education. I do not support the legalization of drugs, but I do believe in education and interdiction rather than wholesale criminalization and incarceration of drug offenders.

We tried the case for nine weeks. I filed an enormous number of substantive motions, most of which I had gotten out of Marty Weinberg's file cabinet, attempting to get Linda Parker's case severed from the others'. She had had no involvement with illegal activities; she had simply been in the house when her husband was home. And as with most motions in criminal cases, these were denied.

The case was heard in Ocala, Florida, by Judge John Moore. Judge Moore, it was widely believed, hated women lawyers, Yankee lawyers, and drug lawyers. So I was batting a thousand and striking out at the same time. While I was arguing, he showed so much disdain for me in the courtroom that his dislike was almost palpable. He was abrupt and we could not get a civil word out of him.

There were so many defendants that the defense table had an "L extension" to accommodate the crowd. Federal indictments are routinely drafted in the order of which defendant the government wants the most. Linda Parker was the last defendant, and I was the last lawyer, way down at the end. The prosecution, in a gesture of equal opportunity, brought a woman attorney to sit at their table as well. Or at least, that was my assumption.

As the lawyer for the final defendant, I was scheduled to deliver the last opening statement. It was ten minutes before one in the afternoon on the second day of opening statements when I stood to address the jury.

"Your Honor, may I approach the bench?" Judge Moore motioned me forward grudgingly. "Your Honor, the jury has been listening all morning and they listened all yesterday afternoon and they are hungry for lunch. I don't want to give my opening statement right before lunch. They are just not going to be able to listen anymore, and my client's liberty is at stake."

"Give it now," he said gruffly. "They will wait for lunch."

I was in trouble. I could not deliver my opening in ten minutes; I had written an extended soliloquy; I had pages of notes full of detail and nuance, and it ran at least a half hour. I looked at the clock. No possible way. I would have to say it like I meant it in ten minutes. I thought, Well, I have talked this case over and over. (If you ask a defense lawyer "How are you?" he'll say, "Let me tell you about the case I'm working on." I had certainly told this story to that crowd more than once.) I would have to deliver this opening as if I were doing it over drinks. It sounded something like this:

"Members of the jury, Linda Parker is guilty." I hesitated. I knew the jury was listening now; how many defense attorneys admit their client's guilt in their opening sentence? "Yes, you heard me correctly. She is guilty of loving and marrying Jim Erp. She is guilty of associating with Jim Erp. She is certainly guilty of traveling with Jim Erp and raising the son of Jim Erp."

Linda's parents were in the courtroom. "The government's evidence is going to show you that when Linda Parker was twenty-six years old she was living in the town of Leesburg. Her family, whom you can see in the audience sitting over there"—I turned and smiled at them—"owned a motel that many of you have passed from time to time. At the time of her arrest she was working as a secretary for the public defender's office in Tavares, Florida. The government's own witnesses are going to tell you that she had absolutely no part in this. The government's own witnesses cannot believe she was even indicted! No, she had no part in this . . . no interest, no drugs, no profit. Her only crime was that she was always around. She was just always around with this person who she met when she was but a girl."

Of the two government witnesses who had turned state's evidence, I knew one liked Linda and would not implicate her, and the other hardly knew her at all. They could place her at her husband's birthday party; they could place her at their wedding; but they could not place her with the money or the drugs. "No one in the United States of America who was married to or who associates with or is in the company of alleged criminal activity can be convicted for that association alone. There is no such crime as guilt by association in this great country of ours, nor should there be."

I was pleased and surprised when I saw a juror tear up during my opening. One of the federal marshals was just gaping at me. I glanced at the judge on occasion and saw that he was listening; previously he had swiveled his chair away from the jury and appeared to be clipping his fingernails.

Promptly at 1:00 I told the jury, "At the end of this case I am very confident that when you go in to deliberate, you will come back and you will hold your heads up high as you uphold the values of the United States of America, and you will look Linda Parker in the eye and proudly say, 'Not guilty.'"

The jury filed out, stomachs grumbling, and the judge motioned me to approach. How had I annoyed him this time?

"Ms. Klieman, I have a lot of respect for you."

And, all of a sudden, I for him. He was tough and arrogant, no question. But it turned out that he had read the motions, and despite appearances, he had overcome whatever bias he might have had to ultimately administer the law. I had shown him respect by adhering to his rules, and from that moment forward he treated me with respect as well.

Big drug trial in Ocala. For nine weeks the press in northern Florida covered it every day. As each witness appeared, I kept hammering away at the fact that no one could place my client with drugs, no one could place her with drug money.

As is standard procedure, at the end of the government's case I moved for a judgment of acquittal, a directed verdict by the judge of not guilty. This is rarely granted, but it is essential to do under the rules of procedure. One attorney in our case, a great trial lawyer by reputation who wore a cowboy hat and drove a pink Cadillac, played possum all trial long. He almost never spoke, though I could imagine his poor client crying, "What are you doing? What are you doing?" He played possum so well that the government basically forgot about his client. He walked out of the courthouse with a directed verdict of acquittal.

So did I.

I was completely thrilled. Not only had I triumphed in a case I'd taken personally, I had won in the eyes of Bobby Lee.

Bobby Lee had a speaking engagement at the National Association of Criminal Defense Lawyers (NACDL) meeting in Jackson Hole, Wyoming. He also had to put on Jim Erp's defense. "Why don't you go give my speech for me?" he asked.

So I stood in for Bobby Lee Cook. That was daunting. If I were attending a conference I certainly would rather have heard him speak than me, but I delivered a talk concerning the concept of theater in the courtroom and was flattered to be well received.

I returned to Florida and listened as Bobby Lee and the other lawyers delivered their closings. When Bobby Lee spoke, he brought forth an encyclopedia of defense arguments, and I pulled out a lined yellow legal pad and took notes like a schoolgirl.

"The United States of America wins its case," he told the jury, "when justice is done." In pulling apart the prosecutor's reasoning, Bobby Lee quoted Mark Twain, for whom he had a natural fondness: "The more you explain it, the less I understand it." He put the government on trial and talked about the country's guiding principles: "We have given up our lives and blood for liberty. Thousands died that we may live on for this republic. Honor, truth, love, and courage are still important in this country, and worth fighting for." To decimate a witness who had done damage to his case but had been caught giving conflicting testimony, he said, *"Falsus in uno, falsus in omnibus:* False in one, false in all." I found that brilliant. In a more colloquial vein, he said, "If you can believe this witness, you believe water can run uphill. If you can believe this witness, you could believe this jury box is in Paris." He was at once folksy and cutting, homespun and erudite, casual and extremely precise.

This was a virtuoso exhibition of lawyering, a brilliant boilerplate of defense. To this day I carry those notes, that exact piece of paper, to every lecture I give. And I was certainly not above using any or all of his winning phrases in my own comments to any jury.

While we tried the James Erp/Linda Parker case, rather than stash us in the splendid isolation of a good hotel, Bobby Lee had rented a large house in Ocala, in which he, I, and another attorney named Steve Sadow lived for the duration. Bobby Lee arranged for maid service, so at the end of the day we were not faced with an empty house that looked like a disaster zone. If we were away from home, at least we had our small, three-person community to return to each night. We would try the case from Monday at 8:30 in the morning until Thursday at 6:30 in the evening, after which the Erp private jet would fly us to Atlanta. Bobby Lee and Steve would go wherever they were going and I would proceed to Boston.

After that trial I was pleased and flattered that Bobby Lee involved me and Steve in several other cases, writing motions or trying high-profile, high-dollar defenses in Georgia cities like Savannah, Brunswick, and Augusta. I can only describe Bobby Lee's life during these times as opulent, and he shared it. We were driven everywhere in his chauffeured Rolls-Royce. (Bobby Lee kept the back of his Rolls stocked with consumer magazines, everything from *Architectural Digest* to women's magazines to *The New Yorker*, and several newsweeklies and daily papers from around the country. He believed he could understand jurors more fully if he kept abreast of what they were reading.) We stayed in first-class hotels; we ate beluga caviar and drank Cristal champagne at sumptuous restaurants. It was a high life, extremely seductive, a life to aspire to, and whether paid for by the client or himself, in the full measure of his generosity Bobby Lee picked up the tab.

My performances at the National College for Criminal Defense and NACDL earned me speaking engagements and teaching assignments at other criminal defense lawyer organizations. Like my colleagues, I did not receive fees for these speeches, only expenses, but I was beginning to become more widely known and to meet some of the notable lawyers in my field.

If you were at the top of your class at Harvard or Yale or the University of Chicago, you entered a corporate law firm, became a partner, worked in the business world of mergers and acquisitions and tax law, and made tremendous amounts of money. Those people were not criminal defense lawyers. Criminal defense lawyers were cowboys.

They were not problem solvers, nor did they provide counsel for everyday concerns. They were not good with numbers or economics. What they did was get you out of trouble. Performance drove them. And high risk. Criminal defense is the roller coaster, the hot-air balloon, the fast car of the legal world. They were dealing with people's lives and liberty: They won and people went free; they lost and their clients went away for long periods of time. They not only wanted to win, they *needed* to win. The competitive edge was always present, from telling stories to putting away the most alcohol to picking up the ever-present bar tab. And all of these cowboys grabbed for the check so they could show the extent of their success, the depth of their pocket.

You wondered, sitting around talking to these men—and at that time the field was made up almost entirely of men—who was in prison? The way they told it, every one of them had never lost a case. The great lawyers truly believed in the Constitution and held the fundamental principles of justice dear, but many of these guys just wanted to win. What was important to them was the contest, the game. They were gladiators. They had their legions, their young supplicant-acolyte lawyers hanging on every word. They wanted a crowd, a circle of admiration for them and their tales. And these older men did like younger women, no question about that.

Sabers, swords, or six-guns, there was a Wild West aura, a gunfighter quality, to the entire criminal defense bar. Many of these men wore cowboy boots; some owned ten or twelve pairs. So it was not at all outrageous that Gerry Spence, one of the most flamboyant of this flamboyant crew, wore suede fringed jackets.

I ran into Spence when we were both teaching at a closing argument seminar at Lake Tahoe in December 1982. I had read his book *Gunning for Justice* and looked forward to speaking with him. A quorum of lawyers was holding court in the hotel bar swapping legends, and at some point he and I wandered away to talk. He had a difficult personal reputation for being highly critical of his students, but I was very curious about him. After all, he was known as one of the great trial lawyers of all time.

I waited for him to speak. He took a swallow of his soda water. The silence was working in his favor, making me deeply uncomfortable. "What makes you think you're a great trial lawyer?" he finally asked.

As much as I knew he was my better, I was not going to be intimidated. I did not think I was a great trial lawyer, but if I had ever dreamed of trying a case with this master, here was my opportunity to impress him.

"I think I'm the most prepared lawyer I know. There is nothing that I miss. If it means lacking sleep, if it means lacking food, if it means doing nothing else whatsoever, I am always working. I think I understand the theater of the courtroom, I understand how to work within a theater with my mind, my body, my voice, my use of props, my use of costume. I use different clothes for different settings, different scenes." I ran down my checklist. "I understand the rules of evidence and the rules of procedure as well as any judge or prosecutor; they are not going to stump me." I took a breath and racked my brain. "I bring passion to my case. I try from the heart."

Spence interrupted my monumental blast of self-promotion. "Well," he drawled to me, "that last comment is the first right thing you've said."

nine THE PRICE OF THE PRIZE, THE PERILS OF BEING PERFECT

HAT A STRANGE LIFE. IN 1983 I WOULD SPEND LONG DAYS AT CHOATE, HALL DOING civil legal paperwork in which I had little interest and on weekends fly off to deliver a speech about which I was passionate to a legal organization or Bar Association. I would constantly battle with the firm to take on more and more challenging criminal defendants, which they resisted, and I would occasionally serve as a highly valued criminal defense lawyer at the right hand of Bobby Lee Cook and live in temporary splendor. The substantial fees I was earning were going straight to Choate, Hall; I was an associate and was paid an associate's salary. And the more I worked there, the more I began to dislike it. I would run around the country at the top of my game and then have to come back and submit memoranda to the senior partners, which would get returned to me red-lined and rewritten as if I were a first-year associate who didn't know what she was doing. I was out there trying the best cases with the best lawyers, who treated me like a princess and respected me as an advocate; I would come back with good fees and be treated by the firm as though I had a disease.

What were all these feelings percolating inside? At first it was simple malaise; on those rare occasions in my office that I would come up for air I would look around and register the fact that I was not happy there. I would duck my head back down and push forward with the paperwork. Then early one morning I was standing on State Street looking up at the Choate, Hall building and found tears running down my face; I just did not want to go inside. I felt like I was outside a prison about to be shuffled into my cell. They were my jailers. After the first episode, I cried in the street often. Then things got more bizarre.

It started as once every eight weeks, then once a month, then every week I was on trial: on Sunday nights I would violently throw up. I was embarrassed, I was upset, but I could not control these attacks. Every Sunday night like clockwork I would vomit. I told my friend Joan Schmidt (now Mrs. Joan Green), who was also a lawyer working herself to the bone. "Oh," she said, "I get hives." That didn't make me feel any better. This was not right.

So, wasn't I surprised when I received a call from *Time* magazine.

A reporter named Joelle Attinger informed me that *Time* intended to publish a piece identifying America's top five female trial attorneys and that I had been suggested for inclusion. Could she come talk to me?

Uh, sure.

When she arrived in my office my first question was, "How did you get my name?" I was tickled and extremely proud even to be considered. Top five? What an honor! There were several other women who could just as easily have been selected. How had this happened?

The reporter and I hit it off right away, just one of those personality confluences in which people are immediately simpatico. Rather than fudge an answer, she told me, "No one knew who the female trial lawyers were in the country, period." Wasn't that perfect. "So we called up famous male trial lawyers and asked for their opinions, and two people suggested you."

"Who?" I wondered.

"One was Gerry Spence."

"Really!"

"He said that in order for a woman to be considered a great trial lawyer she would have to possess the warrior instinct. Then he said, 'Wait a minute, there may be one. I've never seen her try a case but I've seen her teach and do a demonstration. You should check it out with a Boston lawyer.'" The Boston lawyer they asked was F. Lee Bailey. "So," said Joelle, "here I am. . . .

"They are considering several women, so I am not certain whether you will be included. Oh, by the way, they wanted the women to be thirty-five or under. When's your birthday?" I told her. "Good." The date of the issue was May 30, 1983. I was turning thirty-five on the thirteenth.

At approximately the same time that *Time* magazine was calling, the Commonwealth of Massachusetts came calling as well. Governor Michael Dukakis had been elected on a platform in which he pledged to appoint an increased number of women and minorities to the bench, and I received a phone call from the governor's legal counsel telling me the governor would like me to apply for a superior court judgeship. This was a lifetime appointment of great prestige. The people who served on that court were of the highest legal quality. And once within that system, the top rung, the position in at least the periphery of every state trial judge's mind, was Justice of the Supreme Judicial Court of Massachusetts, or the United States District Court. If you got there, you might even get delusional and fantasize about going to the Supreme Court of the United States. Now there was a career path worth pursuing.

Or was it?

My friends were unanimous. They said, "That's a great honor,

Judge Klieman, but why would you want to do it? You just switched to the defense side; you are positioned to become a partner in a prestigious law firm; you could have a meaningful, substantive legal career. And you're thirty-four years old; you could become a judge when you are fifty or sixty; you have years to become a judge." But I always liked being asked to the dance. Plus, there was the added bonus of a judgeship providing a graceful way out of Choate, Hall & Stewart. I decided to apply.

When I told Bobby Lee that I had submitted my application, he was incredulous. "This is insane!" he raved. "This is a terrible move at this time of your legal career. *Time* magazine is going to come out in a month and your career is going to take off like a rocket ship." Joe Balliro, Joe Oteri, and all my mentors agreed. Bobby Lee continued to make his case. "Why do you want to go be a judge and have everybody watching what you do all the time? You're going to have to be in the courthouse five days a week and take home briefs to read, and you can write better than every one of them. You're going to be bored and you're going to be angry because you'll have to watch all these bad advocates. You're alive; you're on the rise; your career has so many places to go! Why would you shut it down now? You'll be an old woman at forty!" That resonated. As usual, Bobby Lee was the most effective advocate. Then he closed.

"Girl, you're going to be a rich lawyer. You're going to make a lot of money. I'm going to make you a lot of money. I'm going to make you even more famous!"

He was right. A judge's salary is not high, and I was entering my prime earning years. And look at the life I could be leading! The life of travel and luxury, combined with the thrill and satisfaction of doing important work, was compelling.

I agonized over my decision for weeks. To sit on the bench and say "Overruled," "Denied," "Allowed," "Sustained" was prestigious, but was it my life's work? My goal had always been to be a great trial lawyer and I would never get there as a judge.

I withdrew my application.

I did it all wrong. I could have told myself, I am flattered to be asked but this is the wrong time in my career for such a move. If I want to, some day I may return and be a judge, but now I want to show the world what kind of trial lawyer I can be. I choose, on the basis of investigation and information, after talking to friends whom I respect, to withdraw this application. Withdrawing my application is a good choice, an honest choice. This is a move forward, toward success in my career, and it absolutely pleases me.

But no. Instead of allowing myself to succeed, I thought, I am a bad girl. I said I would apply and I did not follow through. They're going to think so badly of me. I dissolved my marriage with Sandy; I abandoned my acting career; I left Hale & Dorr after a week; I never follow through. I'm such a disappointment to myself. I beat myself up pretty effectively. Once again I had shown I was not the perfect child.

But life wasn't entirely miserable. *Time* magazine came out.

So I was among the top five female trial lawyers in America? Incredible. That's a tremendous assertion that I was not prepared to make about myself. Such designations are often based not so much on one's work as on the visibility of one's work and the visibility of one's friends and acquaintances. I was honored and flattered to be thought of so highly and placed in such distinguished company. I didn't know, in May 1983, if I was one of the top five female trial lawyers in America. But I did know this much: If *Time* magazine says you are, as far as the rest of the world is concerned, you are.

Requests that I speak at various legal functions snowballed, and the more I spoke, the more lawyers I met who referred more business and bigger cases to me. Bobby Lee was as good as his word, involving me even more intensely in his work. I brought them all to the partners at Choate, Hall & Stewart, who were not pleased.

Choate, Hall was a Boston Brahmin law firm that wanted to do its work with as little publicity as possible. A few colleagues, among them Mark Michelson, a partner and the person to whom I reported in the litigation department, were complimentary. He knew the article would bring more clients and larger fees to the firm. One of the managing partners, Bob Frank, actually said he was proud of me. On the other hand, the corporate partners, of which there were many, simply would not discuss it. They acted as if nothing had happened.

Worse. A Choate, Hall & Stewart corporate partner told the litigation partners, "I know you would have paid ten thousand dollars for that kind of publicity. Well, I would have paid ten thousand dollars to keep it out of the magazine."

This was white-shoe corporate culture at its most insular. They were afraid some banker would call and say, "If your firm is representing drug dealers or organized crime figures, we are taking our bank's business down the street to some other firm where such a thing cannot happen." Whether this was realistic or not, the organizational fear that filled the office every time my name appeared in the paper concerning a criminal case was palpable. The atmosphere, never particularly collegial, turned frosty. I fumed to Bobby Lee Cook, "Do you believe this garbage?"

"What do you expect from these people? Did you ever hear your receptionist answer the phone?" He mimicked the cold, proper Boston accent. From the mouth of a southerner it sounded pretty funny. "You ought to get out of there," he advised.

"No, no, no. I'm about to come up for partner." I had been hired on a three-year track and my consideration for partnership was about to begin.

"Why do you want to be a partner?" he said. "What are you going to do, change your spots? You don't want to be a partner there."

But I did. I came from Depression-era parents and if I became a partner at Choate, Hall & Stewart I would work hard but would be guaranteed a very substantial income for the rest of my life. The allure of that kind of security cannot be overstated. At the same time, I was intent on trying cases.

As the vote on my merits approached, the corporate partners started to make noises about their not wanting their corporate clients in the same waiting room with my criminal clients. Then it got personal.

I was concerned that my application was going to get blocked. According to the firm's bylaws, if two partners blackballed an associate, partnership was denied. Michelson told me that one particularly antagonistic corporate partner was uncomfortable around me. I was too "flamboyant." "He says you have all this sexual energy. He doesn't know how to interact with you; he doesn't like being in the same room with you."

"Mark, it's not like I go into his office with my top button unbuttoned. I don't do anything in his office or in any other office here to make someone feel uncomfortable about my being a woman lawyer in this firm."

"Well, part of it is that you are an attractive woman and he doesn't know how to handle that."

"That is absurd. He better grow up."

"I can't defend him," Michelson said. "I'm not defending him. I'm just telling you that he's very uncomfortable with you in a room."

Here I was, one of the most successful woman lawyers in the United States, and I made my colleagues uncomfortable. Among criminal defense lawyers I was considered playful but practically demure, everyone's daughter, but in the offices of Choate, Hall & Stewart apparently I was one step short of being a hussy.

Some men are indeed uncomfortable working around attractive women; they like the view but don't like the proximity. Having been raised in a culture in which women were objects, these men have difficulty treating us as colleagues. This particular man was a throwback; he felt women belonged in the kitchen. Older men, if they're not dismissive, often go to the other extreme and fall all over themselves trying to be witty and dashing, and end up looking foolish. That foolishness is disruptive to both their business and their self-esteem. Perhaps it's generational; as opportunities open and men and women are increasingly trained and educated together, the fact that some women are both beautiful and smart becomes undeniable and younger men seem less threatened by it.

I was dating one of the firm's associates, Richard Trembowicz, which also caused a stir. "Why?" I asked. There was no corporate policy that forbade intraoffice dating among associates. "He's single and I'm single."

Michelson said, "One of the partners said he is younger than you are." I was eight years older than Richard. Apparently this lawyer thought our age difference gave the appearance that I was taking advantage of a younger man.

"You've got to be kidding. That is the most ridiculous thing I have ever heard."

"I'm just the messenger!"

My partnership was most certainly in trouble. How could I ease concerns and smooth my path, I asked.

Bob Frank, the managing partner whom I greatly respected, felt strongly that if I were going to continue to represent criminal defendants there were at least two partners and perhaps more who would blackball me.

A bookstore in Stoughton, Massachusetts, a Norfolk County suburb of Boston, was being picketed for allegedly selling pornography. The owners came to me for representation. I brought it to the litigation department. The litigation department refused to let me take the case. The handwriting was on the wall.

Gennaro Angiulo, reputed head of the Boston Mafia, had been indicted for several federal crimes. The Organized Crime Strike Force was trying to eradicate the mob. This was huge. If you were a criminal defense lawyer, you wanted a part of this case. I certainly did.

How do people who are supposed to have moral values defend these people? It's the criminal defense lawyer's eternal question. Here is my answer.

My job as a criminal defense lawyer is to represent the values and rights and privileges of the Constitution of the United States. According to the Constitution, every citizen—not only the ones we like and admire but every citizen, no matter what crime he or she has been accused of committing—has the *right* to effective counsel. I offer that counsel; my job is to defend citizens accused of crime. Also according to the Constitution, the government must provide sufficient quality and quantity of evidence to prove guilt beyond a reasonable doubt. I put the government's proof to the test. If the government's proof stands up to that test, it wins; if it does not, the defendant goes free. The Fourth Amendment protects citizens against unreasonable searches and seizures; this is why evidence that was obtained illegally or confessions that were coerced should not be permitted. In other legal systems, one may be maimed or killed without trial. I live in the United States of America; I want the legal system to work. Our system works only when it is based on a foundation of due process — for everyone.

A pure criminal defense lawyer never has moral considerations when choosing her clients. I admire that person. She is usually a public defender or lawyer who tries death penalty cases on a regular basis. She is a better person than I am; she is a pure advocate. She is the greatest pillar of the bar. I admire her; I cannot be her. Sometimes, I admit, my conscience gets in my way. For example, over time, my own personal issues about child molestation have become such that a client charged with the crime would be much better off represented by someone else. Neo-Nazi defendants, the same. All clients have a right to the best legal defense, and in certain situations I am not the proper person for that particular job. However, I have faith that the system will produce someone else to provide the effective defense I cannot.

One fact of life is that if you're a criminal defense lawyer you almost always represent guilty people. It's the innocent ones that make you crazy. The few times I have represented truly innocent clients — people who *did not do it* — the pressure was overwhelming. If I had lost and they had gone to prison for years, perhaps for the rest of their lives, I would have been wracked with guilt and never forgiven myself. If someone did the act, the trial is about putting the government to its proof, and the government wins or loses on its proof.

So when James "Fat Peter" Limone, an accused mob enforcer, came to me and said he thought he might be indicted in a major federal crackdown on organized crime, I read the material he provided and concluded his indictment was likely. I quoted him a substantial fee, which Limone was ready to pay. He had a reasonable defense and I had no problem taking the case to the litigation department for approval. Balliro and Oteri and other honorable lawyers for whom I had the utmost respect had represented people in the mob for years. And that is a significant distinction, representing a person as opposed to advising a criminal organization. I was going to defend Limone; I wasn't going to be the Angiulo family consigliere.

The request was turned down stone-cold. I was told, "You are not going to get involved." Mark Michelson said, "Don't even think about it, and you ought to consider whether or not you ever want to bring up another case like this if you are going to be voted on as partner."

I was in Florida in February 1984 attending a National Association of Criminal Defense Lawyers meeting when the Choate, Hall & Stewart partners met to discuss whether to accept me as a member of the firm. I believe Bob Frank wanted to find some way to keep me. As active as I was with the Boston and Massachusetts Bar Associations, as often as I appeared in the news, I suspect Bob thought it might look bad for Choate, Hall if they dumped me. They couldn't come out and say, "We got rid of her because we didn't want her Italian-named or drug-selling clients in the waiting room with our people" or "We got rid of her because we thought our banking and business clients would go to Ropes & Gray." I was told one partner said during the meeting, "I don't care what the [Massachusetts] bar says about her. We have clients to please, and they will not tolerate this kind of business." So Bob Frank called and asked whether I would forgo my criminal practice and become solely a civil litigation lawyer. If so, I might have a chance to become a member of the firm. If not, the question then was, did I want to force the issue?

"I am certainly willing to do some civil cases," I told him, "which I have been doing. But you brought me in here to be a criminal defense lawyer, which I intend to continue to be." So, yes, I would force the issue.

The partners rejected me. I received a message by telephone that by virtue of my refusal to give up criminal defense —or so they said— I was not voted in as partner.

I felt as if I had been punched in the stomach. I wasn't only disappointed, I was angry, an emotion I rarely allowed myself to feel. I was angry at the firm for being narrow-minded and petty, and I was furious at myself for allowing them to have power over me. I had put myself in this position; I could have left on my own. I had wanted to test them, and for what? For the glory of being accepted into a group to which I did not want to belong and did not feel as if I belonged? I guess I wanted to be asked to the dance so I could say no to the suitor. That was pretty mature. I was returning to my childhood once again. I wanted to get the A on the exam, to be the teacher's pet, to get the best role at the audition even if the part was wrong for me. I did not want to be rejected.

But I knew how to handle rejection and I came out of it with my head high. My public, self-preserving side trumpeted, "I'm glad I didn't compromise my principles. Somehow this will all work out." Fiddle-dee-dee. A Scarlett O'Hara moment.

But how? I was terrified to be without money. How was I going to live? As it happened, Bobby Lee was also at the Florida meeting. He was not perturbed one bit. "Don't take this to heart," he said with great assurance. "I'm going to make sure you have plenty of business. Let the bastards weep."

I quit Choate, Hall. There was no future, and barely an acceptable present for me there. I called around and arranged to rent an office month-to-month in the suite of some criminal defense lawyer friends until I figured out what I would do.

And, of course, Bobby Lee was as good as his word. Without truly needing my assistance he immediately brought me in as cocounsel on a drug-smuggling case in Georgia. Suddenly, instead of my associate's salary, for the first time the sizable fees I was earning were going directly into my own bank account. *Time* magazine turned out to be quite the calling card. I tried cases all over Massachusetts, New Hampshire, and Maine, and Bobby Lee kept me busy down the seaboard. I shouldn't have worried. All of a sudden I was in the chips!

I had been on my own for a matter of weeks when Joel Kozol called. I had heard of but never met Kozol; his reputation as a civil litigator in the business field preceded him. He was supposed to be brilliant, and a scrapper. He wanted to talk about the possibility of my joining his firm, Friedman & Atherton. I was fresh out of a corporate firm and really had no interest. He persisted. He knew my friends, he said, and they thought it was a great match.

"I'm not coming to meet with you. I have just left this nightmare and I do not want to have this meeting."

"What do you have to lose? You'll come meet me for a drink. The worst that'll happen is you'll have a drink. Meet me at the Ritz at seven, in the bar." And he hung up.

I had to admit that was a good move. I called Oteri, who told me, "You know what happens? The Jewish businessmen, they go to some firm like Choate, Hall or Ropes & Gray and they have people manage their affairs. But when they get into litigation they leave and go right to the only guy they know who's just like they are, which is Joel Kozol." Of course, he didn't represent only Jews. The Sullivan family, the owners of the New England Patriots, and politico and race-track owner George Carney were among his many important clients.

So I walked into the Ritz bar at 7:00 on the dot. I didn't know what Joel Kozol looked like, but when I asked the maître d' he said, "Mr. Kozol called to say he is going to be late, but he asked us to take care of you."

The Ritz bar feels like a nice place to have a martini. I ordered a glass of champagne. By 7:15 Kozol had not arrived. I resisted the urge to have another; I didn't want to wind up on my tail. Seven-thirty came and went and I amazed myself by staying. The maître d' kept fussing over me, and I would have been embarrassed to leave. At around 7:45 Joel Kozol strolled in. This guy had demanded that I show up, then kept me waiting for forty-five minutes. My lips were pursed; my fingers were drumming; I felt like a fool.

Kozol was a bit of a wide-body, a solid, well-built squash-player type. He was in his mid-fifties, around five foot seven at most, athletic, tanned, with fashionably long jet-black hair. He had been a wrestler at Harvard and it showed. "I'm really sorry," he said as he pulled out his chair and sat.

"You should be."

"This isn't the way I wanted to start this off."

"Then you shouldn't have."

"Oh, come on," he said, "relax." He refused to rise to my anger. "I told you you could have a drink. I'll even take you to dinner."

"Is this a date or a meeting?"

"It's a meeting. I like to hold meetings over drinks and dinner."

I said nothing and he began his pitch.

"I want to talk to you about what we do at Friedman & Atherton. I've done a lot of research on you; I know a lot about you. I know what kind of cases you try; I know where you speak; I know what kind of money you make. I know it all. I want you to be a partner in my law firm."

This was not the usual way business was done. "Don't your partners have something to say about that?"

"They do, but it's my law firm. If I want you there, they'll want you there because you'd be a great asset. Now tell me you're not interested."

"I'm not."

It was easy to argue with him. He seemed to be enjoying my demurrals, as if he expected nothing less and things were going according to plan. And I must say, he was so good-humored I began to enjoy the banter. It was sport arguing.

"Well," he said amiably, "we could end this conversation now"— he was very good—"or you could go have dinner with me and I'll tell you all about the firm."

How could I resist? "At this stage, I deserve dinner."

He was chatty as we walked to the steakhouse, and even chattier once we sat down. Friedman & Atherton was really a Jewish law firm, he told me. So that's where they all were; almost all the lawyers I had run into in Boston were Irish or Brahmins. He outlined the firm's history and said it was truly a family operation. Kozol's father, Frank, was the revered partner. "My father is my god," he said. "I think my father is the most brilliant lawyer around. I love working with him. Two of my brothers are in the firm and I brought in my son. We have many partners who are not related but we treat everyone like family."

It was a nice sell, but I could have cared less. I wasn't in the market, so I just listened. He enthusiastically described his work and the work he had planned for me. He told me about his life and the people he had represented. We had a pleasant dinner. The next day he sent a dozen roses to my office and arranged another dinner for the following week.

"What time are we going to meet?" I asked.

"Seven-thirty."

"Fine, I'll see you at a quarter after eight." It was a joke, but when I arrived at 8:15 I was just about on time to see him saunter in.

We had a whirlwind courtship—for the firm. He was indeed charming and charismatic, and the work he described seemed enjoyable and worthwhile and highly remunerative. Plus, Joel Kozol had a personal quality that was difficult to describe and more difficult to resist. It didn't matter where he was; he walked into a room and the room was his. He was magic.

So I was in the process of being won over. At one of these dinners I said, "All right, all right, I'll think about coming to the firm if you give me a corner office that's covered with windows on both sides."

"Done!" he agreed.

"How are you going to do that?" I had visited the firm and knew that both corner offices were occupied, one by Joel, the other by his father. I figured I was safe.

"I'll take back the space I subleased on one side."

"Yeah, right."

A week or so passed. Joel called. "Come on over." Sure enough, he had reacquired the space and there was an enormous corner office with lots of windows—the whole thing—just waiting for me.

Bobby Lee said, "Sounds like the right place." Joe Oteri said, "Kozol is never going to curtail you. He's going to let you do criminal law; he might even let you do some pro bono work. He'll also make you into a great civil litigator; he's the best there is." Oteri had that right; Kozol did want me to try large civil cases with him, which I would ultimately find challenging and rewarding. So, in July 1984 I signed on as a partner at Friedman & Atherton.

I proceeded, over the next five years, to work like a dog. Joel Kozol was a taskmaster, a perfectionist. He would bully and prod his partners and associates if he found fault with our work, and he always found fault with our work. He worked like a demon on every case. We may have arrived at the office at the reasonable hour of 9:00

A.M., but his workday routinely ran until 9:30 at night, sometimes
11:00—his only interruption was his squash game at the Harvard
Club—and it was not over then. Joel, his son Matthew, a law associate named John Rosenberg, and I ate as a pack. We drank as well,
spending considerable amounts of time at the Ritz bar. No wonder he
had felt so at home there. And if the phone rang at two in the morning, I knew before answering that it was Joel with a nuance he
wanted to discuss. I didn't hesitate to discuss it with him. If he was
thinking about an evidentiary issue, I should be thinking about it,
too. Joel had such commitment, such blinding enthusiasm for his
work, that I and everyone in his sphere wanted to be perfect for him.
I wanted to please him, to shine in his eyes. If I wanted to be Joel's
favorite child, so did John and Matthew, and Matthew was his real
child!

I was dating men but I was married to Joel. The best hours of my
day and night were spent with him, at the office, traveling together, in
court on cases. He liked to live well, and we did. At the same time, I
was spending my weekends traveling to bar functions all over the
country, speaking before attentive audiences, and meeting increasing
numbers of interesting and important people. If I was invited I could
not say no. I accepted cases in much the same way. I would find the
time. It was part of my character to be consumed 100 percent with
what I was doing. Mostly, that meant clients. Left to my own devices
I found I would work until I dropped. Nothing else was of any consequence. It didn't matter what was in the paper, it didn't matter
what was on the news; my entire world involved my client going free
or my client getting a better deal.

The men I was seeing understood that. I did not have time or
space for personal commitment. My commitment was to my career. I
was always dating and I always found enjoyable and appropriate
escorts, as well as inappropriate but fabulous men, and I must say the
men I found were by and large commitment-phobes. We must have
sensed that kindred spirit. They looked good, they sounded good,
they were lovely people, but they were there for comfort. They were
there to be an escort, to go to the barbecue, to the beach, to bed.

My sexual relationships were intimate relationships. I was a serial monogamist and I cared for the men I was seeing. I knew I needed intimacy. I needed someone to hold me at night, to make love to me and to whom to make love. I was a criminal defense cowgirl. Still, I was not good at having sex without tenderness. Sex for me was a very intimate act, even if I did not think of my partner as a life mate.

Marriage? Who had time for marriage? Why would I want to get married when I was leading this life? I felt young; I was healthy; this was the most fun in the world. I was like the guys.

For the first two years of my partnership at Friedman & Atherton I did everything I wanted to do. I tried big cases; I worked side by side with Joel; I drank with my friends; I dated whomever I felt like dating; I flew around the country. I made friends, but mostly I worked. Every now and then Bill Delahunt, Frank Bellotti, and a wonderful lawyer named Earl Cooley would visit my apartment in the North End and Frank would cook. He was a great pasta chef. While he was preparing the meal my phone would keep ringing with calls from clients. I took them; that was a constant. Frank said, "Can't you stop? You are with three very successful men and we don't do this. You shouldn't have people calling you at home. No client should have your home phone number. You should be able to separate."

I told him, "I can't."

I believe women criminal defense lawyers are more attached to their clients. We are more emotional; that is one stereotype based in fact. Many women think the business of being a trial lawyer is not healthy, or they become psychotherapists and social workers for their clients when they should be advocates. I understand their concerns, but the legal profession needs these women.

But as my caseload mounted and the speaking engagements increased, I started to feel the toll. Slowly at first, then with increasing ferocity. If this is Saturday, it must be Orlando or Phoenix or San Francisco. What had been a joy became a blurred frenzy. Then I started to get sick.

I was eating at odd times, if at all. I used to gauge my cases by how much weight I stood to lose. Was this a two-pound case, a five-pound case, a ten-pound case? My wardrobe varied by the stages of my trials. When I did eat I was on the run and I wasn't eating healthy foods. I was also drinking too much. Why did I have to wind down by drinking every night? Every night. I was so exhausted at the end of the evening I used Valium to get to sleep, then woke up in the morning in a coma and practically drowned myself in coffee to start my day. Once I got to the office I was flying.

I was still throwing up every Sunday night. I'd been doing that for years. I kept getting the flu. My throat was continually sore, and while I never missed a day of work I was constantly exhausted. My medicine cabinet looked like an apothecary. I had always relieved stress by running several miles a day, but my knees—first one, then the other—began giving me so much trouble an orthopedist finally had to order me to bed for a week. The only thing that stopped me from working was my body; I wasn't stopping myself.

By the spring of 1986 I knew I needed a way out. I had attained almost everything I thought I had wanted: I was a known figure in the legal world; I had put away a substantial amount of my earnings and had a nest egg that gave me at least a semblance of security; I had tried cases of visibility and importance. Fortunately, an opportunity presented itself. Once again, a state superior court judgeship became available and I was approached to apply.

I certainly did not want to disappoint Joel, nor did I want my present and future clients to see that I was crumbling, that the only reason I was leaving criminal defense was physical illness. I kept all that hidden. And again, rather than see my application as the culmination of a life's work I defined it as a recognition of failure. I didn't know how to get off the treadmill, so I was crying "Get me out of here!" and running to the bench. That's how I saw it.

How badly I treated myself.

Of course, you don't get a judgeship just by filing. I had to enlist the help of many respected people in the legal community who could speak to the Judicial Nominating Council on my behalf. Attorney General Frank Bellotti and District Attorney Bill Delahunt, and Judges John Paul Sullivan, Robert Barton, and A. David Mazzone, the fathers and mentors of my career, lobbied for me. I asked for and received recommendations from several judges before whom I had practiced. I reviewed and added to my 1983 superior court application.

The form one submits to the Judicial Nominating Council is long and detailed. I listed my work experience, the cases I had tried, the courses I had taken and taught. And then there it was, question 38 (a): Had I ever been arrested?

I didn't have to tell them. My record had been expunged and I had the legal right to answer no. And perhaps I should have; no good could come of opening this nickel bag of controversy. But I felt the need to confess, as I did on my bar applications, on my previous judicial application, and to my government bosses. I was a lawyer. I was proud to be a lawyer, and I felt it was my ethical responsibility to be forthright when asked this question. "Although my record has been expunged pursuant to Illinois law," I began, and detailed the Northwestern cast-party pot bust. "All persons present were charged; all charges were dismissed." My shame was ever-present, and clearly no one cared about it as much as I did. I thought I wore a scarlet letter; they thought it was a college mistake.

My interview went well; the issue that concerned me the most turned out to be no issue at all, and from inside sources I was told I was a shoo-in. I was looking forward to a life on the bench, away from the crushing pressures of criminal defense. When I got the call from Stephen Delinsky, Bellotti's man on the Nominating Council, I answered brightly.

Delinsky said, "You didn't make it and you're not going to believe what I have to tell you."

I did not know what to say. I said nothing.

"The women killed you and I'm horrified." What? "Not all of them, but a group of women on the council were out to destroy you because you are attractive. You would have gotten this job if you were thirty pounds heavier and wore thick glasses. I've never seen anything like it." His wife, by chance, was a writer of romance novels. "It's everything I might read about but nothing I believed was real. These women didn't even understand how they sounded."

One woman had said, "Well, how could you ever put her on the bench? She's much too pretty and she has painted fingernails."

Another had said something to the effect, "Even though her résumé shows she is bright, how could you look at her and think such a thing?"

A third: "If Frank Bellotti is pushing her so hard she must be sleeping with him."

I was devastated. First, because my exit from my demanding trial practice was no longer clear. I would have to dive back into that debilitating world. Second, because I was stunned at the behavior of these women. I had always believed that women should promote one another. Apparently these women felt I had not done enough. In a profile in the *Boston Business Journal*, the reporter wrote, "According to one anonymous active member of the Boston Bar, 'She's not really in the network of women lawyers who support each other, nor does she seem particularly interested in doing it.'" Someone else described me as a "Queen Bee." Anonymous sources, of course.

I had encouraged and networked with women at meetings and conferences around the country. In Boston I had groomed some and given business to others. I was an active mentor to so many young women. I called them "my daughters." To be rejected in the face of that was stunning. And to be whacked in the teeth because I was attractive! The pettiness. The treachery. The outright hurtfulness. I was crushed.

ten UNCIVIL ACTIONS

Y MOTHER MOVED TO BOSTON. MY FATHER
HAD DIED EIGHT YEARS EARLIER, AND AS
most of her friends and close relatives also passed away she was
becoming increasingly isolated. She was still in decent shape and was
excited about the move. I was as well. If my life in court was too hectic to see her every day, at least we would be in the same city.

It seemed like a good idea at the time.

I rented an apartment for her in the older Jewish neighborhood
of Brighton, just outside of Boston, and she hated it. "Where are all

the young people?" she complained. "I don't want to be around all these old people." We both had underestimated the difficulty of the move. At the age of seventy-six she was uprooting herself from everything she knew.

So my mother came to Boston and almost immediately I fell in love, or so I thought.

He was a lawyer. Irish. Big blue eyes, salt-and-pepper hair, athletic build. A bit older than I was, of course. I had known him professionally in the past but not socially. Then I got to know him at a function in May, as the days were getting warm, and fell immediately in love, in lust, out of my mind.

I had been dating constantly. The men I was attracted to were charismatic, accomplished, able to teach me concepts and bring me places I had never approached before. I found that sexy. This man had all of that.

I felt completely transported. He was fun; he was smart; he had a successful law practice. He was divorced. We made love that night in May and began the most intense sexual relationship I had ever known. We stayed up all night and I pulled myself out of bed to go to court. He was off to some golf tournament. When I got back to the office, I found he had sent me a dozen yellow roses. I had told him they were my favorites. What an attentive man.

When I wasn't working, I was with him. He traveled a great deal, particularly on weekends when he visited his daughters or moved around the country seeing clients. I understood; I was gallivanting around the country on weekends myself. I longed for him. *Longed* for him! I couldn't think of anything else.

He moved clothes into my apartment. We haunted romantic restaurants and drank together watching the stars twinkle from bars overlooking the waterfront. I just wanted to see him, to be with him. We were drinking a lot, and then I would have to get up at dawn to be back at work. I began to spend less time with my friends; I was either drinking with him or drinking alone.

He met my mother. I brought him to Chicago to meet my aunt Eve. He told them about a wonderful piece of land he had bought on

Cape Cod, where we were going to build a house. He was vibrant; we were all in love with him.

Another work-driven lawyer, he spent his time either with me or at the office. We talked during the day, met for drinks, went back to my apartment. On those nights when he had to go home, I missed him terribly

But occasionally he said he would meet me and he didn't arrive. That was strange. The first time he stood me up I found it rude, and told him, but he smiled and apologized, explaining that he had gotten overwhelmed at the office and by the time he'd looked up the hour of our date was long gone. I understood. I knew exactly how it felt to lose oneself in business.

When he missed a second date he was equally apologetic and I was equally understanding. A third established a pattern, a fourth my acquiescence. Men didn't treat me this way, but he did. Six weeks into the relationship I was confused but pining.

Then he began to miss dates consistently. The reasons changed, but I had to accept them all. I had no alternative; when he was absent from my bed I could not sleep. I needed him. My mother sometimes came by my apartment to find me crying and screaming and yelling at the walls about what this guy was up to. I was drinking more heavily now.

I was looking forward so gratefully to spending a July weekend with him. We had made wonderful plans. He was going to come pick me up and we were heading off for several days of romance. He called that morning to say he was running late. Okay, I told him, I'm here. An hour went by, another call. "I'll be there. I'm sorry. I'm coming." I understood. By midafternoon I was walking the floor. Another call. "I'll be there." By the evening I was sobbing hysterically. He never did show up.

I wouldn't have taken that from any other man, not for a day, not for an instant. What was this power he held over me? I did not know. He was a volatile blend of sex and romance. He was an addiction. I continued to see him and he continued to be unavailable on weekends, when I would drink with increased intensity in his absence.

We became notorious. The courthouse, as I've said before, is a small town, and it seemed as if everybody knew I was seeing this man. I could go to work and function, but my sleeplessness became noticeable and my abilities began to suffer.

Bill Delahunt got ahold of me by phone at my office. We needed to talk, he said.

Yes?

"This man is not divorced." What? Delahunt's words didn't register. "He is not even separated." I didn't believe him. How blind we can be. "I'm going to take you to the courthouse and show you there are no papers on file. You need to stop seeing him; he is killing your life."

Delahunt, of course, was correct. This man, this transforming lover of my life, was married with two children and had been having an extramarital affair with me without my knowing. When I confronted him, he said, "I'm not married; I'm divorced." Then it was, "Well, I'm not married; I'm really separated." Then, "Well, I don't live in the same house as my wife because I spend so much time with you."

At first, in the intense fever pitch of our sexual, alcohol-driven frenzy, I accepted each answer. I did not want to stop seeing this man; I didn't want to throw the switch on our highly charged affair. As he backpedaled, I was ready to believe anything he said. I waited for my yellow roses; I waited for his phone call; I waited for the knock on the door. And when they arrived, on *his* schedule, I was helplessly grateful.

But finally the humiliation took its toll. I woke up one morning and could not get out of bed. No client could rouse me; no partner could interest me; no work could produce the Siren song that would get me in motion. I called in sick and locked myself in my apartment.

Days passed. I lay in bed. I didn't answer the telephone. I didn't eat. The desperation, the humiliation. Finally my friend Joan Green pounded on my door and demanded that I let her in. I dragged myself downstairs and then shuffled back to the bedroom.

Joni sat on the end of my bed and looked at the clothes on the floor, the unwashed glasses scattered around the apartment. She looked at me. I hadn't bathed in several days. Why would I? She was shocked.

"You've got to see a therapist," she told me. "Your life is unraveling."

"No one can know this." I was mortified. How far I had fallen. How badly I had been deceived. "No one can know."

"No one knows, but I know." She moved around my home, picking up after me. "You have to get your life in perspective. You need to get out of this relationship." So she did know. Was I the only one who was unaware that this guy was lying to me? "You need to not work as hard as you're working. You need to find a way to work as a lawyer without killing yourself."

"I'm not seeing a shrink."

"Look at you. You're not eating."

"Stop it."

"I don't know how to reach you. Maybe a therapist will reach you."

She was right, of course. I may have been intransigent but I was not yet suicidal. With Joni's prodding I called the therapist I had seen when my marriage to Sandy had been breaking up. I had also seen her when my father died and I had needed someone to talk to. I saw her again.

Finally I had someone to tell what was happening to me. I was as successful as any woman lawyer could have wanted to be, but I was dying inside. No one knew what I was giving up to be successful, and for what? What had I done with my life? I was exhausted; I was constantly ill; I was working all the time. My relationships with men, I came to understand, were fractured and unsatisfactory and had been merely parentheses around my work. And when I had fallen in love, it was with a fraud of a man whom I had allowed to strip me of my self-esteem.

Through many hours of therapy we arrived at a plan to take control of my life. First, I needed to cut back on my drinking and become more physically healthy, to exercise regularly, to pay attention to what I ate, to save my body. If I carried myself with purpose, I would give myself purpose. Then I needed to end the relationship with this man. A strong engine inside me still roared for him. I needed to run that engine elsewhere.

My mother became involved. "I know you've fallen for him and he's not worth falling for," she told me. "What you saw was a great act. We all fell for it. But you didn't even have enough time to find out what a fantasy world he lives in. Thank God you didn't have a child with him."

"I actually thought about it."

"Oh, Rikki, a good mother has to nurture a child. You can't do that with your life. If you continue to work as a criminal defense lawyer, I don't see how you will have room for a child in your life." She could see she had upset me. "And you don't have to have a child." She was trying to ease what might have been pain. "You just don't have to, to make yourself feel fulfilled. But"—she was not one to soften her sentiments for long—"I would hate to see you have a child and never be there for her, and eventually come to resent your own child."

"I'd never thought about having children until I got into this relationship," I told her. "I would like to be a good mother, if I'm a mother." How very like me. The law, acting, childrearing—If I'm going to do it, I want to be good at it. "But I don't know how to stop what I'm doing and become a mother, unless I just stop what I'm doing."

"You don't want to do that."

"Maybe I do. I just tried for this judgeship."

"Rikki"—my mother was having none of it—"you thrive on performance. You love being in the courtroom. You may not love a lot of other things about your professional life, but your identity is geared to being a trial lawyer. I don't see you thriving as a mother."

Harsh but correct, not unlike my mother herself.

"Do you regret not having children?" she asked. I suspect she had wanted to ask me that question for quite some time.

"You know," I told her, "I don't. I was so busy, it's like I just forgot."

Despite the fact that I was in my late thirties and my biological clock was supposed to be ticking loudly, I hadn't heard it. I had never given serious thought to the idea of having children; they were not even a blip on my radar screen. First of all, I didn't know a man I was even remotely interested in marrying, and the concept of being a single mother had never dawned on me. And who had time for children? I was constantly jetting off to speak or to try a case; I couldn't be at

home every night nursing and nurturing. Most of my friends were
men, and criminal defense attorneys at that, which meant they were a
special kind of driven. If they had families, their wives were taking
care of the home. I was like the men.

Sometimes a woman's biological clock ticks loudest when the
alarm has just gone off on those around her. But none of my five closest women friends had children, so kids had simply never entered my
world nor I theirs. My elementary school friend Bonnie Typlin was
an unmarried pediatrician in Chicago. My college friend Lucie
Grosvenor was working as a designer of multimedia presentations in
New York. My criminal justice friend Brenda Ellis traveled to assist
lawyers like me on matters of sentencing and parole. In Boston,
Cheryl Delgreco was living with a criminal defense lawyer. We
shared joys and sorrows. No kids there. Joan Green had married a
man with children from a previous marriage who was not having
more. So I had no longings, no first thoughts, let alone second
thoughts, about having a baby. Driven men have kids all the time,
but they are not mothers; they have someone at home tending to the
offspring. Women are nurturers, at least the women who are mothers
should be nurturers. I was driven, and there was no space in my life
for a child. There was barely space for a man! Children simply could
not be an issue in my success-driven life.

Finally, I stopped seeing this man. He was killing me, literally.
It's a mark of the depths of my attachment, in my world of work-
induced total exhaustion, that it took me months to eradicate this
cancer from my life. One night when he didn't show up, I called and
called and called. Then I never called again. I reentered the world
like a cannonball. I went back to work with a vengeance and I found
another guy.

I continued to work hard; that wouldn't cease — it was who I was
and it was who Joel Kozol wanted me to be. I had taken two of
Werner Erhard's est training sessions in the early eighties when they
were in vogue, and several follow-up seminars. At each of those sessions, when asked to put on paper what I wanted to improve in my
life, I said I wanted to quit my job as a trial lawyer. Somehow, by

July of 1986, all my protestations to the contrary, I had done nothing on earth except further myself in my profession. Even when I spent time at a health spa, I had my accordion files with me.

As I advanced in my career, I frequented tonier post-work establishments. Now we were drinking at Maison Robert, an upscale French restaurant. One evening over drinks I was introduced to Barry Reed, a drop-dead-handsome older gentleman who had written the legal thriller *The Verdict*. Paul Newman played his leading man in the movie. Some months later Barry introduced me to a young lawyer in his firm by the name of Jan Schlichtmann. I suspect Barry thought this was a fix-up, but it didn't really dawn on me, and I'm sure it didn't occur to Schlichtmann. All he kept talking about was his cases. So he was one of us.

Jan was tall. I'm not even five foot three, so to me everyone is tall, but he was particularly thin and angular and made a habit of using his long arms to reach around the far side of his head when he was expressing himself. With thick, wiry brown hair and a large and pointed nose, he was a Jewish Abe Lincoln at the bar. We became friends, nothing more, and we would call each other regularly and collegially to discuss the details of our work. If he needed a fresh look at some evidence, or I needed an able mind to think around an issue, we would simply grab the phone. I would on occasion watch his opening arguments and he would watch mine. We were a nice support team.

Barry Reed had given Jan his wings on a case involving a number of plaintiffs who were suing the Copley Plaza Hotel over a very famous and lethal fire, and Jan had decided to stage a settlement presentation before all the lawyers and adjusters hired by the defendants. This was the pre–visual aids era, when lawyers routinely drew on butcher paper with Magic Markers to illustrate their ideas in court. "Come on over to the office," he said on the phone. It was Saturday, but of course he was at work. "I really want to show you something."

Jan had developed a photo mural, fifteen feet long and floor-to-ceiling in height, revealing in living color the progress of the fire as it moved from window to window, pane to pane in its devastation. Here was the fire at five minutes, at fifteen minutes, at one hour, at two hours. Here was what it would have looked like if the hotel had installed functional sprinklers, if the hotel's management had put the proper safety devices in service. The difference was shocking. Clearly, lives could have been saved. The visuals were extremely powerful.

This sort of show was simply not put on in the white-shoe, Yankee world of Boston. The Boston bar looked upon Jan as a showboat, a young Jewish whippersnapper. He made his presentation and got their settlement offer, the one they expected him to accept. He turned it down. When he phoned Barry Reed with the news, Reed was apoplectic. Barry needed someone to fume with. He called me. "Let's go have a drink." Drink in hand he did everything but pace the floor, waiting for the case to explode. Barry had no desire to go to trial with this case; there was an acceptable offer on the table; how dare this Schlichtmann reject it. They were never going to get this money. He had unleashed a monster!

Jan called. The case was settled. He had faced the Brahmins down. He had gotten even more money.

Jan's practice grew exponentially, as did his talent. In a case involving a paraplegic who was suing a hospital and surgeons for medical malpractice, his opening was eloquent. I sat in the courtroom and cried. If I had been on that jury he would have made me want to give this man every penny I possibly could. After closing arguments, when the jury had begun its deliberations, the defense made a settlement offer, which Jan rejected. Superior Court Judge Robert Steadman, a gentleman with a decorous manner, attempted to talk Schlichtmann into taking the offer, implying that Jan had rejected it out of hand and had not brought it to his client, a serious breach of legal ethics. Jan denied the charge, and Judge Steadman angrily informed him that because of his hubris, his client stood to lose everything.

My phone rang in the middle of the night. "You awake?" Oh, right. "The jury came back tonight with a question about liability, not damages." Jan was worried. If they were stuck on liability, did that mean there would be no damages altogether? Was he going to lose everything? Should he take the settlement?

"I can't advise you," I said. I was up out of bed by this time, pacing in front of my windows. "I can only talk you through it. What were the reasons you didn't take the offer in the first place?"

"Wasn't good enough. I can do better."

I rattled off all the questions I could think of. "What did you think your strong points were? How do you feel you connected with the jury? How do you feel your client and his family connected with them? How confident were you, because at four this afternoon you didn't take that offer. Was that real or were you just pushing it? That offer may not be on the table anymore. How confident are you in your case, and how confident are you in your passion for this case, should you take an offer you feel is inappropriate?" And all the while I told him, "You've got to talk to your client about this."

"Of course, of course." I had no idea whether he told his client or not. I have to assume he did.

I talked Jan through his anxiety, told him to follow his instincts, and hung up to allow him to make his decision. I was wide awake when I put the receiver down. Was this what being a trial lawyer was really all about, an elaborate game of poker? I knew exactly what Jan was going through; I had lived it myself. It was his case; it was all about him; and he didn't want to lose. Jan had lost perspective; he was on the ledge with an anvil, about to take his clients down if he wasn't offered the right incentive to come inside. My world was his; we weren't so much advocates for our clients as advocates for ourselves. We thought we knew better.

The sun rose, the day dawned, and Jan once again declined to settle. He chose to trust his ability to convince twelve people to see things his way.

The jury came back with a huge verdict for the plaintiff and we all celebrated. His career began to boom.

As he became more successful, Jan developed what he called his Five Rules of Settlement:

1. Be honest with yourself. Do you really want to settle? If the answer is yes, go on to the next rule. If the answer is

no, keep asking the question until the answer is yes—
otherwise, seek professional help;

2. Look for, exploit, or create opportunities to discuss settlement with the other side;
3. Be honest with the other side. Give rational, fact-based reasons for your position;
4. Give as much respect to the other side's rational, fact-based reasons for their positions as you would to your own;
5. Look for, acknowledge, and accept points of agreement until the dispute is resolved. If you feel that after applying these rules you are at an impasse, go back to rule 1.

I would add several of my own: Always be prepared. Research other settlement figures and verdicts that are similar to your case. Never exaggerate the merits of your claim. Stay focused. Stay calm. Stay credible. And most important: Force the other side to make the first offer.

I found myself in Puerto Rico at a judicial conference and one evening visited a casino with some colleagues. I had no sooner sat down to play some low-stakes blackjack than there was an uproar at the craps table. There was Jan Schlichtmann, dice in hand, screaming. He had money to play with. By this time his practice had skyrocketed. He was rolling in dough.

Jan was yelling with abandon, "Come on, baby, give me that six!" and a crowd was egging him on. The chips were coming to him; he was on a roll; he kept throwing and throwing without crapping out. I walked over and stood next to him.

"Stay here, Rikki. You'll bring me some luck."

I'm not a craps player—I prefer blackjack, where I can sit quietly with my little cards and ponder the odds. I like risk with control. That's why I like good judges, the ones who follow the rules, because I know what the rules are. Jan, on the other hand, was in a frenzy. He was hot, and he kept on being hot. When he finally did crap out he waited a beat and started rolling the bones again. He had an estimable stack of chips. I could see, standing beside him, that he was either going to make a lot of money that night or else lose it all.

Jan took a case against W. R. Grace & Co. and Beatrice Foods Co. brought by six families from Woburn, Massachusetts, all of whom had a member who had died of leukemia or was being treated for the disease. The case eventually grew to involve eight families and three corporate defendants. The suit alleged that the companies had contaminated the local groundwater, causing the leukemia and other significant diseases. Jan was convinced of and outraged by his perception of both the corporations' guilt and their brazen disregard for people's welfare, and he was determined to make them pay. He rejected settlement negotiations that reportedly might have reached eight million dollars, believing that the case could be worth several hundred millions, and proceeded to immerse himself in the suit, spending extravagant time and resources to right this wrong. He spent a fortune during discovery. This is the case that was at the center of Jonathan Harr's book and the movie *A Civil Action*.

"Rikki," he told me, "there is no way I'm going to lose the Grace case. There is no way. I have it all. I'm going to get the bastards. What they did is purely criminal. Not only am I going to get them in civil court, I'm going to make sure that they go after them criminally. What they did was kill those people."

I said, "Jan, you're spending money out of control. You're paying experts; you're traveling all over the place. You're not going to have enough money to meet your payroll."

"What are you talking about? I have plenty of money." Indeed his career had been thriving and he was quite wealthy. "There's nothing for me to worry about."

"Just be careful. You're not trying other cases; you're totally consumed. All you're doing is working on the Grace case. If it doesn't go your way, you have other people to think about. You have two partners; you have associates; you have people who have been with you for years and who depend on you."

"You worry too much."

"I've seen you roll the dice."

When the jury came in, he had won a partial victory against Grace; he had lost against Beatrice entirely. Jan had crapped out.

I was late arriving at the courthouse and found it buzzing with the media, so I ran to Jan's office. I knew he would be shaken. I grabbed him by the hand. "You're devastated, right?"

"Yes."

He was going to appear in New York on *Good Morning America* the next day and I said, "You've got to go down there and act like you really won. Like you won it all. Your whole attitude on television is how you have righted the wrong. *You cannot look sad!* You sound disappointed; you cannot *look* disappointed. You cannot look like they've run over you. There is spin here; you won and you lost. You've got to choose to say that you won!"

My pep talk was highly unsuccessful. "Will you go with me to New York?" he asked mournfully. He clearly needed both coaching and simple warmth. "I'm taking Tom Kiley [the attorney with whom he had tried the case] and Anne Anderson [the lead plaintiff]. Can you come with me?"

One of his partners said, "You'd better go. You need to take care of him because he's going to be a basket case by tomorrow."

I grabbed a change of clothes at my apartment (Jan sent someone out to buy a shirt, underwear, and socks) and we drove to the airport. In the lounge as we waited for takeoff Kiley said, "You've got to help him. He's despondent, depressed. He's nearly suicidal."

"I'll take care of it," I promised.

At the hotel in New York, Jan booked a room for Anne and then there were three of us. He took two more rooms and we headed for the bar. I rehearsed him like a media coach for the next morning's appearances, but Jan was inconsolable. He was not simply dealing with the disappointment of a huge financial loss and the embarrassment of being the losing attorney in the face of a frenzied media; he was wracked with guilt for having failed his clients. He believed W. R. Grace and Beatrice had killed those families, and he had not been able to make it right. We were drained, and when it came time to go upstairs it seemed natural that Jan and I would spend the night together.

I understood it and I didn't understand it. I was dating someone, and he had been seeing the same woman for years, but that night we came together as friends. We counted on each other; I was there with warmth and affection, which was what he wanted and needed. I wanted to comfort him and support him and make his pain go away. Most of all, as a trial lawyer, I wished I could erase the verdict so he did not feel as if the world were falling apart and it was all his fault. I knew what that felt like.

We never resumed an intimate relationship, though from time to time I did think it might be a good idea if I were to marry Jan. He was smart; he was fun; he was Jewish; and he was a very good friend. We completely understood each other's mania for the practice of law—he was every bit as crazy as I was—and we talked all the time. It was just a thought.

Several years earlier, my friend Susan Haar had fixed me up with real estate and media mogul Mort Zuckerman. (Susan, an assistant district attorney with me in Middlesex, was a good buddy. In our younger days we had shopped together at Marshall's and Loehmann's and Filene's Basement, and she had showed me how to find bargains like I'd never seen in my life. My mother would have wholeheartedly approved.) Zuckerman and I had met for a drink, and there was no chemistry between us. Then, about five years later, he became a Friedman & Atherton client.

Zuckerman, who was chairman and editor in chief of *U.S. News & World Report,* had purchased *The Atlantic Monthly* magazine but came to believe that the sellers had misrepresented the magazine's financial status, so he was suing them for fraud. Essentially he felt that instead of a magazine with significant growth potential, he had knowingly been sold something quite less. After he stopped payment on his promissory note, the sellers, the Atlantic Monthly Co., filed counter-claims against him. This was about money.

But it was also about ego and style and tradition. This was Boston, an extremely ethnically conscious town, and this Jew had come in and bought a venerable institution of intellectual discourse from a collection of WASPs. No one said such a thing out loud, but it was the primary subtext and difficult to ignore. Mort wasn't one of them, and it was immediately clear to me that the sellers, quiet and sedate people that they appeared, thought he deserved what he got. And here we were, the Jewish law firm, representing him.

Joel assembled his "high-priority" team and I was honored to be drafted as second chair. Economic issues were not my strength, to say the least; I would have to study hard to begin to understand the nuances, but Joel was obsessed with the case and therefore so was I.

Mort Zuckerman was a tough master. He was a lawyer himself, and a very smart man, and he wanted things done his way. You're the plumber, he believed, fix the drain. We obliged. Joel and all of us worked as if it were a death penalty case. I understood the intellectual and financial basis for such devotion—we were lawyers and we served our clients to the utmost of our abilities—but was this in the public interest? A murder trial was one thing, a person's life was at stake. But it seemed to me we were eating up months of the federal court's time and a sizable amount of the taxpayers' money on a case that should have gone to an arbitrator.

The load of work was overwhelming. This was a paper case, and we were faced with room after room of discovery material, a warehouse of Zuckerman boxes. I spent months doing nothing but reading documents, trying to make sense of this thing. I ate at my desk, stayed until midnight, read in bed. I had little other life than this case. Trial fever. I was getting bone thin. As another night fell and I was straining to read through one more deposition, I had only a few thoughts: I'm hungry; I'm tired; I can think of nothing else but what's in front of me; and Joel must be very proud of me. That was most important of all.

One of the lawyers working on the case, John Rosenberg, left the office one evening well after midnight. When he got home, he was quite surprised to see his wife, Shari, standing in the kitchen waiting for him. What was she doing up?

"Joel called. Ten minutes ago."

"I'm sorry, honey." Not only did she not have her husband around at night, now the boss was waking her up. As they were discussing what an unusual character the boss actually was, the phone rang. It was, of course, Joel. He was incredibly chipper and quite pleasant.

"Where've you been?" Joel was phoning from home. "I called you at the office."

"You must have called while I was driving home."

"Well, I've been thinking about the case . . ." Without missing a beat, Joel launched into a new strategy for the case and a new motion we ought to file.

Standing in his kitchen, John thought, This guy is nuts. I've got to get to bed. Then he thought, You know, this is a brilliant strategy he has come up with. When Joel was finished talking, John said, "That is an excellent way to proceed."

"Draft the motion."

"Do you have a timetable?"

"We have to do this immediately. I'd like to see a draft on my desk at nine."

"Uh, Joel, it's two in the morning."

"Oh, that's all right," Joel said obligingly. "No problem. Have it to me by ten."

It was a measure of the respect and affection we all held for Joel, coupled with our own insanity, that John got four hours of sleep, returned to the office, dictated a draft of the motion, tweaked it a bit, and gave it to the boss by deadline. They polished it all afternoon and filed by the end of the day. Some people would hate a boss like that. Not John. He wasn't angry that he was working half to death; he wasn't upset that his family's life had been disrupted; instead, John was excited to be working at such high quality under such unrelenting pressure for a mentor who was teaching him important lessons by lunatic example.

As we approached trial Joel became even more deeply entrenched. "We all have too many interruptions at the office," he insisted. Other clients had the temerity to require our attention during the daytime. Husbands, wives, and lovers actually wanted to see us at night. "Here's what we're going to do. Everybody involved in this case is going to move into the Bostonian Hotel to prepare for trial." This was not up for discussion. We took a group of rooms on one floor and started the Zuckerman work farm. I remember think-

ing, Will we ever get out of this hotel? I don't think we left the building except to go to court.

In addition, I had been teaching a class in trial practice one night
a week at Boston University School of Law. No matter where in the
country I found myself, I would come home to teach that class. Students were depending on me and I did not want to disappoint them.
Joel was not pleased on those nights when I actually left the office at
the unconscionable hour of 4:00 P.M. to preside. I was back by 7:00
and would put in several more hours before I finally turned in.

I had created a tradition of hosting an end-of-semester cocktail
party for my students at my apartment, after I had delivered their
grades. The party was catered by Debbie Sampson, Joe Oteri's girlfriend, and I made a practice of inviting my lawyer friends to meet
them, a big hit for third-year law students who would not otherwise
have many opportunities to talk shop informally with real trial lawyers.
In May 1987 the Zuckerman trial had started. I was not examining a
witness the following day. I told Joel on the way out of court, "I'm having this cocktail party for my students at my apartment; I need to go."

"You can't go."

"It's my home. It's my students!"

"We have to work."

This was nonnegotiable, or at least I couldn't negotiate it. My
mother had intended to help out, so she would be there. I called the
man I was dating. I had been seeing him for about two weeks, after
ten at night, of course. "Will you help my mother out? Joel is not letting me leave." He said not to worry.

I went back to the office and worked and paced. How dare he!
Were we chattel? Did we have no lives whatsoever? Finally I found
Joel. "Can I go for a half hour?" I asked meekly.

"All right. A half hour. Go."

I lived the better part of a half mile away and I ran to my apartment. I apologized to my students and spoke briefly, but they were
fine; they had lots of lawyers to talk to. My mother spoke with them
all, of course. I couldn't have been home fifteen minutes before I ran
back to the office and worked until midnight.

I was furious. How unfair to me, how unfair to my students. But if I had been first chair, I probably would have felt the same way. Of course, mine would be a murder case with more riding on it than pride and money, but the principle was the same: We work.

When I cross-examined a key financial player, Arthur Gooderal, the Atlantic Monthly Co.'s treasurer, he looked at me and saw a girl he could get the better of. I looked at him and saw the arrogance of power. He treated me brusquely, which no jury likes to hear. I responded by coming to court wearing feminine dresses and light suits in pastel colors; I wanted to establish in the jury's mind that he was the bully, I was the nice girl. And when I arrived in court with huge blowups of company documents, including a directive to Gooderal to "shave a point here and there," he wasn't as tough a witness as he wanted to be.

After months of aggressive research, Bostonian confinement, high-risk cross-examination and seventeen-hour work days, I had lost ten pounds and developed an infection I didn't have the strength to fight off. I was woozy during Joel's closing argument, but I could not allow the jury to see me as anything but intensely concerned. I concentrated on his words, which were brilliant. For a moment the room began to spin. Please, not now, not in front of the judge, the jury, the press. Then I refocused. Joel finished speaking. I stood to greet him as he returned. The jury filed out. I collapsed on the table, crumpled, and passed out. When I came back to life I had only two thoughts: Did I make a fool of myself? and Did I disappoint Joel? He was so euphoric from his brilliant closing that I don't think he even noticed!

The jury found the sellers liable for misrepresenting the magazine's financial condition but not liable for fraud. Mort Zuckerman was found to have defaulted on the promissory note. To many observers it looked like a draw. I came away with the realization that I couldn't do that again, ever.

The real question was, Who won? It was back to the mixed verdict and the ultimate media spin, just like Jan Schlichtmann all over again, and again, and again.

eleven

MY FRIEND
BECOMES MY SAVIOR

I N 1981 A BOATLOAD OF CASH LED ME TO
PHILIP BRADY.

When I was at Choate, Hall & Stewart I was approached by one
of my first potentially big clients in the world of crime and drugs. My
assignment, should I accept it, was to review the work being done by
another lawyer representing this man's friend, John Dickinson, in a
passport violation trial to be held in New York. Dickinson, the government suspected, was the financier or kingpin of a marijuana-

smuggling operation. But the government had no proof of that. My guy wanted to make sure his friend was being well represented.

This was an unusual proposition, but it did happen from time to time. There was nothing sinister about it, just a man who was worried about the state of his friend's defense. And considering all I was doing was observing and making an assessment of the job being done by a fellow criminal defense lawyer, this seemed an ethically proper and easy way to make some money. I observed, found, and reported no complaints, submitted my bill for my time plus expenses, and was paid.

Time went by. About two years later I received a call from a man named Kenneth Leonard who had been arrested in Singapore. He had gone to the American authorities to renew his passport and had been detained when a background check revealed he was a fugitive from justice. He had then been brought to the nearest U.S. territory, which was Hawaii, and arrested. Leonard was about to be shipped back to Boston to face charges. The problem was, he had been unaware that he was a fugitive. If he had known, surely he would not have waltzed into a U.S. government office in a foreign country and asked for assistance. The stamps on his passport showed he had been in and out of the United States several times since he was originally charged with making a false statement to a government official.

Kenny Leonard had my number in his pocket. How? He was a boat captain who claimed (falsely, according to the government) to have worked with famed oceanographer Jacques Cousteau on various vessels, and he was aware of the work I had done for my other watchful client. Apparently my name was getting around in certain navigation circles.

At the time of his call I was in Atlanta, working with Bobby Lee. "I can't be in Hawaii or Boston right now," I told him, "but I'll do two things for you. Number one, I'm going to get you a lawyer in Hawaii. Number two, I'm going to get you a lawyer in Boston for purposes of your arraignment and bail hearing."

I called Brook Hart. If you get in trouble in Hawaii, that's what you do. I explained the case. "He's going back to Boston, but I don't want him to go back in shackles," I said.

"Don't worry, I'll take care of it," he told me.

"I'm not worried. I know who he's associated with. There will be money to pay your fee."

"Thank you very much."

The feds are not generous with fugitives from justice. They play with them. Left to their own devices they would have flown Leonard from Hawaii to California, then bused him from one federal prison to another to another, all the way across the country. It would have taken weeks. Brook Hart did what he does and Kenny Leonard arrived in Boston, by air, unshackled, in record time. Bill Brown, a Boston attorney whom I also called, walked him through his arraignment, and Kenny Leonard was out on bail. When I returned, he came to my office.

He was the sweetest guy, almost cherubic, with curly red hair, a light in his eye, and a crinkling smile. I am, of course, bound by attorney-client privilege to maintain silence about our conversations. However, this is what he permitted me to tell the government:

Years earlier, Kenny Leonard had worked on a boat in Nova Scotia and left Halifax with a briefcase containing fifty thousand dollars in cash. When he came through Boston's Logan Airport, he had not checked off the box on the Customs form that asked whether one had more than five thousand dollars. During the course of a simple questioning, not an interrogation, he was asked what he had been doing in Canada. He answered that he had been working on a boat that was dry-docked there. When the Customs officials ran the name of the boat through their computer, bells and whistles started sounding. According to their records, that boat had been involved in drug smuggling. They opened Leonard's briefcase and found the fifty grand. Jackpot.

Kenny thought he had been forthright; he didn't have more than five thousand dollars because it wasn't *his* money; it belonged to the boat's owner, who had not been in Nova Scotia at the time he departed. He was traveling with it so as not to leave such a large and enticing amount of cash unattended in Canada. He hadn't realized he was supposed to check that box.

The Customs officials had confiscated the money and let Kenny go. He returned to Singapore, where he had a lovely wife and later a baby. In the intervening years he had come in and out of the United States regularly without incident, and because no one had stopped him, and he had given up the money, he had assumed everything was fine. He had no idea he was a fugitive.

What he didn't know was that, after letting Kenny walk, Customs filed an indictment against him for making false statements to a Customs official. The indictment was sealed and at some point they went looking for him. When they couldn't find him, the whole case went into the files, where it stayed until he walked into the government office in Singapore to renew his passport.

This was foolish. Kenny Leonard didn't need to go to jail. I was going to plead him guilty, agree to have him pay a fine, and let him go back to Singapore to his wife and child. The government could keep the original fifty thousand dollars. This was not a hard case to make.

I spoke to the prosecutor, John LaChance. "John, come on. He didn't know he was a fugitive. The evidence is clear by his passport. So he had some cock-and-bull story about the money, so be it. No one can say he is in the marijuana business now or that he has been in the marijuana business for years. Look, let's plead him guilty, let's get him some probation, let's get him back to Singapore, and we are done with him and you've got the money."

John, who was a nice guy, said, "I really can't make this decision myself. I need to talk to the Customs agent. Better yet, you go talk to the agent."

"I don't want to talk to the agent. I'm talking to you; you're the prosecutor."

"This is a Customs case," he explained, "and Customs has strong feelings about it. You need to talk to the agent, Philip Brady."

I didn't know Brady so I called around. A Bureau of Alcohol, Tobacco, and Firearms agent with whom I had worked as a prosecutor said, "He has a good reputation. He's really straight, very tough."

"Will you say something to him? Will you vouch for my credibility?"

"Yeah, sure."

Twenty minutes later I got Brady on the phone. He was pretty straightforward.

"What are you talking to me for? You should be talking to the prosecutor."

"I just did, but he really would like it if I would talk to you. And I would really like to talk to you now."

"I'm not going to plea-bargain a case with you. That is for the prosecutor to do."

"I would like to see you," I said, "and I'm coming over right now."

I thought I simply walked into his office. Brady says I came in knocking down walls with a bulldozer. "May I sit down?" I asked. He glared at me. Glared at me!

"Who do you think you are, Joyce Davenport?" *Hill Street Blues* was in full swing, and she was the attractive yet cantankerous public defender. I laughed it off—*ha, ha, ha*—but thought, Uh-oh, this is not going to work out very well.

Brady was another redheaded Irishman: white-white skin, big green eyes, a wide-body fellow with an athletic, masculine air about him. I gave him my whole spiel verbatim and all the while he was drumming his fingers on his desk. He didn't like me one bit; I was one of "those" people, criminal defense lawyers coming to law enforcement looking for civilized treatment for their scum clients.

He asked the obvious question. "Okay, you want me to do all this for him. What is he going to do for me?"

I said, "Nothing."

"Yeah, right."

"He is not going to do anything."

"You're telling me you want me to give this guy a pass. You want to send him happily home to Singapore, and he is not even going to cooperate with me?"

"Well, you can talk to him; I don't think he has anything to tell you. He doesn't know anything."

"He knows plenty. John Dickinson is a big marijuana smuggler. He knows John Dickinson, and he knows he knows John Dickinson. He either cooperates with me about Dickinson or I have nothing to say to you."

"Well then, we have nothing to say to each other. And I'm going to tell you, he is going to get a plea and he is going to walk out and you are going to give him his passport."

"It is time for you to leave."

"Fine."

"Fine."

That didn't go well at all.

Logic won out. I pleaded Leonard with LaChance. He got his passport back—I made Brady get him his passport back—and he went off to Singapore. Brady, of course, was furious.

Years went by. I would occasionally run into Brady in the street. He would nod at me, I would nod at him. We did not think highly of each other.

In 1984 a boat called *Ramsland* was stopped by Customs officials as it headed for Boston Harbor. Onboard were thirty-six tons of marijuana. Five Americans and the British crew were charged. Everyone hired a lawyer, and many of my Maison Robert friends were involved in the case. I was not. It went to trial. I was in my office when I received a call from one of the attorneys, my dear friend Brian McMenimen, saying that the crew members had been acquitted. The bales of marijuana had not been in plain sight but were buried in the ship's hold under 321 tons of gravel, and the prosecution had not been able to prove that all the members of the crew had knowledge the pot was onboard.

"This is amazing," I said.

"What is amazing about it," said Brian, "is that there was an agent in the case who could have shaded his testimony one way or the other, just stretched it a little bit, and it would have shown that somebody on the crew could have seen or smelled or might have known the marijuana was onboard. He didn't, and as a result, these people walked. They walked!"

"Who was the agent?"

"Philip Brady."

"No way! Brady is tough as nails."

"Well, he is a tough guy but he told the truth."

"Incredible."

"We're having a victory party over at Maison Robert right now. Drop whatever you're doing and come on over." Being the true criminal defense lawyer that I was, that's exactly what I did.

The bar was hopping. It's not often that you get a whole group of people off, and there were lawyers, clients, friends, relatives, all hooting and hollering in jubilation. I dove right in. An hour or two later — who was counting? — who walked in but Philip Brady.

This was a pretty gutsy move, a federal agent dropping in on a defense lawyer's victory party. What could have possessed him? Brian had invited him, and my guess was that Brady was curious how this side actually lived. I had had enough to drink that I approached him.

"I heard you were really honest on the stand. I think that is really commendable." He looked down at me with disdain. "I always respect an honest law enforcement officer, and my clients have always said to me that if they're convicted for something they did, fine. They understand, especially in the marijuana business, that if you did the crime you do the time. What they can't abide are law enforcement agents who lie to get convictions and steal drugs in the process. I really respect you."

Brady was moving through the crowd like an icebreaker. He barely stopped for me. "Thank you very much," he said, and kept on going. He didn't stay long.

From then on, when we passed each other in the street, instead of nodding curtly we would say, "Hello, how are you?" and go on our ways. I ran into him several times at a late-lunch, burger-and-beer joint called Clark's, where public servants routinely finished their day. As we became familiar faces, we stopped and talked and the old hard feelings finally eased away.

In the early winter of 1987 I got a call from one of our group, Tom Heffernon, who said that Brady's wife was very ill and in the hospital, and he and some friends had become a support group for Philip, keeping him company after his day at the hospital, taking him out for a drink, buying him dinner on the weekends. The man was going through a hard time and his friends were trying to be helpful, so they invited me along. He wasn't a bad guy, so I joined the gang.

Brady was very drained when we saw him, but we all had the feeling that we were doing him some good. He became one of our crew. The tough agent, it turned out, had a soft side.

Brady's wife died in early May. Her illness had dragged on for months and he had come to terms with the fact of her leaving. We consoled him as he grieved.

At some point he said to me, "Do you want to have dinner this weekend?"

"Are you asking me on a date?" I wondered.

"Yeah."

"That's ridiculous. You and I are colleagues and friends. I'm not going on a date with you."

"Well, you should try it; you might like it."

"Philip, don't be crazy. We're pals."

"You'll be able to see that our relationship has unlimited potential." What an extraordinary declaration of intention! "Let's go do something on Sunday afternoon." Well, we had certainly spent time together before; maybe a Sunday afternoon would put this foolishness to rest.

Sunday dawned bright and beautiful. Philip picked me up at my apartment and we walked to Charlestown, where we visited the Bunker Hill Monument. He turned out to be a history buff and as we walked Philip filled me full of Boston lore, of which I was quite ignorant and which I found fascinating. We ambled from place to place, the air crisp, the hours passing with ease. For dinner he took me to the Front Page, a lively and casual steak-burgers-BBQ-chicken place. Then he walked me back to the North End and home.

In front of my building he said, "See. You had a good time, didn't you? Didn't hurt, did it?"

"I had a very nice time."

"We're going to do this again." He was quite convinced.

"Well," I demurred, "let's think about it. We really are friends. You're going through a lot of trauma. I want to be there to help you, but I certainly don't know that this is the right time for you to be thinking about going out with somebody."

"That's my issue," he said evenly. "That is not your issue."

"Let's think on it."

He kissed my cheek and walked away.

The following week I was in Washington, D.C., for a meeting of the NACDL. Philip sent a dozen roses to my hotel.

My friend was courting me.

I was more than a little confused. I was dating somebody, for one. But I was always dating somebody. I was never ready for a committed relationship, and that seemed to be what Philip was after. And no matter how prepared he thought he might be, he was still extremely vulnerable.

I was out one night after work, sitting in Maison Robert having a drink with a girlfriend, taking the long view. "You know," I told her, "my life is so screwed up. I'm exhausted. I'm tired all the time. The only thing I live for is trying cases. That's the only time I'm truly engaged. My medicine chest looks like a pharmacy. I'm tired of jetting all over the country. I'm tired of having some fancy man in some fancy car take me to some fancy place when it has no meaning." I think I actually sighed. "Maybe I should just go out with Philip Brady and marry him."

My friend said to me, "It would not be the worst thing that could happen to you."

I sat there and thought very rationally, If I marry Philip, my life will get straight. He was a decent person who was thankful to me for saving him from falling to the depths of despair. He would value me as a person. He had seen me through many crises from afar and from near. I was already very open with him; I could tell him my problems and listen to his.

Clearly he was attracted to me. And clearly he had liked being married. I think many widowers, if their marriage had been strong, want to remarry. They enjoy that style of living; they like married life. Philip had said many times that he did not want to be alone. He wanted a stable relationship. I'd never actually tried that, so who knows—maybe I would, too. Philip owned an idyllic red house on a dead-end street in the leafy Boston suburb of Milton. There were horses at the house next door. I could calm down and discard all my daily garbage and escape the dread and just settle down.

This could be a good match, one in which I might actually sur-vive and thrive. Otherwise, I thought, there's a real chance that I might be dead before I was forty.

In the early summer I was invited to travel to Australia and New Zealand with a group of lawyers on a People to People program to exchange ideas concerning criminal justice with lawyers and judges Down Under. I was honored to be invited and was excited about making the trip, not least because since I was eight years old I'd had a pen pal who lived in Sydney and this trip presented a wonderful opportunity for us to meet. I told Philip about it and he said he would love to go.

All the program's literature spoke of "you and your spouse," so I contacted the people in charge and asked if I could bring someone who was not my spouse. They hesitated. No one has ever asked that question, they told me. (Or certainly no woman had dared to ask.) "We think it would be more appropriate to bring a spouse," they said.

Meanwhile, I was in the middle of the Zuckerman trial. It was Philip whom I called to help my mother at the law students' party, and it was Philip with whom I recuperated.

Philip was working with a large number of law enforcement per-sonnel investigating drug smuggling around Martha's Vineyard, Nantucket, and Cape Cod. His group was stationed on the Vineyard. "Why don't you come with me?" he said.

"What are you going to tell your law enforcement friends?"

"I think it's okay. Obviously you can't take a case, or know any-thing about a case, that might be investigated here."

"I don't want to know what's being investigated here."

"Why don't you come?"

I spent ten wonderful days with Philip on Martha's Vineyard, just hanging around the Westerly, a monstrous, rickety hotel. We were both recreational runners, so we woke up early each morning and ran together. I could go three; he ran six miles at a clip. He had lost his health while caring for his wife and was trying to put himself back together, so we ate carefully and well. I remember Philip going on a search for an apple! While he was working, I spent much of the day sitting in one of the twenty rocking chairs perched on the wooden porch that faced Oak Bluffs Harbor, watching the fishing boat armada sail in. Other times I would go down to the beach. Sooner or later he would join me. I wasn't being a lawyer; I was taking a vacation. So this was what that felt like!

I certainly stayed out of Philip's group discussions. Sometimes they conducted missions, I assume to watch planes and boats they suspected of running drugs. Philip went out once or twice, but most nights, as agent in charge, he sent out his underlings and stayed with me. We were two great friends who loved being together and, quite miraculously, had found we could have a romance in our lives. But I must say, the romance was secondary to this sense of well-being, which was so very appealing to us both.

At some point over that summer it became clear to me that it would be better to be married to Philip than to be married to Joel, which was how I felt. Joel was my life; I worked for him fifteen hours a day and was his in spirit the rest of the time, but I was very unhappy. And here was Philip, who understood my being a lawyer but was not going to make those kinds of demands on me.

We discussed the trip to New Zealand. He said, "Well, why don't we get married and I'll go with you!"

"Okay," I said. "Sounds like a fun idea."

So we were engaged.

I called Cheryl Delgreco, who was thrilled. I called my mother, who loved Philip from the day she'd met him. She said, "I'm very happy you are doing this. He is a good person and he is very stable and you need some stability in your life. But it is way too soon. It is improper."

"That's absurd, Mom. We want to get married. I'm going on this trip. We can get married now. What am I going to do, wait for another year under some false notion of propriety so that someone can say, 'He mourned his wife for a year'?"

"I don't like the way it looks."

"You have an old-fashioned idea about this."

"All right," she said, "but it doesn't look right."

We got married outdoors at his home in Milton on an acre of greenery surrounded by a wonderful gray brick wall. It felt like we were in Ireland. September 20, 1987. It rained all week and the wind was howling and everyone froze to death and ruined their shoes, but all our friends who loved us were there. We ate and drank and told courtroom stories. Our friends saw us as each other's saviors: I had saved Philip from the death grip of loneliness and despair; he had rescued me from all the madness I could not find my way out of. My mother, despite her reservations, was pleased. She said, "I'm very glad that you are fine. This is good for you." She danced at my wedding.

Mom had wanted to die since the day my dad passed away. Her life revolved around her husband and involved him intimately. The only reason she kept on living was to make sure I was taken care of. As soon as Philip and I were married—you could have timed it with a stopwatch—she began to fade. She had moved to Charlestown, where she was pleased to be surrounded by young people, but as time went on she began having trouble even walking out to the benches at the harbor. Her great joy in life had been going to the grocery store; she would intend to shop for ten minutes and emerge an hour and a half later with large baskets of goodies and expansive plans for wonderful meals. She still navigated her way to the supermarket but by December she was using the shopping cart as a walker.

We visited her every week, but each visit found her less mobile until she simply took to her bed. When she was a child, my mother had stepped on a nail, become seriously ill, and was put in a hospital isolation ward. She hated hospitals; she hated doctors. When I was twelve, I came home to find her near death from bronchitis. My father was away on business. She could not breathe, and I had to call my pediatrician to come see her because she refused to go to a doctor. Thank goodness for house calls.

So having a discussion with my mother about doctors fell on deaf ears.

I was beyond despondent. I adored my mother; I could not bear to see her deteriorate. And yet a part of me understood that she was an intelligent, perceptive woman and she was choosing to die. I was in a quandary. Quite selfishly, I wanted her to be better *for me*. I loved

Out on the town with the adults: At age 5, with Aunt Eve, Dad, and Mom.

With my mother in Chicago.

Dressed as Peter Pan for a Jack and Players production in Chicago.

College days: With Alba Houghton Briggs III at Northwestern, 1969.

Acting portfolio photo, 1970.

Getting married to Sandy Wesman,
June 1974.

With a *kvelling* dad, law school
graduation, 1975.

David Levin and his Mercedes at the balloon ranch, Del Norte,
Colorado, 1976.

A true hero for his commitment to causes, Morris
Dees of the Southern Poverty Law Center at
Spence's ranch, July 1994.

Happily married: With (from left) surrogate mom Evan Frances, Bill,
Judge Leslie Crocker Snyder, and my former husband Alex Wesman,
who gave me away, April 30, 1999.

Off to Court TV:
Former DA Bill Delahunt
(now Congressman Delahunt) and
former Massachusetts Attorney General
Frank Bellotti with me at my going-away
party, September 1994.

Going round and round through life:
Our engagement on the Central Park
carousel, February 1994.

"Hello, Aunt Eve!" Making a call from the
Lincoln Bedroom, December 1999.

Can you have it all?
Giving a speech of that name
at a Women's Bar Association
meeting, Fall 1999.

Representing George Washington
in London with fellow
barrister James Doyle at an
ABA mock trial, July 2000.

Young at heart: With Bill
in Chicago, 2001.

With my pals: Mickey Sherman, Ed Hayes, Bill, and Joe Tacopina.

The Quogue visitors: With Andrew Dornenburg, Karen Page,
Evan Frances, and Bill, Summer 2001.

Life is perfect: With Bill, November 2001.

her, and now that I finally was happy I wanted to spend time with her. To be happy in the presence of my mother—that would be a joy.

I called my own doctor. "Whatever it costs, I'm begging you, will you come with me to see my mother and maybe we can get her into a hospital? I can't move her. She refused even to talk to me about a doctor, and it is clear to me that she is dying. You have to come see her."

Dr. Joel Siner met me in Charlestown on a Saturday morning. I let myself in, got her mail, and brought it to her bedside. "Mother," I said as I came into the room, "I have someone to see you. Can I bring him in?"

"Yes."

She looked dreadful. She was bone thin but her stomach was bloated and enormous. Dark rings sunk her eyes and she just looked so tiny. My mother peered at the man who entered the room behind me.

"You must be Dr. Siner," she said.

"Yes." He smiled. "How did you know?"

"I knew Rikki would not be satisfied until she brought someone here."

"May I examine you?"

She agreed and he asked her questions and touched various parts of her body. She did not resist.

"Mrs. Klieman," he said, "I don't know what is wrong with you. I'm sure that if we could take you to the hospital we could make you feel much more comfortable than you are now. We might even be able to get you better. Why don't you come with me and your daughter. We'll just drive over there."

"No, Dr. Siner, I'm not going to do that."

"You really are causing your daughter a lot of worry."

"I'll think about it." I knew she wouldn't.

The doctor tried to discuss her diet but she wasn't listening; she was sweet but she wasn't listening. I asked if there was anything I could do. Could I get her anything—a sandwich, the newspaper, a glass of juice? "No, I'm all right," she told me. "I know you feel much better now that you brought Dr. Siner over."

"I do, but I wish you would take him up on his offer. I'd be happy to take you. Philip and I will drive you over and this will be good for you."

She wasn't going anywhere.

I left town Sunday night to handle some case for Joel, a civil proceeding having to do with Archer Daniels Midland somewhere near Springfield, Illinois. I called my mother but she wasn't picking up the phone. That didn't mean much. My mother could go for days without answering the phone; she couldn't care less, she talked when she felt like talking. That was my mother, her way of life. I wasn't alarmed but I did miss her. I just wanted to say hi.

One day passed. Two days passed. I returned to Boston and something inside told me things were not right. I called the next morning and got nothing but a premonition. I called Philip at work. "We've got to go to my mother's apartment now. She hasn't answered the phone in three days, we have to go there now."

Philip drove me to Charlestown. I picked up her mail from the box and let myself into her apartment, expecting to find her very ill.

I did not expect to find her dead.

We opened the front door onto her body. She was lying half on her side on the floor of the galley kitchen, her feet toward the door. There was some red Jell-O spilled on the kitchen floor next to her; there were stockings soaking in detergent in the bathroom sink. The last moments of her life preserved. I screamed.

Philip had been a police officer in Providence, Rhode Island, before he'd become a federal agent. He had seen dead bodies before. "Just take my hand," he said. "Don't look down." I did as he instructed. He had me step over the body and then sat me down in her bedroom—"You sit right here"—and returned to the kitchen. When he came back he said, "Your mother is dead."

"I know." I couldn't stop crying.

My mother didn't drink, but she kept a bottle of scotch in the apartment for Philip and me. He went and poured me a drink straight up. "Just take a couple of sips of this," he said.

Philip took charge. I could not speak. He called the police, who took forever to arrive because the woman was deceased, so what were they going to do about it except ship the body to the morgue. I was afraid to go out; I did not want to see my mother's body. Neither did Philip. We were prisoners in the bedroom. When the police did finally arrive, he dealt with them.

We would hold the funeral in Chicago, where she would be buried next to my father. But you cannot ship a dead body unless it has been embalmed—a piece of information you really only find out when you can least handle it—so Philip called the funeral home who had tended to his wife. Leave it to Philip to have experience in such things. But that was a Catholic home, who told us we ought to contact a Jewish funeral home in Chicago because they might have differing requirements. Through it all, Philip handled every detail. He called Joel and told him I would be gone from work. He called my secretary and said, "Cancel everything for two weeks." He was very efficient, very reliable. He was that kind of guy. We had been married four months.

Whatever relatives were left came to my mother's funeral. My friends from high school and other days came as well. It was a terrible day for me. My whole vision of the world had begun through the eyes of my mother. I had the strength and confidence to stand up in front of a crowd and act on stage, or in front of a judge and jury and deliver a closing argument, because she had told me from before I could remember that I was wonderful, that I was beautiful, that I was remarkable. Now who was going to tell me I could be anything I wanted? Who was going to tell me to pursue my dreams? Who was going to love me? I hoped I could do that for myself, that my mother had not simply swaddled me in confidence but had imbued me with it. What a wonderful gift she had given me.

The rabbi spoke with each one of us. "Jeannette was a person who not only lived each day to the fullest," he eulogized, "but was also able to live her life very much on her terms. She was a vibrant, charismatic personality. Highly intelligent. Spirited and strong-willed, Jeannette took life by the horns. She could be opinionated but she could laugh at her stubbornness as well. She nurtured a love of learning and an eagerness to continually grow intellectually throughout her life."

I was devastated by the absence of her. I determined at that moment that when I died I would be placed next to my parents so I could be with them for eternity. They loved me unconditionally — no one could ever love me as they did — and I wanted to remain in that circle of love forever. I could not bear to be put to rest without being near them.

My mother never ceased to amaze me. Knowing she was going to die, she had left a piece of prose for me to find next to her bed. I read it at the end of her eulogy:

"Climb more mountains, eat more ice cream, go barefoot more often, swim more rivers, watch more sunsets, laugh more, cry less."

My mother, to the day she died, saw that in my quest for success I had lost touch with the beauty around me. I didn't watch sunsets, and I saw sunrises only when I had been up all night working on a case. I certainly wasn't going barefoot anymore. I wasn't eating very much ice cream; I didn't have time. I wasn't climbing mountains, save legal ones, which I was scaling constantly. I was crying far too often and I was hardly laughing at all.

I vowed to change. My mother's wish for Philip and me was that, by virtue of his being such a steady anchor, he would provide me with the stability that would enable me to find the beauty of life that I had lost. He already had the ability to make me laugh out loud and the drive and desire to help me find my core values.

I told Joel, "I need to take four weeks off. I never mourned my father; now I can do both. I have to clean out my mother's apartment and maybe in that space I can mourn my father as well." He understood. In his fervent pursuit of the law there was still a place for family. He revered his father, and although he was really only with her when he wasn't working, his wife remained special to him. His children were his pride and joy. So Joel was gracious. I think he saw this as a time for me to come to peace with myself, after which I would be able to work even better.

Without understanding quite what I was doing, I structured my grieving. I woke up, saw Philip off to work, worked out at the health club, took a steam bath, then drove to Charlestown. In my mother's apartment I had a task of the day, and I performed each task painstakingly. I went through everything in her closet. I went through her box of letters and read every one. I cried a lot. I called the therapist I had seen several times before and saw her again. And I luxuriated in the exquisite sanctuary of Milton.

If it had smelled of baking bread, the house could not have been more perfect. Idyllic, bucolic. That February the yard was covered in snow. We put up feeders in the trees and I watched birds flock to them. I went next door and fed apples and carrots to the horses. I read books, I checked in with my friends, and I waited for Philip to come home so we could have dinner. I had never learned how to cook well. He would say, "So is it tuna, pizza, or Chinese?" We would watch television, play *Jeopardy!*, read voraciously, and go to bed. I truly indulged myself in mourning.

And in the middle of the day, or at the beginning, or at the end, I would shriek at my mother and father being taken from me. Alone in the house, I would question God out loud. "How could you do this to me? How could you do that to them? To my father? How could you take him away from my mother? Why did she have to live all these years without him? Why couldn't my father meet Philip? Why couldn't my father see how successful I was?"

And then, of course, it came time to go back to work. I was petrified. I had stopped throwing up. Now I started again. I really didn't know if I could do this.

twelve ZEALOTS

THE STATE OF MASSACHUSETTS, IN ITS INFI-
NITE WISDOM, DECIDED IT WAS GOING TO
put the Church of Christ, Scientist out of business.

The prosecutors didn't say as much; they were quite pious in
their denials.

There was a statute on the books stating: "A child shall not be
deemed to be neglected or lack proper physical care for the sole reason that he is being provided remedial treatment by spiritual means

alone in accordance with the tenets and practice of a recognized church or religious denomination by a duly accredited practitioner thereof." *G. L. c. 273 § 1.* It is known in legal circles as the Christian Science exemption. The Suffolk County District Attorney's office, in the persons of DA Newman Flanagan and his assistant John Kiernan, both staunch Irish Catholics, chose to do an end run around that exemption and prosecute Christian Scientists David and Ginger Twitchell for the death of their two-and-a-half-year-old son, Robyn.

In April 1986 Robyn Twitchell had not been feeling well. He had flulike symptoms, his stomach bothered him, and as the pain grew, his parents became increasingly worried. They didn't want their boy to be in pain, so they did what all devout Christian Scientists do when faced with a medical difficulty: They prayed. Christian Scientists look to God as a source of inspiration for everything in their lives. They pray and read religious texts every day. The Christian Science religion is founded on the doctrine of spiritual healing, and the Christian Scientists' faith tells them that God literally heals all wounds. The Twitchells were devout believers. They had faith. As Robyn's pain grew more intense they prayed more intensely.

If you ask a Catholic whether she believes in the virgin birth, certainly she has no empirical evidence of it, but she believes. If you ask whether she believes in Christ's crucifixion and resurrection, she again has no empirical evidence of it, but she believes. So if you ask a Christian Scientist whether she believes that praying and communicating with God will heal a medical, an emotional, or a psychological condition, while she may not have empirical evidence, she has ample anecdotal evidence, and she believes that it does. Christian Scientists have extensive anecdotal evidence that prayer alone can heal. David Twitchell's own mother tells of how he was healed through prayer when he was a boy. David and Ginger truly believed in the efficacy of prayer and had an expectancy of healing.

As one would call for a doctor in times of medical emergency, when Robyn's condition worsened they called for a Christian Science practitioner, who used her spiritual experience to guide them in further prayer for the health of their boy. Within the confines of their religion, they did everything they could do to bring their child back to health. They worked with a Christian Science nurse and continued to communicate with people at the Mother Church.

Four days into his illness, Robyn seemed to take a turn for the better. He sat up and played with his brother, and crawled up on a table and toyed with a flower. The Twitchells hoped the worst was over. It wasn't. Robyn had a relapse. He suddenly began projectile vomiting and went into convulsions. Robyn died in his father's arms. They all prayed, then David called the church, a funeral home, and emergency services, who instructed him over the phone on methods of resuscitation. The resuscitation failed. It was too late.

Boston is an intensely Irish Catholic town. Many of its politicians are Catholic; a large percentage of its police and public officials are Catholic; the ruling culture is Catholic to the bone. Boston is also the city in which Mary Baker Eddy founded the Christian Science religion. It is home to the First Church of Christ, Scientist, the "Mother Church," one of the great architectural wonders of Boston; it's on all the tours. The tension between the hierarchy of the two religions, in a town of rigorous affiliations, was enormous.

The case came to me from Bill Homans, one of the great bleeding hearts of clients with impossible causes. A hulking man with round shoulders, furry eyebrows, and a large nose, he had defended many civil liberties cases. Bill was the model of the lawyer that most people say they want to be but never will be because they want to make some money. Although he wanted to defend the Twitchells, his plate was full. "There may never be a dime out of this," he said, but he felt I would care for these people the same way he did. I was "just the right person." That was one of the greatest compliments I have ever received.

Joel Kozol agreed that our firm would take the case pro bono, but I was working on Zuckerman at the time, so I referred part of it to a good friend and medical malpractice specialist, Steve Lyons, with whom I had previously worked as cocounsel. Steve was always interested in First Amendment and freedom-of-religion issues, and we agreed to work it together. Stephen was the primary attorney during the inquest hearing. The prosecution understood the issue of the religious exemption law and wisely sought the advice of a judge.

We learned that Robyn Twitchell died of Meckel's diverticulum, a congenital birth defect. The umbilical cord pouch on most babies dissolves, but if it does not it may serve as a pocket inside the body for waste and germs to gather, which may then ulcerate and leak into the abdomen, causing infection. The pouching may also in rare cases become a full-fledged bowel obstruction. The associated pain may come and go as the obstruction comes together and dissolves, but the festering waste inside the body may lead to peritonitis and ultimately death. This is what happened to Robyn. It is a difficult condition to diagnose because it mirrors so many other diseases.

Suffolk County DA Newman Flanagan, a proud Irish Catholic with a full head of gray hair, a pronounced Boston accent, and a closet full of his trademark wild ties, and his assistant John Kiernan, another proud Catholic with many children, thought the Twitchells and Christian Science were barbaric. After an inquest at which a judge took no position on prosecution, we sent the district attorney a letter attempting to communicate and find a solution. The answer we received was this: They impaneled a grand jury, which came back with manslaughter indictments against both David and Ginger. The prosecutors then set the media dogs on them, doing their best to portray the pair in the public eye—and the potential jury's mind—as cold-blooded child killers. "We're talking manslaughter," DA Flanagan said, "which is a degree of homicide." The papers were wild with the horror story of a couple who spent five days watching their son die.

David Twitchell, in his early thirties, was possessed of an almost childlike deference. He was a third-generation Christian Scientist, a true man of faith, almost otherworldly in the degree to which he trusted his life to the orthodoxy of his beliefs. He was thoughtful, gentle, obedient. He never for a moment thought about breaking any law. He wouldn't have run a yellow light. He and Ginger were devastated by the loss of their child, yet as far as they were concerned they had done no wrong; they had followed the word of God. And if God had ordained all this misery, David and Ginger felt that they needed to seek God more deeply.

Steve and I drove to the Twitchells' home to explain the indictments and suggest how to handle the couple's arraignment, which was scheduled for the next day. We needed to advise them of their rights. We wanted to break the news to them gently; we didn't want David and Ginger to be unduly upset, but we had to inform them of the seriousness of their situation. They could go to prison for years.

David brought us into the house with the solemnity of a church usher. He was thin and bookish; his brown hair combed to a sharp part on the left side of his head, a walrus mustache hiding his upper lip. He looked like Jimmy Stewart, minus the pizzazz. We sat in the living room and I read the indictment aloud, explaining the single count of manslaughter with which he and his wife were being charged. I then proceeded to explain the entire process, moment by moment, that they would have to endure the following morning.

David sat very still at the side of the couch, leaning forward, his elbows on his knees, scowling as if deep in thought. In fact, he was wracked with guilt. "I feel that if I had been better, or had a better understanding of God," he said later, "[my son] would not have died." What a burden with which to live.

Ginger was nowhere in sight.

Perhaps she had more important work to do in the home, maybe she was taking care of her two other young sons, but I thought she might want to meet the lawyers who were going to try to save her from prison. When Ginger did finally appear, a full fifteen minutes after we had started talking, she set up an ironing board in the corner of the room and began to run a steam iron over her basket of laundry. She was wearing large, purple-tinted rimless eyeglasses on her soft and pretty face.

I walked them through the timetable. "You're going to court tomorrow," I told them. "There's going to be an arraignment. This is what happens in an arraignment. They will advise you of the charges against you. You will enter a plea of not guilty. You're then going to go down to Probation. A probation officer is going to interview you, and you're going to be very open and honest with your probation officers. Of course, you would be." David didn't look up.

"There will be a question of setting bail, by virtue of what the probation office investigates about your roots in your community, your family, your work experience. But you have nothing to worry about because you're law-abiding citizens; you've never been in trouble before. I really don't expect the Commonwealth to ask for you to put up monetary bail." No sigh of relief. David appeared to be concentrating on taking this all in.

"We will file motions. The most important motion is going to be to dismiss the charges on the basis of the child-neglect statute, which I've explained to you before. We're going to file written papers, which are called briefs, and there will be some kind of oral argument and whichever side loses undoubtedly is going to want to go up to the Supreme Judicial Court, the highest court in the Commonwealth of Massachusetts."

I spoke for almost forty-five minutes, and as I moved from point to point Ginger ironed more intently, more furiously, her tongue sticking out of the side of her mouth so hard I thought she might bite it, her arm a righteous piston. The ironing board was sizzling with starch and still she said nothing.

One of the Twitchells' young sons was climbing all over me, but no one moved to restrain him. "First you arrive at the courthouse . . ." A finger in my ear. "Don't talk to the press. There will be a lot of jostling. Just walk with dignity through the crowd." The child tumbled across my lap. I picked up the indictment and read on. David continued to stare at the floor, making no eye contact. Ginger ironed.

God bless these people. David and Ginger were playing by different rules than everybody else. They never had a bad intention in their lives, but they were as blind to what had happened to their child as they were to the legal consequences of their own actions. They didn't have any ill will toward the government. The newspapers and television news were full of terrible caricatures of them, but they never got angry; they simply felt that this was what the district attorney believed and he had a God-given right to his beliefs, *as the Twitchells did to theirs!* They were the most tolerant and naive people; they simply preferred to ignore the adversarial nature of the American judicial system. I would say, "David, they are trying to put you in prison for years!" "It's just what they believe," he would tell me. "They just don't understand; if they understood, it would all be fine." I wanted to take him by both shoulders and shake him.

I hate defending the innocent; I always feel the need to be their guardian angel.

The case dragged on for years. Robyn Twitchell died in April 1986; David and Ginger pleaded not guilty to manslaughter in front of Superior Court Judge Sandra Hamlin in May 1988. Judge Hamlin was no stroke of good fortune for us. For starters, she owed her judicial career to DA Flanagan. She had been an assistant in his office; she had gotten her judgeship because of her relationship with him. From the day she was assigned the case it appeared to me that she was determined to deliver a verdict against these parents. The forces were being aligned.

The Christian Science Church was under siege, or so it must have felt to those inside. Around the country, four similar cases had been brought against Christian Scientists in the past several years. A court in California had ruled that Christian Science parents who attempted spiritual healing and failed could be tried for manslaughter. This was a legal and religious nightmare.

When it became clear that the church's interests were highly at stake in this particular trial, a group of people significantly involved in the religion formed a defense fund and stepped in to pay our fees. They felt their entire way of life was on trial and by defending the Twitchells they were also defending themselves and the church itself. They were remarkably gracious. They paid the two years of legal bills we had previously accumulated and encouraged us to do everything in our power to win the Twitchells' freedom. We agreed. This looked to be a long and difficult period of discovery. The trial was still two years away. There were motions to argue and pretrial appeals to be heard.

In the summer of 1988 Steve Lyons said to me, "Why don't we go have a drink? I want to talk to you." We repaired to one or another of our favorite bars.

"You and I have been friends since the early eighties," he began. "We've worked together a lot; we've shared a whole bunch of stuff." I had spent many hours listening to tales of his love life, and he had been privy to my own continuing saga. He had also served as a guest lecturer at my Trial Advocacy courses. "We have a great history; we love working together; I think you married a really good guy; your life seems to have some stability to it now. Why don't you and I form a law firm together?" That stopped me. He continued, "We won't have to work these kinds of crazy hours; we can take the cases that we want. You can put away a lot of money; I can put away a lot of money. We could really have a great boutique law firm."

He was absolutely right. Steve was an excellent civil litigator with a specialty in the areas of medical malpractice and catastrophic injury; combined with my criminal defense experience we could offer wide coverage. We would have to find some other lawyers who worked in real estate, corporate, tax, and bankruptcy law to broaden the firm's scope and make it a going concern, but this sounded like an excellent idea, and I told him so.

"But I don't know the first thing about running a business," I said.

Steve did. We agreed to consider this remarkable concept with all deliberate speed.

Philip and I had often talked about finding a way for me to work fewer and less arduous hours at Friedman & Atherton. I wanted to spend more time with my husband, but I was always behind the eight ball, trying to catch up with my caseload. As of yet I hadn't been able to find a means to that end. Maybe if I worked for myself. . . .

Over some six months Stephen and I seriously pursued the idea of forming a law firm. Rather than form some huge operation, we came to the conclusion that what he and I really needed was to form a partnership of our own, and as a means of sharing expenses, share offices with several other lawyers and create a revenue agreement under which we would arrange to feed each other clients. Finally, we made a decision: Let's do it.

I told Philip one night, "I really need to talk to Joel." He thought that was a great idea.

I was extremely anxious when I broached the subject with this dynamo. Joel was always in motion and I needed to capture his attention. I spoke with him in his large, corner office overlooking Quincy Market out toward the harbor. I started slowly and quietly. I had no idea how he would react. Was I going to get a big hug or would I be escorted out of the office?

"I've been married to you all the time I've worked here," I began. "All I did was work for you, and I've loved working for you. But it was at great cost to my health, as well as my general outlook and well-being." Joel, being an adept attorney and negotiator, said nothing and listened. "I really thank you for the time you gave me to mourn my mother, because it allowed me to see what I needed at some stage in my life. My marriage to Philip, I think, has a solid foundation and it would be better for me if I could have a small law practice where I can set my own time within reason and take as many cases, or not, as I choose. I'll make a lot less money, but I'll have a personal life."

I waited.

Joel said, "I completely understand." I could have kissed him. He remained behind his desk with his hands folded. He was not smiling but he was being sincere and compassionate. "I love having you as a partner. I would love to have you stay. But I've watched what you've gone through this year, and I'm not going to keep you here against your will." I was so relieved. "I'll be happy to feed you business when I can," he told me. "I hope we can do cases together in the future. But you're miserable here, and it shows. Your performance in these last few months has not been good because you're in this tug-of-war between wanting to go home to your husband and wanting to stay here and do your job. I completely understand. We'll do this in an adult fashion."

Joel became a mensch. I reverted to being a little girl inside. Although I had every good reason for making this move, I felt that I had failed him in a fundamental way. I felt guilty and disloyal.

When we opened our new offices in January 1989 the sign on the door said KLIEMAN, LYONS, SCHINDLER, GROSS & PABIAN, but we were actually two separate partnerships: Klieman, Lyons and Schindler, Gross & Pabian. I had a fabulous corner office overlooking the tall, white Customs House with its familiar clock tower, a treat since Philip was a Customs agent. I was determined to maintain some sense of balance between work and home life. I had great faith that we would be a success. We attracted several good clients immediately, and it didn't hurt that we had the Twitchell case to pay our bills. So I was out from under the intense demands of Joel Kozol, and my desire to fulfill them. Now all I had to answer to was myself. Or so I thought.

In order to defend the Twitchells properly, Steve and I became conversant not only with the facts of the case but with the religion itself. We divided it up. "You do the medical," I suggested, "I'll do the rest." He and I visited one Christian Science trial in Jacksonville, Florida; we went to Santa Rosa, California, and heard the openings and some evidence in another. We spoke with many people within the hierarchy of the church. We read all the books. At some point I knew more about Christian Science than I did about Judaism.

Stephen and I also spent a significant amount of time with Nathan Talbot, the top legal and public relations person in the Christian Science Church. A smart, articulate, gentle man, his place in the Christian Science hierarchy was head of the Committees on Publication in the country. Nathan Talbot was a committee of one. His job was to give advice to practitioners and to interact with the media worldwide in an attempt to have the religion understood and thereby portrayed in a positive light.

"This is how the media views this case," I told him. "They think it's voodoo. Society has decided that innocent children must be protected, and it believes that the way to protect them is by medical care. Christian Science runs completely contrary to exactly that belief."

Several issues were in play. Were we going to try this case in a court of law or were we back to heresy trials, to the Spanish Inquisition? How can we try, in a secular court, issues of someone's deeply held religious beliefs? Who were we defending? Were we defending the Twitchells, or was our client the Christian Science Church?

We were the Twitchells' advocates. I was very forthright with Mr. Talbot. "This is my defense," I told him. "First, David and Ginger never appreciated that their child was in a life-threatening situation; in fact, Robyn had appeared to improve at various times. He even went outside only days before he died. Second, if this child was under medical care, he would still quite possibly have died. Meckel's diverticulum is an extremely difficult defect to diagnose because it is an insidious anomaly. You cannot diagnose it physically. A physician cannot put her hands on a patient and feel it; she cannot measure signs clinically because it mimics so many non-life-threatening illnesses. Even radiographically it is almost impossible to detect until it is in the final stages. Even the best-prepared doctors might not have found this obstruction unless they had opened up Robyn's body.

"I also have the legal religious exemption, and I want the jury to understand that every action the Twitchells took was with the explicit approval of the church." I looked at him. "You understand, we're not here to carry the mantle of Christian Science; we are here to defend two people. You, the church, could become the enemy in this trial. We will not make you the enemy, and we will present Christian Science as a well-recognized, well-respected religion. But everything the Twitchells did was according to what the church told them to do, and the child died. We don't intend to put Christian Science on trial, but the prosecution surely does."

"I understand," Talbot said. "I face that every day. I only ask that you continuously communicate with me."

In Los Angeles all the lawyers from the various pending prosecutions met with representatives of one of the church's law firms, O'Mulveny & Myers, in their sumptuous offices. Warren Christopher, who was deputy secretary of state under Jimmy Carter and later secretary of state under Bill Clinton, was among their distinguished partners.

The place looked like a palace. Polished floors; long, arched corridors. Among Stephen's most vivid memories of that meeting was the fact that their kitchen was larger than our entire law firm. At lunch one expected guys to appear in paper hats wheeling stainless-steel steam tables.

We were two independent legal practitioners defending David and Ginger Twitchell; they were generalists serving as the clearinghouse for the several ongoing Christian Science trials, as well as those that would undoubtedly occur in the future. We were talking about the nuts and bolts of one manslaughter case; they were looking over our shoulder, more interested in Constitutional issues that would have an impact on the freedom of religion. We had information and strategies with which to win individual cases; they were looking at a far larger picture throughout the country. Our mandates were different: We were charged with getting David and Ginger acquitted; they were determined to defend and protect the interests of the church.

But greater even than those issues, the Christian Science Church saw the Twitchells' trial as an opportunity to educate the public about a misunderstood religion. Its representatives could not have a primary interest in David and Ginger's rights; their focus had to be on the interests of the church. We were attempting to try this case cleanly, without making religion an issue whatsoever. We knew that if we tried the case on religion alone we stood a good chance of losing. What we needed to do, and what was well within our reach, was to win this case on the medical issues.

They kept suggesting expert witnesses whom we should call to the stand to explain the Christian Science religion to the jury. We thought the worst thing a witness could say to a Boston jury would be, "I'm a Christian Scientist. Let me explain my beliefs," but that is exactly what the church and its lawyers wanted its believers to do. We tried to explain that if we put on Christian Science expert witnesses, things would only get worse: This theological sidetrack would not only drive up the price of the trial—adding extra lines of defense to the lawyers, extra witnesses, and extra time to each witness—but could also get the church's true believers, the Twitchells, tossed in prison. It seemed as if they might actually want to duke it out in court with the Catholic Church in Boston.

The attorneys with whom we met were hardly trial lawyer cowboys. They were litigators—brilliant but very straight and proper. They truly did try to help us, but their efforts were taking us far afield. We needed doctors as witnesses, not theologians. We received support from the grass roots and the church hierarchy, but while well intentioned, they did not perceive their own needs in contrast to the Twitchells' needs. They tried so hard and had such good hearts, but they were making things more complicated.

In December 1988, long before the trial started, *60 Minutes* ran a piece titled "They Call It Manslaughter," which cast the case as a battle between religions. Both sides were portrayed as zealots. I was criticized substantially by my criminal defense lawyer friends for allowing David Twitchell to be interviewed before trial, but I felt secure because his story was the truth; it would never change, whether told on a news magazine show or in court. What I did not consider was that his interview would be edited. I thought I knew how to handle the media; clearly I had overestimated my talents.

Nineteen eighty-nine was the year I almost died.

It should have been a very good year. Stephen and I opened our new law practice, Philip and I settled into a comfortable routine, and my period of mourning my mother had come to a close. However, I still found myself having the impulse to call her from pay phones in airports, and in my dreams she was trying to reach me. Clearly I was trying to reach her.

The office looked great, and revenues were coming in, but I was continuing to work like a dog to prepare the Twitchell case. Then I got really sick. My difficulties began when I had trouble swallowing, then moved to intense pain in the center of my chest, then to shooting pains down my left arm. The attacks were intermittent but intense. I could not eat; I could not breathe. I went from doctor to doctor, enduring barium X rays and so many EKGs that I could administer them myself. My medicine cabinet, already a pharmacy, began to look like a supply depot. Philip was always picking me up and taking me to some treatment center. We never knew when these attacks would occur.

Finally the pains started to incapacitate me, although, of course, I kept working. Among my problems was the fact that I was having trouble flying. In August Philip traveled with me to San Francisco to make sure I would be able to deliver a speech to the NACDL. I remained in bed except when it was time to deliver my address. We flew home via Dallas, and as we were landing I was convinced that my body would explode before we hit the ground. I rushed to a pay phone and called Kenny Marshall, a friend whom I had met when I had taken Werner Erhard's est training, who was working with some holistic team that he was constantly touting. I begged, "You have to get me to your doctors. I think I am going to die." He assured me he would have an appointment for me the next day. And he did.

I drove to Weston, Massachusetts, and met Barry Taylor, a naturopath who worked with foods and supplements, and his wife, Elizabeth Spark, an M.D. who worked in a psychotherapeutic fashion with people in chronic pain. I filled out forms for hours and talked with them just as long. Barry gave me a book, *Love Your Disease,* by Dr. John Harrison, which stated that any doctor who saw my symptoms should know I was having esophageal spasms brought on by both stress and improper eating habits, which could be cured in three weeks by a diet of steamed vegetables and brown rice. Oh sure, right!

I'll be damned, in three weeks the whole thing was gone, never to return. I marched into my internist's office holding a brown paper bag packed with pill bottles and dumped them on his desk. How little we know about certain illnesses.

I continued to work with Barry and Elizabeth, taking their programs called "Love Your Body" and "Stress Management." All of the participants were type-A folks totally maxed out and striving to find a means to health. We were paired up with a buddy and became each other's monitor; we established goals for food, exercise, relaxation, and reading. I took food allergy and sensitivity tests. I revamped my body and therefore my life. I participated in these programs whenever I needed a tune-up, which seemed to occur every few months. Without their work, I am sure I'd be dead. Because of them, I can eat virtually anything without consequences.

I used Barry Taylor as a coach through the ordeal of the Twitchell trial. He monitored my eating, and I had the best boil-in-a-bag dinners delivered to my office by one of Boston's top chefs, Stan Frankenthaler. I might not have eaten them until midnight, but sooner or later they got in my body. I ran every morning; I meditated every night. I even had this snowflake obsidian stone that I carried into the stall of the women's bathroom at the courthouse and held so I could clear my mind during the afternoon recess. I simply had to remember to breathe.

After almost four years of run-up, we finally went to trial on the day after Patriot's Day, April 17, 1990. Jury selection took three weeks. Though I should not have been, I was shocked by the response. Prospective jurors who had heard about the case brought with them vast amounts of misinformation: They had no idea what the child had died of; they thought he had languished for months. "I can't be unbiased in this case, Your Honor; I am a good Catholic and I know they are guilty." We must have heard that seventy-five times—"I am a good Catholic." Some prospective jurors said they wished there was a death penalty in Massachusetts; they thought David and Ginger should be hanged.

This is what happens when people are afraid, when they are presented with people different from themselves, ideas different from their own. Rather than learn, many tend to react in fear and ignorance. I regret that we could not overcome that. The prosecution had done a masterful job of manipulating the jury by manipulating the media. They knew how to play the game.

My faith in humanity was pretty shaken by the time we had rejected hundreds of Boston residents for cause—bigotry—and seated the jury. We actually accepted the deacon of a church in Charlestown because, while religious, he seemed to be tolerant, which was the best we could ask for.

Judge Hamlin allowed a prosecution request for the court to travel to the house where Robyn Twitchell had died. I was adamantly opposed; the Twitchells no longer lived there; their furniture was gone; someone else occupied the house now. The jury could get no real sense of the place at the time of Robyn's death, I argued, only a titillating sense that they were standing in a place where someone died. But this was exactly what ADA John Kiernan, who was trying the case, wanted. I kept asking, "Why are we doing this?" but the judge allowed it.

Every Christian Science witness called by the prosecution was a fact witness. "I came to the house and this is what I saw." That's all they should have been permitted to say, just the facts. Judge Hamlin, again over my strenuous objections, allowed Kiernan to interrogate each of these fact witnesses about their deeply held religious beliefs.

I found it appalling then; I find it appalling now. We went into chambers and protested to the judge. Could I question Catholic fact witnesses about whether they believed in the factual nature of the virgin birth? Would she find it permissible for me to question such witnesses about whether, when they go to confession and they say their Hail Marys and novenas, they actually believe they will be absolved of their sins? Could I ask a Jewish witness whether he believes that if he fasts on Yom Kippur he can truly atone for his sins? I was outraged! What did this have to do with a court of law, unless the prosecution was trying to put religion on trial? It offended every ounce of my being.

"Judge, this is a fact witness. He can't ask him about that."

"Yes, he can."

"No, he can't."

"Well, these people don't see things the same way as others see them. They see them and interpret them in light of their deeply held religious beliefs." The prosecution was allowed to probe religious beliefs on the pretext that such probing would shed light on the witnesses' powers of observation. Garbage.

"Your Honor, if they are telling you that they are having visions, maybe you should question them about their perceptions. They come into a house, and they make observations about the room, the child, and two parents. They are not in some trance state; they are telling what they saw."

"Well, you know these people. . . ."

Obviously, the prosecution wanted to make Christian Scientists look crazy: They believed in this wacko religion; no wonder the child is dead. To make matters worse, when the Christian Science witnesses did testify about their beliefs, the judge rolled her eyes and turned her back to them. Her intolerance was completely apparent to the jury.

I was working untold hours a day, part of them in a bar room late at night, talking to my criminal defense lawyer friends. "I don't think I understand the rules of evidence anymore," I told them. "I think I've lost touch. Every time I object, nothing is sustained. Everything Kiernan wants gets in. She is absolutely penalizing me just for representing these clients."

My friend Marty Boudreau, a former-federal-prosecutor-turned-defense lawyer, said, "Oh, come on, Rikki, you're overdramatizing."

"I am not. Come into court."

He came. "Oh, my God!"

Despite the fact that we had the exemption statute on our side, we were going down in flames. We needed someone to provide a medical overview for the jury to make them understand how difficult

Meckel's diverticulum was to diagnose. Steve, with his background in medical malpractice trials, found a radiologist at Massachusetts General Hospital who happened to be a specialist in the field. There are some people who practice medicine like statisticians and others who are led to the practice because of its humanity. This doctor was a most caring and sensitive man. He knew better than anyone how difficult this medical anomaly was to diagnose, and it was out of that concern, and out of his compassion for these parents, that he was motivated to testify.

Before he was to appear in court, our doctor was called by other physicians at Mass General and told, in no uncertain terms, that his testimony would not be looked upon favorably. He was on track to become chief of pediatric radiology. His career was at risk. We were stricken; without compelling medical testimony our case was lost — it would be *The State v. the Baby Killers.* Our doctor, being a man of conscience and a conscientious practitioner of medicine, at great personal risk and sacrifice, put his career on the line and testified for us strongly and effectively. What a courageous man.

There were cameras in the courtroom, and every time Judge Hamlin wanted to make a ruling and yet avoid their gaze she took both sides' counsel into the lobby. These rulings, of course, went uniformly against the defense. At the end of the court day, in one lobby conference concerning an evidentiary issue, John Kiernan said something concerning the Twitchells that truly concerned me and that I thought could be viewed as bordering on prosecutorial misconduct. (At some point I carried a list with me of all the statements a prosecutor was specifically not permitted to make during a closing argument. I would keep a checklist, and at the end of a closing move for a mistrial. I would never get it, but at least I would keep my record clear.) I don't allege prosecutorial misconduct lightly or often, and I did not make my statement aggressively. I wasn't being angry; I was going to protect and put it on the record. If a lawyer does not raise certain issues at trial, she loses them forever. So I made the statement that what Mr. Kiernan was suggesting bordered on prosecutorial misconduct.

Surprise. Standing in the lobby, Judge Hamlin came to Kiernan's defense. She said she did not believe he had violated anything, but she did agree with my position that he could not introduce this particular piece of evidence. We reentered the courtroom to pack up our briefcases.

It was 4:30. The jury was long gone, the courtroom empty save for the lawyers. Steve had exited through the rear doors and I was following when Kiernan turned on me and growled. *"Don't you ever say something like that about me again!"*

I'm not even five foot three; Kiernan is a big, tall, muscular guy. I thought to myself, Please hit me. Oh, please hit me! We'd get a mistrial and get out of here. This nightmare would stop.

Kiernan stormed out.

When I got home and related the events of the day, Philip said, "I'm going to court with you tomorrow."

"You're what?"

"I'm going to sit right there in the front row." He was as good as his word. Philip came to court the next morning and sat there and just glared at the prosecutor.

The key moment of this trial was the confrontation between John Kiernan and David Twitchell. Kiernan is a very good advocate—smart, powerful, sincere, emotional when necessary. He is a commanding presence in a courtroom, a formidable adversary. He clearly thought these defendants were worse than criminals. In his opening statement he had re-created in graphic detail Robyn Twitchell's dying moments, and tears were streaming down Ginger's face by the time he finished. I felt he truly had taken the knife and twisted it.

Under normal circumstances I would not put a defendant on the stand, but these circumstances were not normal. If the jury believed that David Twitchell was a religious fanatic who had seen that his child was dying and still had not called a doctor, they would have convicted him no matter what the law said. For being a barbarian, for being a member of a cult, for doing what the prosecution said he did, which was standing around for five days letting a child die. But David had said to me and to Stephen that he had had no idea his child was mortally ill, and that if he had he would have done anything—*anything,* including calling a doctor—to save his child's life. When faced with a choice between his religious faith and his child's life, he would have blinked.

The jury needed to hear that.

They also needed to hear what had actually happened inside their house, the steps David and Ginger had taken to try to save their child's life. David was so guileless that I felt the jury would see and respond to his innocence.

"I wish my son had lived," he said during his fourth day on the witness stand. "If medicine could have saved him, I wish I had turned to it." It was a remarkable admission, not the words of a barbarian or a cult member, but of a grieving father. "If I try a method of care I think is working, I will stick with that. If I think it's not working I will try something else." Because Robyn had seemed to take a turn for the better on the fourth day of his illness, David had felt his prayers were being answered and had not taken the drastic step of calling a doctor.

Kiernan took great pains to inform the jury that David had gone to a dentist for root canal work but had not extended that level of medical attention to his son. The pain, David explained, began to affect his relationship with his family and his work as an administrator of a Christian Science retirement home in California. After discussing it with Ginger, he said, "I decided I could not continue to impose it on those around me." And he did not take the prescribed medication after the procedure. David was a brilliant witness. He spoke the truth. He was a spiritual man and a good human being. "I don't understand the virgin birth," he said, "but I believe there is a heaven." Nevertheless, Kiernan scored mighty points in his brilliant cross-examination.

I wrote my closing before the trial began, using all the best arguments I planned to pursue, but a trial is a living, breathing thing, and it changes over time, and so did my closing. Lawyers have to do things backward. I have a ritual. First I create a trial notebook, including jury instructions. And it doesn't matter how many times I have tried the same charges — rape, drunk driving, murder — I always photocopy the jury instructions and I always photocopy the law. I have to know the law before I can figure out where the facts fit into it. I also put each idea for my opening and closing arguments on an individual page. Although I have a preliminary theory of the case, over the course of a trial I constantly revise my themes and therefore constantly revise my closing.

The night before I was to deliver it, I diligently wrote out my speech in longhand. When I was a child in the theater I memorized scripts the same way. There is something about the physical act of writing, putting pen to paper, that solidifies words in my head.

But something was not right. I was writing, I was walking around our house speaking the speech out loud, and it wasn't working. I told Philip, "I really need a favor."

"What? It's late."

"Can you go down to the video store and pick up a copy of *To Kill a Mockingbird*?"

"You've seen it a hundred times."

"I've got to see it again."

Philip dutifully got into the car, drove to town, came back with the videotape, and fast-forwarded it to Gregory Peck's closing. I watched it over and over, ingesting the passion, the power. When he finally intoned to the jury, in that majestic voice, "In the name of God, do your duty," I was ready.

"They loved their child," I told the jury the next morning. "They suffered the greatest loss imaginable to parents. They did everything they were supposed to do and they listened to everyone else. . . . Could you find, beyond a reasonable doubt, that David and Ginger Twitchell were so uncaring, so unfeeling that they just let their child die?"

I spoke for two hours. I don't think I delivered my best closing that day, but it was the most heartfelt.

Then Judge Hamlin decimated our defense. Her instructions to the jury eliminated almost in its entirety the Christian Science exemption. In her charge, as with her rulings, she just took the guts out of it. Although we wanted to try the case on the basis that even medical-care parents would not have seen that their child was seriously ill until it was too late, the case had turned into a trial about the Christian Science religion because the judge permitted the prosecution to use this tactic, witness after witness, question after question.

I looked at Stephen. "Why were we here? We have no defense under these instructions. *I'd* have to vote guilty, if that's the law." The jury had no choice but to convict the Twitchells under the charge she gave them.

They were out fourteen hours over three days. When they came back, on July 4, they were clearly distraught. With lips trembling, the forewoman delivered the verdicts: "Guilty," "Guilty." The Twitchells held hands. Three jurors began to weep and broke into loud sobs.

"Your Honor," I requested, "may the jurors be polled?"

This is a common request. It is always granted in homicide and other serious cases. The judge simply asks each juror, "Is this your verdict?" and the juror responds.

I thought I could bust this verdict. I'd never seen it happen, but I've heard it can be done. Jurors were convulsing in tears; there was every chance that when asked directly they would not be able to face these lovely parents and send them away.

Judge Hamlin said, "No." She waved her hand, dismissing me. "Take the jurors out of here," she instructed the bailiff. She left the bench like a thief in the night. Her chamber door slammed.

The jury was whisked away; they didn't understand what was happening. The courtroom erupted with cheers and jeers.

In the hallway Stephen and I explained to the press what they and the jury never got the opportunity to hear. Judge Hamlin had rejected so many of our motions that the jury had been denied information and our clients had been denied a fair trial. If the jury had understood that these parents thought they had been abiding by the exemption law, they might have come to a different conclusion. Stephen explained provisions in the law which showed that Christian Science was recognized by the Commonwealth of Massachusetts as a reputable religion. For instance, you are excused from jury duty if you provide a note from a doctor saying you're ill; well, you are excused from jury duty if you get that same note from a Christian Science practitioner. Basic Blue Cross/Blue Shield care covers Christian Science practitioners, so they are recognized as legitimate care providers. Judge Hamlin had excluded many such pieces of evidence which showed that this religion was regarded by other parts of society as being completely reputable, and therefore David and Ginger Twitchell had been following the law.

Back at their hotel, the jurors saw our press conference. One of them, the jury forewoman and a legal secretary, took it upon herself to write a scathing four-page letter to the presiding justice of the superior court detailing Judge Hamlin's actions and behavior. She wrote that she had an "uneasy feeling that the judge was biased." Even the judge's "facial expressions," which included "rolling her eyes . . . led me to feel she was being unfair. . . . Had she also told us about the religious exemption and had we still come back with a guilty verdict, then that verdict could have been viewed as precedent. But Judge Hamlin obviously didn't want to take that risk, so she set the precedent herself, but needed twelve jurors to sign off on it in order to make it appear legal. . . .

"The one and only thing I learned from this trial is that the criminal justice system doesn't work, or at least it doesn't work fairly."

Stephen and I believed if the jurors had been in possession of the evidence that Judge Hamlin had specifically refused to admit, they may have acquitted the Twitchells or we may have had a hung jury. We used the letter to challenge the verdict.

We expected sentencing to take place within thirty days. That's standard. There were probation investigations to be done; we had letters to prepare. Normal procedure. We informed the court clerk that the Twitchells, who were out on bail pending appeal, were going to visit relatives.

However, on July 6, two days after the verdict, Judge Hamlin suddenly ordered me and Stephen to produce the Twitchells for sentencing. I wasn't even in the office. Stephen had to send for me at the Christian Science church.

The press had started to pay attention to the jurors' reactions, and reporters might get volatile interviews. A month of those kinds of stories would have been devastating to the court. Stephen and I believed the judge was afraid she was going to see her whole case unravel. To make the verdict stick she wanted a quick sentencing, and she gave the Twitchells probation. And in a bizarre coda she made it a condition of their probation that they take their remaining children, *and any children yet to be born,* to a doctor for regular medical checkups in addition to those times when the children appeared seriously ill. This was outrageous, considering the Twitchells' deeply held religious beliefs in a well-recognized church.

We filed a motion for a new trial, which was denied. The Christian Science Church brought in a powerful Washington, D.C., law firm to handle the appeal, and ultimately the Twitchells' convictions were reversed. The Supreme Judicial Court of Massachusetts decided that the Twitchells should have been entitled to present an affirmative defense of reliance upon the attorney general's opinion regarding the Christian Science exemption. But rather than lay the responsibility at Judge Hamlin's feet, the court laid it at ours; it found we did not press the issue sufficiently. I was furious and wrote a letter to the court with every reference from the trial. We got no satisfaction, but the ultimate justice was done: David and Ginger Twitchell's case was reversed in 1993 and the district attorney's office, under a new leader, decided not to retry the case.

Immediately after the emergency sentencing hearing, I left to teach at the Western Trial Advocacy Institute in Laramie, Wyoming. Philip went with me. On my first free morning we drove up to a panoramic hilltop for a picnic lunch. I couldn't remember the last time we had done such a thing.

I fainted dead away and could not get up. Philip drove me to the hospital, where I was delirious. I knew who I was, but I didn't know where I was; I couldn't hear; I could barely breathe. They put an IV in my arm and started nourishing me. I had lost more than ten pounds; I was gaunt; I was completely exhausted. I looked like a refugee. Maybe it wasn't just Joel Kozol who was working me so hard.

I made it through Twitchell. I said I would change my life.

I didn't.

When I was on trial I had no other thought than my case. This is a disease common to many trial lawyers. We have no time for our spouses, our friends, any other part of our lives. On trial, we are 100 percent focused on our case. Our lives are our clients' lives and nothing matters but winning.

I thought that by marrying Philip I might change all that. I liked going home to the same person every night and waking up with him every morning. I had a constant companion, a good friend. Philip knew my maniac dedication and could help me with it. He was my anchor; he would keep me grounded.

I tried to slow my pace, to ease the work and curtail the travel— I paid lip service to changing my life—but I found I couldn't do it. Not if I wanted to be a success. I knew no other way than to work hard, and I had to travel, so often I took Philip with me. He was pleased to come.

I was highly visible, Philip was not, but that truly did not seem to bother him. Philip never for a moment suffered a lack of self-esteem. He knew who he was. He was happy with his life and proud of his wife; he took pleasure in my successes and was happy to bask in my reflected glow. It was the fabric of our relationship, the male-female inverse of most traditional relationships. I was a successful lawyer with a very demanding life; he was there to make sure all the pieces were in place, or to put them back together should I fall. Philip was so willing to be accommodating because he didn't see any of it as a sacrifice. And by no means was he uncomfortable; my aunt Eve said Philip Brady was the most secure man she had ever met.

Philip was fun. His basic outlook on life was, "Where are the laughs in this?" One of his goals was to teach me to laugh, because I was working so hard I rarely did. On summer Saturdays we would drive down to Rhode Island, where he had been raised. We would bring a change of clothes, go to Scarborough Beach, then stop at his sister's house in Cranston and shower before heading off to our favorite restaurant. After dinner we would drive back, singing along with our cassette tapes all the way.

Philip was the life of the party. Gregarious, funny, a hale fellow well met. His attitude was "roll with it"; that's who he was. We hosted barbecues and volleyball parties and all kinds of fun functions in our backyard in Milton. He would buy all the fixings and do all the grilling so I could be a guest at my own party.

Yet he was a serious thinker, a big reader in the field of politics. At the drop of a dram, he would expound on the Harry Truman/Douglas MacArthur confrontation during World War II and the cause of Irish freedom in Northern Ireland. I had tremendous respect for him as a federal agent, and when he left government service in 1992 to become a private investigator, he continued to demonstrate his dignity and integrity.

We really only communicated with each other on weekends. I worked late at the office every night, then went out drinking. Philip certainly participated in that arena nightly. My friends were his friends—a very tight circle—and Philip was completely comfortable swapping stories and tossing back drinks at Maison Robert or wherever we were convening. Often we were at Barsanti's, later called Alicia's, a dark, smoke-filled room with a great jukebox. Maison Robert was light and airy; Barsanti's was our hole. We all vacationed together on the cape in Truro and in Provincetown. We went to Ireland together; we spent New Year's together; we were a happy group having high-intensity fun.

Philip and I were also best friends. His late wife had been the love of his life. He and I were not passionate, but we were happy. I was his savior when his wife died, and he was my savior from my own life, and I could not imagine life without him.

From afar, everything seemed well in order. Klieman, Lyons was prospering; the law firm was getting high-profile cases and substantial fees; I had appeared on *60 Minutes* and all the talk shows; I was known.

But I was shot out of a cannon every Monday morning, and every Friday night I was completely spent. It's the trial lawyer's lament. I loved being on trial in the courtroom; I hated every night afterward and every morning before. In the courtroom I was flying, but as soon as the gavel came down and I had to prepare for the next day I became extremely frightened: I hadn't done enough for my client; I hadn't had enough time to prepare; we were going to lose; my client was going to jail and it was my fault. My world controlled me; I tried to put my hands on it but it lurched away. I drank too much and took sleeping pills, then shook off the daily coma. I shone in the spotlight, then felt like a black hole in the dark.

The prize I was after was fame, fortune, success—not peace of mind. And despite my apparent success, I was so rarely happy. The only difference between winning and losing a trial was that if I won I had forty-eight hours to be elated before I became depressed again. I could not enjoy my free time because I was either worried about my next case or worried about the business. Steve and I were making money, but it's a fickle world. Would we continue to attract clients? What if I couldn't meet my financial obligations? I needed to keep getting more work in order to pay the bills—I could not afford to turn down a case—but with more cases came more demands on my time. It was circular. I had to keep working; I had no time to breathe. No time to eat. No time to sleep. I would drink too much on Friday night and awaken Saturday morning feeling god-awful. "Philip," I would moan, "I just don't want to get up." He would open the blinds and start singing "High Hopes" at full volume. I would close the blinds, crawl my way back into bed, and pull all my pillows around my head until he couldn't see me—he called it my "pillow cave." I wouldn't come out.

Some hours later I would wake to the smell of Philip's cooking me a grilled cheese sandwich, one of my beloved comfort foods. I would take my little plate, pad into the den still wearing my pajamas, turn on the television, pull the coverlet up to my neck, and watch cooking shows on PBS until I fell back to sleep again. Philip would putter around the house, or work in the garden, or work out, or read. Sometimes we would have dinner and drinks with friends; at other times that was too much to handle. Often I was so exhausted that Philip had to ease me out of bed and stand me in the shower, then take me for a walk as one would an invalid. In the summer he would carry, drag, somehow move me to the car. I would sleep all the way to Rhode Island. He would put a lounge chair out for me and I would sleep all day at the beach. That was our Saturday. That was my life. At the courthouse and at events around the country I took care of everybody—I smiled, I performed—but at home I barely functioned. Philip became my caretaker. All he needed was a white coat and a stethoscope.

Sunday night I would throw up. Violently. Monday morning I was shot out of the cannon again.

In January 1993 I was teaching a trial advocacy course at the University of Virginia with Jack Curtin, a past president of the American Bar Association whom I deeply respect. Bill Clinton had just been elected president, and whenever a new president comes in, with him come new United States Attorneys and federal judges. Jack told me, "Ted Kennedy has said publicly that he is looking for qualified women candidates." (A group of three candidates for U.S. Attorney is selected by a nominating committee and presented to the senator. The senator makes his selection and recommends one candidate to the president, who makes his nomination, which is then confirmed by the United States Senate.) Curtin was familiar with my credentials and was aware of the 1986 federal judgeship fiasco. "I think you would be the perfect candidate to be the United States Attorney."

I was terrifically flattered. There are few jobs I would like more than being U.S. Attorney. In a lawyer's world, if you are a district attorney or a state's attorney you are a prosecutor; if you are the U.S. Attorney you are *the* prosecutor. The prestige is estimable. You need a presidential appointment and serious pull to get that job. You really have to know somebody. Only the best and the brightest and the very well connected become U.S. Attorneys.

I immediately reminded Jack of my marijuana arrest. "Oh, come on." He smirked. "That was 1969. It's on your bar application, your judgeship application. Nobody cares!"

I told Philip about the approach. He was less impressed.

"You're not serious," he told me. "Don't you know that nothing the federal government ever does is on the level?"

Philip had been a gung-ho federal agent for decades, but his years at the Customs Service had ended on sour terms. "You're going to be a showpiece. They're not going to give you this job. They're going to put your name out there; you're going to be the front-runner; the press is going to love it—and you're not going to get the job. This is a fantasy. They're using you."

I did not listen to my husband; instead, I discussed the possibility with Steve Lyons. We had been partners now for four years, and my serving in the government would mean my leaving the law firm. "I would hate to lose you as a partner," he said, "but I love you and you would be the perfect United States Attorney. So if you want to apply, I will do everything in my power to support you. We'll have to find out who's on the nominating committee. I'll call people."

We would campaign. I knew how to do that, I'd done it in one fashion or another since freshman year at Northwestern.

I called Curtin. "Is this really serious?"

"Absolutely."

I spoke with Philip again. He just shook his head in disbelief. "If you want to do this, go waste your time."

I prepared for my interview as if I were going to trial. I discussed it with my mentors, with people who knew the personalities on the nominating committee and understood how the process worked. I honed my opinions on prosecutorial discretion, relations with the state and local governments, diversity in the office. I was very well prepared and practiced by the time I was called for my interview.

There were no trick questions. The approximately twenty people around a long conference table in one of the prestigious white-shoe corporate law firms were curious to explore all those issues plus legislation, guns, and juvenile crime. We had a substantive discussion and I left feeling quite satisfied.

Committee member and former U.S. Attorney for Massachusetts Wayne Budd became my buddy. "Terrific interview. I'm sure you're going to get invited for another."

Rumors began to circulate. There were many people who wanted this job and the *Inside Baseball* analysis had it that the selection would be made between me, Wayne Budd's protégé Deval Patrick, former secretary of state Dean Acheson's granddaughter, Eleanor Acheson, and my colleagues and progenitors Alice Richmond and Andrea Gargiulo. I was indeed brought back for a second interview. Acheson landed a job at the Justice Department, and word had it that the choice was down to me, Alice, and Andrea. It was all very exciting. Philip said, "None of this is on the level. I can't believe you've fallen for it." He shook his head in disgust over and over again.

The committee was voting on which names to send up. I was in Washington for a meeting of the Advisory Committee to the United States Supreme Court on the Federal Rules of Criminal Procedure when I called Wayne Budd for the final results.

"I don't know what to tell you."

This was not good news.

"What do you mean?"

"There are three names going to Ted Kennedy and yours is not among them." He tried to soften the blow. "But neither is Andrea Gargiulo's or Alice Richmond's."

Philip was so smart.

"That's a disgrace," I said flatly. "Do you know how people voted?"

If he knew, he wasn't telling. "But I will tell you, it's an interesting thing to observe what women do to women. The problem is, all three of you are attractive."

I'd had this conversation before.

He said the committee felt Andrea was too political, Alice was too controversial because of her relationships at the Bar Associations, and I had been a criminal defense lawyer too long; none of us had distinguished herself sufficiently to become a federal prosecutor.

I was furious. "Wayne, please don't tell me this stuff. Tell me that the women on the committee voted against us. Tell me we were too attractive, too controversial." I was close to sputtering. "This is such nonsense. Alice Richmond and Andrea Gargiulo would both have been excellent U.S. Attorneys whose selection I would applaud, and you're going to give me some rational reason why they weren't chosen? Forget about me, take me out of this equation. This is a disgrace to those women."

Three men's names were sent to Senator Kennedy, and the man who ultimately was appointed to the job was Donald Stern, who just happened to have served as Governor Michael Dukakis's legal counsel. Philip handed me the newspaper the day the nomination was announced. "You'll never believe me, will you? You were a token; you were a showpiece; you were used. So was Andrea; so was Alice. I'm sorry you got suckered into this. I'm sorry you allowed yourself to get suckered into this."

Andrea, Alice, and I had all been asked to apply for this position; we had not initiated the pursuit. If we had not been sufficiently distinguished to begin with, why had they invited us? The answer was obvious. The committee wanted to appear inclusive while not actually being inclusive. I was so angry. I was so disappointed. I was so naive. "You were right," I finally admitted.

thirteen **THE FUGITIVE**

WAS HAPPY WHEN THE PHONE RANG.

AS AN ATTORNEY, MY RULE OF THUMB
was: You take the calls from people you don't know. You can
always call back your friends, it's the strangers who will walk into
your life with business. Especially lawyers. They might be lunatics
and I might be sorry I answered the phone, but half the time they
had either a legal question or a case for me. So, sitting in my office
on Custom House Street in Boston in July 1992, when my secretary, Paula Kimball, said a lawyer named Steven Black was on the

line and he wanted to speak with me, I picked up the phone with pleasure.

He was calling from Corvallis, Oregon. "Do you remember someone by the name of Katherine Ann Power?" he asked.

"Yes," I told him.

This brought it all back. Katherine Ann Power and Susan Saxe were two Brandeis University students who had gotten involved with radical politics, culminating in a 1970 Brighton, Massachusetts, bank robbery in which they took part. A Boston police officer, Walter Schroeder, was shot and killed. Power and Saxe and the three ex-convicts–turned–radical politicos they were running with had fled. Boston, a conservative city in the best of times, was livid.

The convicts were soon captured and convicted, and one died in prison when he blew himself up making a bomb. Saxe had been arrested in Philadelphia a few years later and served more than five years in prison. Power hadn't been seen or heard from. For fourteen years she was on the FBI's Most-Wanted List before being removed in 1984, presumably because the sixties peace movement was no longer an issue and the heat of her pursuit had cooled. Or they simply thought she was dead. The home of Paul Revere and Samuel Adams, however, held no truck with radicals, no romantic attachment to the sixties politics of liberation. The Boston Police Department named its award for outstanding bravery the Schroeder Brothers Medal of Valor and the city held a grudge. (The first police officer to win the Schroeder Medal was a cop-on-the-rise named Bill Bratton.)

When Susan Saxe was arrested in 1975, I was at Boston University School of Law and my own background made me wonder what had happened to her. How had a nice Jewish girl from Brandeis wound up with a set of criminals who not only robbed a bank and set fire to a National Guard armory, but also shot a cop? I could not understand how she got there, so I read about Saxe voraciously, which was easy to do. The case was all over the newspapers for months and was a huge cause célèbre. Boston was out for blood.

Saxe was represented by Nancy Gertner. I just thought that was the greatest thing in the world, a woman operating at the center of a legal whirlwind. I was a young woman just starting out, knowing full well that the legal profession was not particularly hospitable to women and that within that profession the Boston legal community was not among the most enlightened. So I watched Nancy Gertner with admiration, awe, and a keen sense of appreciation. I wanted to see how this was done.

She did it well. The case was huge, and as much attention as it won, Nancy Gertner's reputation grew proportionately. A season in the media will do that for you. Gertner went on to become one of the leading lights among Boston's women lawyers, and eventually became a judge. In the moment Steven Black asked for my recollection, clippings and headlines flashed through my head. I thought, Nancy had Susan; I'm going to have Katherine!

So, yes, I remembered Katherine Ann Power.

"Would you like to represent her?" Black asked.

"Absolutely."

Black explained that he had met Power recently. If she had once been a dangerous fugitive, now, twenty-two years later, Black said, "She reminded me of the woman who is on the box of Keebler cookies." But more than her looks affected him. "She is really a remarkable woman," Black said. "She wants to come back and face her punishment. I need you to find out what you can do for her."

"How did you get my name?" I asked.

"I'm a public defender in Corvallis. Katherine found herself clinically depressed, suicidal, and she went to see a psychologist for help. After some therapy, the psychologist brought her to me.

"When we first met, Katherine didn't remember much about everything that had happened. She was severely clinically depressed. She knew that she had been involved in radical activities, she knew that she had been involved in a bank robbery, and she believed that a police officer was killed, but she didn't know what the charges were against her. I've since contacted a lawyer in another state to find out what she is facing. She seems to have some federal problem in Philadelphia concerning a bank robbery, she has a federal indictment in Boston for theft of military equipment from some National Guard armory, and she has a murder indictment in Boston for being part of the group that killed this cop.

"I believe from my conversations with this other lawyer that the Philadelphia thing is no problem. I don't even think there is an indictment. The real problem is going to be Boston, both federal and state, and this is how I found you. I don't know any lawyers in Boston; I called some big-time criminal defense lawyers on the West Coast and asked them for some names of credible people they believed could negotiate a deal for Katherine, who could actually work with these prosecutors' offices and, if worst came to worst, if there was no deal, who could try the case. Your name just kept appearing on everybody's list. At that point it made sense to call you."

"Well, I'm flattered," I told him. "I think I can do this job." There was no question that I wanted to. I explained to Black that despite the Twitchell case I had a good relationship with the Boston district attorney's office but that Newman Flanagan was coming to the end of his tenure. "There are all kinds of rumors afloat that the next DA is going to be a fellow named Ralph Martin. I know Ralph well."

Ralph Martin was an Assistant United States Attorney for the District of Massachusetts whom I respected enormously. I had represented a defendant accused of participating in an around-the-world con game, and in the course of negotiating a deal in which my client eventually cooperated with the government, Martin and I had developed a truly collegial professional relationship. Recently, when Ralph had wanted to become district attorney, I had made some calls to people in positions of influence to try to help him out. If Ralph did get the job, and it was looking very likely that he would, those calls would certainly not hurt me when I was negotiating with him on Katherine Power's behalf.

Black wanted to be very clear about all the issues and took his responsibility extremely seriously. "There is no money in this case," he informed me. "I can send you a hundred dollars to retain you."

I would have to find money elsewhere. This was too good a case to turn down because of finances.

"You can't talk to anybody about this case," he continued. "You can't talk to your partner, you can't talk to your secretary. This woman is a fugitive from justice. She was on the FBI's Top Ten Most-Wanted List for many, many years. From the day you say 'yes' —

today—she is in danger of being found. Everything you do is now going to have to be secret. You are going to have to be watching your back, because if something you do causes her to be arrested, that's got to be on your conscience. Can you handle that?"

For Steven Black this was an intensely serious question. I said, "I can handle that." I was a tough criminal defense lawyer and I thought I could handle anything. I had represented fugitives before; in fact, I had represented a few people who had been indicted, either escaped or ran away, and whom I had brought in. I was pretty cavalier back then.

I said, "Steve, I need to tell two people about this."

"No."

"Wait, hear me out," I said quickly. "I need to tell my husband because I need his help."

"Why is that?"

"My husband, Philip, is a former federal agent. . . ."

"Are you out of your mind?" Black was almost sputtering.

"He just retired from the U.S. Customs Service. He was an investigator."

"I don't believe this."

"I have to tell him because I need his help," I explained. "If anybody can tell me things I need to do when dealing with a fugitive, I'm sure he can. Plus, I really don't want to keep this from him because I imagine this is going to take some time. I don't know that I can do this otherwise and stay married."

If Philip had still been a federal agent, I'm certain Black would not have gone one step further. But Black took a great leap of faith and agreed. I appreciated his gut sense that I was trustworthy.

"The other person I need to talk to is my investigator," I told him. As a criminal defense lawyer, investigators are part of the daily existence, almost like a professional appendage. "I need help here; I need to get up to speed. I need someone to get the newspaper articles for me. I need him to get the microfiche information for me. I may need him to locate witnesses and just help me out in whatever it is I am trying to do here. I would trust my investigator with my life. If I killed somebody, he would bury the body." Black was a professional; he understood and agreed immediately—much more quickly than he had concerning my husband—and didn't give it a second thought.

"Let's consider it a done deal," I said. "Let me go read all the background stuff first and I'll call you back in a couple of weeks."

"Good."

"And I do not want to know where Katherine Power is," I stressed. "I don't even want to have the slightest notion of where she is." This was not evidence I wanted to have to withhold when asked by prosecutors.

"Okay, I think that's smart. Though at some point you need to talk to her."

"Of course, but I won't be ready to talk to her until I know what to talk to her about."

"I'm going to send you the money. No one in your office can know about this. I'll make a notation that it's for some other case."

"I look forward to it."

I hung up the phone and took two steps toward the window. I had been standing for a good part of the conversation; I get that way sometimes, pacing as if I'm talking to a jury. I was pretty wrapped up in my work, but I loved the view out my window. I had a corner office on the ninth floor of 21 Custom House Street and directly across from me stood the Custom House Tower, a mid-nineteenth-century stone edifice with its huge clock with faces on all four sides. It was my favorite building in Boston, old, proud, and full of history. Philip's having been a federal Customs agent made it an even more perfect building from which to find inspiration. I looked at this beautiful structure and thought, *This case is going to be the top of my career. Bigger than the Twitchells'. This is going to beat that by a mile!*

I called my investigator, a marvelous character named Charlie Moore. "Charlie, come meet me. I have a case I need to talk to you about." I gave him no details over the phone. He showed up in about an hour.

"Do you remember a person by the name of Katherine Ann Power?"

"Sure," he said poker-faced. "Schroeder brothers. Brighton bank robbery. Susan Saxe."

"I was just contacted to represent her and bring her in."

Charlie had a great grin. He was a Vietnam vet. Green Beret. Special Forces. Went out on a disability, having been shot up pretty badly and by some miracle having crawled out alive. Hospitals for months of rehab. He was the best witness in the world to put on the stand, even for something as mundane as identifying a photograph, because jurors always thought he was a hero. Despite our being on different sides of the Vietnam War barricades, he and I were good friends. "Good for you." He beamed. "This is going to be the best thing that ever happened to you. You are going to be the name on everybody's tongue."

"I can't pay you for this."

He shrugged and grinned again. He clearly liked the clandestine nature of what lay ahead. "Are you kidding? This is a gas!"

I told Philip that night. He, of all people, understood the need for secrecy. After the Twitchell case I could sneeze in Boston and it would wind up in the papers. He, too, said it would be the greatest case of my career.

I studied up, kept in touch with Steven Black over the course of two months, and in the fall visited with Brian Kelly, the Assistant U.S. Attorney in Boston. Kelly had already been contacted, via Steve Black, by an attorney from Alaska, Greg Cook, who let the government know that Katherine Power was alive and had representation. A sweetheart of a guy, Kelly was very deferential to his law enforcement colleagues in Boston. The federal charge was robbery of an armory; the local charge was the killing of a cop. The death took precedence. The feds would love to have Power back, he said, but it really was a Boston case.

It was an easy conversation. I told Kelly, "I want to try to negotiate a deal. I want concurrent time." I could save Power years of her life if federal and state sentences were to run at the same time, not consecutively. He said, "We don't have a problem with that. We would like her in. We would like to clear this case off our books. I'm not going to commit to it, but concurrent time seems fine right now. But it is Boston's case; let's see what the state is going to give you."

So I called Ralph Martin, who had indeed been appointed district attorney. On September 14, 1992, I walked the half mile to his office.

The district attorney's office in Boston, in the old courthouse in Pemberton Square, was a very old building, one of those places that is always dirty. The criminal courts are housed there, and you really didn't want to wear a light-colored jacket inside. It was a state courthouse in a big city.

I had been in the DA's office many times during Newman Flanagan's reign. According to tradition, all visitors were made to wait, then passed through security before being ushered past the paper and processors of the Suffolk County prosecutorial system all the way to the back of the dingy suite, to the big office. There one was confronted with a large desk that belonged to the district attorney of Boston. This was one imposing piece of furniture, over which the legal dealings of the City of Boston had been hammered out for decades. Ralph Martin was an articulate, talented, and thoughtful man, but unlike Flanagan, who had been a rather robust physical presence, Martin was relatively small of stature. He looked very small when I walked in.

Ralph and I were comfortable with each other. "How does it feel to finally be in the big seat behind the big desk?" I joked. He surveyed his new realm and said, "You know, I think I'm going to like this." Still, he said, he thought he was going to have some problems with the Boston Police Department. They were all great fans of Flanagan, but Martin was an outsider coming from the U.S. Attorney's office, a man who had gone after Boston cops. As much as he might enjoy his work, it was not going to be easy.

What he wasn't saying was that he was the first African American district attorney in this city with a truly difficult racial history.

"Well, I have another police issue for you. Do you remember a person named Katherine Ann Power?" Ralph knew who she was immediately. "I would like to bring her home to you."

"You really have her?" he said.

"I think I do."

"You don't know where she is."

"Of course not."

"Of course not." He had asked and I had answered.

"I'm working with an intermediary," I told him, "and Power would like to come back and face her punishment, so I need to talk about what would be appropriate."

Ralph was all business. "I won't be able to determine what is appropriate until I review her file."

We agreed on the need for absolute secrecy. "I haven't told my law partner, who is like my blood brother," I volunteered. If the FBI arrested Power because of a leak during our negotiations, not only would we ruin our chance for a plea-bargain deal, which was clearly the proper resolution to this case, but we would be faced with a public relations nightmare. The Boston Police Department would be out for both her blood and Ralph's—a cop killer was brought to justice by another organization while a black Boston DA cut her a deal—and then I'd have to take the case to trial, which would certainly inflame the city even further.

We started to work. Just as I'd had to include Charlie Moore in my small circle of intimates, Ralph had to bring in his chief trial counsel, Jack Cinquegrana. That was okay; I knew Jack.

Smart and charismatic, Jack Cinquegrana was a tall, lean, handsome man with high cheekbones, very structured features, and a full head of thick brown hair that fell over his eyes. He wore tortoiseshell glasses that added to the distinctiveness of his face. He might have been Cuban or South American, or he might have been raised in the barrio of some American city, but he carried himself like a Brazilian aristocrat. Jack and I always had a nice professional rapport; we had encountered each other at social functions but had never had more than a perfunctory conversation.

As attractive as he was, it was very clear to me that when I was dealing with Jack regarding legal matters he considered me to be just like a guy. When working on a case, I was never above using flirtation, using my charms, or even carefully considering how I was going to dress when I negotiated with male colleagues. But Jack was all business, and we went *mano a mano*. He was an able prosecutor and I totally trusted him. So having Jack in the mix was fine with me. Ralph, Jack, and I agreed to immerse ourselves in the details and speak again when we were more fully prepared.

As I read the transcripts of the Susan Saxe trial, I found some important facts. Whereas Power had been half a mile away driving the getaway car, Saxe had been in the bank with a machine gun. The prosecutors had not convicted Saxe; instead, they'd gotten a hung jury and then pleaded her to twelve to fourteen years for manslaughter. Charlie found a news clipping during the Saxe trial in which the DA at the time, Garrett Byrne, said in substance, "If Katherine Power turns herself in, she will probably get probation." I tucked that quote away for the proper moment.

It was clear to me that if I could find a couple of witnesses, assuming they were still alive, I could try this case and perhaps win it. The trial lawyer part of me had green lights flashing: "Try! Try! Try!" A significant portion of my ambition was saying, "This would be just the best!"

But there was another side to me as well. I learned of conversations between Katherine Power and her therapist, Linda Carroll. (In an odd confluence of politics and pop culture, Linda Carroll is the mother of rock star Courtney Love.) When Power, in the depths of her depression, had told her therapist that she had been involved in something truly terrible involving the death of a cop, Carroll had analyzed her feelings and told her, "You need to make this right." This was not simply a desire; this was a *need*.

That phrase resounded in me. The more I learned, the more I felt that I was the chosen messenger. *I* needed to make this right. In the day-to-day battle of my career, my nurturing, compassionate side had been long dormant. Now it stirred. Forget about a plea bargain, forget about the law; as a woman I felt that I was being given a gift. I could help someone who had probably spent every day of the past twenty-two years wondering when she was going to be captured, who had become clinically depressed, who had become suicidal—I could help make her whole again. I could bring her together with her family. I could also help bring some sense of justice and finality to the Schroeder family. Walter Schroeder had been the father of nine children. His brother John, also a Boston police officer, had been killed in the line of duty four years later. That family needed some finality as well.

How naive I was in the midst of my grandiosity.

In the autumn of 1992, while Ralph Martin was doing his homework and I was doing mine, I spoke at a criminal justice conference in San Francisco. I delivered my "Theater in the Courtroom" address and was wending my way to the back of the room, fielding questions as I was moving, when I was faced with a tall, wide-bodied, broad-shouldered man wearing a tweed porkpie hat, light shirt, khaki pants, and beige angler's jacket with a bunch of pockets. *Sports Afield* meets Paul Bunyan. He had an open face and a twinkle in his eye. Whoever he was, I liked this guy viscerally. "Hi, Rikki," he said. "I'm Steven Black."

We sat in the roof bar of the hotel and talked about the case. He had a soft drink; I had a glass of wine. Steven adored Katherine Ann Power. "She has worked in soup kitchens," he told me. "She helps the poor . . . she feels as if she has lived her life as an act of contrition."

"An act of contrition": with that phrase I understood the enormity of my task. The FBI hadn't been able to find her; they'd thought she must be dead, Black told me. But she herself had decided she should go to prison. I had to help this woman.

At that moment I got scared. Really scared. What if she got caught? What if my phones were going to be tapped? What if I was going to be followed? How was I going to do all this? What if I couldn't sell it to Ralph? What if he couldn't sell it to the police? I had a cascade of "what ifs" going through my head, and I hadn't even talked to her.

I was used to getting "what ifs" when I was on trial: "What if I haven't asked the right question?" "What if I've forgotten a phrase?" But in my mind this was much more monumental. At trial, I always found the confidence to say to myself, Who could do this job better than you can? You are supposed to be here. This is your destiny. I found that strength at this moment, too.

I told Black that I needed to talk to Katherine. (By now, despite the fact that I hadn't met her, I was calling her by her former and true first name.) She had lived for years under an alias, but to me then and now she was always Katherine Power. I could not go into the DA's office and say "This is what I want" without first having a conversation with the client.

I was on my way to Washington, D.C., for a Friday dinner meeting of the Advisory Committee to the United States Supreme Court on the Federal Rules of Criminal Procedure. I was booked into the Hay-Adams Hotel. I asked Black if we could arrange it so Katherine could call me there between 5:00 and 7:00 in the evening, and he agreed to try.

I flew in to Washington, took a taxi to the hotel, and found they had no room for me. Not only was my reservation not in their computer, but they had no record of my staying with them whatsoever, and the place was completely booked. I am convinced that hotels always have rooms. I'm a true believer in that old saw, "If the president of the United States arrived, you'd have a room for him, right? Well, he's not coming; I'll take his." So I stepped away from the front desk, called my office, and put them on the case. But no amount of strongly worded contact between my secretary, the federal government travel agency that booked the reservation in the first place, and the desk clerk helped. I realized there had been a screw-up and that I did not have a room.

At that point I started to panic.

I could live without a room at the Hay-Adams; there were other hotels in town. But Katherine Power was supposed to call me *in my room at the Hay-Adams* between 5:00 and 7:00 that evening, and I had no way of contacting her.

One's first meeting with a client is vital; it sets the tone of the relationship, establishes trust and confidence, and provides both client and attorney with an immediate sense of the person he or she will be working with so closely on matters of great urgency. Katherine Power needed to have confidence in me as her protector, let alone her messenger and advocate, and I couldn't even get a secure line. This whole thing was going to get blown before it even began.

I was inconsolable. I approached the desk and said, "I am expecting a critically important phone call. You can put it through to me in the lobby." The clerk said, "We can't do that."

"Why not?" This was beyond unthinkable. One more automaton and I would scream.

"We at the front desk are not the people who get the calls," I was told.

"Fine. Can you talk to the operator who takes the phone calls and ask that person to transfer it out here?"

"You know," the clerk informed me, "we have more than one operator."

"How complicated can this be?"

I asked for the manager and finally got some satisfaction. I am not one to throw a tantrum in public—if a dry cleaner stains my clothes, I have to get my husband to argue with them; I can't. My way of dealing with people is usually to empower them and try to make them act on my behalf. I told the manager that I knew this was not his problem—it was mine—but I needed a room and I needed to take this phone call. Could he please help me? He was quite gracious, considering. He found a room at the Carlton Hotel and said they would get a taxi. "We can transfer your call to the Carlton, if you like." No, I would wait here, thank you.

So with my luggage piled by a cart in the lobby, I began to pace. It was the witching hour. I had to attend the Supreme Court Rules Committee dinner before the meeting the next day, which was the reason I was in Washington to begin with; I had no hotel room; I had not yet changed my clothes; and I was in danger of missing perhaps the most important telephone call of my professional career.

The phone next to me rang.

I did not mention her name out loud. I introduced myself and said, "I feel really bad about this." I was as contrite as I could be. "This is the first time we are going to speak and I'm in the lobby of a hotel because they didn't have a room for me. I feel very foolish. I know this is a very important phone call for you. It is for me, as well." I turned my back to the room and shielded my mouth. No one was looking, as far as I knew, but who really knew? "We need to reschedule this conversation for a time when I am in a private place to talk. I'm terribly sorry."

Katherine Power was calm. "I understand," she said. "You don't

have to keep apologizing." It didn't occur to me until sometime later
than she was probably quite experienced in these communications
operations, that as a notorious fugitive she had certainly called a
given number at a given moment more often than I had. She was better at this than I was.

I rode to the Carlton, dropped my stuff, went downstairs, got a
load of quarters from the gift shop, found a pay phone, and began to
slug them in. I needed to call Steven Black immediately. I could call
him from my office with impunity; it would show up in my phone log
as time spent on our designated case. But there was no reason for me
to call him from the Carlton, and I did not want a record of the call to
appear on my bill. Already I was thinking like a fugitive.

I quickly told Steven what had happened and asked that he
please make sure Katherine was not unsettled by the experience. I
had been on the case for only a few months and the tension was
almost unbearable. The call ended, I went up to my room, lay down
on the bed, and stared at the ceiling in disbelief. Everything had gone
wrong, but this made me even more determined to make it all right.

Making contact provoked major anxiety in me. Philip had
warned me about using the telephone; as a federal agent he knew
how well it could be monitored by court-approved wiretaps or high-
powered microphones, and how extremely simple it would be for the
FBI to get my phone records. My office and home were no longer
safe to speak from. The car phone was out of the question; not only
could those calls be intercepted, those records, too, could be
attached. I opted for pay phones.

Philip would get rolls of quarters for me at his bank and I'd get
rolls of quarters from mine. They weighed so much my shoulder hurt.
Steven would call me at the office and I'd say, "Hi, how are you? I'm
busy now, I'll call you back in ten minutes." Then I would grab my
quarters and head outside. There was a row of pay phones in the
bank building, but I would never use them; I was convinced that people were following me. I would dart into one building after another,
watching my back. I didn't know whether I was acting in my own
paranoid movie or I was being smart. To this day I don't have an

actual clue whether I was being followed, but I still feel I was not irrational to behave that way.

Not long thereafter I received a call at work from a woman who identified herself as Kathleen Branigan, Special Agent, FBI, with the fugitive squad. Could she come see me at my office? I said, "Sure."

So Special Agent Branigan showed up, one of the loveliest women I have ever met. Perfectly Boston Irish: reddish brown hair, very fair pale skin, freckles. She was both all business and an Irish lass, and she had exactly the right attitude.

"I have been contacted by the U.S. Attorney's office about the fact that you are representing Katherine Ann Power and are trying to make a deal." No question about it, the FBI had been notified as soon as the U.S. Attorney's office had received that first phone call from the lawyer in Alaska. Probably the moment after they got that call. "I am," I said.

It was clear that Agent Branigan was here because she wanted to be the agent who brought Power in. Everyone was after his or her own bit of glory in this case: I wanted to represent Power; Ralph Martin wanted to be the hero who brought the fugitive to justice; Agent Branigan wanted to be the person who walked her in. She told me it was perfectly all right with the Bureau if I was the person who gave Power up. Better, in fact; that way they didn't have to go find her. She knew I had been negotiating with the district attorney's office. "I hope we can do this sooner rather than later," she told me, "because you understand that we are looking for her."

"I do."

"And there is always the chance that someone is going to want to put you in front of a grand jury to find out what you know about her whereabouts."

"I don't know where she is," I told her.

"And you know that kind of information is not privileged." Agent Branigan was being very sweet while she was threatening me.

"I'm well aware of that. That is why I don't know where she is."

"You say you are dealing through an intermediary," she continued. "We can put him before a grand jury."

I assured her, "There is no question in my mind that if you put the intermediary before a grand jury, that person would take a contempt. They're never going to tell you where she is." We were being amiable; we were smiling. My grammar was incorrect, but I did not reveal whether my contact was a man or a woman. This was not information I needed to provide to the FBI.

"I would like to work this out with you," she said, "but if we find her first, it is just done."

"I understand," I told her. "But I would ask you to hold off a little. We are working." Agent Branigan gave me no assurances. I said, half joking, "Well, I guess I ought to be careful about my phones."

She smiled at me. "No, we won't, and yes, you should."

During my speaking trips to various bar and student groups I would also speak with Katherine. I would tell Black where I was — a two-hour window was usually sufficient — so she could call. I needed to get to know her and establish a rapport. I needed to tell her what I had learned, both from reading the transcripts of the Saxe trial and others and from talking with the district attorney, before I could ask her what she really wanted. Katherine was not a difficult woman to talk to, and by our third or fourth conversation, in early 1993, we started to formulate a strategy.

I asked how much time she thought she deserved to serve. Susan Saxe had received a negotiated sentence of twelve to fourteen years, and I felt there were strong arguments that Katherine should get far less. Saxe, as I've said, was in the bank with a machine gun; Katherine was unarmed and driving the switch car, parked six blocks away from the bank. I recognized that in the eyes of the law, one physical position was the same as the other, but in terms of moral and social culpability I felt there was a substantial difference.

Katherine was talking about a very short prison term; other advisers had told her she could possibly get probation. I told her probation was impossible, that too much had happened for the DA to do that. Since she was prepared to accept her punishment, she might do a short term in prison.

It did not appear to me that she had come to grips with the reality of prison yet. It's one thing to say, "I have to turn myself in." That takes a great leap of moral and intellectual courage. But I don't know that she had followed that leap with a grounded sense of what it actually entailed, leaving her family. I told her that it could be a long process and that I had no idea what the DA would offer.

I called Steven Black immediately and told him since it was not a probationary case that he needed to talk to her. I didn't know Power's location, but I was under the impression she lived somewhere near him, perhaps in Washington, Oregon, or California, even Alaska. At that point I thought she was in Alaska. "I can't hold her hand," I said. "You can." He accepted that role. He liked that role.

I met with Ralph Martin and Jack Cinquegrana after we had all done our homework. I opened by saying, "Let's try to figure this out. This is a woman who everyone in law enforcement thought was dead. She is making your case for you; you don't have to do anything except take her in and make things right with the Schroeder family. And this is a great gift for them."

I felt I was dealing with rational people, and my selling point was the appropriateness of the sentence.

Jack did most of the talking, and he was tougher than Ralph. "You're not talking about probation," he began.

I admitted the thought had crossed my mind, and if they would accept such a proposition I was fully prepared to put it on the table. Jack raised his eyebrows and rolled his eyes. I smiled at him and said, "Let's be serious about what we are dealing with here. Susan Saxe got twelve to fourteen. That is your ceiling. Before we start this conversation, you can never think of anything higher than twelve to fourteen."

"Yes, I can," Jack said. He was giving up nothing.

"Jack, we're not going to play this game. I am not here to nickel-and-dime you, and I don't want you to do it to me. Let's come to a reasonable conclusion."

"I don't know if we are ready to give her a twelve to fourteen," he said.

"Well, then, I'm leaving. Why did I even come here?" Did we have to play this out?

"All right, all right; let's talk about what you want."

"I think three to five is reasonable." In Massachusetts at that time, sentences included the minimum and maximum amount of incarceration; for a violent crime, the client has to serve two-thirds of the minimum. I didn't think there was any way I could ask for less than a three to five, which is about the lowest prison sentence a lawyer can propose without looking foolish. I did not want this to be a protracted negotiation, since I knew that every day that passed was a day Power could get caught. Of course, they would reject it, but I had to try.

"Well, fine." Jack shuffled his papers. "You can leave."

We were playing pro forma high ball–low ball. I argued that I needed a low bottom number because Katherine was voluntarily surrendering and therefore should not have to do a huge stretch in prison.

"We have nothing to discuss."

"Okay," I said. They weren't moving at this first session and neither was I. I picked up my bags, said good-bye, and left. But we both knew I'd be back. When I called Steven Black, I told him that we had made our opening gambit and they had laughed at me and I had laughed at them.

Ralph Martin stepped out of the picture temporarily, and Jack became the point man for the negotiations. Even though we both wanted to bring Katherine in, this was not going to be easy. He was playing tough prosecutor, I was playing tough criminal defense lawyer, and we just could not get to a number.

Jack and I met regularly, talked on the phone, and about once a month I would go to his office for negotiations. I would have a number and a reason; he would have a number and a reason. Sometimes we would actually deal with evidentiary questions, assuming the case would be tried. Other days we would simply propose and counter-propose. Where could we get to today?

Neither of us budged early. I felt that after more than twenty-two years of being a model citizen, three years in prison for driving a get-away car was sufficient. He said that three years for a crime in which a cop was killed was simply impossible. Power had had nothing to do with the killing, I said. He reminded me that, under the law, she was equally responsible as the man who pulled the trigger. In real life, I told him, she was not responsible. In real life, he told me, she was not going to get three years.

By springtime we had each moved a bit, but it was clear that we had reached an impasse; neither of us was willing to go any further. "This is really a pity," I said. "It's unacceptable to me and unacceptable to you, and we're not going to make a deal. Why is this? I can't understand."

Jack was clear. "This is a political decision for this office, and we will come under a great deal of criticism if there is not an appropriate disposition."

I tried to push him. "You know, I'm going to go talk to the Schroeder family."

Jack blew up. "Don't you dare! Who do you think you are?" He was furious. "Don't you go near them!" I shelved the idea.

During one of my calls with Katherine I told her we were at a standstill. "What shall we do?" she asked. "You have to make this choice," I said, "but my best advice is to let things chill for a while. There is a rumor afloat that a person who is very respected in the Boston Police Department may come back as police commissioner. A man named Bill Bratton. I've only barely met him once but I have an enormous amount of respect for him, and the department trusts him. The Boston Police Department is heavily involved; one of their own was killed and they want to see you go away for a long time. There may be a way for the DA's office to have this new commissioner approve the negotiated plea if we can convince him that your coming in is a good thing for the Boston PD and for the Schroeder family.

"I can't make this decision for you; this is something you need to think about. I don't think you should accept their present offer, it is too much time, but it is your life. If the FBI finds you, you are going away for a long time. You are at risk, and you should know how much you are at risk, but maybe we need to wait a little longer."

Katherine said she would think about it. She wanted to talk to Steven Black and needed to talk with her husband. Then she asked about the possibility of a trial.

I thought it was a bad idea but agreed to consider it. I felt that the state wasn't going to trial on a manslaughter charge and that she would be charged with felony murder of a police officer in the commission of an armed robbery. If they convicted her of murder, she would be in prison for life. This was gambling with her life, and I didn't want that responsibility. It didn't matter that Susan Saxe wound up with a manslaughter plea; if Katherine had to do ten to fifteen, it was a lot better than life. Right?

I needed to familiarize myself with the state's evidence in the event we actually did go to trial. There were two key witnesses around whom a trial would center, and I needed to know whether they were alive and if they would testify. Charlie Moore came back with information on each.

Robert Valeri been one of the three bank robbers alongside Susan Saxe. He had been captured almost immediately after the event and had flipped over on everybody, turning state's evidence in exchange for a plea bargain. He served a lengthy sentence. Charlie found out that over the years, Valeri had had a variety of problems. He had already testified at the Saxe trial, and the jury hadn't convicted her on his testimony. Not a credible witness, not a grave concern.

Another man had not taken part in the robbery, but in 1970 his apartment had been used as the staging area, with plans and guns coming in and out, and he had been there for all of it. This man had had money to pay for good lawyers and had managed to get himself a sweetheart immunity deal and avoided prosecution altogether. We investigated him and found that he was not only clean but respectable. This guy was going to be a problem for me if I had to try this case, and Katherine was in trouble if he got on the stand.

I called Ralph. "Do you think Bratton is coming back?" I asked.

"Sounds that way. So what?"

It had been a while since my last negotiating session with Cinquegrana. I said, "Jack and I are at an impasse here. If Bratton comes in and we can create a deal that is acceptable to the police department, will that help you?"

He was quite abrupt. "I don't have a clue. We are at one place;

you are at another. The DA is plea-bargaining this case, not the police commissioner!"

Not long thereafter I found myself at a Ralph Martin fund-raiser. District attorney is an elective office, so DAs are constantly running and holding fund-raisers, and defense lawyers attend because they need access. This particular party was being held at a lovely place on Park Street, overlooking the Boston Common. It was a springtime early evening, the trees were blossoming, flowers were everywhere, the Common looked extremely peaceful. I was there to pay my respects to Ralph; I certainly did not intend to discuss a case that no one was supposed to know about.

So who do I see in the room but Bill Bratton, who had ascended to the position of Boston police commissioner in March. Drink in hand, I buttonholed him near the picture window overlooking the park. "Commissioner Bratton, may I talk with you for a minute?"

Bill Bratton had been a home-grown Boston cop-on-the-rise. He had received a lot of publicity for his innovative work in the Boston Police Department and his rapid ascension in its hierarchy, but had run afoul of department politics and gone elsewhere to pursue his career. He served as chief of the New York City Transit Police and had returned to Boston as superintendent in chief. The insider's word had been that he would get the top job, and he did.

He looked at me blankly but pleasantly. I had received a certain amount of publicity myself, and we had met briefly the previous year at an Anti-Defamation League luncheon at which he had spoken against the establishment of a Civilian Complaint Review Board of police actions, but the look on his face made it absolutely clear to me that he had no memory of it. "I don't know if you remember me," I began.

"I think I know who you are," he said.

"This is the wrong place to do this, but if I don't talk to you now I might never have another opportunity. Do you remember a person by the name of Katherine Ann Power?"

"Yes." It was a rhetorical question. What police official would not remember a fugitive cop killer?

Bratton knew better than most. Although I was unaware of it at the time, when Bratton joined the Boston Police Department in 1970, his first police funeral had been for Walter Schroeder. Bratton was the first recipient of the BPD's Schroeder Brothers Medal of Valor. So, yes, he knew the name of Katherine Ann Power.

"I'm negotiating to bring her back to Boston."

If I was expecting some conversational help, I got none. He said nothing.

"I really need your help," I said.

Bratton was quite direct. "There's nothing I can do."

"Now that you've become the police commissioner," I continued, "your belief that her coming in is a good thing for the Schroeder family and the police department would be very helpful in getting it done."

His voice was pleasant but he was quite firm. "That's the district attorney's job, not mine."

"But you really could help."

"I'll be happy to listen to what Ralph Martin has to say," he offered, "but you really shouldn't be talking to me about this."

He was totally distanced, totally appropriate, but where other police commissioners might have slammed the door that I was putting my foot in, I thought—or prayed—that Bratton had left me some room.

"Well, that is fine! I'd be happy to set up a meeting with you and with Ralph in the future."

"Ralph Martin and I can talk about it if he chooses. You don't set up meetings with the commissioner and the district attorney."

As noncommittal as he had been, I still thought this was tremendously good news. One of the major obstacles to our negotiating a successful plea arrangement had been the district attorney's sensitivity to the reaction of the police department. For its part, the Boston Police Department as presently constituted wasn't going to be satisfied with anything Ralph Martin did. He was black; he was liberal; he had prosecuted cops. The department was sabotaging him daily. They were at war. Any deal I struck with Ralph, the department was going to dismiss by saying, "He's a sell-out. Forget it." As a result, Martin probably felt compelled to take a harder line with me so as not to alienate them. Three years for Katherine Power? They preferred the guillotine.

But I had been led to believe the cops loved Bratton, and apparently Bratton was a reasonable man. He also believed in Ralph Martin, which was a huge plus. If Bratton were willing to discuss and ultimately accept a negotiated plea, I thought the cops would say, "If Bratton thinks it's good, it must be good." (I had no idea the police union and Bratton had had great difficulties in the past. He had lots of enemies. Ignorance was clearly bliss.) Ten minutes earlier I had been stymied. Now I walked out of that party feeling as if a star were shining on me. Either I was delusional or I had supreme trust in my own instincts.

I strolled through Boston Common to the Public Garden. Filled with flowers, this place had always been a sanctuary for me. I was living day-to-day in a world of negativity; every piece of energy in the courthouse was about distress and disaster and murder and mayhem. In the garden I felt like Dorothy in the field of poppies. The sun was setting orange. I felt wonderful.

I called Philip. "You got a jacket on?"

"Yeah. What's up?"

"Meet me at the Ritz. I'm going to buy you a drink." How could he say no?

We sat in the bar drinking Dewar's. I told him, "I'm going to close the Katherine Power deal." I recounted my conversation with Bratton.

"He didn't tell you anything positive at all," Philip said.

"We are doing this deal."

"You are out of your mind."

"This deal will be done."

I went to a pay phone in the basement and called Steven Black. "She's going to do more time than she wants," I told him, "but it will be sufficient." I told him the Bratton story. "Nothing happened; you're dreaming," he said.

I called the DA's office the next morning. I didn't want this to fester. I met with both Ralph and Jack that afternoon. I repeated my Bratton conversation. They looked at me. "So?"

"Look," I told them, "you and I can reach some sort of agreement here, and if Bill Bratton will back you up and the department will not explode in your face, you are in a position to eliminate much of the political fallout."

Ralph understood, but he said, "That is all very nice, but we don't have an agreement."

I laid out my case for them, explaining that Charlie Moore found out Valeri had his share of problems. I knew I could rip him up on the stand. I didn't mention the other man. I also told them that since, by everyone's account, Katherine Power drove the switch car they could not make a case that she had any knowledge that Walter Schroeder had been killed, period. Moreover, the fact that she decided to turn herself in made her very sympathetic. I promised that when she testified she would be a fabulous witness.

"You are going to lose," I told them, "so let's talk about the plea deal."

They listened.

I reached into my briefcase and pulled out the clipping in which former DA Garrett Byrne said Katherine Power would get probation. I had been waiting for just this moment. "You are worried that the media is going to criticize you unless you give her extensive jail time. Here I've got the DA who had the case from the beginning saying she should get probation."

Jack has a better poker face than Ralph. Jack showed nothing. Ralph showed a flicker of understanding.

"Let's work this out," I said. They told me they'd get back to me with a number.

Philip picked me up outside the courthouse. We were going down to a barbecue function at Marshfield, which is on the south shore on the Atlantic Ocean. I needed to convey the day's events to Steven Black, so we got off the highway and pulled over at a small-town general store, a real throwback of a place. I went inside and asked for ten dollars' worth of quarters. The old-timer behind the counter looked at me as if I had three heads, but he gave me the change.

The pay phone was outdoors, not even in a booth. Trying to be both organized and inconspicuous, I stacked my quarters in ten groups of a dollar on the little shelf underneath that held phone books and dialed Black's number. As I began to dial I brushed the stacks and they went sliding all over the place. Here I was with the receiver tucked under my chin, Miss Clandestine negotiating the fate of a famous fugitive, while Philip and I were crawling on the ground gathering coins.

"They're going to come up with a decent number," I finally told Steven. "One we are going to live with. But we are going to have to talk Katherine into it." The longer the negotiations had gone on, the less malleable and more resistant she had become, which is natural. Negotiation raises the hackles in most people.

"We'll work it out," he said.

I then made sure that Black and I could talk regularly by arranging for his law firm to hire Philip's son as a summer intern. Finally I had a reasonable basis to call anytime.

Within a week, Ralph and Jack called and asked me to come see them. They came in at eight to twelve but would let me argue for less time to the court. I would argue for six as the bottom number. They felt confident with eight; they were throwing me a bone with six.

"This is the final offer," they told me. We had both come a long way.

"I think it is reasonable, under the circumstances," I told them, "and I'm going to recommend it to my client."

I arranged a call with Katherine right away. "Katherine," I said when I presented her with the offer, "this is it. If the judge accepts their position, you would serve two-thirds of the minimum, minus time off for good behavior, or about five to five and a half years. It will never get better than this, and my advice is that you should take it."

She was not pleased. "I really hoped it would be less," she said.

"We all did," I answered, "but I have done everything anyone could possibly do. Although I can argue to the court for less time, it's a real long shot. We can put together a great package about your life, but you need to be prepared for the eight-year number. I think you need to think about it; you need to talk to Steven about it, you need to talk with your husband. But I think this is a good offer for both sides."

Katherine was a very smart woman. Within days she called to deal with details. She accepted the length of her sentence but wanted to make certain that the state time would indeed be concurrent with her federal sentence. It was. She had concerns about where she would be located because she wanted to serve her time in Oregon, near her family. We had been through this before and I said I would try. I had no idea whether I could get this done but I was determined to do it. In my world, all things were possible. Clearly I could not mention her preferred location to the prosecutors without compromising Katherine's security, but even without my being specific, if the primary case against her was to be local, her sentence would most likely have to be served in Massachusetts. There were such things as prisoner trades, but given the highly visible, highly volatile nature of this case it seemed a long shot to think she might be given special consideration. I could only try to make that happen long after she surrendered.

Katherine was on vital and necessary antidepressant medication, and she wanted absolute assurances that she would have access to that medication throughout the corrections system.

I negotiated all of these issues with Jack Cinquegrana. Location of imprisonment did turn out to be a sticking point and bogged us down. Time was going by and Special Agent Branigan was getting antsy. I really needed to get Katherine in, but she did not want to return until September. It was by now the beginning of summer and she wanted to spend one last season with her son. He would go back to school; she would go to prison. I called Jack and told him.

"That is ridiculous!" He was apoplectic. "I won't even entertain this conversation."

"It's only a couple of months."

"Rikki, we are done."

"We've got issues we have to deal with. She really needs this time."

"You're playing a high-risk game. We've reached a deal." Nevertheless, Jack realized it would take time to get this complicated plea agreement in writing and signed. "September," he finally agreed.

I woke up early one Sunday morning, June 27, 1993, picked up the *Boston Herald,* and found the basis of our negotiations on the front page. Although the *Herald* did not have my name, they had much too much information.

My mother told me when I was around twelve years old, after I had dropped something on my foot and uttered a single expletive, "Rikki, there is nothing wrong with the word 'fuck.' It's just a word. Words won't hurt you. But it is an inappropriate word for a person to use at most times. It is a word to be savored. You should keep it close inside, so when you really need it, sometime other than when you stub your toe, you are allowed to let it out."

I called Jack Cinquegrana at home and woke him up. *"Did you read the fucking* Herald *today?!"*

"What happened?"

I read him the clip. In an extremely unfavorable article about Katherine that rehashed the bank robbery, the sixties, and the Schroeder murder were details of the plea negotiations and a prophesy of the already building anger of the Boston Police Department. "I want to see you. This came out of your office!" I was livid. "We are in a mess now." We had worked so hard to be able to present Katherine's return to our advantage in the press; now that opportunity was lost forever.

Special Agent Branigan called. "Did you see the *Herald*? This is not good."

"The only thing I can hope is that it begins and ends with this story." That didn't seem likely. "A public relations battle is bad for everybody." Branigan was no longer going to be a heroine; Ralph was going down the tubes; I was going to get sacks of hate mail. If only to be able to respond that it was on the case, the FBI would be forced to step up its efforts to find her.

I contacted David Weber, a *Herald* reporter. "I've got to talk to you. It has to be completely off the record." I tried to make an arrangement. In exchange for his not following up the article with several days of continuing coverage, in exchange for no more coverage at all, I promised him the first story on Katherine when she came in. He agreed. I breathed a great sigh of relief. For now, the story had been effectively quashed.

Or so I thought. Other reporters and columnists at the paper would not let it go, and the story raged for days.

And Katherine still wanted to stay out until September. We kept negotiating. Jack wanted to work out the details of where and how we surrendered her. Then there was, Who got her? Did the feds take her in? The Boston police? Turf wars.

We ultimately agreed that Katherine would turn herself in to Special Agent Branigan and a Boston police officer on September 15.

I wanted Katherine's family to see her before she gave herself up. They had not seen or heard from their daughter in twenty-three years. I planned to wait until the weekend before the return to contact them because I could not afford any more leaks. I first called Special Agent Branigan.

"I want to notify the Power family that their daughter is returning and that they should come to Boston to see her," I told her, "but the only way I can do so is to use your name to vouch for me; otherwise they're going to think I'm some nut case and not a lawyer."

Agent Branigan had been busy. She had already contacted the family who, though wary, had given a list of questions to be put to Katherine Power to assure themselves that the woman was who she claimed to be. Agent Branigan had passed that list to me along with family photos to be transmitted to Katherine, a ploy I'm sure the government hoped would help break security and run the fugitive to ground. She gave me the Powers' phone number. I called.

"Mrs. Power, my name is Rikki Klieman. I'm a criminal defense attorney in Boston and I've been in touch with your daughter Katherine." There was silence. "I would like to have a conversation with you and I think it will be a really good one." More silence. "But, so you don't think that I'm just a crazy person harassing you, I'd like you to call FBI Special Agent Kathleen Branigan, who will verify who I am." I gave her the agent's telephone number and said I would call back in fifteen minutes. When I did I said, "Your daughter is alive. She is well and she is going to turn herself in in Boston."

Mrs. Power just started to cry. "I can't believe it," she sobbed. "I can't believe it. I never thought this would actually happen." She cried for a considerable length of time. I don't know how you tell someone that, after twenty-three years, their daughter is alive and well and coming in from the cold. I cried with her.

"You should be very proud of her," I said when I could. "She is really a remarkable woman. She has worked in soup kitchens; she has worked with the poor. She is the person who made this choice to return and you really gave her some wonderful values."

"What should we do? What should we do? Can we see her? What can we do?"

"I would like you and your husband and whichever relatives you want to fly to Boston on September fourteenth. We will make arrangements at a hotel for you, and I will try to work it out so that you can visit with her before you see her in court."

"We have to see her."

"I can't guarantee that, but I'll try to make it work. I must stress to you, you can tell *no one* except the people you will bring with you. There is a chance that someone will try to get Katherine between now and then. It is critical that, no matter how much joy you have, you can't tell a living soul beyond the people getting on that plane."

Mrs. Power did not answer quickly. I wondered whether she was planning phone calls or was simply so dazed by the news that she couldn't speak. "Did you hear me?" I asked.

"Yes."

"I want you to repeat that back to me." She was in shock but I wanted her to have her wits about her.

"I'll be back in touch with you about hotels."

"I'll never know how to thank you," said Mrs. Power.

I adored my mother. We were so very close, and I can't imagine what it would have been like for me to be separated from her, unable to write or receive a letter, unable to call or be called, my mother not knowing if I was alive or dead for twenty-three years. I was overwhelmed. I would have paid Katherine Power for that moment. "I'm just so happy I can do this," I said. "This phone call was thanks enough."

"God bless you." Mrs. Power was crying again when she hung up.

As a lawyer my job was to offer people options, but I don't know if I'd had half a dozen opportunities in the course of my career in which I knew I'd made a real difference in the complete quality of another human being's life. The hotel room was very quiet as I sat down on the bed and looked out at the mountains, understanding with my heart as well as my head that I was doing a very important and deeply meaningful deed. I was clear about my commitment. I really missed my own parents so very much.

I had arranged for Katherine to call me later that day between 4:00 and 6:00. I knew her voice well when I picked up the phone. "I talked to your mother," I told her. "They are going to come to Boston to see you."

I had never heard Katherine cry.

Jack Cinquegrana felt we needed to see the judge who would be handling the case. I agreed. The presiding administrative judge at the Suffolk Superior Court was Robert Banks. As it happened, he and I had shared an office years earlier when he had been the first assistant district attorney in Norfolk County under Bill Delahunt. Banks had been a great trial lawyer and was a well-regarded judge. We had a lot of respect for each other.

Jack and I explained that we didn't want a media circus when we brought Katherine in. Because she was being charged with both state and federal crimes, we needed to get her to the state courthouse and the federal courthouse in one day. We needed a good judge to make sure things ran smoothly, and we got the right man. We would surrender her to the authorities at 6:00 in the morning, have her processed immediately, and get her through the state court system and over to the federal court by noon.

"Since you have an agreement," Judge Banks said, "I think we should plead her and sentence her on the same day."

I disagreed. Because I knew this case would attract tremendous media and legal attention, I felt the record should be absolutely clear as to why this plea agreement had been entered into. Since I was asking for less time, I felt I needed to provide the court with a full report, including letters and documents, and I could not prepare those documents beforehand because I could not let anyone in my law firm, let alone people around Katherine, know what I was doing.

Judge Banks told me I had gotten the best of the DA's office, and the longer the time between the uproar of bringing her in and the time of sentencing, the more he would be criticized for accepting this deal. I said, "Judge, you are not going to have any problem. This is a good, solid deal for everybody."

"Rikki, you are trying to con me."

"I am not. I think everybody thinks this is a good deal." It was clear that he was not convinced. Still, he delayed sentencing to accommodate the paperwork.

The judge wanted my word that I would not engage in any prereturn publicity. I agreed easily. "Why would I possibly jeopardize her surrender, Your Honor?"

"I think this is going to be a problem. I still think we should sentence her that day."

Judge Banks was angry. He clearly thought Katherine should do more time. There were plenty of reasons why—a police officer had been killed, the group of defendants had been violent, and the system should not be seen as rewarding fugitives.

I called Ralph Martin and said, "I'm bringing in the Power family, her parents and siblings. I would like her to meet with them the night before we turn her in."

"You can't do that. Although I trust your word, I don't have any doubt about it, if somebody finds her, you are at your peril."

I called Agent Branigan and asked her the same thing.

"Absolutely not," she told me. "Under no circumstances could I possibly permit that. When she enters the Commonwealth of Massachusetts, she must surrender immediately."

"Well, you have to admit, since I am surrendering her at six A.M., she is going to be there the night before."

"She is at risk."

"Kathleen, this is crazy."

"I am telling you, it is not only that the FBI might find her; now, with the leak in the press, the Boston police and the state police could all be looking for her. I can't guarantee her safe passage. I want you to give her to me as soon as she comes in."

"Kathleen, for God's sake, she hasn't seen her family in twenty-three years!"

"Not on my watch."

"I'm going to do it anyway."

"I have no sympathy for you. You might get *yourself* arrested. How could you even think about this?"

"Because I spoke to her mother."

Agent Branigan was furious, and I was defiant. We'd established a relationship of trust, and I'd just told her I didn't care what she asked. As far as she was concerned, I was asking the FBI's permission for a fugitive cop killer to have a party. As for me, I felt Mrs. Power ought to see her daughter before Katherine was slapped in handcuffs and put behind bars. I was doing this for the mother, and nothing was going to stop me.

So I did what any headstrong person would do: I went to the one person I knew who knew how to move people around—Philip—and asked his advice. We booked the Power family by name into several hotels from Providence to Maine. We arranged for Katherine, her husband, and her son, accompanied by Steven Black, to fly in two days early. Changing cars and taking evasive action along the way, Philip and I drove up and met them at an out-of-the-way bed-and-breakfast in Newburyport. I asked at the desk for Mr. Black's room, walked down the hall, knocked on the door, and there I was, face-to-face with Katherine Ann Power. She had an extraordinary grin.

I hugged her; she hugged me. She is barely four foot eleven, even shorter than I am. She held me by the shoulders and actually looked up at me and said, "Thank you for everything you have done." I broke down and this fugitive held me.

Katherine's husband, Ron Duncan, looked like a sixties relic. He had long, stringy, strawberry-blond hair and an unkempt beard and was wearing old jeans and wire-rimmed glasses. Katherine was wearing overalls. They really looked like an Oregon hippie couple out of some other era. Next to them, Steven Black looked like a banker.

We went to dinner and talked about what she had done in Oregon—her cooking, her work in restaurants, her friends—everything but her surrender, because we were in public. She had a gentle and secure quality about her, speaking slowly and deliberately, without hesitation. She was at peace with her decision to face her punishment, and I found her remarkably courageous.

A day later Philip picked up the Power family at the Providence airport and, putting his federal training to work once again, drove them around to lose whoever might have been tailing him before eventually checking them into the Sheraton Commander Hotel in Cambridge. I went to work and tried to act normal. I didn't want any part of greeting them; I had made myself very public, and if anyone was being tailed, it was me.

Philip was at the hotel when they met, but he left them alone. The meeting must have been overwhelming for this reunited family. Tears, laughter, memories . . . a toast to the future. Photos, smiles . . . too many smiles.

On the morning of September 15, we scrambled cars and all wound up in the parking lot of Boston College Law School in Newton, Massachusetts, at 6:00 A.M. The FBI was waiting; the Boston police were waiting. I had barely gotten out of the car when Steven Black arrived with Katherine and her husband.

I'm sure there was some major turf battle between the Boston police and the FBI. I don't know how they resolved it, but they ran the surrender by the book. Law enforcement agents from both organizations surrounded the car, took her out, cuffed her. Boston police Lieutenant Detective Timothy Murray got to do the cuffs. Agent Branigan was given the choice assignment to bring her in, and she was visibly nervous when reading Katherine her rights. Performance anxiety, I assumed; her voice was shaking. She must have wanted desperately not to screw up.

The scene was tense, actually a little frightening. I had been lulled into the sense that I could just pass Katherine along; I had never given thought to the physical act of transfer. The agents and officers were dealing with a former member of the FBI's Most-Wanted List, and they were by no means casual. They were very brusque, all business. The whole exchange took about thirty seconds.

Steven Black and I had worked for hours constructing a multipage press release telling the story from our perspective. Reporters are notoriously lazy, so if you give them an angle that is intelligent, interesting, and responsible, rather than do their own legwork they are very likely to run with yours. We had high hopes. The bank rob-

bery, the death, the fugitive—we had worked hard to explain everything properly, and we had developed a great document. We had
also asked Katherine to write a one-page statement expressing whatever she felt was appropriate. In my office that morning we stacked
perfectly stapled piles of these releases, to be distributed to every
media outlet at 9:00 A.M., after Katherine got to the courthouse.
However, Steven had leaked one to the *Boston Globe* earlier, and they
put what was essentially our version of the story on the front page
that morning.

Black had not made the no-publicity agreement with Judge
Banks, but I had. When that story leaked, I knew I would have to
take what I deserved. The judge, I knew, would be furious, and not
only that, I had made a promise to Dave Weber of the *Herald* to give
him the first Katherine Power story after her surrender. I owed him,
and now it would appear that I had betrayed that trust. Forget the
Herald for positive stories from here on in.

I thought I had handled everything right—thirteen months of
negotiations, one leak that I quashed fairly quickly, a well-crafted
press release that turned into a front-page article in which Katherine
Power came through very favorably—but as I entered the main
police station on Berkeley Street, the men and women in uniform
were angry. As a defense lawyer, despite the fact that I was representing people they had arrested and basically thought were scum, I
had always gotten along with cops, but now they were extremely
unfriendly. As sophisticated as I thought I was concerning law
enforcement personnel, I had completely misjudged their reaction.
There is a huge difference in their mind, I was made to understand,
between even the most heinous criminal and a person involved with
someone who kills a cop. It was very apparent that I was going to
have a problem with the police.

Judge Banks was even more furious than I had imagined. The
story in the *Globe* stood in complete disregard of his direct order. He
called us into chambers immediately as we entered his courtroom,
steam as much as coming out of his ears. "You gave me your word. I
trusted you. You betrayed me. How dare you! I've known you for all
these years. How could you do this?"

Steven Black stepped in. "It wasn't her; it was me. I didn't know."

Judge Banks wasn't buying it. "You didn't communicate that to him?"

"Your Honor," Steven continued, "with all due respect, we've been trying to do so many things in the last twenty-four hours. . . . If I had understood that this would have affected you this way, or that you had issued an order, I would never have done it."

"Your Honor," I sputtered, "I'm sorry."

Judge Banks's face was bloodred. "I don't believe either one of you. Rikki, I will never trust you as an advocate again."

I was devastated, but he was right. Bob Banks and I went back a long way; I had tremendous respect for him as a jurist and a man and now our relationship was in tatters. Jack and Ralph stood stone still, didn't say a word. You don't chance a confrontation with an angry judge. Not a word.

The judge reiterated his belief that he should impose sentence immediately. I again respectfully disagreed. Now, more than ever, I felt I needed to document the reasons for the agreement.

"So be it," he said.

What happened next was a blur. I have no memory of entering the plea or of Judge Banks putting it over for sentencing, or of taking Katherine to federal court. Only one thing is clear in retrospect. When Katherine left her holding cell and entered the courtroom, she saw her entire family, old and new, sitting in the front row. Her passive face broke into a beatific grin. That ear-to-ear smile was captured by photographers and wound up in *Newsweek* and countless papers across the country. She should never have smiled. Taken out of context it was a public relations disaster. It appeared that Katherine was dancing unrepentant on Walter Schroeder's grave.

Black and I and Ron Duncan did every morning and evening news show, every morning magazine show. I did the *Today* show and *Good Morning America* in the same morning. At that moment Katherine Power was the most famous criminal defendant in America, and therefore Steven Black and I were America's most famous criminal defense lawyers. It was very heady.

I had intended to deal with reporters one by one, but the demand was so instantaneous and overwhelming that it would have taken all day, so we decided to hold a massive press conference in my office. We arranged a *Newsweek* interview; we organized *Time*; we were unceasing and relentless with the press in service of our client that day.

After that day, however, it was the press who was unceasing and relentless with us. The phones started ringing and didn't stop for months. The other lawyers in my office were furious with me: Not only had I sprung this case on them, but they couldn't get client calls; they couldn't get business done. I had never seen anything like this.

It is very flattering when Diane Sawyer, Katie Couric, Barbara Walters, and Peter Jennings all call you themselves; that high-volume star power is how they get their stories, and it works. Steve Kroft flew in to sit down with me. Connie Chung arrived and afterward sent about $250 of white roses and lilies. Barbara Walters was gracefully persistent. I got a little taller each day. This was pretty cool.

My office became cluttered with stacks of books, manuscripts, and movie scripts from writers, publishers, and producers all over the country who wanted to do the Katherine Ann Power story. My entire day became managing this public relations and book and movie life. My partners were not happy, because I didn't have time to bill work.

The television magazine people were the most aggressive. They figured they had three entries to get to Katherine: me, Steven Black, and her husband, Ron, who was the most naive and vulnerable. They would send their producers up to see us; they would take us in limousines to eat in tony restaurants; they would give Ron plane tickets. And all they wanted was to see Katherine first and get that interview. Ron and Katherine had no money, and the amounts that the TV people were offering were very seductive.

Movie people and agents called: Abby Mann wants to do the story with Oliver Stone. If only I'd been an actress! Part of me thought this was the greatest thing in the entire world. It was nice to be the center of attention, even if I could not eat or sleep.

I made it clear that Katherine would give no interview until after the sentencing, and that she would choose to whom she would speak. I tried to keep a lid on publicity because I felt our initial splash was plenty and that we needed time to sort this out, but Steven Black was a public defender from Corvallis, Oregon, and I could not control him. The story was everywhere.

I thought I had done a terrific job. We had positioned Katherine as a woman of conscience, a person who after two decades of depression and attempted restitution had at last come home to accept her punishment. That portrait played for a while, at least. Times had indeed changed in twenty-three years, and Katherine received an enormous outpouring of sympathy from certain members of the press, some even calling for her to be spared jail time and given probation. The Schroeder family was prepared to accept her apology and obtain some measure of satisfaction that the final person with responsibility for Walter Schroeder's death was finally being punished. Katherine herself was adjusting to incarceration better than any client I'd ever worked with.

The sentencing hearing was put off for a month, and in that month things turned. At the same time that Katherine Power was being portrayed in some parts of the media as a heroine of redemption, a backlash was gathering in Boston that threatened to undo all our hard work.

COP'S WIDOW LASHES OUT AT EX-FUGITIVE read the *Herald*'s headline. Under it the story talked of Mrs. Schroeder's "honesty and perspective" and the "strangely 'triumphant' spectacle" of Power's return.

"Richard Nixon made her do it? Oh, how perfect," opined the *Herald*, "how very convenient. And how absurd! . . . But Power is oh so sorry now."

"After twenty-three years she wants to cleanse her soul and make it right?" asked Walter Schroeder's son Paul, now a Boston police detective. "She don't make nothing right with us."

I had not expected such reaction; the ensuing torrent of negative publicity made life difficult for the attorneys in my law firm who were working on other cases. In plotting the course of action for Katherine Power I really had never thought about how it would play out in the press to the detriment of my client and all we had worked to achieve.

The Boston police would not stand for the beatification of a cop killer. The Schroeder family backed off from their acquiescence and became more and more hostile. The media hostility fed on itself, turning the press and the public increasingly against her, and by the time of Katherine's sentencing the atmosphere was wild. Headlines were blaring; papers were selling: More than a person, a radical past was put on trial in Boston, and Katherine Power was made to signify all that was wrong with the sixties.

In the face of this backlash I was having difficulty negotiating the fine points of our deal. Her medication, which should have been simple to obtain, turned into an issue. Because the publicity had reinforced Katherine's image as a cop killer, neither the Federal Bureau of Prisons nor the Massachusetts Department of Correction was going to do me any favors. Forget finding her a cell in Oregon; usually the state can't wait to get rid of the expense and responsibility involved in housing a prisoner, but Katherine Ann Power must have been the first prisoner that a state actually wanted to keep.

I had made a terrible mistake. If I had agreed to have her sentenced immediately, as Judge Banks had counseled, we would have eliminated all this. But walking into the courthouse on the day of sentencing, we were in the middle of a firestorm.

Judge Banks had told me in chambers a day earlier, "She has a right of elocution at her sentencing hearing. I'll give her seven words and she better not say 'Vietnam.' I don't want to hear any of that stuff or, I'm telling you, I won't sentence her according to the agreement." There were other nonnegotiable terms: No one could speak on her behalf, including her husband and son. While Katherine was given seven words, the Schroeder family would be allowed unrestricted time to speak; this was their final opportunity to eulogize and they could say whatever they felt at whatever length. Katherine was also not permitted to look at the Schroeder family. She was not allowed to turn to them and say she was sorry, not even so much as make eye contact. Face front. Of course, that would leave the impression to anyone who saw her—and to those who were reporting the scene— that she was cold and uncaring, but these were the rules.

Katherine was well prepared on the day of her sentencing. She recognized the solemnity of the occasion; she was prepared to accept the court's strictures, her responsibility, and her fate. Her lifetime of action and then remorse and restitution had brought her to this moment. She was somber when she was led into the courtroom.

The jury box was filled with police brass, including Commissioner Bratton, whose attendance was commanded by Judge Banks. The gallery was teeming with press and a very large contingent from the Schroeder family. All that was missing was a twenty-one-gun salute. A Schroeder daughter, Clare, who was also a cop, delivered one of the most eloquent speeches I had ever heard and spoke for around thirty minutes. Katherine kept her eyes forward.

When it came time for her to address the court, Katherine said more than seven words. Judge Banks dared not stop her. She told the court, "Your Honor, twenty-three years ago I undertook a course of action that resulted in the death of another human being." She was choking back tears. "I cannot possibly say in words how sorry I am for the death of Officer Schroeder. My whole adult life has been a continuing act of contrition for my act in contributing to his death. I am here today because I recognize that I also have a debt to my society resulting from my actions in 1970. You will measure that debt and I will begin to discharge that debt, and I will continue to live my life from today forward as a responsible citizen abiding by the law. Thank you, Your Honor." Then she sat down.

Judge Banks tacked on twenty years' probation to Katherine's sentence and issued an order under which she could not profit from her story. Katherine never wanted to profit from her story for a moment. Included in that order were her agents and representatives. Whatever fee I might have thought I could garner from the sale of book or movie rights to cover the fact that I had worked these thirteen months without income was out the door.

Katherine Ann Power went peacefully to prison, and I almost had a nervous breakdown.

From the outside my life must have seemed extremely glamorous. I was a role model for successful women, making the most of my opportunity, shining in the spotlight. To my colleagues I was the most famous and popular criminal defense lawyer in the country. Think of

Roy Black after defending William Kennedy Smith or Johnnie Cochran after O.J. I could not walk down the streets of Boston without being recognized or followed by the press; I was in the papers and on television constantly; it was everything you could want from media stardom.

Except I could control nothing. I had to look like everything was planned and provided for, but my law firm was near bankruptcy because I had brought in no business, and my personal life was almost in ruins.

The alarm rang one morning and I cowered under the sheets, pillows covering my head, refusing to move. Philip said, "You have to get out of bed."

"I can't go to work," I told him.

He began to peel the pillows away one by one. "You've got to go."

"I can't take this for another day."

Joking, he lifted me off the mattress. That was easy; by this time I had lost fifteen pounds and wasn't eating. I was bony. And I was exhausted. "I can't do it."

He placed me back in bed, turned on the water in the bathtub, filled it with bubble bath, came back, picked me up, carried me over, and gently slid me in. "Just lie here for a while. Then you've got to go to work."

I knew I couldn't handle this. I cried amid the bubbles. But I got up, got dressed, put on my makeup, and put in a full day.

Everyone wanted a piece of me, just as I'd always wanted. I either drank or Valiumed myself to sleep each night, sometimes both. I had reached the pinnacle. I had reached the bottom.

fourteen **BRILL'S CONTENT**

 'VE GOT TO STOP THIS OR I'M GOING TO BE DEAD," I TOLD STEVE LYONS IN EARLY 1994. "I'll make you a deal. I'll take five weeks off; you take five weeks off some other time. You cover my cases, then I'll cover yours. It's either that or we dissolve the partnership, because I'm no good to you or anyone else right now." Steve graciously agreed and Philip and I hit the beaches in Hawaii.

Or should I say, I collapsed on them.

The first thing I did was sleep. Just sleep. The idea that I didn't have to get up in the morning, any morning, was so unique that I had a hard time getting used to it. I did nothing. That was impossible, but I did it.

After a few days we eased into activity. We went for a run in the morning; we worked out in the gym; we snorkeled in the clear ocean; we read books; we ate wonderful food. And we didn't drink. Neither of us. That was another first.

Two weeks in Maui, two in Kauai, a final stop in Honolulu. What a wonderful, relaxed place Hawaii was. How completely different from the vibrating stress of Boston. I could stay there forever.

Philip said it out loud. "Your life is just not right in Boston anymore. But you know how to be a lawyer; that's what you do. Why don't we do some exploring about lawyering in Maui or Honolulu?"

Sometimes good ideas are undeniable. I could find no reason to say no. I had hit the wall at the law firm, and I had conceived no plan to recapture my zest when I returned. Boston was over. I said, "Great!" The vision was clear in my mind from the moment he put it into words. Then I did what I always do; I began a campaign.

I looked in my directory and found lawyers to talk to. I visited Brook Hart, who had handled Kenny Leonard for me more than a decade earlier, and wondered aloud whether he had an opening. He asked if I was serious. I was. He didn't need a partner but, he said, "The federal defender's job is about to come up. That's a prestigious job; maybe that's a way for you to get your feet in the door in Hawaii, to get to know the judges and the lay of the land. Maybe you should consider applying for that." I set about to consider it seriously.

Marjorie Ziffrin, one of my college roommates, and her husband were well established in Honolulu. She was involved in several charity and community groups and could introduce us to a whole world of people and situations. So we had the beginnings of a social circle. This was not frivolous. Philip and I began to look in earnest for property to buy in Maui. And the more I thought about living in Hawaii, the more I warmed to the idea. The sun shone; the surf beckoned. We could do this!

Steve Lyons called. A lawyer from California was trying to get in touch with me. "Just give me his number," I said. "I'll call him."

The California lawyer laid it out. His client, a vice president of Honda, was facing a sizable federal indictment in the District of New Hampshire. Bribery, kickbacks—big. He needed a local Boston cocounsel; I'd done a lot of work in the District of New Hampshire; he'd been told I was the lawyer who could handle it. We should meet. This was a big case, a lot of money; we could share it.

Hmmm.

I told Philip, "You know, on the way back to Boston, I'm going to L.A. and talk to this guy."

Philip rolled his eyes. "I'm going out for a walk." He was gone for quite some time. When he got back, he said, "I thought we were looking to move."

"Well, I owe Stephen something. I haven't brought in any money in a year; this is a federal case in New Hampshire; it shouldn't be that hard. . . ." All my usual rationalizations.

Philip was incredulous. And rightfully so. For several weeks he had been seduced by the vision of life in Hawaii; he had actually begun to believe that I was on the road to recovery, that we could live together in paradise. We had looked at houses and had contemplated creating a new home of our own. Now he saw that for what it was. "So this whole venture in Hawaii, in Maui, is a fantasy?" I was silent. He was disgusted. "It was real for me, but it was a fantasy for you, because you can't help who you are."

I had learned nothing. I thought I could live outside the limelight, but I couldn't. The whiff of Boston's legal excitement overwhelmed the fragrance of Hawaii's serenity like a barbecue truck passing a field of gardenias. I was quite aggravated with myself. I had said I wanted to change my life; I had said I wanted to slow down. But every time you change your circumstance, every time you change your location, you take yourself with you. And in that moment I could see that, while I truly would like to be the person I kept saying I was, I was not that person. I needed applause; I needed fame; I needed to live life out loud and hear people say, "She's a great lawyer." Part of me wanted to live in the country, watch waterfalls in Hawaii, sit on the sand and watch the sunset. But I was a trial lawyer. Put me on a beach, put me on a mountain, that's who I was:

Rikki Klieman, Trial Lawyer. If you took that away from me, who would I be?

I could have had a career in Hawaii, but I had worked up to the pinnacle of the legal profession in Boston, and I didn't have the heart or strength to step down from that mountaintop and start over, even in nicer, more peaceful surroundings. The vision of RJK, Powerful Boston Criminal Defense Lawyer, was so clear I scared myself.

I did return to Boston via Los Angeles; I did take the New Hampshire case; and it did make us a lot of money, which calmed me and eliminated the necessity to chase around after other big-dollar opportunities. Disappointed that I had returned to my hectic law practice, Philip suggested, since I enjoyed public speaking and was so well received, that after all these years of doing it for free I do it for money. I put together a packet, bought business cards, made an audiotape, went to conferences to seek representation by a speakers' bureau, and began to think about a nice little cottage industry. I would still be traveling more than I would have liked, but public speaking fees would be found money, and I could try to live a more balanced life. If I had learned nothing else from the events of the past year, it was that left to my own devices I would kill myself for the law. Maybe I shouldn't do that.

I met Steve Brill in early 1994 at a meeting of the Advisory Committee to the United States Supreme Court on the Federal Rules of Criminal Procedure in Washington, D.C. The committee was looking at the issue of cameras in the courtroom. As founder and CEO of Court TV, Brill was vitally interested in expanding coverage to the federal courts. Massachusetts had allowed cameras in its courts since 1980, and I had found it not only exhilarating but helpful. Brill knew of my legal work; his magazine, *The American Lawyer*, had run a profile of me. "You should come on Court TV as a guest," he told me.

"I hate to tell you this," I admitted, "but I've never seen Court TV." It wasn't on our cable system.

He explained that the network aired a live trial and featured an anchor and a commentator who discussed the case on the air. Brill invited me to be a guest on the New York–based show.

I was very interested, and I was bubbling when I got home. "This is great! I'd love to do this!" Philip agreed. "You'd have a lot of fun," he said.

Schedules being what they are, we could not arrange a date until early July, when I agreed to be a commentator for two days in succession. As it happened, O.J. Simpson was charged with killing Nicole Brown Simpson and Ron Goldman on June 12, 1994, and when I arrived the country was rapt in the midst of the Simpson preliminary hearing. I spent several hours on the air with Court TV anchor Fred Graham and another long segment with anchor Jack Ford.

I had a fine time. This was easy! The issues jumped out at me; the personalities were dynamic; the stakes extremely high. All I had to do was watch the proceedings and talk about them. I did that at Maison Robert pretty much every night. I loved being in front of the camera and I chatted up a storm.

At one of the breaks Jack Ford said, "You should do this for a living."

"What?"

"I'm serious. You would be great at this job."

"Well, I have a job and I live in Boston."

"You should think about it."

The next day in a *New York Daily News* television column, Eric Mink reviewed the legal hit list of people who had been on the air commenting on the Simpson trial and wrote, "One of the best experts to date has been Boston attorney Rikki Klieman. Substantive and direct, she strips the complexity from questions and explains what remains simply." I arrived at the studio the next morning to find it buzzing. My cocommentator that morning was former Maine Attorney General Jim Tierney. During a commercial Jack Ford asked him, "Jim, don't you think she should become an anchor on Court TV?"

Tierney went along with it. "I think that's great." Now I had two buddies. They were like my criminal defense lawyer pals championing me.

When I got home and told Philip, he smiled.

Now I wanted it. The work was pretty much everything I could ask for: highly visible, intellectually stimulating, fun. I didn't know how much a job like that paid, but it was television, so I assumed they paid decently.

I called Tierney for advice. How could I position myself? How could I encourage someone who made decisions about such matters to notice me? "Should I send Brill a letter?" I asked.

Tierney, lawyer to the bone, said, "It's always better to be wanted than to ask."

I stood tight.

A month later I was at the first session of Gerry Spence's Trial Lawyers College at Thunderhead Ranch in Wyoming, which was pretty heady. This was the inaugural session, and I was honored to be on the faculty alongside such notables as my idol "Racehorse" Haynes; the hero of the Southern Poverty Law Center, Morris Dees; Al Krieger; Howard Weitzman; Philip Corboy of Chicago; Joe Jamail of Texas. We were living in the main house and cabins on this ranch doing trial advocacy work as well as participating in some of Spence's more avant-garde bonding rituals, such as painting canvases, telling stories around the campfire, and revealing "psychodramas," which left as many as half the people there sobbingly in touch with their pasts. Gerry felt one must exercise the whole person, but that was a little edgy for me.

One morning we were all called upon to find a private moment on a private piece of ground and meditate on our lives. We were to leave in silence, commune with our spirits, write in our journals, and return not as we had left but somehow advanced—and still in silence. Then we would gather and share what we had learned. So as the sun rose I was on my little hill, meditating and freezing, when I saw a hawk glide across the sky. It called to me, not physically, but it made its message known. I was going to travel. And wherever I was going was right for me. I felt strangely peaceful.

Maybe this Spence thing had some merit.

I finished my meditation, ate breakfast without speaking, and walked to the room where we were to share. Someone came running from the main ranch house to intercept me. "You have a telephone call."

It was my secretary, whom I called back immediately. "I'm sorry to bother you but it's a real emergency. There's a man who says he's the executive producer for Court TV and you have to call him right away."

I called the number and a guy answered. "Steve Johnson."

"Hi, this is Rikki Klieman."

"I'm the executive producer of Court TV. I need you to get on a plane and come here to audition to cover the O.J. Simpson case. I want you to anchor the case. Jack Ford just told us that he's leaving today to go to NBC and we need to replace him right now."

"Okay, who is this? Is this a joke?"

"This is not a joke. I am who I say I am. If you want to be our anchor we need to see you now."

"I'm two and a half hours north of Jackson Hole, Wyoming. It's Thursday. I can't even get there tomorrow."

"Can you be here Monday morning?"

"I guess."

"See you then."

After the sharing meeting I told Gerry about the call. "Go. It's perfect for you."

I called Philip and told him. "Wow," he said. And then, "What, did you dream it?"

I called Steve Lyons. "I got this wacko call from someone who says he's from Court TV. What do you think?"

"Oh, come on, the job has your name on it!"

I flew to Boston, exchanged my blue jeans and cowboy boots for a suit, then flew to New York.

I was loose as a goose when I auditioned. I was very flattered, but my business was doing well, my public speaking career was about to begin, I didn't take this seriously one bit.

And, of course, when you're loose and uninhibited, you're at your best. I read from the TelePrompTer, conducted a mock question-and-answer session with Steve Johnson as a guest—yes, he was the executive producer—then threw to a commercial break, came back from a break. I had a ball. This was a fantasy, so why not enjoy it?

At lunch afterward I thanked Johnson for inviting me. "The person you ought to thank is Jack Ford." When Ford gave notice that he was leaving, Johnson said, Steve Brill went off the wall screaming. Ford said, "Wait a minute! I have the perfect person for my job. You know Rikki Klieman? She's made for television!" Apparently that soothed him.

Johnson told me they were auditioning about a dozen people, but that they would keep in touch. They would be making a decision within a couple of weeks, he said. I flew back to Wyoming, finished the session, and returned to Boston. I didn't hear anything, but I didn't give it much thought, either.

In early September I flew to Los Angeles to act in a mock trial of the Simpson case. Television was full of these mockumentaries and in this one I played a defense attorney for O.J. The afternoon before taping, from a pay phone at a restaurant, I called the office for messages and found that Steve Brill needed to hear from me, so I called him.

"We want you to come back and do a second audition."

"Great, when?"

"Friday." There was a clatter of dishes behind me. "Where are you?"

"Los Angeles."

"What are you doing there?"

I told him about the mock trial.

His voice became hard and solemn. "Rikki, if you do that program, don't come here Friday."

"What?"

"We do real trials. We have integrity at Court TV. The idea that you would even consider doing a mock trial where people vote about guilt before he has been put to trial, when he has the presumption of innocence, which you well know as a criminal defense lawyer . . ." Brill fumed. "This kind of program is a disgrace. It's everything I fight against at Court TV. I'm almost tempted to forget your audition because you even considered doing it. The fact that you're out there shows me you have no judgment."

"Steve, I'm so sorry, I didn't realize —"

"Well, you *should* have realized. It's your choice. You have to cancel that appearance, whether you're going to come audition for me or not." This was what I later learned was called "getting Brilled."

"I'll cancel the appearance!"

I got off the phone shaken. Now that they might put the kibosh on me, I realized that I really did want this job. But since I had committed to doing the mock trial, how was I going to get out of it?

I called the producer and bowed out of the show, claiming a vague personal matter. I suggested another lawyer, and when I called him, he agreed to take my place. Then I called Brill. I was breathless, scared, and sweating, my blood ringing in my ears. I told him I was out of the mock trial and coming to the audition.

I flew to New York thinking I was auditioning again. However, I was ushered into Brill's office. "You blew them away. I don't need to audition anyone else. I'm offering you the job." Great! "And we're going to negotiate your deal right now."

I am truly not good at this. I can function at a high level for somebody else, but I am significantly less successful when arguing for myself.

"I can't negotiate my own deal," I complained.

"Do you want the job or not?" Brill was a tough guy. He'd planned this, and it worked.

"I want the job."

"Then we're doing it now."

I was not entirely unprepared, however. Jack Ford had told me that when it came to dealing with Steve Brill I should get all my perks first, when they wanted me, at which point I would be in the driver's seat; once I was inside the organization I was just "talent." But I didn't have a clue what kind of salary to ask for. I had done no research and was caught off guard, since I had no idea what a television anchor made. I didn't want to price myself out of the market, but I also didn't want to be taken for a fool.

Of course, Brill had done his research fully. "I write about law firms," he told me. "I have a general sense of what you make for a living over the last number of years on your W-2."

"You mean my K-1." I was a partner in Klieman, Lyons, not an employee . . . I'd have him know.

"Yes." He pressed on. "I'll offer you half."

"What did you just say?"

"Every lawyer in the country wants this job. I'm giving you the opportunity to comment on the case of a lifetime, a moment in history, on TV every single day. We're going to be the network of record. I could pay you nothing. I could pay you one-tenth of what you make as a lawyer. I'm willing to gamble that I have a sense of what you earn, and I'm going to offer you what I think is half, and you can take it or leave it."

Primary rule of negotiating: Force the other side to make the first offer.

"What's the number?"

He was pretty close.

Ford had made some nonsalary suggestions, so I gathered myself and began to negotiate on my own behalf. "Well, number one, my home is in Boston. I'm going to need some sort of residential allowance; I have to find a place to live when I'm in New York. Two, I'm going to have to commute to Boston on the weekends and I need to negotiate a deal in which either my husband or I fly each way. I teach a course at Boston University Law School this semester and I need to commute to Boston one day a week to do that."

He asked me to get out of the course. I refused because of the commitment I'd made to the school and the students.

I had no idea what it cost to live in New York, so when I based my calculations on Boston prices, my residential allowance was woefully low. I was taking a 50 percent cut in pay. Was I crazy?

No. It was indeed the job of a lifetime.

"When do you want me to start?"

"October first."

"That's three weeks from now! I have a law firm; I have clients."

"Work it out."

"When do you think Simpson's going to start?"

"We don't know."

I got the job!

Philip and I took the train down from Boston. Court TV was putting me up in a hotel while I looked for a rental apartment, and we were laden with suitcase upon suitcase of clothes. We arrived in Penn Station, carted the luggage to a cab, and what should have been a ten-minute trip eight blocks across town took a full hour. There was a parade—Jamaican Day? Greek Awareness? Polish Pride? All we knew was that people were streaming in front of us, we weren't moving, and the meter was running at a gallop. We got to the hotel and the room wasn't ready. Philip, who hated New York to begin with, said, "All right, we'll go for a walk."

I said, "Let's go to the river." Rivers are soothing and sensual. In Paris, a walk to the Seine is a romantic experience. So we were walking east and as we approached a McDonald's on the northwest corner of Thirty-ninth Street and Second Avenue we saw a cop car. There were people yelling. As we got closer we saw there was a man on the ground with blood streaming everywhere. The man was dead or close to it. The incident must just have happened; the police were arresting somebody, and several officers were shoving him into the patrol car.

Welcome to New York.

The word *splayed* does not do a body justice. It is a grotesque sight. It is not natural.

I had never seen a body in the street before. Philip, though he'd been a federal agent, was shaken as well. We turned the corner and headed for the East River.

There was a promenade by the water's edge; we could see it from across the street. But we couldn't get there from here. The FDR Drive had no stoplight: Traffic was shooting by both uptown and down; there were on-ramps and off-ramps and nowhere to cross. We looked to our right and about five blocks down saw a traffic light. We walked toward it and crossed there when the light turned green.

The light had turned red behind us and traffic was blistering again when we found we were in an underpass in the middle of a homeless camp. The signs were unmistakable: The stench of feces and urine was unbearable; the tents and cardboard boxes were barely upright; dozens of people in rags were sitting and standing, mumbling to themselves. For a moment I was terrified.

Philip took my hand and pulled me to the other side. We traversed the camp and emerged on a walkway. Finally. We tried to put some distance between us and this horror story and found a park bench facing the water. It wasn't so very clean, either. I was shaking when I sat.

Philip's face was red, his fists were clenched. Whatever turmoil he was going through, he wasn't talking. I thought, I've landed in a war zone. I turned to him. "Let's talk this through. I don't have to take this job." I got about one more sentence out when a helicopter began to rise from a heliport not one hundred yards away. We hadn't noticed it. The blades were whining, the rotaries whipping New York's riverside debris into wicked projectiles of grime. We couldn't hear a word. We were The Out-of-Towners!

When it lifted off and I took my hands away from my ears, I was in tears. "I'm not taking this job. We don't deserve this. You don't deserve this. This town is crazy. I'm going to tell them tomorrow that I'm not going to start."

"No, you can't do that." Even though he was furious, Philip still thought of me first. "This job has your name on it." He and Steve Lyons were clearly on the same wavelength. "You have to take this job. The Simpson trial will start; you'll get to L.A. This time in your life will never come again. It's everything you've always wanted, and I can't stand in the way. We will make this work."

What a wonderful man.

Steve Lyons was remarkably agreeable as well. We tried to draft documents to dissolve the partnership and then realized that our handshake would do. Our mutual trust and respect was paramount; our friendship was unshakable. We maintained the name of the firm, and I moved from the partner side of the letterhead to the "of counsel" side. It was, and still is, his law firm—but I'm there in spirit.

I finished up cases throughout 1994 and 1995. I transferred many to Steve and to other criminal lawyers in Boston who were caretakers and great tacticians as well. There is nothing quite as liberating as saying good-bye to clients. I had practiced law for twenty years, not seventeen, not twenty-two. It seemed like the right time— a milestone—to move on.

I would always be "Rikki Klieman, Trial Lawyer." It was my

identity, it still is. It was my calling. But it was no exaggeration to say that it had almost killed me. As I moved into a perfect job that combined my strengths as trial lawyer, teacher, and entertainer, I kissed the business of law good-bye. I waved and I broke out in the world's biggest grin. Yes! Yes! Yes!

I found an impeccably furnished apartment on a lovely, tree-lined street near Sutton Place, and Philip drove down from Boston with more clothes, a few artifacts, and some paintings I wanted to put on the walls. We brought them upstairs, went to dinner, went to bed. Around three in the morning we both woke up to the insistent scream of a car alarm. We headed right for the window. Of course it was our car. Thieves had smashed the driver's side window; there were shards of glass all over the seats. A doorman from an adjacent building had heard the alarm and come running out, surprising the thieves, who bolted. Philip threw on some pants and ran outside.

"I hate this fucking city!"

"It was my fault," I told him when he came back in. "We should have put it in a garage."

"You come home to Boston on the weekends," he demanded. "This is a third-world country! I don't want to be here. I can't even pretend. You just come home on weekends."

So I commuted.

During the week, in New York, I was having a blast. I was a full-fledged anchor! The Simpson case had not yet started so I worked on whatever was happening in the United States judicial system at the time. I just loved it. I had always enjoyed seeing how other lawyers approached important cases. I was constantly impressed by the thinking involved in their choices, the options they considered and discarded. I was fully prepared to critique a witness's performance as well as a prosecutor's or defense attorney's line of attack. And with no one's life in my hands, there was no pressure for me whatsoever. What could go wrong—I'd flub a line, swallow a sentence, garble a word? I was free!

Lo and behold, my first Sunday night in New York I slept like a baby. As soon as I stopped practicing law, I stopped throwing up.

At Christmas I took a week off and spent it with Philip in Boston. "Remember when I used to say that if anyone wins the lottery and says he won't quit his job he should automatically be stripped of his winnings?" It was one of my set pieces. What kind of idiot doesn't retire with millions? "Well, if I won the lottery I wouldn't quit my job."

Fred Graham and Gregg Jarrett were Court TV's first Los Angeles–based anchors for the Simpson trial. I worked the pretrial warm-up and from time to time the evening commentary. In June 1995, Steve Brill sent me out there. I called Philip, truly excited. Even though it meant a longer commute between us, I was going to be sitting in court and then on a scaffold outside and above the Los Angeles courthouse, watching and analyzing legal history.

I had initially tried to get on the defense team. It was a natural reaction. I was a defense lawyer, and this was the biggest case of the decade, if not more; everybody wanted a piece of it. When I heard F. Lee Bailey was going to be part of the defense team I had called and said, "You should have a woman at that table. Cosmetically, it would help him. And I would be the perfect person for you."

Lee told me that Robert Shapiro was running this case, and if there were a woman at the table, she would probably be taking notes or, at best, examining some inconsequential witness. "You're a real trial lawyer," he said. "Robert Shapiro is going to decide who gets in this case and it's just not going to be you."

I was disappointed. Guilty or not, Simpson was the highest-visibility client in the world, and his lawyers were going to be well-paid media celebrities for defending him. It was bigger than the Menendez brothers, bigger than William Kennedy Smith. (Any of those highfalutin' lawyers who say they would never have taken this case are lying. Everybody tried to get in; the bigger the lawyer, the more he or she tried.)

Fred Graham and I cohosted Court TV's coverage. Dan Abrams and Kristin Jeanette-Meyers were our reporters. I would get the newspapers at my hotel room door at 5:30 in the morning, drive to the set with Fred at 7:30, get made up and go on the air at 8:30 L.A.

time. We alternated anchoring in the mornings and afternoons, and if we weren't on the air we were either in the courtroom or in the truck watching the trial, because we didn't want to miss a minute. Our broadcast day ended around 8:00 at night, after which we would have a glass of wine, get some dinner, prepare for the next day, and do it all over again. Fred, a consummate professional, patiently taught me the ropes of broadcasting. He was one of the most intelligent and thoughtful mentors of my life and he remains so to this day. His friendship is one of my life's great gifts. In return I gave him insights into the practice of criminal law. This was thoroughly enjoyable.

I had heard about O.J. Simpson's charisma. It was all the buzz among certain elements of the media. I, of course, had seen him only on the television and movie screens. He was a celebrity, he was handsome, but I had been around handsome celebrities before; I was not easily impressed. I had also spent time in the presence of high-visibility criminal defendants, the kind who developed their own brand of attractiveness. No doubt about it, notoriety is seductive, and there is something about having seen a person on television that makes being in his physical presence a notable occasion. So I was prepared.

I found my assigned seat. Court TV was given one seat to the trial each day, and there was a lot of fighting for it within the organization's hierarchy, but that day it was mine. We spectators were waiting for the session to begin when O.J. Simpson emerged from the holding cell and was led into the courtroom.

The room vibrated when he stepped inside. That's the only way I can describe the effect this man had on the place and the people gathered to see him. He walked in with a big grin and he was on top of the world.

Every criminal defendant I had ever seen had come into court scared. There was something about each of them that understood the solemnity of the proceeding and wondered, What am I doing here? What will become of me? Not Simpson. He looked like a winner, as if he had just received a huge trophy and was sharing the victory with everyone in the room. He was electric. Some people have that quality. Simpson had it in abundance. Despite my better instincts I thought, He radiates confidence. He radiates power. He radiates sex!

The entire room, except for those who hated him, had to have been affected by it. It made people want him to be innocent. He was so . . . *vibrational* . . . that people did not want someone who displayed so much promise to turn out to be a murderer.

I was irritated with myself because I was supposed to be a detached journalist and I was reacting viscerally to a man charged with murder. I wondered whether this response would wear off, and thought that if I had reacted like this, how would a juror respond? I still suspect that Simpson's charisma had an effect on the verdict.

But considering the case they put on, the government ultimately misunderstood its audience. They tried it in the wrong place. The prosecution could have assured itself of a more sympathetic jury pool by having the venue in Santa Monica, but for reasons of convenience and fairness, they decided to try the case in the Los Angeles County Courthouse. That choice alone affected the result of the case.

Los Angeles County District Attorney Gil Garcetti was committed to justice. Fundamentally, he wanted to show that a celebrity would be treated in precisely the same manner as every other defendant. However, in practice his ideals did not go according to plan. The assistant district attorneys in charge of the case made the wrong strategic and tactical decisions.

Marcia Clark understood nothing about theater in the courtroom. Although very smart, she had little understanding of who she was and how she communicated. From her initial assumption that the rumored focus groups were wrong and that African American women would respond to her, to her decision to immerse the jury in the issue of domestic violence rather than the specific issue of the murders themselves, she thought she knew better, but she didn't. She capped off her miscalculations with a closing argument in which she effectively said that she wished she could go to the cafeteria and have a cup of coffee with the jurors and talk the case over. There wasn't one person in the jury box who believed that for one solitary second. The last thing on earth she ever wanted to do was go have a cup of coffee with these jurors. They knew it. How were they going to believe anything else she said?

Then there was the matter of strategy.

LAPD Detective Mark Fuhrman's disability application records were in the package of discovery materials Court TV received before the trial began. (Fuhrman was the man who found the bloody glove at Simpson's home on Rockingham.) We found in our reading that he had basically asked the department to take away his badge and gun because he felt that he had become too violent. We also found that he had talked about "niggers" and "spics." Later, the defense hit pay dirt when it located the infamous "Fuhrman tapes," in which he not only used racial slurs but also revealed ways in which the police can obstruct justice when interacting with minorities.

People of color in America, cops, and criminal defense lawyers were not shocked by one syllable uttered on those tapes; we have all heard some cops talk like that. But there was a significant number of people of color on the jury who at the very least were not going to give credence to the testimony of the man who said such things. Their feelings about a prosecution who supported this man were certainly not going to be positive. I said, "Are they out of their minds? They're going to put this guy on the witness stand? Give up the glove!" Instead of introducing the glove found at Simpson's home on Rockingham, the prosecution should have introduced only the glove found at the murder scene at South Bundy Drive. And they should absolutely not have put Detective Mark Fuhrman on the witness stand. If they had tried the case clean, in six weeks, they could have had a victory. What could they have been thinking?

But, no, the prosecution had to embrace Fuhrman. Marcia Clark almost literally touched him on the way to and from the stand. *Are you all right, Detective Fuhrman? Are you nervous today? Have you ever seen a case like this? Have you ever been in a position like this?* With the exception of the talented scientific evidence prosecutors George "Woody" Clarke, Rockne Harmon, and Brian Kelberg, this case was tried so defensively they almost deserved to lose. How the prosecution allowed the defendant to put a stiff, blood-soaked leather glove on over a latex glove that could only interfere with its ease of movement I will never understand; I would *fail* any student in my trial advocacy class who didn't try out an experiment before using it in a trial. And, of course, I eventually said so on the air.

When Johnnie Cochran assumed leadership of the defense from Robert Shapiro, F. Lee Bailey introduced me to him. Cochran was friendly and impressive: Here was a man who understood the theater of the courtroom. He knew how to dress; he knew how to walk; he knew when to face the jury and when to direct its attention elsewhere. He used his voice as an instrument. His phrase "If it doesn't fit, you must acquit" was a work of genius. Not only did it apply to the glove that Simpson tried on, the phrase was a telling metaphor for the case. If any piece of evidence didn't fit into the prosecution's case—for example, their time line or the "plaintive wail" of Nicole Brown Simpson's dog—the jurors could disregard everything else with which they had been presented. It was the Gospel According to Johnnie Cochran, a colloquial equivalent of Bobby Lee Cook's *Falsus in uno, falsus in omnibus.*

Cochran certainly pushed Marcia Clark's buttons to great effect. When he wanted the jury to see her get exasperated, he would orchestrate a conversation at sidebar and turn his back to the jury, making her face him. Marcia would be blowing one gasket or another, gesticulating, her mouth moving, her eyes aflame, and the jury would be afforded a straight-on view of these overwrought reactions over Johnnie's shoulder. And she never caught on to what he was doing.

Each member of the defense team had an assigned role: Bailey cross-examined Fuhrman, which turned the tide of the case by boxing in the witness to commit perjury, while Robert Shapiro took on the pathologist on the government's side and then blew out his conclusion with defense witness pathologist D. Michael Baden. Barry Scheck, Peter Neufeld, and Bob Blasier knew more about science and DNA than anyone in the country. Scheck had a boy-genius appeal to the jury. Shawn Chapman and Carl Douglas worked incessantly on preparing witnesses and gathering facts. Alan Dershowitz and Gerald Uelmen were responsible for the law. Jo-Ellan Dimitrius, one of the best jury consultants in the country, missed nothing. Defense investigators located the so-called Fuhrman tapes, and Johnnie Cochran was the master of communication in the courtroom and on the courthouse steps. That's why they truly were the "Dream Team," quarterbacked and paid for by the football star himself.

The one person in the Simpson trial who received the most media heat for the theater of the courtroom was Judge Lance Ito. He was so thrilled with his celebrity that when *The Tonight Show with Jay Leno* began its continuing segment of the "Dancing Itos"—a kick line of bearded Ito look-alikes—he reportedly called the lawyers into chambers and played them a videotape of it. The fact that everyone in the courtroom waited forty-five minutes for an afternoon session to start because the judge was in chambers with some celebrity actor made many people furious. One day fairly late in the case he actually let the two sides vent their emotional arguments in front of the camera after he had already made his ruling behind closed doors! This kind of behavior gives cameras in the courtroom a bad name. For a long time after this case, Court TV suffered with the public and with judges, who denied camera access because of the fiasco that was the Simpson case.

The jury had been deliberating for about four hours when we heard they had reached a verdict and would announce it the following morning. I was sitting in the trailer and the next thing I knew I heard, "Rikki, get back on the scaffold." I ran up the steps and found myself alone in the anchor seat, talking live on the air for hours with anchor Carol Randolph in New York, with all of America watching. That was just pure fun.

The next morning, Fred Graham and I returned to the studio on the scaffold and watched the mob on the street being reined in by mounted police while we all waited for the verdict. And then it came: "Not guilty!"

I was not surprised. Given the case the government presented, it did not matter whether Simpson had committed the crime or not; they had blown it. That was hard for the national audience to hear, considering the DNA, blood, hair, and fiber evidence, but for the lawyers who watched every single moment, the verdict was predictable.

If I had been known only in Boston before the Simpson case, I was known nationwide after it. Anchoring the trial made my face recognizable, and being the face of Court TV for those many months was a thrill. I was sitting buck-naked in a steam room when a woman on the shelf to my right looked up and said, "Oh, my God, you're Rikki Klieman!" I wrapped myself pretty quickly but apparently I was a star at my gym. Early in the trial, on one of my weekend commutes home, Philip and I were having dinner at a little Italian restaurant when a lovely blue-haired older woman approached our table and said, "Oh, my darling, I just love your work. May I have your autograph?" I suppressed a giggle, but this was pleasing . . . and cool. I had never given an autograph. I was about to step through a revolving door into a department store in Chicago when a well-dressed, very attractive African American woman in her sixties swung out, dropped her bags, and said, "My dear, let me give you a hug! I watched you every day during that trial. You are a champion of the people! You are the only one who understood the presumption of innocence. My hat is off to you." I signed her shopping bag. I was in Orlando, Florida, giving a speech when Philip and I decided to spend the afternoon at Disney World. We were waiting in Fantasyland for the parade of characters to begin when a woman in her forties, toting her kids, bustled up to me and said, "I have to have your autograph. It's more important than Mickey Mouse!"

fifteen A WOMAN'S RIGHT
TO CHOOSE:
CAREER OR LOVE?

LOVED MY HUSBAND. WE HAD THE PER-
FECT MARRIAGE. HE WAS MY BEST FRIEND,
my lover, my caretaker; he constituted my entire sense of stability.
But by the summer of 1997, our marriage was in crisis. We palled
around a lot but we just weren't talking about anything of substance.
There were no cataclysmic battles, just a sense of distance even when
we were near.

Philip and I had been living in different cities since 1994, and the
cracks were showing. During the Simpson trial, I would take the red-

eye across the country, land at six Saturday morning, Philip would pick me up at the airport and we would make our drive to Rhode Island. I would sleep in the car; I would sleep on the beach; I would wake up in the early afternoon and then we would have the rest of the day. Saturday night we would go out drinking; Sunday we would have an Italian meal in East Boston, and he would put me on a plane back to the coast. There wasn't a lot of talking going on. Once in a while he would come to Los Angeles, but I was so wrapped up in my work that I thought of little else. The intense focus of my world was "Who had the latest Simpson story?" The pressures of my job and our need to support two households, added to the physical separation, created a deep divide. Philip and I needed to be together. We needed to make our marriage a priority.

After the trial, when I arrived back in New York a Court TV celebrity, I thought I would cruise on upward into the prestigious and high-paying job of nighttime anchor, but I was passed over for that position on Court TV's nighttime show *Prime Time Justice* in 1997. Then Steve Brill sold his interest in the network and left. I had truly wanted that anchor job, and I felt I was positioned perfectly. When I didn't get it, I began to question my future at the network: Was my work valued by this new management? Did the people in charge have any regard for my work or my career? Did I have a chance to rise here? I didn't know, and I wondered whether my time at the network was coming to an end.

If I wasn't going to work at Court TV, I certainly didn't need to live in New York. Although I had learned how to survive in the city and had begun to enjoy it, Philip truly hated New York and refused even to consider living there. Since he had always accommodated my career advancement, I thought that now I should make the sacrifices, so I considered moving back to Boston.

I was very scared of losing Philip. He was my anchor; without him I might just float away. My ability to function in the world depended on his being there. We were supposed to grow old together. He may not have been the passion of my life, but he was my savior. Without Philip I had no vision of a future life at all.

A couple needs a home. Philip was raised in Rhode Island; he showed me the physical beauty of this small state surrounded by water. What a treasure. To please him for a change, we went house hunting on the island of Jamestown on Narragansett Bay. We saw every piece of waterfront property on the market and found a lovely contemporary house with a two-story fireplace, open space, skylights, colorful gardens, and a beautiful frontage on the bay. Philip was a sailor, and it had a mooring for a sailboat. I knew when I walked in that the place was ideal, so we bid on it.

As the negotiations progressed, we were twenty-five thousand dollars apart. Now, in the scheme of things, when you're talking about a big house on the water, twenty-five thousand dollars is not normally an impediment. We could reasonably have split it down the middle, but I wouldn't budge. They wouldn't move and I wasn't buying. I wanted to live there but . . .

If we were going to buy a new home in New England, what would I do for work? I knew I didn't want to return to the practice of law; I would very soon have made myself just as crazy as I'd always been. I considered working in the television industry there as well, so I started to look for a job with some degree of apparent earnestness. (That is, I made a couple of calls.) Philip took this as a sign of respect and affection, and he could not have been happier or more accommodating. No sooner had I said, "Maybe I should look for a TV job in Boston or Providence" than this wonderful man said, "No, no, no. You have another year on your Court TV contract. I'll come down to New York and we'll make it work." So we didn't buy the house in Rhode Island.

Philip was working as a private investigator and almost immediately as he settled in New York, he found a good case. He'd barely been in the city three weeks when I got a spectacular promotion.

Fresh off his victory in the Simpson trial and now a smoking-hot media figure, Johnnie Cochran had signed with Court TV to be host of a nighttime talk show, *Cochran & Grace*. While Nancy Grace was a true TV personality, somehow the chemistry between Johnnie and her did not work, so he was hosting alone. I had substituted for him during a week in May. Now it was autumn and I was invited to share the stage with him as coanchor on the new show, *Cochran & Co.* This was going to be Court TV's featured presentation. Philip was working days, and at first the show was live from 9:00 to 10:00 at night, so we wouldn't have much time together, but I expected him to understand. After all, this was my career. It never occurred to me to turn it down.

How selfish, how rude, how extraordinarily self-centered of me. I was always the person making the choice, and it was always for me: my career, my fame, my life. They were always opportunities of a lifetime—my lifetime—and I always took them. This time was no different.

I threw myself into the show. As the actress that I have always been, I was determined to shine in the show's bright spotlight. I was enthralled with the work; the staff was large and efficient; the issues were more than trials. We were truly breaking legal news. This was the big time for me: a job that met so many of my needs. This was huge.

But all our determination to work on our life as a couple went by the boards. Philip and I saw each other in the morning and occasionally met for dinner or drinks at night, but the distance we had created when I was commuting from New York to Boston or from Los Angeles to Boston didn't get any smaller when we were in the same room. We talked all the time, but we didn't have much to say. Although he was in my home, he wasn't in my world.

There's nothing lonelier than being present but not there. For two people who were best pals, we were drawing further and further apart. During a Christmas party at a friend's home in the Boston suburb of Lincoln, I was hanging out in the kitchen when my friend Laura came in just bubbling. "That Philip. What a funny, witty man!"

I was unimpressed. "You can have him if you want him." I scowled.

It was an awkward moment, and Laura looked at me strangely. On the surface, Philip and I seemed to have a perfect marriage, but my reply was a clear indication of trouble.

Or so I'm told. I have no memory of this conversation or this evening whatsoever. I only know about it because Laura told me. I find it interesting that I've blocked it out.

Every New Year's Eve, Philip and I and the same group of friends would drink champagne at the Harvard Club on Commonwealth Avenue, walk to the Boston Common to see the ice sculptures, and then proceed to Locke-Ober, one of Boston's finest restaurants, for a celebration dinner before fireworks on the harbor. This year was quite the same: We laughed as we always did, made our annual toasts, then ran down to a friend's house overlooking Boston Harbor to see the fireworks display. We were all living good lives.

Philip and I didn't sit next to each other. We didn't walk outside together. When the year turned, we barely acknowledged it with a peck on the cheek. Surrounded by friends, we were alone in the crowd.

The next morning Philip and I flew to Pasadena to the wedding of his eldest son from his first marriage. On the return trip, shockingly, I actually accepted a first-class upgrade so I did not even ride home in the same cabin with him. What could I have been thinking? I flew back to New York alone the next day.

One day later I called him at dawn, hysterical. I was in bed crying. I could barely speak between the sobs. I told him I needed to talk to him.

I took the 6:30 shuttle to Boston and he met me in the Delta terminal. We didn't even go to his car; he insisted that we sit down in the airport.

"I want to separate," I said shakily. "I want to get counseling for us."

"You want to separate, we'll separate. No counseling, we don't need counseling. An official separation." Philip shut down. As far as he was concerned, if I wanted to be separated, I was out of his life. That was it, marriage over.

It was 8:30 in the morning; the day had hardly begun, and already my marriage had broken up. I don't know how I got on the shuttle back to New York. I certainly don't remember doing it. Philip had been my anchor, but now I was adrift.

By 9:30 I was back in New York. I was shaking uncontrollably when I got out of the cab and into my apartment. How odd am I—I can remember exactly the clothes I was wearing: black turtleneck, black Gap jeans, a pair of black flats. I called in sick, crawled into bed, and, fully clothed, folded myself into the fetal position and

cried. I was freezing, but no amount of blankets could make me stop
shaking.

Sobbing in bed I thought, This was a stupid decision. Why did I
do this? I can't live without Philip; he's the only thing in my life that
is really stable. Maybe I can still make it work.

But I didn't call him. Nor did I tell anyone we had separated. I
thought that if you say it out loud, you make it true, and I just wasn't
ready for it to be real because I was embarrassed. My perfect marriage had collapsed, and, invested in perfection as I was, I didn't want
anyone to know.

I sobbed and shivered and could not focus for twenty-four hours.
Then I got up, because I knew it was the right decision, even though
it terrified me.

How did I handle it? I worked. I got up the next morning and
immersed myself in my daily routine. I opened the front door, picked
up the papers, and read them with an eye toward what they could do
for the show. We had an 11:00 A.M. conference call, which I did from
home. I got a little something to eat, arrived at the office at 2:00, put
in my eight hours until 10:00 at night, went home, stared at the ceiling for hours, and at some point, exhausted, fell asleep. Got up the
next morning and did it all over again. That was my life. No one
knew.

A. Thayer Bigelow, Court TV's boss at the time, and the man who
had pushed my promotion to the Cochran show, was taking the network's anchors to breakfast one by one in an effort to get to know
them personally and to discuss his vision for the company's future.
He was taking them to the Frontier Coffee Shop, a Formica-tabletop
kind of place across Third Avenue from our offices. That's fine for a
quick snack, but we were discussing significant themes, and I felt we
should be discussing them in better style. When he called me to
schedule a time, I said, "Thayer, you are an important guy; you
should be going to an important place for breakfast."

He laughed. "What do you want to do, go to the Regency?" The
Regency is the originator and home of New York's power breakfast.

So there we were at the Regency, having just finished our state-of-the-network morning meal and standing to leave, when I saw Bill Bratton across the room, sitting at a table with Lester Pollack, a prominent investment banker. As I moved toward the door I excused myself and stopped at Bill's table. I thought this would earn me big brownie points with my boss. Bratton had ascended from the Boston Police Department to become commissioner of the NYPD. He had appeared on the cover of *Time* magazine and was widely credited with personally reversing New York's crime epidemic before being forced out of office for reasons of personal pique by New York's Mayor Rudolph Giuliani.

Bratton rose from his seat and kissed me on the cheek. He smiled. "You look so beautiful," he said. "If you were single, I'd marry you."

Was this the thunderbolt from *The Godfather*? I was immediately and enormously attracted to this man.

"You should call me for lunch," I said.

By the time I got back to the office, he had called.

Between his schedule and mine it took several weeks to arrange to meet. In that time he was in my thoughts every day. Every day. He came to mind at odd moments, whether I was writing some copy for the Cochran show or in the middle of a meeting. I thought of him each night when I went to bed.

And these weren't idle musings — they were young, lustful, sexual thoughts, that feeling of high school desperation.

This was startling. My hormones weren't just running; they were at a gallop. I was having adolescent sexual fantasies. I couldn't get him out of my head. I was forty-nine years old. This was preposterous!

And still, despite a series of phone calls, we could not organize our schedules to be in the same place at the same time. One night he called me from the airport. "If we can't get this lunch together, why don't we try to meet after work?" he suggested. Lunch and drinks are different invitations altogether, I knew that. So it hadn't been all in my mind. We arranged to meet in the King Cole Bar at the St. Regis Hotel the following week.

The St. Regis is no roadhouse. Its darkened bar stands down a long and wide lobby corridor, plush carpets absorbing footsteps as if each step were a secret, flanked by several rooms with comfortable corners in which to settle. It's a nice place to be.

In the car on the way over my heart was racing in taxicab tachycardia. I rushed in looking for him, uncharacteristically frazzled. He was sitting with another gentleman, drinking champagne, and as I walked toward them I didn't know if I could speak. The gentleman soon excused himself, however, and Bratton and I were alone. I was wearing my best black suit; he was in navy blue, with a tie that had a pattern of quarter moons. Not that I noticed, or anything. I ordered a glass of wine and we sat and talked and talked and talked.

We had first met back in 1992 when as superintendent in chief of the Boston Police Department he had come to deliver a lecture about the Civilian Complaint Review Board at an Anti-Defamation League luncheon. I remembered him as one of the smartest, most charismatic people I had ever met. His presence had only intensified over the years. I have no idea what we talked about at the St. Regis, only that we were engaged in a dance of romance and sexuality and that we moved well together. It was clear to me that if we continued to see each other there was no way for me to turn away from this man. This was a wonderful feeling, but dangerous. I was still married and I was not quite disconnected from Philip.

He put me in a cab.

What I didn't know was that he walked home through Central Park that night, looked up at the moon, and thought of the movie *Moonstruck*—*la bella luna,* Cosmo's moon. His first gift to me was a quarter-moon pin from Tiffany.

Bill and I started dating, if we could call it that. There is an old phrase: "We never went out, we stayed in." We went out but it felt as if we stayed in. Whether we were walking down the street or talking on the telephone or he was buying me little presents, everything we did was electric. It was a fabulous courtship.

The passion I felt for Bill was overwhelming. I had no choice; I was his in all ways. I would walk down the street singing. When I saw him on a corner, I would literally run toward him to be crushed in his embrace. I could not control myself; he was in my thoughts day and night. In the madness of a romantic affair, at first I did not trust my own feelings, let alone his, to have any degree of permanence. I thought that passion had to be fleeting, that people could not fashion a lifetime on lust.

Bill was going through a difficult divorce; I was separated from my husband; these were not the first unsuccessful marriages for either of us. Bill said, "I am not going to tell you I love you right now, because once I do there is no turning back for me." We were rushing headlong toward each other but still somehow holding back.

I spent a few weekends in Boston with Philip, trying to reach some conclusion. He may have been done with me, but I just didn't know what I was doing. I was supposed to be with Philip; we had taken vows, and I had taken those vows seriously. Through all my trials, Philip had taken care of me; how could I leave him now? In April, he and I drove to Rhode Island, walked on the beach, ate clams together in the open air. The setting was beautiful; the weather fresh and clear—for any normal couple this would have been a weekend of romance. Philip was truly trying. And I was so very not present.

Though Philip attempted to make everything right, it was clear to us both that we would never close the distance that had grown between us. "If you are not ready to be with me," he said, "we can't act like this anymore. We should face facts and get divorced." I knew he was absolutely right. I felt relieved and terrified and excited.

I returned to New York that night. I met Bill for dinner. He said, "I've shared you as much as I'm able; I can't share you anymore. You have to choose."

I was a month away from my fiftieth birthday. I adored this man and wanted to spend the rest of my life with him, but I was paralyzed with guilt.

Bill took control of my fiftieth birthday. He sat down and asked whom I wanted to celebrate with. I chose several close friends and he booked the back room at a very fine restaurant, Picholine. We hosted a one-table party on the Saturday night of my birthday weekend that was simple and wonderful. My best friends, the man with whom I was wildly in love—what better company to keep while I was hitting this daunting age? I have photographs of that night; in some I appear ecstatic, in others I look clearly concerned. I loved this man, but was I done with being married?

On the actual night of my birthday, Bill took me to one of our favorite restaurants, Campagnola, for a lovely, private meal to celebrate this milestone. I walked in and all my friends were there. Bill had coordinated with Johnnie Cochran and my friend Joe Tacopina, the only one of my criminal defense lawyer friends Bill knew, to throw me a surprise party. I fell for it completely—walked in and had no idea. They were all hooting and hollering, and I was warmed by their attention and thrilled at this demonstration of Bill's love. It was no small concession: He was a former police commissioner sitting at a table full of boisterous criminal defense lawyers.

Philip never called to wish me happy birthday. I'd turned fifty and he hadn't acknowledged it. I called him the following day. "I guess you wanted me to get the message," I said.

"That's right," he said coldly. "You are already gone. I'm going to make it easy on you. Let's figure out the finances. Let's get it done." He informed me of how we should divide our assets. I said, "I guess you've thought this through."

"You just want me to say it's over," he told me, "so you can rationalize the whole breakup." Oh, he knew me very well.

And so I was going to be divorced again.

Since Bill had a speaking engagement in Rome, we made a vacation out of his trip—another fiftieth birthday present. Johnnie Cochran, who knows how to live, offered me his travel expertise: "Positano. The Sireneuse." I knew a travel agent who was Italian, and I called her with Johnnie's recommendations. I researched our trip obsessively, the way I would have worked a case, down to the last detail, finding just the right combination of out-of-the-way places and upscale hotels. The opportunity to leave my work and my troubles for ten full days was a blessing.

Bill and I traveled to Rome, then through Tuscany to Florence. We walked the cities; viewed art, cathedrals, and historical sites; ate very well; and shopped a lot. But it was in Positano that my life changed.

Positano is a famed storybook town built into a cliff on the ruggedly beautiful Amalfi coast, and we were giddy as we walked to our elegant room in a hotel that had been a private villa in the eighteenth century. We brought a portable CD player, put on Pavarotti, and slipped into this glorious, enormous bath just to relax. Bill and I both go nonstop, and we both had made a life of constant movement, so neither one of us was good at this "relaxation" thing. The music resounded, a candle flickered; nothing else moved. We were so still.

Terry cloth robes with great hoods had been laid out on the bed next to each other; we slipped them on, then reclined on chaise longues on the balcony and watched the sun set over the Amalfi coast. As I sat there peacefully next to Bill, I felt the palpable weight of guilt and care lift itself from my body and float away. I knew that I was free of the past, free to move forward with the man I loved.

It was then that Bill told me he wanted to marry me and bring me back here. It was our place, speaking to us of love, romance, and commitment. We took a day trip to the Isle of Capri, a mere boat ride away from Positano, where we strolled the town. We took the obligatory ride to the Blue Grotto and experienced the hilarity of watching large boats moving people to small boats to even smaller boats to move them into the cave. In the United States there would have been dozens of regulations to stop these boats from running into each other—it was wildly unsafe—and we could not stop giggling at its absurdity. People packed to the brim on a large boat recognized Bill, waved to us, and started singing "I Love New York."

In Capri we passed a jewelry store where a beautiful bracelet, a ribbon of yellow and white gold, caught Bill's eye. The owners were on their afternoon siesta; the doors were closed. Before we boarded our boat to return to Positano, we took one last stroll. As the store's doors opened Bill took me by the hand and pulled me inside. He placed the bracelet on my wrist, did not even consider bargaining for it since we had to run like the wind to catch our boat to the mainland, and paid for it immediately. It is on my wrist now; it is on my wrist always.

My mother had been desperately in love with my father, and I was blessed to have grown up in a household filled with affection and desire. My mother had told me, "I pity you. You've had too many men. You will never know what true love is, not the kind of love I've had with your father." For years, that last sentence haunted me. Through two marriages I suspected she was right. Now I could tell her I knew, too. I was fifty years old and had finally found my soul mate. In Yiddish they would say he was my *beshert.*

It is my greatest single regret that my parents did not live to meet Bill.

We returned to New York and were happy. My show was a success, and both of us were working constantly. The country was immersed in the Monica Lewinsky scandal, which guaranteed active television for the entire year. My work was fun and intellectually stimulating; it sparked my creativity. I was thrilled that Johnnie and Bill had a great rapport. Listening to them talking about the relationship of the police department to the minority community was fascinating, since it was such a significant issue for them both. Among Bill's regrets at being forced out as commissioner was that he did not have enough time to build the bridges he had designed to connect the two. He had plans to develop a career ladder into the NYPD for inner-city kids, including a mentoring program, an expanded Scout Explorer program run by each precinct to introduce them to the workings of the police, and a police high school that would track into City University's John Jay College of Criminal Justice. His goal was to broaden the department's hiring practices to, as he said, "make the NYPD look more like the community it polices." He had been commissioner and created the turnaround in "wartime," he said, and now that we were in peacetime, the minority community deserved to reap the benefits of the peace dividend. Imagine the strides New York could have made if he had remained to do this work.

My job's hours—8:00 to 9:00 at night, four nights a week—made it perfect for me. Bill and I rented a charming, secluded little house in the Hamptons and spent every summer weekend at the beach. I was used to getting away, as my home in the woods in Milton had provided the peace and privacy I needed. When Philip and I broke up I had lost both my anchor *and* my sanctuary. Somehow, lucky me, I had regained both.

In September 1998 Philip and I went to court to finalize our divorce. The night before, we slept in our house: me in the bedroom, he in the den. We drove together to the courthouse, then he drove me to the airport. Philip and I, miraculously, had parted as friends, or so I thought. I was so glad. (Philip's feelings later changed.)

I was moving forward; my life was total perfection. I signed a new two-year contract with a good raise in pay. Court TV, which had struggled for years as part of a dysfunctional tripartite marriage between NBC, Time Warner, and Liberty Media Corp., with a bare-bones marketing budget and no promotion budget to speak of, had been in danger of going down the chute. Now the partnership had bought out NBC, and Court TV was finally going to get an infusion of money from Time Warner that promised to bring it even further forward in the American media consciousness. How could life have been better?

Court TV's executive vice president of programming, Sheilagh McGee, and the new prime-time executive producer, Andy Regal, came into my office one night around 6:00 as I was preparing for a show and closed the door behind them. This was not good. I had watched in August 1998 when the same pair had walked into our producer Donna Vislocky's office and closed the door; the next thing I knew, Donna was out of a job. You don't get a visit from two of the top network executives for them to tell you they love you; that's not the way television works. Their visit could only bring bad news.

"Rikki," Sheilagh began, "you've been great on *Cochran & Co.*, couldn't be better. We value your star power here. But with the new arrangement, we need to use that star power to raise the level of the other evening show." *Prime Time Justice*, the program that now aired from 9:00 to 10:00 each night following our taping, had gone through several incarnations, none of them terrifically successful. "It is time for Johnnie to make it on his own. For the money the network is pay-ing him he has to come to the plate and produce. He needs to bring in ratings, and he simply cannot depend on you anymore for support. Either he makes the show or breaks it, but he has to do it by himself."

Johnnie Cochran and I had developed a nice professional rela-tionship over the year we had worked together. I understood it was my task to set up an issue and it was Johnnie's to knock it over. My job was to make Johnnie look good. I did that easily and happily; he was smart, quick, and made great television.

"This will be fabulous for you," Andy continued. "We want you to coanchor *Prime Time Justice* with Gregg Jarrett. We have great plans for the show: We're going to give it a new title; we're going to give it tremendous promotion; we're really going to build it up. This will be our signature nighttime news and talk show, and we want your star power to run it."

"And when we're successful," Sheilagh added, "we'll have two shows in the evening that will be excellent; Johnnie will be excellent and you and Gregg will be excellent. This is a win-win all the way around, but we need your pizzazz in another place."

This was tag-team flattery, but as they were making their pitch my mind was racing. Sheilagh was a master at spinning events toward the positive, and it was nice to hear the kind words, but this was the worst news I could have received. No matter what kind of a promotion Sheilagh made it seem, it was effectively a demotion because I was being taken off the network's most visible show and being told to go start over and prove myself again. Plus, I enjoyed working with Johnnie and loved the job.

Worse, *Prime Time Justice* aired live from 9:00 to 10:00 at night. For the past several months, Johnnie and I had worked out a schedule that allowed us to tape our show from 7:45 until 8:45, even though it aired from 10:00 to 11:00. I would be losing an hour and a quarter each night. Now, the difference of an hour and a quarter may not seem significant, but in this case it was crucial because Bill was working at a background screening security firm in Smithtown, Long Island, and had at least a two-hour commute each way. He got up at 5:30 in the morning and picked me up after work each night at 9:00. Getting out at 9:00 was difficult but doable. At 9:00 you can still go out to dinner; often I didn't take off my makeup, I just walked out the door and was at a restaurant by ten past. That was a quasi-normal life for New York.

But going out at 10:15, your life shifts. It's one thing when you're in the early days of love and lust, when it doesn't matter what time it is, you're just happy to see each other, but Bill would be tired from a long day and he'd have cooled his heels for an extra hour before he saw me. Coming out of the studio after having been performing on the air, I'd be wired for sound and he'd be at the end of his tether. No good could come of this.

I was smiling through their barrage, politely listening. When they paused, I told them, "I would love to work with Gregg, he is a real professional, but I truly don't want to leave Johnnie and I don't want to leave this show." Sheilagh and Andy looked at me as if I didn't understand. They weren't asking my permission; they were telling me how it was going to be. There was an awkward silence.

"Do I have any right of protest on this? Do I have a choice?" I asked.

"No."

"Henry is coming in a week," I said. Court TV's new CEO, Henry Schleiff, was being installed the next Monday. He was a man with a reputation for having supreme ability and vision. "Why are you making these changes now?"

"These are changes Henry wants." Of course. How naive could I have been?

"Does Johnnie know this yet?"

"We are coming to you first. We are going to him next."

"What if Johnnie doesn't like it?"

"Rikki," Sheilagh said directly, "this isn't a democracy; this is television. You are being moved. You are doing this other show and it is going to go on from nine to ten at night."

"When is this going to start?" I wondered.

"Next week." My pretense at a smile disappeared. "It is really best if you stop doing Cochran and start doing this other show. To drag this out does not help you."

The Jewish holidays were coming up. "Why don't you take a week off?" Sheilagh suggested. "Go up to Boston or wherever, do whatever you need to do, and come back and get to work on the new show."

"Do you mind if I talk to Thayer Bigelow about this?" My friend A. Thayer Bigelow was the outgoing Court TV CEO.

"Go ahead. It's not going to do you any good."

They left to inform Johnnie of the new regime. I had to prepare for that night's show, but I called Johnnie after they had left his office and asked him what we could do about Court TV's decision.

"We have to do something," he told me.

Needless to say, Johnnie and I put it all aside and did a good show that night. When Bill picked me up after work, however, I was a wreck. We went to dinner, but I was totally distracted and couldn't find a way out of this situation short of damaging both my career and our relationship. I really didn't want to do either.

The next morning I was in Thayer Bigelow's office. He and his wife and Bill and I had spent some summer evenings together in the Hamptons. Thayer had championed my career at the network, and while we had a professional relationship, I felt comfortable with him and felt I could be frank.

"Thayer," I said, "I don't want to do this." He was no longer the executive in charge. He was out and Henry Schleiff was in, so I was not challenging his authority.

"You have to do it," he told me.

"I can't. It would kill my relationship with Bill. This is going to take us right down. We're going to be exhausted all the time and we're not going to be able to communicate. I just can't work five nights a week until ten o'clock."

He looked at me. "Don't say that to anyone else."

"Of course I wouldn't say that to anyone else." I began thinking out loud. "Maybe I should go back to daytime. At least then I could have a life."

"It's not your choice what you do here, Rikki," he said evenly. "Court TV owns you. Your contract says you are a Court TV anchor. You're going to work at whatever time Court TV says you're going to work." The only rider I had included in my contract was one that prevented my being on the air before 1:00 P.M.; I was teaching a morning class at Columbia University Law School and did not want to abandon it. "Just relax," Thayer told me, "take the week off. I know you'll deal with it correctly." His years in the business were telling me to accept the inevitable because that is what you do in television.

I went to Boston with Bill for a few days, completely in turmoil. We spent most of our time either considering the possibilities or studiously avoiding them. Finally, I developed a plan. "When I get back I'm going to go in and see Henry Schleiff," I said. "I'm going to tell him that I am going to give up my nighttime salary, my whole huge increase, and go back and anchor daytime." Then, as always, Bill's first impulse was not to speak but to listen. He said nothing. "Maybe I can work out a way to make the show run earlier," I said hopefully.

"What are you, a magician?" Bill said finally. "You're not a programmer, you don't decide when the show airs." The voice of reason.

I obsessed about it until it was time to fly home. "Bill," I told him, "our relationship is what matters most. I've got to go to Henry and tell him I can't work till ten o'clock."

"You're going to lose your job." He was not reprimanding me but just stating a fact. I think he was frightened for me, not that I wouldn't eventually land on my feet, but that I was making a dangerous professional choice. "Remember, you love this job."

He was right, I did. "I love the job," I told him, "but I love you more. I've been making this same choice over and over, all my life, and I've always done the right thing professionally and I've always ended up killing my relationships, my happiness, my health."

"Well," he said calmly, "it's your decision." I knew Bill didn't want me to work until 10:00 each night, but I am equally certain he didn't want to prevent me from choosing to do so if that's what I wanted. We were freshly enough in love and still filled with Pollyanna certainty that we could make any situation work, but at my core I knew better and probably so did he. "I'll support you," he said, "whatever decision you make."

I could picture Philip right next to me on the couch in our Fifty-fourth Street apartment a year before, when I had told him I had been offered the job at *Cochran & Co.* He'd said to me, "We'll never see each other." That scene played out as if in front of me. I was not going to let it happen twice.

"In reality, Bill," I said, "our relationship will be injured if I work like that."

"Well," he agreed, "it wouldn't be the best way to have a relationship."

As they say in New Age philosophy, my paradigm shifted. My father had worked at one job for thirty-two years. As far as he was concerned, you didn't change jobs. He told me so over and over. Throughout my law career, as I moved from firm to firm with a fair amount of regularity, I always felt I was being somehow professionally inappropriate. Every time I made a move, even if it was onward and upward, I still looked down on myself because I wasn't being the perfect child I felt my parents and others expected me to be.

So when I decided to speak with Henry Schleiff, to ask him to reassign me to daytime in order to save a budding romance, I felt it was the most unprofessional thing I had ever done. As far as my career was concerned, it could only be a suicide move.

If a friend had come to me in the same situation, seeking advice, I would have told her, "Why don't you wait a month, see how it plays out?" That would have been sound and constructive professional advice. I ignored it. I felt compelled to go down that rabbit hole, and if I didn't do it that day, I felt I'd be lost.

In the week I had been away, Henry Schleiff had been installed as CEO of Court TV. Schleiff was extremely well regarded in the television industry. He had previously served as executive vice president of Studios USA and chairman and CEO of Viacom's Broadcast and Entertainment Groups and had a reputation for innovation, creativity, and humor. I called his assistant Yvette at 9:00 on Monday morning to set up an appointment for sometime that day. I realized that I was not exactly the first thing on Henry Schleiff's mind, since his mandate was to pick up this struggling network and rebuild it from top to bottom. He'd only been on the job for seven days; I was the "talent" and was expected to do what I was told. Yvette told me she would see what she could do to squeeze me in.

My huge seventh-floor office was gone and I was now in a temporary office the size of a closet on the third floor. Gregg Jarrett, my proposed cohost, had a large office at the other end of the hall. Gregg and I had shared an office and worked together on daytime and we had a pleasant professional relationship, but he must have thought I was a raving lunatic that day as I popped up every ten minutes or so and paced the narrow hall in front of Schleiff's office. Three large plate-glass windows gave the new CEO full view of the area, and he could not possibly have missed me: I felt as if I were in high school waiting for the principal. I prepared for my first show with Gregg that night, and finally, late in the afternoon, there was an opening.

"Rikki Klieman, I'm so glad to see you! I really wanted to see you today." Henry Schleiff walked from behind his desk and came into the hall to greet me. He took me by the arm, brought me inside, seated me in a chair in front of his desk, and closed the door.

His office was like a playland. What was at core a standard, characterless room with fluorescent lighting and a regulation-issue breakfront and desk had been given life by his array of toys gathered from his years at work in the entertainment industry. An old Victrola stood in one corner, a jovial ceramic fellow leaned against a lamppost on a table, and behind his desk hung a large primitive, childlike painting of a house wired with real coaxial cable. Against all odds, the room felt playful.

Henry Schleiff sat behind his desk as he spoke. He had an animated way of getting his points across. A tall man, he put both elbows on the table and ran one palm through his ample head of silver hair while running the other across the desk toward me. He looked up at the ceiling as if considering his words as he chose them, then came down and made penetrating eye contact. He seemed in constant forward motion.

"I wanted to tell you what a great job you've done on *Cochran & Co.* You were just terrific, and I think this new show is such a great vehicle for you. You and Gregg are going to be terrific; this is going to be wonderful. We are going to give it the advertising and marketing it deserves to make this a show of star quality."

Several months earlier, at a dinner at a leadership conference in Colorado at which I had been Bill Bratton's date, I had been seated next to a public relations guru named Paul Flaherty. Over the course of the evening, in discussing our jobs and lives, I told him I worked at Court TV. "My best friend just became the CEO," Flaherty told me. "Henry Schleiff. We've been playing tennis for years. He's so funny.

And so smart. Here . . ." He took my place card, turned it over, and wrote on the back, "This woman is your greatest talent. Give this woman a raise." He signed it.

"When you have an opportunity sometime, just give this to him," he told me.

Now I stood and handed that card to my new boss. "I knew I was going to hold on to this for the right moment. I just didn't know it would be this soon." Mr. Schleiff looked at it and genuinely laughed.

I know how to position myself physically for success, how to move forward when making a point, how to sit or stand to my advantage — I even teach a class about it. But at that moment I didn't know how to get comfortable. I felt as if I were in free fall, as if I were tumbling down. I was putting my career and my professional reputation at risk. This was a defining moment: Schleiff was moving toward me over his desk, while I was in essence backing up. The whole dynamic was wrong. In my class I use the Tony Robbins maxim: "If you want to change your emotion, change your motion." I stood because I wanted to stand on my own two feet and get centered. I needed strength and I could not say what I had to say sitting down. Then I sat down because Schleiff would not get up.

"Henry, I want to thank you for your confidence in me. I am going to tell you something that I think is the most unprofessional thing I've ever done, and I won't blame you if at the end of this conversation you tell me to leave. I'll accept that if you do. If an associate, male or female, said this to me in my law firm, I'd show them the door before they had finished." In fact, when I was practicing law in the mid-eighties and was in the middle of preparing an important brief, one of my associates had told me he couldn't work past 6:00 that night because he had a music gig that was important to him. I felt betrayed and I couldn't believe this man was deserting me in the midst of a trial to go play music, so I became furious and threw him out of my office. I knew how this could end up.

"But I need to talk with you," I told him. "I need you to listen." Schleiff, who was already sitting forward, hunched toward me intently.

"I think I have always been, throughout my life, very professional. I love my job at Court TV and have always done what was asked of me here. I've always made choices for my professional life ahead of my personal life." I became self-conscious. This was not how one spoke to a CEO, but I knew if I stopped for even a moment I was finished. "I know how this may sound to you, but I have to just say it and get it out of my mouth.

"I have a relationship that I believe in with all my heart. I have met a man who I really think is the person I am supposed to be with."

"Oh, I know," he said. "You're dating Bill Bratton."

"Yes."

"He's a great guy. Great guy. Terrific police commissioner."

"Thank you." I started again. "This relationship is of critical importance to me. I think this is the relationship that is going to last my lifetime, and I will not, at the age of fifty, do what I have done in the past. If I were twenty or thirty and on my way up in this business, this would never have even dawned on me. But at this stage of my life I will sacrifice *nothing* for this personal relationship. Working at night and getting off the air at ten o'clock, which doesn't get me out of here until ten-thirty and keeps me up until two-thirty in the morning because I am wired for sound, won't work in a relationship with someone who has a more normal schedule." As I spoke I thought, What an inane way to begin this conversation. I was like a girl saying, Sorry, I can't do this job; I have to go out with my boyfriend. And yet, it was the truth.

"I appreciate your giving me the opportunity for the show"—that was better, that was a strength move—"but I cannot work until ten o'clock at night." I knew if I stopped there and gave him a chance to talk I was gone, so I pressed forward. "I know what the consequences are. I understand that you can simply say to me, 'That's the way you feel and you have to go.' You could fire me today or another day. I accepted that risk when I came in here." I felt stronger simply for saying that out loud, for not being a namby-pamby girl but for accepting the consequences of my actions. I was telling the truth and I felt the strength of that truth.

Schleiff looked at the ceiling and I thought, I'm dead.

He looked at me. "This is a pretty brave thing for you to do."

"You know," I said, still breathing, "I think you are right. It is also a very foolhardy thing for me to do. Some might say this is a stupid thing to do. I haven't told anyone about having this conversation with you except Bill, because my friends would tell me not to. And part of me is ashamed of myself because this is *so* unprofessional, but part of me is really proud because I am doing the right thing for me, maybe for the first time in my life as a professional woman. I need to make my life work for me now in a way that I haven't chosen in the past."

Had I gone too far? I really didn't know Henry Schleiff at all, and here I was confiding in him as he was considering whether or not to fire me. I plunged ahead. Henry Schleiff is a smart man, smart enough to say nothing and listen.

"If, as you look through your prime-time lineup, you want to change the time of the show and make it earlier, I'm perfectly willing to continue to do it. Logically, it should follow directly after daytime trials because it is a wrap-up show of the day's legal events.

"You can also let me go back to daytime. I could be a really good anchor for you in daytime. I would not have this personal issue in my life, and I could still continue to contribute to Court TV in a way that is good for the network." (I wanted to say, "And you can take away my raise," but some innate sense of self-preservation made me resist the urge to give back my nighttime salary.)

I had filibustered. Now I was done. Henry Schleiff looked at the ceiling, then ran his hands through his hair, around his eyes, over his forehead. He was very quiet and he didn't look at me. I sat there thinking, I'm a goner. He's just going to fire me. He's going to make Gregg do this show alone and I'm fired for cause.

Finally his hand slid over the desk. "I agree that this is unprofessional," he said. My heart sank. "But I also respect your honesty. This was difficult for you to do, I'm sure. I admire you for coming in. I have a happy family; I have a great wife and kids; I work hard; I try to have some balance in my life. So I know what you're talking about."

Maybe I was going to survive.

"We value you here. You and Bill Bratton are a great couple," he told me. "You're a very public couple. I understand why you don't want to lose this relationship." I was waiting for the other shoe to fall.

"How about this for a compromise: It's October. We are going to put in a lot of new programming in January. The time of the show might change; the format might change. But we need it up and running now. Why don't you stay and do the show till ten o'clock until the end of the year? After January first we'll look at it and work something out." He looked at me. "It may mean you're not doing a prime-time program."

I took a breath. I had promised myself that I wasn't going to work under these conditions. No ten o'clocks. Not one.

"If you need me, I can do three months," I told him, "but that's all I can do. I understand, in the world of television, that would preclude me from ever thinking about doing news at six and eleven, but I'm not looking for those kinds of jobs anymore. I can do three months. I think that's appropriate. If you want to fire me at the end of the year because that's all I can give you, I can understand it. But I am no longer working late nights."

We had a deal. Schleiff put his arm around me and walked me out the door. The whole conversation had taken perhaps seven minutes. Maybe I had saved my job. But had I saved my relationship? Would Bill go along with it? I was trembling.

I didn't want to risk anyone seeing me in this state so I took the elevator to the seventh floor where my office had been, went to a bathroom where no one would hear me, and cried like a baby. I had been so knotted with worry that when I broke down I released a true torrent of tears. I just stood there and shook. Finally I washed my face, pulled on my mask, and dove back in.

I called Bill from my office. "I told him I couldn't do it anymore and I didn't get fired! He was great. He listened. He doesn't think I'm being a bad girl. It's okay. I can't believe it!" Bill said with a laugh, "Slow down."

"But we have to do this for three months," I said. I told him about my agreement to do the show from 9:00 to 10:00 at night until the end of the year. "I know I said I wouldn't, but I didn't see any other way out. I'm sorry. Can you do this?" I was babbling. Had I just sentenced our relationship to death by neglect?

Bill laughed. "We'll be just fine. After what we've been through this year . . ."

I kept apologizing. I felt that I had let both him and our relationship down. In my concern over losing my job I had agreed to put us in peril for three months, just as I'd put every other relationship I'd ever had in peril because of my work. I was relieved that I had taken action to protect us, yet scared that I hadn't gone far enough.

But maybe there was some release from this work prison. "Three months. I've had clients tell me they can do three months standing on their head. So can I!"

Bill picked me up at the station at 10:00 that night and took me out for champagne. What better way to finish this long day? We sat again at the King Cole Bar and this time toasted our life, our good fortune, our future. We both realized that the quality of our lives was what we treasured . . . professionally and personally. This was a new prize—a good and happy life with the man I love—and no price was too great.

sixteen LOVE IS A MANY-
SPLENDORED THING

NINETEEN NINETY-EIGHT AND **1999** WERE
THE YEARS OF OUR EXQUISITE COURTSHIP.
We tried to avoid the gossip columns early on in deference to the
spouses we were divorcing—they were decent people who did not
need us to flaunt our relationship in front of them. We traveled to San
Diego, Chicago, Washington, Nantucket, Philadelphia, and London,
and spent New Year's Eve in Paris, dancing at the Hotel Le Bristol.
We found our special places and restaurants in New York City. Jog-
ging in Central Park, strolling up Madison Avenue, holding hands in

the movies, sharing popcorn and sloppy slices of pizza and those special stolen moments. We could not stop touching and looking at each
other. He has a glance that is so filled with love that it causes all of my
emotions to roll out of my eyes as tears of joy. They have to flow out
somewhere.

We knew we would get married as soon as our divorces were
final. We could not bear to be apart. If I could have been his Jiminy
Cricket, I would have traveled with him 24/7.

I was adored and adorned by him: Tiffany earrings, bracelets, pins,
a Cartier ring, a Cartier pen that I won't appear on television without.
And the teddy bears! I have always collected teddy bears, and now I
have only those Bill gave me, from my Vermont police bear with the
gold half-glasses like the ones he wears, to the bear from the Rainbow
Room, to the Hampton Maid fluffy white bear, to the Blue Shalom
Hanukkah bear, to the bear he placed in his room at the Regency Hotel
so I would feel welcome. He even bought the tiniest brown travel bear
that fits in my bag of toiletries so he is always with me.

Bill moved into a charming, furnished sublet in the East Sixties
filled with beautiful Latin art. I spent time with him at his apartment
while holding on to my own apartment and, most important, all of my
closets. His place was perfectly cozy, with a Murphy bed that we
kept perpetually open in the bedroom. Bill called it our "love nest."
He bought a ridiculously huge brown teddy bear that lay across the
bed as if it were his lair.

Bill called me his "many-splendored thing." He bought a videotape of the classic William Holden–Jennifer Jones movie *Love Is a
Many-Splendored Thing*, and we watched it over and over again, sobbing away in the warmth of our affection and our understanding of
how fragile love can be, how potentially short-lived. He actually
crooned to me: "Your fingers touched my silent heart and taught it
how to sing." I said I would settle for twenty-five years and a day; it
would satisfy me if at fifty, I could get to seventy-five by his side. I
would be so very blessed.

Time passed and our divorces eventually became final. We were
aware then, and that awareness never leaves us, of what we left in
our wake. It has been said that one must know great pain in order to

find great pleasure, and there is not a day of our lives when we do not count the blessings of our being together.

At the end of the summer of 1998 I knew I needed a rural home to replace the sanctuary I had had in Milton. The privacy of the woods was essential to my life. I told Bill that I wanted to look for a house to buy in the Hamptons. I had breathed a deep sigh each time the Hampton Jitney had turned into the Village of Quogue, with its wide main street and majestic trees that spoke of pastoral moments, so we looked there. Quogue was only seventy-eight miles from my office and would take hours less driving time than the far reaches of the East End, where many of our friends lived and complained of the weekly commute.

In August I began looking in earnest. Bill and I visited a home we saw listed in the newspaper, made a wrong turn, and found ourselves on a lovely street lined with well-groomed contemporary homes. Barely idling, we passed a house with a FOR SALE sign on the lawn, and I screamed, "Stop the car!" No one was home, so like burglars we walked up to the windows and peered inside.

The house was beautiful. I wrote down the name of the broker and called him the next day. Ron Scala, a friendly talker with a deep tan, who looks like he should be in *The Sopranos,* met me the following Friday. "How much do you want to spend?" he asked. I gave him our price range. "Oh, then you can't see that house; that house is at least a couple hundred grand more. I'll show you some property within your budget." After he had toured me through those homes, all of which needed several hundred thousand dollars' worth of work, he said, "Well, I guess you should see that house you liked." He was good.

When I walked in, I knew this was where I wanted to live and die. The house called to me. The landscaping was breathtaking, the interior tasteful and meticulous. The original owners had put all their love and skills into creating a secluded retreat. The grounds in the rear were completely private, bordering on a Suffolk County wildlife preserve so no one could ever build near us. The house stood on one acre, with three hundred acres of privacy. A pool, a gazebo and matching birdhouse, a sunken tennis court surrounded by fences lush with purple wisteria vines all added to the magic. From a pond on two levels, a waterfall gurgled with the soothing sounds of a Zen moment. The perennials flowered for most of the year in all conceivable colors and shapes.

Inside, the furniture was stunning yet simple, the light magnificent. Trompe l'oeil ivy climbed beneath a skylight and in subtle places on the walls. And when I walked into a guest room I gasped. The black-and-white bedspread was exactly like one my mother once owned, and the poster on the wall was by one of my favorite artists, whose work hung above my bed in New York. I felt as if I already lived there.

Bill returned with me the next day and the place captured him as well. I kept babbling to the owners about my feelings, and he gave me "the look" to shut me up, since I was driving the price even higher. But my feelings, my absolute love of this house, won the owners over. They knew I would care for it as they had.

I bought it and took almost every piece of furniture that they would sell. I only added the art, the collectibles, and all of the toys.

The house in Quogue was our paradise, its privacy our sanctuary. We thrived there alone. No guests, no makeup, no phone calls. Feeding the birds and the squirrels; finding turtles and rabbits; watching the ubiquitous deer—we loved it all. Our answering machine actually said, "We are not answering the phone right now."

Quogue was my heaven on earth, my salvation, my serenity. It was our home, our roots, our life. I could not imagine ever living anywhere else on the planet. I wanted to die there. It surrounded us, embraced us, with joy.

I knew Bill would ask me to marry him, and I suspected he would make a production out of it. I thought he might take me to the top of the Empire State Building, or plant his proposal on the news zipper that encircles the building in Times Square. I was simply waiting. I didn't have a clue how clever he really was.

On Monday, February 8, 1999, Bill called me at work and told me to wear something nice for dinner. He picked me up in a town car with a driver. This would be the night, I knew. There was a dusting of snow on the ground as we started driving north on Sixth Avenue. I thought perhaps we were going to Petrossian, a favorite of ours, for champagne and caviar, but then we turned west into Central Park. Were we going to Picholine? No, we turned south. I thought, Oh, no, don't tell me he is going to propose at Tavern on the Green. It was such a touristy thing to do.

I took a breath as we turned down a dirt path. I had no idea where we were, but I could see a cluster of police cars with their headlights on and their roof lights spinning. They were creating a glow around the Central Park carousel. We got out of the car and as we passed, the group of police officers standing around the gazebo like real-life toy soldiers applauded and hooted and hollered. Bill took my coat and walked me into the well of the merry-go-round. He lifted me onto a masterfully crafted white horse and held me as the carousel began to move. He looked into my eyes and said, "I want to go round and round through life with you!"

"Oh, yes, yes, yes!"

There was never such a magical moment in my life. Then he added, "Wait, that wasn't the question . . . that's simply the statement." I had continued to underestimate his romance.

"We're on our way to act two," he said. I was happy to be along for the ride.

We drove to the superb restaurant Daniel where the magnificent chef and his staff awaited us, applauding as we entered. Daniel Boulud himself cooked a special tasting menu for us. We drank champagne and a grand Bordeaux. And for dessert they brought out a marvelous confection that asked, in chocolate letters, "Will you marry me?" *Then* Bill asked the question. As tears of joy rolled down my cheeks and I whispered, "Yes," Bill presented me with a beautiful engagement necklace — strands of gold, each with a floating diamond. It looked like a waterfall of love.

News of our engagement appeared in all the New York papers. They seemed to love our romance almost as much as we did. I think we gave people hope: You can find love in your fifties! You can be middle-aged and ecstatic!

Our wedding could only be for twenty people or five hundred, because choosing a guest list would have been difficult for any number in between, so we decided to have a small ceremony and take our celebration on the road. We visited what was left of my family in Chicago and took them out for a loving and glorious dinner. We went to Boston and celebrated with Bill's family as well. In New York, one set of friends threw us a cocktail party and another a "lingerie shower," though in truth Bill got the best of that deal.

We were married on April 30, 1999, a Friday. I took the day off (how rare), treated myself to a massage, had my hair and nails done, and went to Court TV, where my makeup artist, Jill Spector, made me look like a movie star. Bill wore a tuxedo. He looked breathtaking. I chose a long gown of white velvet from Suzanne's of Boston. My Tiffany earrings were Bill's gift; and I finally had an occasion to wear the extravagant pearl necklace and bracelet I had been given by Big Jim Williams of Savannah. Our cake was surrounded with real flowers and topped with a gold quarter moon, our symbol of our love.

Bill and I decided our two witnesses would be Evan Frances, my surrogate mother, and Alex Wesman, my first husband. Before we were wed, Alex (he was no longer known as Sandy) had written to Bill:

"We received your wedding invitation last night and I suppose that is what focused my thoughts. I have been both flattered and impressed by your ability to extend friendship and trust to me, given the complexity of my relationship with Rikki. It is precisely because I have known her so long and so well that I want you to know how good I think you are for her. She needs someone who will encourage her to be more, to go further and continue to grow; not someone who simply can't stop her from doing what she wants. Yours is the kind of marriage I always assumed Rikki would ultimately find. I suspect (although I am obviously guessing more here) that the same may be said of you.

"When I look at it, I think my relationship with Rikki has always been largely paternal in an asynchronic way. In that role, let me finish by simply saying that it will be my distinct pleasure to give the bride away and to share in the joy of your wedding."

Since 1979, Alex had become my closest friend. When he had left his second wife and fallen in love with another woman, Ellen Lederer, he came to see me in Boston to try to understand what had gone wrong with our marriage so he would not make the same mistakes again. (My mistakes were hardly mentioned.) I met Ellen and I adored her. We had so much in common, including but not limited to Alex. Ellen became my friend, my confidante; she opened her heart and her home to me. Along with Alex, she took me in at various times in my life when I was quaking. I envied their love, their relationship. They had what I always wanted. Suddenly I realized that I now had precisely the same thing. I adored them, and Bill and I loved their precious son, James.

The wedding was full of joy. Tears, of course, but tears of joy or those provoked by gales of laughter. Judge Leslie Crocker Snyder, who presided, began by saying that she would "like to talk about the bride and groom before they talk about each other. There's a lot to say, but Bill said that I can't talk too long because Rikki is in a hurry to get married."

Who, me?

"Try to get information from Bill about himself," she joked, "and you begin to understand what the 'blue wall of silence' really means!" How well she knew him.

Her wedding quote came from George Eliot's *Adam Bede:* "What greater thing is there for two human souls than to feel that they are joined for life—to strengthen each other in all labor, to rest on each other in all sorrow, to minister to each other in all pain, to be with each other in silent unspeakable memories at the moment of the last parting."

How well she knew us and our love.

I rarely winged it in court and I was certainly prepared on my wedding day. Reading from a card adorned with two hearts joined, I said to Bill, "Truly you are my *beshert*—my fate, my destiny. In one moment of time all of my lifetime of searching, feeling, and reflecting came together. In that moment I fell so in love with you. The process of loving you is truly spiritual for me, for I know only God could have sent you to share and enrich the last half of my life.

"I have lost myself in you and found myself again. You are the reason for my being on this planet. As it was written: 'In a universe of ambiguity, this kind of certainty comes only once, and never again, no matter how many lifetimes you live.'"

Then it was Bill's turn. He looked into my eyes and spoke: "Throughout my lifetime, I have always envied and sought the love that my parents have for each other, a love that was born at first sight when they were teenagers so long ago and has continued for over fifty years to this day. I had reached a point in my life when I felt that 'true love' like theirs was never going to happen for me. No possibility of magic, no possibility of being swept off my feet. And right about the time when I was ready to finally close the door to these dreams, you walked into my life and everything changed. The more I learned about you, the more amazed I became at how right we were for each other. The more I was with you, the more I wanted to be with you. My dreams had come true.

"And now every time I have you in my arms, or whenever I look at you as I am doing now, I realize that life saved the very best . . . for last."

All tears. All smiles. All joy. All the meaning of life for everyone in that room.

And then it was some kind of party!

We lived our love affair every day. Twenty-four hours would not go by without a phone call to tell the other "I love you." The cards, notes, and flowers continued. We were mindful of what we had and we worked never to forget it.

Yet, we also led complex and very public lives. From 1999 through 2002 we dined out or attended functions almost four nights a week. On weekends we went to Quogue religiously and kicked back . . . just us, no frills, no glamour, lots of workouts and movies and books. On weekdays, I worked on television and taught at Columbia Law School. Bill opened his own shop, The Bratton Group, which then joined forces with the acclaimed international consulting firm Kroll Associates. He remained in the news as a commentator about police, public safety, and terrorism issues. I attended his public speeches, he attended mine. When I was a keynote speaker, he would even introduce himself as "Rikki's husband."

We traveled together often and made it a point to return to Positano and Capri every year. He brought me on consulting trips to Lisbon, Brazil, and beautiful Buenos Aires, where we even took a tango lesson. We were a perfect complement. I liked how magazine writers put it: I'm the fire, he's the ice; he's the salt, I'm the pepper.

In the fall of 1999, as she prepared to run for the Senate in New York, Hillary Clinton called Bill to seek his advice about crime issues. While police commissioner in Boston and New York, Bill had developed a relationship with President Clinton and his staff while aggressively lobbying for passage of Clinton's Omnibus Anti-Crime Bill. He met with her over breakfast and as he was about to exit, she asked whether he would be attending the White House Christmas party. She suggested he bring his wife and "be our guests." He looked at her quizzically and she said, quite clearly, "We would love to have you stay overnight as our guests at the White House."

Bill called me and asked if I could take a day off from work in December.

"Impossible."

"We were just invited to stay overnight at the White House."

"I'll get the day off."

I called my scheduler and asked for a day off in December.

"Impossible."

I told her the reason.

"Consider it done."

We entered through the oval driveway at the rear of the White House under the awning we had seen so many times on the news and were met by Mrs. Clinton's chief of protocol who saw that our bags were taken by two tuxedoed ushers and conducted our tour. As we walked along the corridor on an upper floor, I gazed at the amazing rooms and then noticed that our luggage was sitting neatly in the Lincoln Bedroom. It was unmistakable.

After I ran my hands along each piece of furniture in complete amazement, we changed for the cocktail party. Then I called my aunt Eve and screeched, "I'm calling you from the Lincoln Bedroom!"

Christmas trees were everywhere, and the decorations were something out of a fantasy. The food, the china, the silver all displayed the majesty of the place. We stepped into the Oval Office and visited the Cabinet room. We danced to an orchestra. We later met President Clinton, who had been involved in Israeli-Syrian peace talks all day; he shook hands with hundreds of people in a receiving line, conducted a dinner, and still had private time for just us when he and

Hillary personally escorted us to our room for the night. Incredibly, they stayed with us for another twenty minutes at the end of what must have been a very long and tiring day. He spoke to us as if we were diplomats and discussed the vital issues of the Middle East conflict. It's all about water, he explained.

President Clinton's charisma lived up to its legend. The room did vibrate when he entered, and no matter what one thought of his politics or his personal life, one was entirely drawn to him.

Bill and I were the only guests in the White House that night. We walked into the famous quarters of FDR with its ramp entrance and its view of the grounds. We stared at portraits, in awe of the majesty.

And, yes, we did make love in the Lincoln Bedroom. Afterward, Bill slept soundly, but I stayed awake, hoping to see the famous "Lincoln ghost."

Sadly, life is not paradise. In December 2000 I had serious lumbar surgery after a chiropractor blew a disk out of my back. I was in intractable pain for months afterward and feared I would never have any physical vitality again. I have remained in physical therapy for years. Bill was there every step of the way, stroking my forehead, comforting me, never impatient with my protracted recovery but frustrated with his inability to make it all better.

It's funny what I remember: the wonderful folks at Campagnola sending flowers so large that they could have filled a hotel lobby and the restaurant's owner, Murray Wilson, actually delivering dinner to me himself; lawyer "Don't Worry, Murray" Richman sending Jewish care packages from the Second Avenue Deli; my friends Andrew Dornenburg and Karen Page bringing homemade meals, flowers, and books.

Of course, after two weeks of incapacitation I refused to miss any more work. I spent mornings lying in bed in agony, reading scripts faxed to my apartment. The doorman then practically carried me to a cab, and when I arrived at the studio I hobbled out and made my way upstairs to makeup and hair, did the show, and returned directly to my bed. I was so out of it, if I didn't review the tapes of the shows I would not even remember that I had done them. My producers,

Vicky Pomerance Neer and Gideon Hayes, kept me on the air without anyone else knowing my pain.

I thought I would never get better. In April Bill and I attempted to go to dinner, but by the end of the appetizers I could not sit for another second and did not know if I could even move to exit. The maître d' gave me the name of a healer named Jiei Atacama and told me about a pastry chef who had come to work shaped like a corkscrew, in so much pain that he could barely speak, who after a few hours with this man had come back to work upright and smiling. Yeah, right. I put the card in my wallet, but a week later I called; I had to try something more. The morning after my first visit with his son, Aaron, I had two hours pain-free. I worked with the Atacama Healing Center as well as my physical therapist three times a week, and by May I actually had one full day without pain. Against all the rules and everyone else's predictions, by August I was able to run. This was a miracle.

Since Bill was no longer in public life, I became his priority. I felt true peace of mind, perhaps for the very first time. And yet I loved Bill's life of celebrity. We would walk into the noted East Side restaurant Elaine's and hear "Run for mayor!" "Come back as commissioner!" "You changed our lives!" "We miss you!" "We love you!" People never stopped coming up and shaking his hand and schmoozing.

I watched him. There was no doubt he was tempted by his own power, and from time to time I would join in that fantasy. What could he do with this? But at the same time I wanted to hold on to our private life, our love, our togetherness. I was scared that this peace, this life, might be taken from us—I was afraid that he might take it, that I might choose to give it away. Please, I told myself, contentment is so fragile, don't screw it up again. What a grand thing this love is. Every day, our love grew deeper and even more passionate. I loved middle age!

In her wonderful book *Wouldn't Take Nothing for My Journey Now,* Maya Angelou writes, "Being a woman is hard work. Not without joy and even ecstasy, but still relentless, unending work. . . . Women should be tough, tender, laugh as much as possible, and live long lives." Some of us are foolish enough, and brave enough, to believe we must be the best at what we do. And then, when we have a moment to kick off those uncomfortable shoes and stare at the ceiling, we ask, "Can we have it all?" Can we be lawyers, leaders, writers? Can we make partner or become a CEO while we date, marry, have children, exercise, eat right, get to the dentist, see the doctor, have annual Pap smears and mammograms, do our nails, get our hair styled, call Mom, call Dad, call the kids, write thank-you notes, read, sleep? Do we ever get to smell the roses? It was not even a balancing act anymore; it was juggling.

I came to the conclusion that you can have it all, just not all at the same time. We women had to choose our priorities according to the time of our lives. One's goal at twenty-two may well not be one's goal at forty or fifty. For some that meant career first; for others it was family. We needed to set reasonable goals and stick to them as best we could. We needed to monitor ourselves and see if the goals we had set were still the ones we wanted to achieve, and if they weren't, we needed to set new ones. If we failed, we needed to acknowledge that failure and start again. We needed not to beat up on ourselves, but to use the benefits of our mistakes. I certainly needed to, in any case. The sacrifice of family, time, and health to charge ahead with my career? I had paid dearly, but I didn't regret a minute of it, because now my life was perfect.

In 2000 Bill considered running to succeed Rudy Giuliani as mayor of New York City. Because of his positive public persona and notable accomplishments, he was encouraged to run by people from both political parties. Bill was an Independent; his friends thought he was a Democrat; and the polls showed that since his fame was inextricably intertwined with Giuliani's the majority of New Yorkers believed him to be a Republican. He was uncertain how to position himself. He held countless meetings and ran several polls with my dear friend Larry Kaagan, who had learned his craft from the master pollster Daniel Yankelovich, and with Kieran Mahoney, a major campaign adviser to New York's governor, George Pataki, and Senator Al D'Amato, to gauge public interest.

It did not take long for Bill to realize that he was not ready to head out on the campaign trail. He would not lock himself in a room and make phone calls to raise money. He just could not bring himself to do it. As time went on and we attended social functions, I would work the room relentlessly and he would be uncharacteristically withdrawn.

Bill would have been a great mayor. Getting there was the problem. He did not have the fire in his belly at that point in his life.

Before 8:00 A.M. on the day it was announced in the *New York Times* that Bill would not be seeking the nomination, our telephone rang. It was Mark Green. Green wanted Bill's support for his own mayoral candidacy, and he was smart and aggressive enough to be the first person to call. It was September 2000, and the Democratic primary election for mayor was one year away.

Mark Green was a longtime political figure in New York City and in the state, having run unsuccessfully as the Democratic nominee for senator in 1986; seven years later he had been elected overwhelmingly as New York City's Public Advocate. He was articulate, progressive, well funded, and media savvy. Green was the early odds-on favorite, and like so many liberals, he was perceived to be soft on crime.

Mark was smart. He invited us to his apartment to watch the presidential debates. He courted Bill slowly, deliberately, skillfully.

We thought this was a brilliant stroke of both politics and public policy. Bill was a solid figure, well liked and well respected by all segments of the city. He had left the police department with a 71 percent approval rating, and he offered all the inoculation Mark Green might need against accusations that he would coddle criminals.

Bill gave it considerable thought. He certainly was interested in running a police department again. His work in the private sector was remunerative and allowed us to live a life of comfort he had never attained before, but he felt there was so much more he could have given the city and achieved in his job had he not been forced out by the mayor. Bill gathered his crew and consulted with his advisers. Could they reconstitute Camelot? Jack Maple, one of the prime architects of Bill's NYPD turnaround, had contracted cancer and was always in our prayers, but many of his former colleagues were eager to finish the job, and in the years since Bill had left, a new layer of talented police professionals had moved into place and would be eager to sign on.

The boys had the fever. Bill was going to be police commissioner,

John Miller was going to return to his role as deputy chief for public information, and Jerry Hauer, the guru of emergency management, was going to be fire commissioner. They had it all figured out. Bill was working day and night on transition plans with the best police minds in the country. Everyone wanted to work with him and be back in the game.

Bill agreed to support Mark. They campaigned together and Bill produced exactly the results that had been anticipated. Mark never actually asked Bill to be the police commissioner until the very end, but he campaigned on the issue of crime with Bill at his side for every relevant campaign stop. The electorate had to assume that Bill would get the job. And so did Bill.

Then all hell broke loose.

The day of the Democratic primary, which polls showed Green winning, was sunny, with a bright blue sky, a day promising a good turnout for Mark. It was also September 11, 2001. In the aftermath of the terror attack everything changed. For the citizens of New York City, nothing would ever be the same. The election was postponed, and the behavior of the candidates during those highly charged times affected voter allegiance. Green ultimately won a runoff but sufficiently alienated another Democratic candidate, Fernando Ferrer, so that he and his organization essentially sat out the general election. It was New York City politics in a nutshell.

The terror attack pushed the issue of crime to the background. Although Bill and Mark did one fine commercial together, after September 11 the campaign foolishly dropped it in lieu of ads concerning the education issue and others attacking Republican candidate Michael Bloomberg. After his truly heroic leadership in the aftermath of 9/11, Rudy Giuliani became "America's mayor" and he endorsed Bloomberg big-time.

Green lost.

So Bill wasn't going to be police commissioner. Camelot would remain a memory. What a shame. What a loss for New York City. On election night we went down to Green campaign headquarters at the Sheraton Hotel, where Bill smiled, Mark smiled, and I cried. The dream was gone—*poof*.

seventeen

MY HOUSE, MY HOUSE,
MY HOUSE, MY JOB,
MY JOB, MY JOB

ILL HAD BEEN OBSERVING THE LOS ANGELES
POLICE DEPARTMENT CLOSELY FOR MANY
months. After the scandals of the Rampart Division—in which
numerous LAPD officers in that division's antigang unit were found
to have either participated in or known about and not reported a pattern of corrupt practices including assaults, narcotics trafficking, and
the shooting and framing of civilians, resulting in more than one hundred criminal convictions having to be dismissed—the City of Los
Angeles agreed to enter a five-year consent decree with the Justice

Department, making the LAPD the largest law enforcement agency in the nation to come under federal oversight. A federal monitor, with access to all of the LAPD's files and investigations, would report the city's progress in implementing the consent decree to the federal court. The company with which Bill was working, Kroll Associates, won the contract to be that federal monitor, and Bill was on the monitoring team as one of three chief of police "subject matter experts."

Bill was in his element and he loved this work. If anyone could help to reform the LAPD, it was my husband. Separate and apart from the federal monitoring, people in the office of Los Angeles Mayor James Hahn expressed interest in having Bill's company, The Bratton Group, put together a proposal to develop anticrime strategies and a Compstat management system similar to the successful model that had worked so well in New York and other cities. Bill was interested and excited about the prospect. There was one problem, however: LAPD Chief Bernard Parks's contract was not being renewed, so the position of chief of police was in play, and there was some noise that Bill wanted the job. Believing that the mayor would not go with an outsider, Bill told them, "Look, I'm exactly what you need as chief of police, but you won't hire me. However, I'll put together a crime-reduction proposal for you to consider. I'll bring in my people for three or four months and we'll give your new chief, whoever that turns out to be, some plans and recommendations." (Bill had been through this twice before in L.A. He had applied in 1991 but dropped out as one of twelve finalists when it became apparent to him that Philadelphia Police Chief Willie Williams, an African American, was the favorite candidate. He had been approached once again in 1997 about applying for the chief's job, but when it became clear that this time they wanted someone from inside the force rather than a complete outsider, he had decided against it, and Bernard Parks, also an African American, was appointed by Mayor Richard Riordan.) He gathered his troops over an intense two-week period—many of the same people who had helped him turn around Boston's and New York City's problems, including consultants Bob Wasserman, John Linder, Richard Aborn, Bill Andrews, former NYPD Chief Pat Harnett, and Joan Brody, who had served as his special assistant in both the Boston and the New York police departments—and put together a proposal.

Bill flew to the West Coast several times in an effort to get this consulting proposal approved. The mayor's office liked it and wanted to take it to the police department. Instead of Acting Police Chief Martin Pomeroy coming to the mayor's office to discuss the proposal, however, in a power play of territoriality he requested that the mayor's deputy for criminal justice come to him instead. And when the LAPD saw the Bratton Group proposal they didn't want any part of it. In essence: "Forget about this. We don't want Bratton. We don't want an outsider. He doesn't need to tell us; no one needs to tell us what to do; we can do it ourselves." Bill felt that the acting chief would even resign before he would allow this group of "outsiders" into the department.

Bill thought that the mayor's office had not anticipated this level of resistance and hostility. Rather than fight the issue and create a political crisis that the mayor did not need, Bill chose to withdraw his proposal, recognizing the futility of trying to force a consultancy on a hostile client. The department was in desperate need of reform, but this reticence made it even more clear that if the new chief came from within the ranks, in all likelihood the LAPD culture would remain intact and nothing would change.

So I was sitting quite happily at our home in Quogue on the first day of summer in 2002, when an application for the job of chief of police of the City of Los Angeles came over the fax machine. I picked it up and walked it over to Bill.

"Don't tell me."

"No, no, no," he said. "My office simply sent this to me for my awareness, as part of the monitor's responsibilities."

"You are not applying, are you?"

"No, I'm not applying. It's part of the project."

That was comforting. As far as I was concerned, everything was ideal. I was married to the most wonderful man in the world; I had a great job that allowed me to be at my best using so many of my strengths in public; I loved my house in Quogue; I loved my life.

Bill flew back to Los Angeles and I did what I always did when he was traveling—I waited for him to come home. I had an American Bar Association meeting on Saturday, June 29, in Washington, D.C., and told Bill I was sorry it was spoiling the beginning of our vacation together. "Tell you what," he said, "I'll go with you. We'll have a nice dinner. You have your meeting on Saturday, then we'll take a plane back and we'll drive to Quogue. We'll look at it as a great excuse to have dinner in Washington."

We did indeed have a nice dinner with friends; I attended my meeting and Bill played tourist. He walked all over Washington, visiting the Vietnam War, Korean War, and Lincoln Memorials, as well as the Holocaust Museum. Then he picked me up at the hotel. We flew back to New York, got in the car, and drove to our glorious home in the Hamptons. That Sunday, as we were driving back from a friend's party, Bill said, "Let's cancel all our plans for the week and just have the time together."

"Great!"

It was a spontaneous honeymoon. We stayed in Quogue and went to the beach, read, played tennis badly, watched DVDs. We spent an extraordinary, relaxing seven days together. We were very, very happy.

With extremely rare exceptions we never had houseguests in Quogue. It was our place, time, and space. The only exceptions were Bill's family, my surrogate mother Evan Frances, our friends Karen Page and Andrew Dornenburg, and our friend Mickey Sherman, who spent all of two nights in our guest room coming back from some late Hamptons parties.

On Sunday, July 7, Andrew, Karen, Bill, and I were sitting by the pool, sipping wine, when I said, "My life is now perfect. I hope nothing ever changes."

Famous last words.

I was blasted into reality that Monday morning. It's amazing what a week of marital bliss can do. Bill went back to Los Angeles and I spent time with my women friends. I waited up for him on Thursday night, when he came home after midnight, no time for serious conversation. He was waiting for me in the car outside the Court TV offices at a quarter to four the next afternoon, and we began our weekly Friday-afternoon drive to Quogue. I was still in work mode, finishing up the day's telephone calls, returning messages, on the phone with a real estate broker because I was in one of my periodic quests for a larger apartment. I arranged an appointment for the next Wednesday. When I put the phone down, Bill said, "Before you go out with this broker I think we should talk about something that happened this week in L.A."

I didn't have a clue. "Sure. What's up?"

"Politics have changed and I have been approached about applying for the job of police chief." He told me the details but I couldn't hear him.

"Tell me again, you're not going to apply."

"Well, I think we should talk about this. I think I have a good chance of getting it." I didn't say a word. He went on. "I think we can make this work." Then he proceeded to tell me all the wonderful things he could do to make the LAPD function the way it should again, all the changes that needed to be made and how he would make them, all the projects, all the plans.

I didn't hear a word. It was as if a metal bar had been placed between my temples. All I could think was, What's going to happen to my job? Am I going to have to move to Los Angeles? Are we moving to Los Angeles? What about our house? How am I going to earn a living? How am I going to deal with this? My life is over.

At some point Bill took a breath and I said, "I don't want to talk about this now. I'm taking a nap." I pulled the seat back and lay down flat on my back, arms crossed as if I were in a coffin. If I'd started talking I would either have begun to scream or broken down and cried, so I closed my eyes and willed myself to sleep.

I woke up a half hour later, groggy and barely syllabic, and we really hadn't gone very far. The Long Island Expressway on a Friday barely moves on a good day, and this was a particularly slow one.

"When is the application due?" I asked. Much as I hoped the topic would go away, there really wasn't anything else to talk about.

He explained the process in far more detail than I was interested in hearing. He was already immersed in the details. Once the applications and résumés were filed a head hunter sifted through them and culled the top fifty. From them, twenty were culled. Of those, a group (it turned out to be thirteen) would be interviewed by the Los Angeles Police Commission, and three names would be sent to the mayor, who would interview the finalists and select a police chief.

"When do you have to apply?" I asked again.

"Friday the nineteenth."

"You mean a week from today."

"Yes."

"What are your chances?"

I knew the answer to that one. If they hadn't been good, he wouldn't be applying. "I think if they are looking for an outsider there is no one better qualified than I am." Bill has never lacked for confidence.

I asked the true question. "Do you really want to do this?"

"I do."

Boy, I didn't.

"I have a contract with Court TV until a year from October. This means we'll have a commuting relationship. We said we would never do that. I've had one marriage break up over that already. And if we are going to live in Los Angeles we have to live nicely, which requires money. We would have to sell the apartment; we would have to sell the house."

"Oh no, we can rent Quogue."

"Bill, if we have to move we are never going to be *in* Quogue."

"I don't want to give it up."

"When are you going to come back here if you're living in L.A. for the next five years?" It was a five-year contract. "In the meantime, I have a contract at Court TV and I'm not going to have a job in Los Angeles." The network did not have a studio in Los Angeles and wasn't about to open one. The more I talked, the more anxious I got.

"I have a lot to think about," I said. "We'll talk about it over the weekend."

"Fine."

"Fine!"

Anger had torn through me immediately. He had told me he wasn't applying. How could he go back on his word? How could he do this without discussing it with me? He knew I thought of myself as a New Yorker/Bostonian/Chicagoan, that for all the time I spent in Los Angeles during the Simpson trial I'd thought the L.A. lifestyle existed in automobiles, not on foot as I chose to live, since I hate to drive and cannot see a damn thing at night. And yet he had ripped the rug out from beneath my entire existence. He was thinking only of himself. How selfish could he be?

But then I really hit the depths; I was petrified. My whole life as I had known it was over. How were we going to live? What was I going to do for a living? God help me if I had to go back and practice law; I would be better off waiting tables. I would have no job, and he would be on a fixed income from the city—where was the money going to come from? How could I give up Quogue, the one place in the world where I felt completely and totally safe and happy? My God, how could I give up Quogue? I was in a panic.

And, of course, it was not lost on me that this was Rikki and Philip in reverse. I had pursued my career to New York and Philip had sacrificed his feelings and finally attempted to come join me— and look how that had worked out. I had no experience making this kind of sacrifice. I hoped this wouldn't kill our marriage. Would I resent him? Would I resent this move? Would he resent me?

My house, my house, my house. My job, my job, my job.

We drove three hours in silence. I could not get words out for fear what those words might be. Every mean, hurtful, ungenerous thought I had ever harbored against my husband came to the forefront of my mind. My mother had a wonderful phrase: "Words are like birds; once you let them out of the cage you can't get them back in again." I was about to open the aviary on him.

But I had enough sense to keep that door and my mouth shut. There was no point to screaming red-faced in the car and wailing, "Look what you are doing to my life! I have a job, why can't you let me keep it? I have this house that makes us happy, why can't we stay here? You're breaking our pact, our relationship agreement! How dare you?" It would have felt good to disgorge all this venom, but I had retained enough rational thought to know that I needed time to think, to work through the thunderclouds of my emotions and see what might be shining above them. I knew enough about myself to actually force myself to shut up, which is no easy task.

When we arrived at our house we had no time to talk; we had been invited to a fancy dinner party in Southampton. We changed clothes in silence and got back in the car. I made a calculated decision to talk about landscaping, restaurants, anything but what was really on our minds. At least that way I wouldn't yell at him.

Bill and I are good in a crowd; we normally find plenty to talk about with the people around us. We toured this fabulous home with its expensive art and talked with people one normally sees on television or reads about in the newspaper. At some point I realized that both Bill and I had done our best to be both present and pleasant, and as we talked to other people, some of the tension between us began to fade.

"We're going to the beach tomorrow, right?" I asked in the car on the way home.

"Yes, we'll go to the beach."

"Great, fine."

Sooner or later we had to discuss the major issue in our lives, but we held off. Knowing me, I had to take notes. I needed to write things down on paper in order to look at them objectively. That would take a day. When we reached our house, I said, "We need to talk about this on Sunday. I don't want to talk about it from now till then."

"All right."

We went to bed but I could not find sleep. I picked up a book and moved to another bedroom to read for a while. I could not concentrate because the words had no substance; I could not capture them in my mind. From tiny tears to the histrionic sobbing with which I was entirely too familiar, I couldn't stop crying. The house was still, as if breathing in repose. I thought, I love this house. How am I going to leave this house? We were so happy here a week ago; we had never been happier. What is going to happen to us? Finally I simply passed out.

I rose at dawn, put on my running shoes, and took off with Madonna blaring in my ears. I pounded the pavement hard, harder, harder still. I wanted to punish my body as I was punishing myself.

We didn't talk all morning outside of "Would you like some coffee?" We sat next to each other, reading the paper on the deck in the fresh air, and more than once I teared up and had to leave. I was just so . . . sad. I took a shower, put on some clothes, and took Bill to the Riverhead Kennel Club All-Breed Dog and Obedience Show, a cultural event he had never seen the likes of; as two dog lovers we could genuinely smile. We had been invited to a barbecue at the home of Beau Dietl, a Runyonesque former NYPD detective, so we dropped by Beau's. We ate a ton of very delicious, very unhealthy food, laughed with friends, and had a warm time. Walking down a path to our car, Bill said to me, "We went to this fancy party last night with a lot of fancy people. We went to this simple barbecue with really entertaining, down-to-earth folks today. Interesting, the worlds we travel."

This was one of the reasons I loved him. "Bill, no matter where we have risen in life it all comes back to our blue-collar roots." We both smiled.

I napped in a hammock and dreamed about falling out.

Coming home that night from a dinner we bolted down in twenty minutes, I began to cry again. "You can't do this to us." I tried to keep quiet but I couldn't. "I can't deal with this. I don't want you to do it. This is terrible for our lives. I don't want to move there. I don't want to give up my job. How can you give up Quogue?"

"We're in the car," Bill said flatly. "I don't want to talk about this." We walked into the house in total and complete silence, got into bed, turned our backs to each other, and went to sleep.

Again I woke up in the night and paced the floors as if I were preparing a closing statement. I argued with Bill in my mind: "We made a deal. You are breaking our deal. You are not supposed to be able to announce that you are going off to some city; this is supposed to be something we talk about. How can you make me give up everything I have when I am finally happy in my life?!"

I woke up with sharp pains in my back and neck. I could not turn my head. "You go to tennis; I can't," I told him. I didn't want to be with him. I was going to be a brat. I reminded myself of the Roy Lichtenstein painting of a woman with her hand on her forehead, saying, "Oh my God, I forgot to have children!" I had the pose, but my thought bubble said, "My home! My sanctuary! My job! My life!" Great melodrama.

But as soon as he left I washed my face, looked in the mirror, and didn't like what I saw. I had thought only of myself; I hadn't given Bill his proper consideration. I might have gotten away with that in my younger days, but my husband was entitled to pursue his dreams as far as I pursued mine, and rather than getting in his way I ought to have been supporting him. I was ashamed of myself, and of the way I'd carried on. My love for Bill made me stop the drama-queen antics: I was not going to whine; I was done with the flamboyant mourning; I was going to act like a grown woman. I put in my contacts, poured a cup of coffee, threw on a T-shirt and shorts, sat down at the round table outside on the deck, and made a list.

- *Sell house?*
- *Rent house?*
- *Check prices in Quogue and NYC*
- *Call accountant re capital gains*
- *Call Tarlow re real estate* [Barry Tarlow was a lawyer in Los Angeles who could tell me prices off the top of his head]
- *Call Andrew Frances in L.A. about neighborhoods, lifestyle, costs*
- *Talk to Henry Schleiff about future possibilities*

I didn't want to have a conversation with Bill from a list of talking points. I crumpled up the paper and threw it away.

When Bill came home I was calm. He tossed his tennis clothes in the hamper, took a shower, put on some shorts, and took a cup of coffee and the newspaper outside. I sat next to him. Sunday had finally arrived.

"Bill, I want to talk about Los Angeles."

"There is nothing to talk about."

"No, no, no. We have something to talk about."

"I cannot see you like this." He looked at me directly. "I love you. You're the most important thing in my life." I began to speak but he continued. Tenderly. "I'm not going to do this to you. Forget it. I don't need to do this." He was smiling.

What a sweet man. And he meant it! He was going to forgo his dreams so that I would be comfortable. That anyone could love me so much to make that sacrifice—it was a miracle. I was infused with a warmth I had never felt before. I shall cherish that moment for the rest of my life. I patted my heart.

"Bill"—it was all I could do to speak—"I can't tell you what this means to me."

"So it is done. Our life is together. Everything we do is together."

"Well," I said, "maybe we should look at this in a different way."

"No, Rikki, we are not going to talk about it." He turned to his newspaper. I could only marvel at the strength of my husband's generosity. He had sacrificed his vision of his future for our vision of ours. How I loved this man.

Bill and I knew each other's rhythms. I waited a half hour, got another cup of coffee, and sat next to him again. He was reading an article in the Long Island section of the *New York Times* about the Nassau County Police Department. After the autumn elections, he had been approached about that job, too.

"I really want to talk to you." I took the newspaper from his grasp and put it on the ground. Then I held his hands and leaned toward him. "I truly love you." My eyes held his; I needed to be sure he understood me. "That was the nicest thing anyone has ever said to me. You may actually love me more than my parents, and I didn't think that was possible." He smiled. "But I love you just as much. I've thought about this long and hard. I have been impossible this weekend. I don't blame you for being furious with me."

"I'm not angry."

Then I went into lawyer mode.

"Listen to me." I went through the list in my head and then out loud: L.A. real estate prices, neighborhoods, capital gains benefits/ detriments to selling the homes, pension, job benefits, my work. "My contract is up a year from October. I'm willing to commute if I have to, and I'd be the one doing the commuting. We should look into air fares and plane schedules to see if it can be done. But is that something we want? If Henry tells me he will commit in writing to an additional two or three years, I will tell you, Bill, I would prefer to stay in New York." Television is a fickle industry; people fall by the wayside constantly and jobs are not easy to come by. It would be very difficult for me at the age of fifty-four to walk away from the security of four more years of Court TV anchor work.

"If Henry tells you that you have a lengthy job commitment, that may make a difference."

"I think you need to look into the Los Angeles job. If you have five years and a pension attached, that would make a big difference to me financially. Let's try to get answers to our questions by Friday, then we can decide together on the objective evidence whether this is a good idea."

He smiled again. "I can't believe you came out of this so quickly."

"Well, it's because I love you. If this is best for you, we should go. What I'd like to hear is why you think this is best for you."

Bill knew exactly why. Clearly he had not endangered our wonderful New York life on a whim. "I'm not getting work done," he told me, "not the kind of work I want. I'm not satisfied in my work as a professional because I want to work in the public sector to accomplish things that impact people's lives, and in the private sector I cannot do that. I can't create a system; I can only advise. Right now I go in; I make some recommendations; I leave. The implementation is done by somebody else. That's not enough; it's not satisfying to me. The only project where I could set a goal and meet it was Venezuela." He had been an adviser on policing issues to Caracas Mayor Alfredo Pena and his police chief, Ivan Simonovis. Bill was taking the methods developed during his tenure in New York and Boston and turning the Caracas department around. However, his project had been aborted when an attempted coup of the government of Venezuelan president Hugo Chavez disrupted that country's political stability.

"I'm always scrambling for the next contract. The two most important deals I had this year were Caracas and L.A., and neither

turned out the way I expected. As many times as we bid on a proposal, we're lucky—as any company is lucky—if we get fifty percent.
And because I'm in the private sector, and I don't know when the
contracts will come along, I can't afford to turn down the travel.

"All I'm doing now is traveling," he said. We'd been lucky that
sometimes it was only eight days a month in two groups of four, with
an extra trip for a day or two here and there. "Let me just tell you the
places I have to go in the next six weeks." He reeled off England,
Brazil, Peru, back and forth to L.A. "Out of the four weeks of the
month, whether you are commuting to L.A. or I am on the road, we
may be in the same position.

"I am fifty-four years old. I'm going to be fifty-five. I don't know
if I can keep doing this for the next ten years. I don't know when the
money is going to run out; I don't know when the business is going to
run out.

"But it's more than the money. Who am I? Who am I now? I
knew who I was when I was police commissioner. I knew who I was
when I turned around five police departments. I knew who I was in
Caracas, because I could see the results of what I was doing. But I
don't know what my identity is anymore.

"I felt powerless after September eleventh. I want to be part of
the change. I have much more left to contribute. I know I can go into
this L.A. job as the only person in America who will turn this department around, the only person who knows what to do. The contract
will be over when I'm sixty, and I'll know at the age of sixty that my
team and I will have changed people's lives, that we will have made
the city safer, that we will have saved hundreds of lives. I can make
those police officers proud again. They deserve it. The community
deserves and needs them at their best. I want to forge a partnership
built on trust. As corny as that sounds, that's what I want to do. It's
what I do best, and I miss it. I can prove in L.A. that cops can reduce
crime and improve race relations. Giuliani lost that opportunity in
New York. With Jim Hahn in L.A. I can prove we can have both."

By this time tears were streaming down my face. How selfish I
had been, how blind to Bill's goodness.

"You have a job that you love," he said. "I know what that means to you. I've had jobs that I've loved. And the more challenging this police chief's job is, the more I would thrive on it.

"I don't want to ask you to leave Court TV; I know how important that is to you. We'll make this first year of commuting work somehow. And, you know, I'm fine if you are not working, if that's what you want to do in L.A. I'm fine if you're teaching; I'm fine if you're speaking; I'm fine if you're writing. I'll do whatever it takes to make sure that the two of us are together." He got a little twinkle in his eye. "You know," he said, "it might not be so bad to be in California in our sixties."

I thought, I am so lucky I married this man. I am so blessed. I had never seen this side of Bill. I'd thought he just wanted another police job, another professional accomplishment; I hadn't looked beneath and realized what that profession meant to him; I hadn't realized the depth of his commitment to other people, to changing the face of crime, to bridging the racial divide.

I crawled into his lap and gave him a big hug and a kiss. "We'll make this work."

Bill laughed. "Well, let's get the questions answered and we'll make a rational decision."

"Come on, Bill." I was smiling now. "You know you're going to apply." This would be Rikki and Bill's Excellent Adventure!

The next day, I paced outside Henry Schleiff's office once again. He told me, "As long as Court TV has daytime programming, you have a job here. We love and value you. That said, no one has a contract beyond the end of 2003." So, no long-term written commitment for me in New York. The word on Los Angeles real estate was that it was expensive; we would have to sell both our apartment and the paradise home in Quogue in order to live the way we wanted, assuming Bill got the job. And Bill did apply.

This was certainly the flip side of all the choices I had ever made between family and career in my past. I was faced with selling my two most significant financial assets, picking up and moving my life to another coast without a clue as to what I was going to do, with no security except the love of my husband. How daring. What a trial. How very postfeminist.

 OW ALIKE WE WERE. BILL APPROACHED
HIS PURSUIT OF THE CHIEF'S JOB THE
same way I approached a trial, with complete and meticulous attention to detail. While some of the applicants, because they had other
jobs, asked that their candidacy be confidential, Bill had no such
need. He openly declared his interest in becoming the chief of police
of the City of Los Angeles, and he sent the Police Commission his
autobiography, *Turnaround,* along with a large stack of articles and
news clippings outlining his career. One of the knocks on Bill is his

fondness for media attention; this fondness was said to be the basis of
Rudy Giuliani's difficulty with him and, coupled with Giuliani's
unwillingness to share credit with Bill and the rank-and-file cops for
New York's policing success, may have ultimately cost Bill his job.

So when the original group of applicants was whittled to thirteen
and stories in the press began to focus on my husband's ego — *See, Bill
Bratton is a publicity monger; he sent all these clippings* — I became wife-
lioness. Bill didn't deserve that rap, and he certainly didn't need to
have the initial perception of him in Los Angeles colored by this old
news. I was angry with the press for drumming up controversy
where none existed. This was a career move of vital importance to
Bill, and there was no way of knowing how Mayor James Hahn
would react to Bill's constantly being criticized *by* the press for constantly being *in* the press. It would have been a deal-breaker for Giuliani, but perhaps this mayor was more generous of spirit.

Bill didn't divert his attention to this swirl. He went about the
business of getting the job. He studied for his Police Commission
interview as if he were taking the bar exam. He was going to be the
best-qualified and best-prepared candidate they saw. He read books
on the history of the LAPD and position papers concerning the consent decree, and he reached out to people who had both knowledge of
and influence in the life of Los Angeles, such as John Mack of the
Urban League and Rabbi Abraham Cooper, associate dean of the
Simon Wiesenthal Center. While he was supremely qualified for this
position, there was no reason to believe he had a lock on it. The selection process was a fragile thing. Would the commission want someone from inside the department with intimate knowledge of its
personalities and workings, someone to whom the rank and file had
already responded favorably, or would it want an outsider with a
first-class track record, fresh ideas, and few ties to a difficult past?
And exactly how secure was Mayor Hahn? Would he tolerate a
police chief who used publicity to carry a message? None of these
questions had a definitive answer, which was why the process was so
fraught with uncertainty. Several names were floated in the press,
and the job search became a nightly news saga as reporters and City
Hall sources handicapped the candidates.

Bill was extremely anxious when he met with the Police Commission. He was so chock-full of information and insights, there was so much riding on his performance, that he was uncharacteristically nervous. But Bill being Bill, he went out there and aced it.

And then there were three. And among the three finalists to be interviewed by Mayor Hahn was Bill's former NYPD first deputy commissioner, John Timoney. Timoney had been languishing in the department when Bill had come in and jumped him from a one-star to a four-star chief, the youngest chief of department in NYPD history. They had written NYPD history together, and Timoney had gone on to become police commissioner of Philadelphia. (Mayor Ed Rendell had wanted Bill for the job, but Bill had not been interested; instead he recommended Timoney, who he knew wanted desperately to get back into policing.) John and Bill were good friends; in *Turnaround*, Bill called John "a cop's cop . . . the NYPD personified." I found myself angry at John for applying.

Maybe it's a female thing. If a close woman friend and I were looking at a job that was interesting and desirable to us both, but one of us *really* wanted it, one or the other would say, "Okay, you go ahead." I could not get over the fact that John knew how passionately Bill wanted this job, and not matching that passion with his own, didn't step aside.

Bill thought I was nuts.

"Aren't you angry?" I asked him. "Aren't you angry that he's doing this?"

"He wants the job. He has the right to apply. He is a well-qualified candidate; he is certainly somebody to be reckoned with. I understand why he's applying."

I was very conflicted. I love John Timoney. He is great company and one of the most straightforward, honorable, and funny men I know. He had been intensely loyal to Bill in the past. But I am a competitive person, and there was a part of me that was saying, "This is my husband we're talking about. Get out of the way!"

Bill, John, and Art Lopez, the Oxnard police chief, were the last men standing. Lopez had spent twenty-eight years on the LAPD, eventually rising to deputy chief before leaving four years earlier. All would be interviewed by Mayor Hahn, who would then make his decision.

By the time Bill met the mayor his anxiety was gone. Mine wasn't. I waited all day for his call. Finally it came.

"How was your day?" he asked me. Was he joking?

"Okay, okay," I said. "How did it go?!"

Bill is an unusually measured man. He rarely gets excited, and he wasn't effusive now. Just calm. "I really like this man," he told me. "He knows more about community policing than I do and he's really committed to reforming the LAPD. We talked for three hours. I really believe in him as a mayor. If I don't get this job, it's too bad for the City of Los Angeles, because I am the person who can make a difference. But I'll tell you that I've learned a lot from this process. The Police Commission was fair; I believe this mayor is fair. Everything about the guy tells me he is totally straight and has a lot of integrity."

The decision was to be made soon. By this time I was Bill's biggest cheerleader; I fervently wanted my man to get this job.

Bill flew back to New York. The waiting around was making me crazy, so to take our minds off it, he and I had planned to go to the movies, something we usually did only on weekends. On Monday, September 30, I picked him up at his office after I got off from work and found him at his desk in front of a stack of papers, busily taking notes. He had gotten a call from Mayor Hahn's office saying that the mayor wanted him to review several articles and that he would be calling to discuss them sometime that evening.

"Well, then, we're not going to the movies," I said.

"No, I've read these articles before." He gave me a quick overview of the need to create a partnership with the community in the effort to rid Los Angeles of its problems with gangs. He was completely on top of his subject, and I listened with pleasure and appreciation. "I'm perfectly happy to go."

We went to see *The Four Feathers,* an epic movie. Bill loves epic movies. When we got to the theater, I said, "You better go in and let me call you on your cell phone to make sure you can get a signal in there."

"Great idea."

He went in; I called; the phone vibrated. Everything was in working order. "Okay, come on in." We bought a bag of popcorn and sat down for the previews. He seemed calm, but Bill had brought with him the mayor's articles and his notes in a blue cloth pouch. I noticed he was holding on to his cell phone, so maybe he wasn't quite as sanguine as he seemed.

About twenty minutes into the movie I heard the phone buzz. He stood up and left. I figured I would watch until he got back, but that was foolish; I couldn't concentrate even a little. So I was looking but not seeing, tapping my foot nervously. It took me more than a moment to realize I was drumming on my left thigh with my right hand. On screen people were dying very bloodily, but I couldn't tell you how.

Over an hour later Bill plopped down in the seat beside me.

"Okay," he said, "I'm watching the movie now."

"No, you are not!"

I had to know what happened. We walked into the lobby. "Where'd you do it, in the car? I was going to come looking for you."

This was one of the few remaining one-screen theaters in New York. It actually had a balcony alcove outside the theater doors, where one could sit and wait for a movie to begin. These used to be the norm, but the multiplex has killed off most of them. "I sat here on the bench." He showed me. The bench was red lacquer. The nook was quiet enough when everyone else was in front of the screen.

"You did the interview on this bench, in a movie theater?" I was incredulous.

"I had perfect reception."

(I have to buy that bench for him.)

We walked to the car. "How do you feel?" I asked. You have to ask Bill those questions; he will not spontaneously volunteer the answers.

"I feel great. I think I was right on my game—assertive and confident. I know—and I conveyed this to the mayor—that this is a historical moment and the Los Angeles department can either change its face and its policing and its relationship to the community now or it can't, and I may be the only person in America who can do it. Shame on them if I don't get this job."

Bill had abandoned any attempt at modesty. He was so filled with a sense of mission that he wanted to start that evening. He knew how to get there from here. That is a most astoundingly valuable character trait, and I loved him for it.

We went to dinner. I couldn't eat; Bill chowed down heartily. I hadn't been sleeping well; Bill was sleeping the sleep of the dead.

Bill flew off to Oregon the next day on business. I was driving him crazy, pestering him anxiously about whether they had called, when they would call. A day went by.

I was in my office at dawn and called Bill very early. While we were talking, my friend Brenda Ellis e-mailed me. Had I seen Page Six? I hadn't.

Page Six of the *New York Post*, the tabloid's gossip section, was stating definitively that Bill had been rejected. An unnamed source said Timoney was getting the job because the mayor "was annoyed by [Bratton's] self-promotion and his media manipulation." Under a picture of Bill smiling broadly was the bold-faced line **"Pushed too hard."**

I went crazy. Bill said it was absolutely not true, and that he had spoken with the mayor's office about substantive issues after that edition of the *Post* had been put to bed. But I was still rocked by the piece, and I went into high gear, telling Bill we had to do something about this outrageous article, which certainly showed that he was not the media manipulator here. I called my friend Gerry Chaleff in L.A., where it was 5:30 A.M. "Help! People in L.A. need to know about this—now!" Gerry, a longtime friend and fellow attorney, was familiar with all of the players and said he would look into it immediately. His wife understood my spousal loyalty and forgave the early-morning intrusion. I was fierce. This was my husband, after all.

People came into my office as if I were holding a wake. "I'm so sorry." "I can't believe it." "How sad." That's New York for you: Everyone believes Page Six.

I called Bill again before I went on the air. "If you hear anything," I said, "would you leave me a voice mail?"

"I'll leave you a voice mail if I get it. I won't leave one if I don't."

"No, no. I'll call at the breaks. I just want to know."

"Fine." He went back to his business meeting.

I went on the air very distracted. My guest that afternoon was a criminal defense attorney I had known for a long time, Dino Lombardi. He could see I was only half there and did a nice job of covering for me. At about 1:30, at my anchor desk during a commercial, I called for messages. On my voice mail I heard, "Break out the champagne and caviar!"

"He did it!"

I was on the set, celebrating. "Oh my God! Oh my God! Yes, he got it! He got it!"

The voice mail continued, ". . . And you can't tell anyone."

Oh.

"Dino." My face fell. "No one can know. I, I, I . . ."

"Rikki, it's attorney-client privilege. No one will know."

I looked at our floor manager, Dave Liebeskind, the man who keeps the show moving. "Dave, you didn't hear this."

"Hear what?"

I returned from the break bursting with energy. I became the most engaged anchor on Court TV.

I kept my fist in my mouth all evening. I even went to a party and accepted condolences over the Page Six article. I got home to find a white shopping bag waiting for me in the lobby. Inside was a bottle of champagne and a note from my friends Karen Page and Andrew Dornenburg: "Congratulations to you and Bill." Upstairs, my answering machine was overflowing with messages. How did everyone know?

While I was trying to be cool about it, the *Los Angeles Times* had announced the appointment on its website. The news was on CNN. The next day Page Six published a major retraction, with my picture in the same place Bill's had been two days earlier over the headline HAPPY ENDING. They wrote, "We were only 100 percent wrong." Then they quoted me: "It was a great shock for me to discover that Page Six is not infallible." The article continued, "Bratton's wife, Ricki Kleiman [*sic*] . . . [t]he vivacious Court TV anchor, said she wanted to reach through the phone and rip out our larynx." Well, at least they got that right.

Bill called. He was on cloud nine, joking that the Page Six screw-up reminded him of the famous headline DEWEY BEATS TRUMAN! He demonstrated a level of enthusiasm I had never seen in him outside of our wedding day. I had never known Bill when he was NYPD commissioner, when he was truly in his element. Now he was so confident, so excited, so possessed with the desire to make Los Angeles safe for its citizens. We were going to have a great time, he said. I luxuriated in his excitement.

My boss, Henry Schleiff, called with hearty congratulations. Understanding that a cross-country commute could damage me and Bill's relationship, he offered to let me out of my contract. His generosity was overwhelming, but I couldn't think about it then. It was only later that night, as I remained in the office answering hundreds of congratulatory e-mails, that I realized I was terrified. I called Brenda Ellis for comfort. I was becoming hysterical and hyperventilating. All this talk about opportunity and challenge was one thing; finding a life for myself was quite another. Was Bill going to be working seventeen-hour days? Would we be able to spend the kind of time we were spending together now, enjoying each other, going to familiar restaurants with good friends at night? Were we going to have a romantic weekend ever again? What about my job? Where was I going to go? What was I going to do? Where was I going to live? What about my identity? Who was I going to be?

Brenda calmed me down. But she lived in Florida, I couldn't drop by her house and talk this out. I pulled myself together and called Karen Page. Karen and Andrew lived on the same block as Court TV and asked whether I would like to stop by for a glass of wine on the way home. I sure would. Of course, by the time I got there Andrew, a food writer and chef, had cooked a full meal that they demanded I eat.

"Karen," I said, "I'm very scared. I am frightened that all these wonderful, romantic times are never going to happen again, that he is just going to be working. What's going to happen to us? I never thought about the fact of commuting for a year. Sure, I said we could do it, but Bill and I can't do that; it's not who we are. We want to be together. I want to be there now. I want to go there now. That is what I want to do."

Karen and Andrew knew me well. "This is a big change," Karen said calmly. "This is difficult. You can't be thinking about all of it at once; you just need to break it down into increments."

"You and Bill are the most romantic couple I know," added Andrew, "outside of Karen and me. You should never fear. No matter how hard Bill is working, he will always have the time for you that you want." I believed that and glided home.

I flew to Los Angeles the next morning, a Friday. Bill said we had a function to attend that night. What to wear? I packed his suits, socks, underwear, handkerchiefs. What if it were hot? What if it were cold? I did the best I could.

I set two alarms for 4:30 in the morning; I was not going to miss this flight. I arrived in Long Beach around 10:00 in the morning and was driven to the hotel by one of Bill's old friends, Mike Berkow, chief of police of Irvine. Knowing I love fine hotels, Bill had booked us into the Four Seasons under my name. This was a big occasion. But we were going to be private. Right. As I was checking in, the concierge introduced herself and said, "Mrs. Bratton, congratulations! If there is anything we can do for you, please let us know. Everything is at your disposal."

This was new. No one had ever referred to me as Mrs. Bratton, and that certainly wasn't how I saw myself. I had never been "Mrs. *Anybody*." Earlier in my life I might have bridled, corrected her, taken the title as an affront to my own identity. Isn't that the feminist doctrine, and hadn't I accepted it? This new role of mine would require some adjustment on my part.

As I was talking with the concierge I caught a glimpse of myself in one of the lobby mirrors. I looked like a dog. "Do you have a hair salon in the hotel?" I asked.

"No, but there is one around the corner. Would you like us to call them for you?"

"Please."

"When would you like an appointment?"

"Now. Ten minutes. I have to go to an important meeting with my husband."

"Well, of course."

By the time I hit the door the phone was ringing. "Rafael will take you in ten minutes."

It's good to be the wife of the king.

The room was beautiful. I hung up my clothes and scooted downstairs. Bill called me on my cell. "Where are you?"

"I'm getting my hair done."

"You're *what*?"

"Don't worry, don't worry, I'm going to be ready on time, I promise."

"You are something else, my love." I could almost see him shaking his head. "There is a fellow who will pick you up in about forty-five minutes. His name is Officer Manny Gonzales. He is about six foot three, and he looks like an Aztec god."

"Okay, I guess I'll find him."

So this fabulous Parisian Rafael did my hair. It looked dynamite. I hurried back to the room and dressed very conservatively—I was, after all, the chief's wife—in a taupe sleeveless dress with a matching suit jacket and bone faux-alligator shoes. I was ready when my ride arrived.

I came out of the elevator into the lobby and up walked this six-foot-three Aztec god. Head of Bill's security detail, Manny was smart and very professional. He drove me to the mayor's office, where we swooped into the parking garage and rode up in the mayor's elevator; as the big doors opened, people began introducing themselves to me. Into the room walked a very tall, silver-haired gentleman, Mayor James K. Hahn. I shook his hand as Bill approached. "Mayor Hahn," I said, "thank you so much for making such a wise choice. You are really going to be proud of what you did. It is so nice to meet you."

Bill greeted me with a big hug and a kiss. "I'm so happy you're here, my love," he said. The mayor seemed to enjoy this public display of affection.

Mayor Hahn is a walker, so he and his aides and his security detail, as well as Bill and I, hand in hand, strolled the few blocks from the mayor's office to the *Los Angeles Times'* building, where he and Bill were scheduled to meet with the newspaper's editorial board. I was surprised and honored to be allowed to sit in, and I listened with tremendous affection as Bill answered questions with confidence and vision. He shone in ways I had not yet seen.

The officer who drove me back to the hotel was a handsome and smiling triathlete named Randy Yang. L.A. cops apparently aren't eating a lot of doughnuts; these guys were spit-polished and muscularly fit. I was getting a quick sense of the culture.

That evening we attended a fund-raiser with the mayor for the Gene Autry Museum. Everyone there wanted to meet and talk with Bill. The television cameras were rolling; the press followed us everywhere we walked; and people whose faces were immediately recognizable from stage and screen all wanted a moment with him. The warm and enthusiastic applause my husband received was very gratifying. Bill was not simply an incoming civil servant, but a white knight, royalty, and I was his Guinevere. The mayor seemed very pleased that his choice for chief was well received and reflecting well on him.

At the function we were seated with the honorees, the actress Melissa Gilbert and her actor-husband, Bruce Boxleitner. She had grown up since her days on *Little House on the Prairie* and was now president of the Screen Actors Guild. I mentioned that I was a SAG member and in her acknowledgment of Bill she mentioned it to the crowd, which I thought was rather sweet. Later that evening one of her assistants came by and asked that when I moved to Los Angeles I shouldn't hesitate to get in touch with them. I thought, This is divine providence!

In the hotel that night the chef had prepared beautiful little candies surrounding a Los Angeles chief of police badge that he had created out of pastry. The power of Bill Bratton was beginning to dawn on me.

The *Times* assigned a reporter to write a profile of me, the New Chief's Wife. Where would we like to be photographed? On our hunt for a new home? I don't think so. At a private dinner party on Saturday night? No. Instead I suggested we go to a carousel on Sunday,

Bill's fifty-fifth birthday. As luck would have it, there was a carousel within the city limits of Los Angeles, in Griffith Park. The officer assigned to us that day, a tall, quiet, very military fellow named Tim Swift, had probably never escorted a chief spinning around on a carousel getting his picture taken with his wife.

When I mentioned to the reporter that as well as being a lawyer and a broadcaster I had been an actress, she featured the fact in her profile, and the day the article appeared I started getting calls from important talent agencies with projects to suggest and offers of representation. I began to think that my career concerns had been a bit overblown.

Bill's schedule was awhirl—he had people to meet, hands to shake, meetings to participate in. For my allotted two hours I broke away with a Realtor to look at houses.

I found out immediately that prices for a rental were outrageous. We're not rich, and the more I saw of unfurnished houses, aging appliances, and general disrepair, the more demoralized I became. Bill was the toast of the town, and certainly could not come home each night to a dump. As I saw one completely unacceptable place after another I began to think that we could never afford a nice enough home, and I began to doubt the wisdom of the move all over again. By the time I reunited with Bill I was in a panic.

Bill was meeting with Los Angeles City Councilmember Tom LaBonge, a proud lifelong Angelino and a delightful nonstop talker. He knew everything about the city, its history, and its architecture. He was very proud of his town. As we were being driven to our next destination, a restaurant in Hollywood in the district of Councilman Eric Garcetti, son of former district attorney Gil Garcetti, Tom was giving us a guided tour out the window. At the end of a windy road on the top of a hill in the Los Feliz section, Councilmember LaBonge pointed to a house and said, "These are great friends of mine. This house is on the market. You should see it."

"Great!"

Tom told the security detail driver, a quiet but wickedly funny officer named Russ Vincent, "Stop!" Russ gave him the "What's going on here? This wasn't in the plan" look but pulled over. Behind him, a caravan of vehicles pulled to the side of the road as well. Tom bounded out and rang the doorbell.

"We want to show these people your home!"

He conducted a whirlwind, five-minute tour, and it was indeed a wonderful house. It overlooked Silver Lake, all the way to downtown Los Angeles. I could see Bill's eyes lighting up. Councilman La Bonge said, "Well, Chief, what do you think?"

"Oh my God," exclaimed the home's owner, "you're the new chief of police. Wait, you really have to slow down; I want to show you this house!"

On Sunday, Bill's fifty-fifth birthday, we attended the Latin American Law Enforcement (LA LEY) organization picnic at the Police Academy. I shook a lot of hands, ate a lot of Mexican food, and was fascinated to observe myself be "Mrs. Bratton." This was the way I had been introduced all weekend and this was how I was perceived. And I enjoyed it! I was proud of Bill. I don't know that I had ever played a truly subservient role in my life, and here I was, truly an appendage. There were a few people in these crowds who had heard of me, but the vast majority didn't have a clue. And I didn't mind; instead, I watched myself saying all the right things and taking a step back when he spoke. I didn't need the spotlight now, because I was perfectly pleased to let Bill shine in it alone. And Bill, to his everlasting credit, brought me into focus with every group he met, declaring that we were a team and that Los Angeles was getting two for the price of one. I could have kissed him. I did.

A Latino officer who said he had been on the job through seven different police chiefs told us this was the first time he had ever had the opportunity to share a beer with one. They were excited at how down-to-earth Bill seemed. For Bill, it was only natural. "How does it feel to be Mrs. Bratton?" the officer asked. "Pretty good!" I answered. At the age of twenty, thirty, forty, forty-five, or even forty-nine I would have said, "You've got to be out of your mind if you think I could ever play this role!" But I was enjoying it now because this was Bill's moment, not mine.

We went back to that marvelous house in Los Feliz with a broker and this time took a long tour. Then we attended a cocktail party

hosted by the Stonewall Association, the gay and lesbian organization of Los Angeles. Bill and the mayor were staying for dinner, but
I had a red-eye to catch back to New York because I still had a job I
had to be at Monday morning. I kissed my husband good-bye and
was swept away.

I was driven back to the airport, where Manny Gonzales the
Aztec God was waiting for me. His children called him to say good
night. "Go home," I told him. "I've waited in plenty of airports alone."

"I can't leave you, Mrs. Bratton."

"Would you just call me Rikki, please."

That wasn't likely.

"What would happen if something happened to you between the
time I left and the time you got on the plane," he asked. "The chief
wouldn't want me to leave." So he stayed, then walked me up the tarmac and saw me onto the plane. "Your husband is quite a guy," he
told me. "We all really want to work for him."

And I wanted to be with him. But I had a contract that would run
for another year. I would commute. I could do that. We were solid as
a rock.

 *nineteen* TURNAROUND

WHAT WAS I, JOKING? I COULDN'T LAST A YEAR. I COULD BARELY LAST A DAY.

I had hardly slept in the four nights since Bill got the nod. I never stopped moving in three days in L.A. I arrived in New York on Monday morning, blew into work, and stayed until midnight. Then it was October 8, and I had to get on yet another plane after my television show was over.

I had been invited to improvise a closing argument in the fifteenth-anniversary performance of *Shear Madness,* a comedy/

murder mystery play at the Kennedy Center in Washington, D.C. Bill Clinton's lawyer Bob Bennett, noted Washington lawyer Robert Barnett, Fox News's Greta Van Susteren, and I were to appear as lawyers for each of the suspects and the audience would vote to convict or acquit. I was honored to be in such distinguished legal company. As exhausted as I was, I prepared my closing and delivered it with passion. "Boy," said Bob Bennett, "the trial bar really lost something when you stopped practicing law." That was a nice compliment because it had been a long time since I had faced a jury.

Bill had originally planned to attend, but couldn't leave Los Angeles in time to make it. I received flowers at the stage door, but they were from Karen and Andrew. At the party following the show I realized this was the first time since Bill and I had started seeing each other that I had gone to a major function by myself, and I didn't like it. I didn't even check into the hotel until 1:00 A.M. and had to rise at 5:00. No sleep again. As it happened, the one day I was out of New York City, Bill had flown in, on the way to give a speech out of the country. I called him at 5:30 in the morning, out of control, sobbing convulsively, barely able to form words. "I can't live this way," I choked. "We can't do this. I don't know what to do."

"You have to call your doctor," Bill said quietly. "You can't be this way." I calmed myself enough to take a shower and somehow got myself on the shuttle and made my way to work. I was stretched so thin I was fraying.

I needed to be tethered or else I would blow away. I answered the hundreds of e-mails I had received, and I tried to distract myself, to prevent myself from visiting all of this misery on Bill whenever I saw him. I called my therapist, with whom I hadn't spoken in quite some time, and set up a schedule of sessions. I joined a new gym and contacted a personal trainer; Lord knows I would need to be in shape to appear in Los Angeles. I put in a standing appointment at the physical therapist to soothe my bad back.

In the weeks he was away I lost eight pounds off my little body. I went back to my old patterns. I was eating a lot but whatever I ate came out of me. I drank too much; I didn't sleep. It was like being a lawyer all over again.

Bill returned to New York to close his office at Kroll, put his financial affairs in order, and to pack and move to Los Angeles once and for all. We spent a sad weekend in Quogue, where I mulled over so many achingly fond memories. I was going to leave this marvelous house that I adored, my close friends, my wonderful job.

We swirled through going-away parties in New York and Boston. Bill's celebrity status had exploded with his becoming LAPD chief. If he had been respected during his tenure in these cities, he was now treasured in his loss. Though I knew this was foolishness, I somehow felt I was losing him as well. I was certainly losing the life we knew, and I was uncertain about what kind of life faced us. I was used to being Rikki Klieman; despite my introduction in Los Angeles, I had no idea what it was really like to be Mrs. Bratton. What did that mean? Was I to be a ceremonial wife? I am not a woman who is adept at hosting cocktail parties. I work. Well, what if there was no work for me? What if I didn't get a job in television? What if, despite the agents who were putting together packages, I couldn't find a way to make a living? What if I wasn't successful? What if I didn't have any money coming in? What was my future?

Our last night in our apartment, I couldn't stop crying. It wasn't as if I would not see Bill for a while; he was leaving for Los Angeles on Thursday, and I was joining him on Friday. He was going to be sworn in as police chief on Monday. It was the fact that this was his last night in New York and I was worried sick. He packed his bags and joked, "Well, you'll have another closet now!" My loss was overwhelming. I couldn't even watch.

Bill finished late and we fell into bed, but we weren't able to think about being intimate. We just held each other for dear life.

He was out the door and gone by 5:15. As soon as I awoke I took his pillow and buried my head in it, just to smell his being there. I got up and looked in the closet and was so grateful to find he had left a few jackets and sweaters. I still had something of him, though I felt as if my heart would break.

But I came off that plane the next day strutting, looking as if I didn't have a care in the world. I knew how to do that; I'd had so much practice. Fake it till you make it. Officer Gonzales picked up my bag and drove me to the restaurant where I was meeting Bill. In the car all the way there I said a silent affirmation over and over: "I'm happy. I'm fine. I'm happy. I'm fine." I wanted to bounce out of the car and show Bill I was the person he needed, as well as the person I wanted to be.

As I approached him, his smile was electric. "Wow," said Manny, "what a grin!" Bill took me in his arms, and it was as if we had been apart for weeks. We had been apart one day. He buried his face in my neck and told me, "You know how much I love you. Do you know how happy I am that you are here and that you let me do this?" I melted.

Freshening up in the bathroom, I looked in the mirror and said, "Rikki, just get over it. This is the man you love. You knew how hard this would be. Just let yourself be."

We relaxed; we talked; he told me about his day. Although there would be a public swearing-in on Monday, he had been sworn-in privately that morning, after which he and the mayor had flown by helicopter to a conference on emergency preparedness. He was in the process of selecting his inner circle and new chain of command. Gangs and graffiti were at the top of his list of problems to solve. He was excited to be running a department again.

Bill had put me in charge of finding and buying a home. The hilltop house we had seen was wonderful, and I had a Realtor searching for others. We had been corresponding by e-mail and narrowed the selection down to five, and now we had between 9:00 and 10:50 A.M. to see them.

Bill and I visited one after another. The first was wrong, the second possible, the third I can't remember. The fourth house could truly, in my heart, replace Quogue. It was way up in the foothills above Los Feliz with a wonderful sense of privacy, which was my first concern. I wanted a home where Bill and I could be alone. With its Spanish Mediterranean architecture, tiled kitchen, inviting pool, and sculpted greenery, this house was an oasis. It opened onto a redwood deck from which we could see the entire city of Los Angeles. I would love living there. In my great love for my old sanctuary, how wrong I had been to think that there could never be another Quogue. A house does not create tranquillity; instead, you bring your own serenity and peace of mind. In sense and sensibility, this house was everything we wanted: a sanctuary, a home.

We drove from our house hunt to a "Women in Blue" LAPD recruiting session held outdoors at the Police Academy. Booths had been set up for female members of the department to explain and recruit for divisions like helicopter, traffic, motorcycle, mounted, diving, and the bomb squad. Bill shook hands with every officer at the event. As he was talking, one young civilian asked whether I would introduce her to my husband. We waited and then she said, "Chief Bratton, I came here to join the LAPD today because of everything I've read about you." The *Los Angeles Times* had run a huge article the day before in which Bill had described his vision for ridding the city of gangs, starting with graffiti, which followed the "Broken Windows" philosophy of policing. James Q. Wilson and George Kelling had created the theory, which held, as Kelling wrote, "Untended disorderly behavior can . . . signal that nobody cares about the community and lead to more serious disorder." Fix the broken windows, and make sure they don't get broken again, and you will establish just who is in control of society. "You make people proud," she told him. "I want to be proud. I want to join the LAPD."

Both the women in the department and the women recruits were vital and strong. Here were dozens of women who would change their lives because my husband had inspired them. Despite my status of "wife" in this particular situation, I was proud to be part of this project to bring order to Los Angeles, and to empower both the men and the women of the LAPD to do so.

This visit to the Police Academy confirmed that Bill and I had made the right choice. Bill was an inspiring leader, and these visions of his success at the LAPD were enough to calm the doubts and fears I'd had about the move, enough to make me stop second-guessing my decision to be "Mrs. Bratton." I was now inhabiting that role fully, happily.

On Sunday we hosted a luncheon for the fifty friends who had come from the East Coast to celebrate Bill's swearing-in. Al Sweeney, Bill's friend since the age of five, who served with him on the Boston Police Department, prepared a poem for this occasion, as he had done for Bill's previous ceremonies. He called it "Ode to the Chief":

. . . We can see him now at the Academy Awards
Wearing his pearl-handled pistol
He'll probably end up hosting the thing
Move over, Billy Crystal.
Enough of this nonsense, I must slow down
Before you declare me delirious
So let me take a moment or two
To get a bit more serious

Bill has a way that motivates folks,
He lights their creative fire.
It makes you want to work all that harder
He truly does inspire.
It's a brisker step, a sharper look
Your walk becomes a stride.
The head tilts back, the eyes lock in
He instills a greater sense of pride. . . .

Bill stood and told a story about every person in the room. Men and women from his past growing up as a street cop in Boston, people he had worked beside in police headquarters, at Massachusetts police departments and the New York Transit Police, at the NYPD and beyond. By this time I knew them all, because Bill's life was policing and these colleagues were really Bill's extended family.

Bill choked back tears twice, an extraordinary thing for this reserved man to do in public; first, when he acknowledged Jack Maple's widow, Bridget O'Connor, and spoke of the professional and personal bond he and Jack had shared, and second, when he spoke of former Boston Police Commissioner Bob di Grazia. Now in his seventies, di Grazia remains Bill's inspiration and mentor, without whom Bill would never have had his career. There was not a dry eye in the house.

Coming back to the hotel, we drove through sections of Los Angeles with which neither Bill nor I was familiar. We were as yet strangers to this town; we knew where we were going, but we didn't know what these places were called. "Where are we, Russ?" Bill asked.

"This is your city, sir," he answered.

And so it was.

Unlike the NYPD commissioner, the Los Angeles police chief wears a uniform virtually every day on the job. Bill hadn't worn a uniform in a decade, since his time as Boston Police superintendent. As head of the chief's security detail, Officer Gonzales supervised the ritual of Bill's dressing in our hotel room on the day of his swearing-in. Put on the blues, put on the stars, put on the medals, put on the nameplate, put on the belt shined with black shoe polish that holds the gun, the spare ammunition clips, and the handcuffs. Wash your hands and scrub your fingernails. Make sure everything is just right. Don't give the troops anything to criticize. *60 Minutes* was taping it; *20/20*'s John Miller stayed out of their camera range. Bill's son, David; his sister, Pat; her partner, Val; and their son, Kyle, looked on with love and support.

Bill was uncharacteristically nervous. He had risen early to work on his speech, and he had butterflies, but the tension was evidence that this was a day of importance, of promise. A day of success.

We reached the meet-and-greet at 9:15, thinking we would be among the first to arrive. Hundreds of people had already filled the Police Academy. New friends, old friends, East Coast, West Coast, police officers, dignitaries, everyone wishing Bill well. I introduced myself to everyone in blue I could find.

At some point Bill took a left turn and we lost sight of each other. A few minutes later he asked, "Where's Rikki?" Someone told him, "She's standing next to the mayor."

"Why am I not surprised?"

But I wasn't rainmaking for a firm anymore; I was working the room for my husband—a much bigger payoff.

At 11:00 we gathered for the swearing-in ceremony. California Governor Gray Davis, Mayor Hahn, Police Commission President Rick Caruso, Bill, and I walked in one line. The entire entourage included the department command staff, the Police Commission, and the City Council. We marched onstage to the haunting sound of bag-pipes and drums. As if reviewing the troops, we walked through the Police Academy parade grounds before a long row of saluting officers, then climbed the steps to a stage and took our seats. The pomp and circumstance made the warm air feel charged with anticipation.

The governor spoke, as did the mayor and Mr. Caruso. They were saying wonderful things about my husband and I was *kvelling,* a Yiddish word meaning soulful beaming. People used to say my father *kvelled* when I walked into a room, that he lit up like a beacon when he saw me. I *kvelled* for Bill.

At some point during the speeches my husband took my hand, infusing me with energy as I did for him. We held hands for about fifteen minutes, and people later commented on what an extraordinary act that was, what a remarkable gesture, that a big tough police chief would have the romantic nature, the confidence, the sheer audacity to hold his wife's hand at such a public moment. He hadn't thought about it. For us, such displays of affection were completely natural.

Bill also displayed his affection for his job, his mission, and his new home. When he took the podium, he spoke with feeling and, as he always does, without notes. He had planned to speak about the changes he would be putting into place, the alterations in the way the LAPD would be going about its business from now on. But when he looked out at the crowd of men and women in blue, he recognized that this was not only his day but theirs. This was not a time to criticize them but to make them feel proud.

He talked about "a commitment to the profession of policing. An understanding that police count, that police can, in fact, make a difference in a democracy.

"This is a new day," he told the crowd. "Cops have to work with their community. . . . There is no police department in America that needs the community more than this police department." To the cops he said, "You cannot do it alone, but with them you can do anything. We're outnumbered ten to one; one hundred thousand gangbangers out there. Ten to one. And I wouldn't trade one of your lives for any of theirs."

But he was more than a cheerleader. "I want to talk very bluntly to you," he told his force. "The citizens of this city need you back in those streets. They don't need you smiling and waving. They need you out of those cars, on those corners, in those parks—taking back those streets, that, unfortunately, so many have been lost. You have the ability to do this. You are America's best. You are Los Angeles's finest."

He told the cops he needed them to embrace the concept of community policing. "When you've pinned this badge on your chest you've committed to going where others do not have to go; you've committed to going when others do not have to go; you've committed to being there so long as you wear this badge, this shield, so proudly on your chest. . . .

"We all need to be about the prevention of crime, and to that end we will take on the gangs. . . . You need to get in the business of problem solving—putting cops where the crime is. And if it's on weekends, if it's on nights, if it's on the late hours, that's where you have to be."

They wouldn't be there alone. "You're going to see a lot of me," he told them, "nights, days, weekends. But when you see me, I will not be there checking up on you. I'll be there shoulder to shoulder with you. . . . We'll be out there as partners."

"To the communities of this wonderful city—" he concluded, and in a reference to the concept of secession that was roiling many in Los Angeles, "this *one* city—my commitment to you is to work night and day with the finest cops in America to truly make this city the safest and greatest in America. That's a promise that I intend to keep."

As Police Commission President Rick Caruso was pinning the chief's badge on Bill's chest—Bill had been brought up on the TV show *Dragnet*, and this must have been quite a moment for a boy enamored of "Badge 714"—he said, "If I stab you, it's only a sign of things to come."

Bill replied, "Mr. Caruso, you can stick me anytime, as long as it's not in the back." Serious Bill Bratton also had a sense of humor. The audience roared.

He was magnificent. When he finished, the crowd was enthusiastically applauding. He turned toward me and opened his arms and hugged me and beamed. He had no second thought about showing such emotion in front of all these people. He loved me, and he was happy I was there with him. I put my hands on both of his cheeks and told him, "I love you so much. I am so proud of you." I felt a geyser of joy explode inside me. We were as high as the helicopter fly-by salute that thundered above us. Being Mrs. Bratton and basking in his glow bathed me in the most glorious light.

At a party for 350 guests at Rick Caruso's magnificent home in Brentwood that night, after a few words from the mayor and the president of the Police Commission, Bill spoke for several minutes and then said, "I've been talking enough. I think it is time for you all to hear from my wife."

He hadn't told me he was going to do this. I was completely unprepared. But I was a born actress as well as a lawyer, and I knew how to close on my feet.

I spoke from my heart. I told them that on Fourth of July weekend I had told my good friends that my life was perfect and I wanted nothing to change. I told them how I had acted like a brat for hours on the Long Island Expressway when Bill told me he wanted this job, and how I had cried with admiration when he had explained why. I told them how proud I was of him, how blessed I was to have him. "He will make this city the safest in America." I turned to the people in uniform. "For all the men and women in blue here tonight, I want to tell you that he will give you back your pride, that you will wake up every day of your lives as a police officer and put on that uniform and know that you are the heroes of the city and that Bill Bratton, my husband, made it all possible."

I hugged the mayor. I hugged Rick Caruso, who told me I should run for office. Then I turned to my husband. "You were wonderful," he said as he kissed me.

"Why didn't you tell me you were going to do this?" I whispered.

"I didn't want you to be nervous," he told me. "Remember, I need you by my side. You are my best asset in this community. We are better together than we are individually. And besides," he said with a smile, "there are agents and producers in the room!"

The moon was shining over Los Feliz when Bill and I stepped out onto our new deck and surveyed the lights of Los Angeles. We weren't scheduled to move in for several weeks, but we had never seen the view at night and made a special visit to take in this vista.

The house was still, as if waiting for us to breathe life into it and make it our own.

I watched the lights twinkle and I watched my husband's face. He was peaceful, calm in the midst of the million demands of this new life we were forging together. Who would have believed that, in my fifties, I would find a fairy-tale ending?

When I was a girl, whether I was playing Snow White and feeling that someday my prince would come, or Emily in *Our Town* reflecting on the fragility of life, I truly believed that fairy tales did come true. As I grew up I put those feelings in a box inside me, tied a great big ribbon around it so tight I couldn't unwrap it, and then tucked that box away so deep I couldn't find it. When I took off on my journey toward fame, success, and wealth, in order for me to remain focused on those goals my personal life had to stay in the background. It was only when I met Bill that I recognized how far I had fallen from those dreams, and that the way I was going they never would come true.

Since her death, my mother has rarely been far from my thoughts, and she became ever-present after I fell in love with Bill. For so much of my life I could never find what she wanted for me — the love she felt from my father, the love he felt from her — and now finally I have found that transforming affection. How well she knew, how often she tried to tell me, that a sunset is so much more beautiful when you are holding hands with the one you love and can share it in words. When you live life out loud, the telling deepens its colors. Somewhere up there my mother doesn't have to feel sorry for me anymore; she would be so proud. I have that love in this relationship, this partnership, this companionship with my magnificent husband.

Do I think this new life will be easy? Do I think it will be without struggle, without difficulty, without pain? Of course not. I worry every day about my career, my ability to earn a living. I am accustomed to working; it's in my soul. Los Angeles is full of opportunities — movies, television, public service, teaching — and I will pursue them. I don't know how I'll fit into life in a new city, whether it will break my cycle of overwork, exhaustion, and collapse, or, like an open freeway, it will make my drive easier. I do know I won't sit still. It would be nice to take a rest from the driven life and make Bill my primary focus, but even then I have no doubt I will want to be the best "Mrs. Bratton" possible. Now, who is this Mrs. Bratton that I'm supposed to become?

I know who she is. She is me. I love Bill unconditionally, the way my mother loved me. I didn't know I had it in me, this desire to nurture a person I love. I wasn't at Bill's side when he was New York's police commissioner. I had never seen him in his full glory as a working police chief; it's a sight to behold. I will be proud to stand next to him now. I want to serve as his source of support; I want to be an asset for him while he helps good triumph over evil in Los Angeles. I've never felt this urge before. And at the same time I'm the police chief's wife, I will have the opportunity to involve myself in projects that serve the passions of my own life: issues of fighting domestic violence, mentoring kids, feeding the elderly.

And I will get work. It's who I am. Mr. Bratton is working hard and being a wonderful husband, so who's to say that I can't be Mrs. Bratton and also work hard in the field of my choice?

Do I think I have it all? I do! But—and this is the key element— not all at the same time. What we have changes from moment to moment. Is my life with Bill always perfect? Not a chance. And isn't that a relief for me, because all my life everything was always "perfect"—until it wasn't. Now I understand that life can only be perfect in moments, and that we have to recognize those moments and live in them with all our heart. We need to move slowly through life, to observe and savor the present—it will never happen again—rather than dash to get to the future. With Bill, I once again believe that fairy tales can come true, that life is sweet, that life with him is sweeter. He has given me a gift, one that I possessed long ago but had lost until he found it and shined it up and returned it to me. What he has given me . . . is me. And more than that: us.

ACKNOWLEDGMENTS

We would like to thank our cheerleaders, our supporters, our colleagues in this venture. Judith Regan is a fierce champion—she is everything one could want in a publisher. Her staff at ReganBooks was with us from day one: our editor, Lisa Hamilton; Carl Mark Raymond; Jennifer Suitor; Paul Olsewski; Mark Jackson; Conor Risch; Mac Hawkins; Angelica Canales; and so many others whose work and enthusiasm helped bring our book forward. Thanks to Lynn Goldberg and her colleagues at Goldberg McDuffie Communications for their solid support.

Our thanks to John Taylor ("Ike") Williams, my loyal agent, who has cheered me on to do a book since 1986 and waited patiently until I was truly ready to share my story. None of this would have been accomplished without him. And to Peter's agent, Esther Newberg, who allowed him to work on this project with me.

To transcribers Nadine Wolf and Joycelyn Furginson, who worked hard and quickly and let me know how much they appreciated this book.

My life has been made remarkable by so many people around me: my extraordinary parents; my aunts, uncles, and cousins; my surrogate mother, Evan Frances, who remains with me to this day; all the members of Bill's family, who have accepted me as their own; my mentors in the law and in television, who shaped my careers; Fred Graham, who helped me hone my craft and nurture my marriage; my students and those I have mentored, who have enriched all of my days; my law partners, particularly Steve Lyons and Joel Kozol; my dearly beloved friends, women and men, who want me to succeed and want me to be happy—for the latter, I cannot thank them enough. Thanks to two special young women on their road to success and happiness, Allison Simpson and Katie Maxwell, who helped with their research and enthusiasm. Thanks to all the doctors who took care of me throughout the years when my job was killing me. A special thanks to Professor Franklyn Haiman of Northwestern University, who dramatically changed the direction of my life and didn't even know it.

I have the gift of my wonderful husband, Bill Bratton. He is my life. He is my reason to be. I thank him for his unwavering support of this book and his inner strength to permit me to reveal my past. I will love him for the rest of my days—there is no life without him.

And, finally, my thanks to Peter Knobler. I consider him my partner, my voice, my conscience. He has made me realize more about myself than I ever dreamed possible. He also allowed me to appreciate my whole life, the bad with the good, the pain with the pleasure. He became a trusted confidant, a therapist, a true friend. He not only lived the book with me, he lived life out loud with me. I would trust him with anything, anytime, anywhere. Thanks is too small a word.

PHOTOGRAPH CAPTIONS AND CREDITS

All photographs courtesy of the author unless otherwise noted.

ABOUT THE AUTHORS

RIKKI KLIEMAN has been an anchor at Court TV in New York since 1994, analyzing trials and legal proceedings throughout the country. A practicing attorney for twenty-eight years and member of the Adjunct Faculty at Columbia Law School, Kleiman was named one of the five most outstanding women trial lawyers in the country by TIME magazine. She remains of counsel to the Boston law firm of Klieman, Lyons, Schindler and Gross. Prior to becoming an attorney she was a theater major at Northwestern University and a professional actress. Klieman is also a motivational speaker, lecturing on "Powerful Communication from the Courtroom to the Boardroom," "Theater in the Courtroom," and "You Can Have It All, But Not All at the Same Time." She lives with her husband, Los Angeles Chief of Police William Bratton, in New York and Los Angeles. For more information, visit www.RikkiKlieman.com.

PETER KNOBLER wrote the bestselling political memoir *All's Fair* with James Carville and Mary Matalin. With Daniel Petrocelli he wrote *Triumph of Justice: The Final Judgment on the Simpson Saga*. He has collaborated on the autobiographies of Governor Ann Richards, Kareem Abdul-Jabbar, Peggy Say, Thomas "Hollywood" Henderson, Hakeem Olajuwon, and Sumner Redstone. Knobler wrote *Turnaround* with Los Angeles Chief of Police William Bratton. He lives with his wife and son in New York City.